2004

The Future of American
Democratic Politics

The Future
of American
Democratic Politics

Principles and Practices

GERALD M. POMPER

MARC D. WEINER

EDITORS

RUTGERS UNIVERSITY PRESS
New Brunswick, New Jersey, and London

Library of Congress Cataloging-in-Publication Data

The future of American democratic politics : principles and practices / Gerald M. Pomper and Marc D. Weiner, editors.

    p.   cm.
   Includes bibliographical references and index.
   ISBN 0–8135–3297–3 (cloth : alk. paper) — ISBN 0–8135–3298–1
(pbk. : alk. paper)
   1. Democracy—United States. I. Pomper, Gerald M. II. Weiner, Marc D., 1959–

   JK1726 .F88 2003
   320.973—dc21

2002037013

British Cataloging-in-Publication information is available from the British Library.

The publication program of Rutgers University Press is supported by the Board of Governors of Rutgers, The State University of New Jersey.

Manufactured in the United States of America

Contents

Contributors

LANCE CASSAK is special counsel for the U.S. Department of Treasury's Office of Thrift Supervision. He has taught at Rutgers University, Rutgers Law School, and Seton Hall Law School. Cassak is the coauthor of several law review articles, including *Profiles in Justice? Police Discretion, Symbolic Assailants and Stereotyping* (with Milton Heumann) and *Hearing the Cries of Prisoners*. He is also the coauthor of a forthcoming book *Good Cop, Bad Cop: Profiling, Race, and Competing Visions of Justice* (with Milton Heumann).

WILLIAM CROTTY is the Thomas P. O'Neill Chair in Public Life and director of the Center for the Study of Democracy at Northeastern University. He has published a number of books and articles on political parties, elections, and campaigning and is a former president of the Parties and Political Organizations section of the American Political Science Association, the Policy Studies Organization, and the Midwest Political Science Association.

ELIZABETH GARRETT is professor at the University of Southern California Law School. She has written on the legislative process, the law of democratic institutions, direct democracy, the federal budget process, and administrative law. She is the coauthor, with William N. Eskridge Jr. and Philip N. Frickey, of the third edition of the leading legal casebook in the legislative process field, *Cases and Materials on Legislation: Statutes and the Creation of Public Policy*.

JOHN MARK HANSEN is the Charles L. Hutchinson Distinguished Service Professor in Political Science and dean of the Division of Social Sciences at the University of Chicago. He is the author of *Mobilization, Participation, and Democracy in America* (with Steven J. Rosenstone) and numerous other research articles and monographs. He received his doctorate from Yale University in 1987.

MILTON HEUMANN is professor and past chair of the Department of Political Science, Rutgers University. He has written extensively on case disposition processes, civil liberties, and criminal justice concerns. He is the author and coauthor of numerous books and articles, including *Plea Bargaining* and *Speedy Disposition* (with Thomas Church), and has just completed (with Lance Cassak) a forthcoming book on police profiling, *Good Cop, Bad Cop: Profiling, Race, and Competing Visions of Justice*.

NANCY J. HIRSCHMANN is associate professor in the Department of Political Science at the University of Pennsylvania. Her books include *The Subject of Liberty: Toward a Feminist Theory of Freedom*, *Rethinking Obligation: A Feminist Method for Political Theory*, *Women and Welfare: Theory and Practice in the United States and Europe* (coedited with Ulrike Liebert), and *Revisioning the Political: Feminist Reconstructions of Traditional Concepts in Political Theory* (coedited with Christine Di Stefano).

JENNIFER L. HOCHSCHILD is professor of government at Harvard University, with a joint appointment in the Department of Afro-American Studies. Until 2001, she was William Steward Tod Professor of Politics and International Affairs at Princeton University. She is the author, most recently, of *The American Dream and the Public Schools* and is the founding editor of the new journal of the American Political Science Association, *Perspectives on Politics*.

JANE JUNN is associate professor of political science at Rutgers University. Her research interests include political participation, education, race and ethnicity, and social science methodology. Her first book, *Education and Democratic Citizenship in America* (with Norman H. Nie and Kenneth Stehlik-Barry) won the Woodrow Wilson Foundation award from the American Political Science Association for the best book published in 1996.

RUTH B. MANDEL is director of the Eagleton Institute of Politics at Rutgers University and Board of Governors Professor of Politics. Mandel developed and, for several years, directed Eagleton's Center for American Women and Politics. Her most recent publication is "A Question About Women and the Leadership Option," in *The Difference "Difference" Makes: Women in Leadership*.

WILSON CAREY MCWILLIAMS is professor of political science at Rutgers University. He is the author of *The Idea of Fraternity in America* and, most recently, *Beyond the Politics of Disappointment?: American Elections, 1980–1998*. He is a frequent contributor to *Commonweal* and other journals of opinion.

NELSON W. POLSBY is the Heller Professor of Political Science at the University of California, Berkeley. His next book will be *How Congress Evolves: Social Bases of Institutional Change*.

GERALD M. POMPER, Board of Governors Professor of Political Science at Rutgers (emeritus), was director of the Walt Whitman Center during the symposium "The Future of Democratic Politics" at Rutgers University. He is the author of *Passions and Interests*, a forthcoming volume on *Ordinary Heroes and American Democracy*, and a quadrennial series on U.S. national elections from 1976 to 2000.

ALAN ROSENTHAL is professor of public policy and political science at the Eagleton Institute of Politics, Rutgers University. He has published a number of books and articles on state politics and state legislatures. He is the author of *The Decline of Representative Democracy* and *The Third House*. His latest book, coauthored with Burdett Loomis, John Hibbing, and Karl Kurtz, is *Republic on Trial*.

GORDON SCHOCHET teaches political and legal philosophy and the history of political thought at Rutgers University and is one of the founding directors of the Center for the History of British Political Thought at the Folger Shakespeare Library. He is the author of *Patriarchalism in Political Thought* and the forthcoming *Rights in Contexts*.

DANIEL J. TICHENOR is associate professor of political science at Rutgers University, New Brunswick. He is author of *Dividing Lines: The Politics of Immigration Control in America* and coauthor of the forthcoming *Representational Bias, Organized Interests, and the American State*. His current work centers on the presidency, social movements, and democratic politics in America.

MARC D. WEINER is the assistant director of the Princeton University Survey Research Center. He holds a J.D. from Widener University, and his forthcoming doctoral dissertation is "The Bureaucratic Effect: Toward a More Comprehensive Measure of Party Responsibility." During the symposium "The Future of Democratic Politics" at Rutgers University, he was assistant director of the Walt Whitman Center.

Preface

THIS VOLUME RESULTS from the year-long symposium "The Future of Democratic Politics" at Rutgers University. Giving particular attention to the United States, the writers of these chapters examined this general theme through paired presentations over six sessions during the 2001–2002 academic year. After the individual presentations and mutual review of the papers, they came together for a daylong seminar, leading to further revisions of their arguments. The outcome is a printed dialogue on vital issues affecting the principles and practices of American democracy.

The symposium was developed by the Walt Whitman Center for the Culture and Politics of Democracy of the Department of Political Science at Rutgers University, in cooperation with the Eagleton Institute of Politics. We appropriately thank these institutions for their financial and organizational support. We are indebted to Rutgers University for the resources provided through Deans Doug Blair and Holly Smith and to Vice President Joseph Seneca.

We are particularly grateful to individuals who gave special support to this work. Carmen Diaz devotedly handled the diverse logistical details, from travel arrangements to organizing the paper flood. In his role as chair of political science, Milton Heumann vigorously supported the work of the Walt Whitman Center. As the symposium developed, we gained from the stimulating thoughts of Kerry Haynie, Robert Kaufman, and Dan Kelemen. Ruth Mandel, Eagleton's director, was an avid participant in planning and implementing the symposium. Michelle Horgan and Michael Soga efficiently administered our public meetings at the Eagleton Institute. Sophia Mihic served as a year-long critic and as a rapporteur during the closing seminar. Marlene M. Pomper expertly revised, edited, and indexed the manuscript. Jessy Thomas voluntarily and professionally developed vital audio- and videotapes of these discussions and provided assiduous editorial assistance. Marlie Wasserman effectively brought the work to publication by Rutgers University Press.

In a more personal vein, Gerald Pomper thanks Marlene Pomper for her encouragement, advice, and, where necessary, reminders that love is more important than publication; his children and daughters-in-law—Marc, David, Miles, Rayna, and Erika—for their commitment to a full and democratic life; and his grandchildren—Aidan, Jacob, Zachary, Daniel, and Nora—for their promise of a bright future. Marc Weiner thanks his mentor—*il miglior fabbro*—for much guidance, many opportunities, and countless insights; his family—Bruce, Nansi, Julie, and Adam Weiner—for many years of support and laughter; and Patrick Simon, for all manner of things, great and small.

Our greatest obligation is to the scholars whose work this volume comprises. They have taught us much; it is our privilege to bring their insights to a wider audience.

The Future of American
Democratic Politics

Introduction

A Dialogue on American Democratic Politics

GERALD M. POMPER
MARC D. WEINER

AT THE BEGINNING of the twenty-first century, democracy is both triumphant and troubled, caught in an ambiguity that provides an opportunity for innovative scholarly analysis. Using that opportunity, the authors of this volume engage in a spirited dialogue on the future of democratic politics, particularly in America. The democratic future will inevitably parallel the future of the United States, the world's most influential democracy. These discussions illuminate those twinned prospects.

Democracy appears triumphant. The United States led the world's democracies in the defeat of the totalitarian doctrines of Nazism and Fascism. The ensuing cold war ended with the disappearance of the authoritarian Soviet Union. Today, there is no ideological rival to the doctrines of representative democracy. Its institutions of free elections, civil liberties, and market economies encompass all of Europe and are increasingly evident throughout the world. In Latin America, notably, there are no military governments in power for the first time in the recorded history of the region. For over half a century—a period termed the "democratic peace"—international conflict has been restricted to local conflicts and civil wars.

At the same time, there are serious uncertainties about the long-term viability of democracy. Its basic principles of equality, liberty, and mass participation remain contested. Economic failings, social inequalities, ethnic conflicts, and religious fundamentalism threaten the stability and longevity of political institutions. Political parties, the traditional hallmark of free politics, are in decline in both established and emerging democracies. Legislative and judicial institutions precariously attempt to control executive and military power. The character and quality of public participation are uncertain. Over the past half century, the population has steadily increased, but overall participation rates have steadily declined. As a result, smaller segments of the population, with parochial interests, engage in a politics increasingly affected by the technologies of the mass media, computers, and the Internet.

The terrorist attacks on the United States on September 11, 2001, transformed these concerns from intellectual doubts to deadly threats. The airplanes that crashed into the twin towers of the World Trade Center, the Pentagon, and the national heartland carried hatred and fanaticism that cannot be controlled or, it seems, even moderated through democratic dialogue and processes. The American response carries its own worrisome implications. Can an open society protect itself from its enemies? Does a government strong enough to protect its citizens from foreign attacks also endanger their liberties?

While the problems of American democracy did not materialize from the dust of terrorist targets, it has now become even more critical to analyze and resolve them. Inevitably affected, even shaken, by the events of September 11, these scholars bring a longer and deeper perspective to their discussions. In this volume, they look at three principles fundamental to democratic politics: equality, liberty, and participation. They examine these principles within the context of the basic institutions of American democracy: Congress and the state legislatures, the president, political parties, interest groups, and the Supreme Court.

Several related themes connect these discussions. Three are especially pertinent: the health of the formal institutions in our traditional system of checks and balances, the attractions and threats of increased public participation, and the achievement of both equality and liberty for future American citizens.

The Madisonian System of Checks and Balances

James Madison provides a core reference for these essays. Madison presented the basic framework of American politics in two major papers in *The Federalist*, no. 10 and no. 51. With the Constitution's framers generally, he attempted to combine two goals: the creation of a strong central government and the protection of liberty. In brief, the methods they developed included "a dependence on the people"—the political process of popular participation and elections; "auxiliary precautions"—the elaborate set of separated institutions and checks and balances; the filtration of popular passions through the selection of representatives and a federal union; and social diversity—the elaboration of competing factions to prevent the tyranny of any particular interest.

Contemporary America may be seen as a more complete realization of Madison's description, as Jennifer Hochschild argues in the first chapter. But it is also different from that Founding Father's ideal, because politics has become less attached to place, less local, and more nationalized. As a result, democracy incurs both gains and losses. As John Mark Hansen analyzes, national majorities are better able to work their will, but, as Wilson Carey McWilliams makes plain, the egalitarian face-to-face interaction of involved citizens decreases.

The authors of this volume raise important questions on the continued viability of the Madisonian system of checks and balances among the formal institutions. They have particular concern about the position of the legislature, designed as the most democratic branch of American government but now challenged by its rivals in the judiciary and the executive.

The leading instance is surely *Bush v. Gore*, the case that decided the presidential election of 2000, discussed in the chapters by Elizabeth Garrett and by Milton Heumann and Lance Cassak. Beyond its immediate impact, that decision is significant because of the Supreme Court's evident distrust of Congress and the political process generally. The following dialogue among this book's authors underlines their concern with the current conflicts among the three branches of government.

POLSBY: It is absolutely right that *Bush v. Gore* was an all-out assault on Congress. The question is, Is Congress powerless to respond? And the answer is, No, they are not powerless to respond. An artifact of *Bush v. Gore* is that a fair number of expected retirements from the Supreme Court have not taken place. And they won't for probably a while. And Congress is stalling confirmations to the appellate courts. It is, in other words, one of the things that is "fun" about our system, the interrelatedness of it all, but it means there are lots of different places you can look for consequences.

CASSAK: What may be starting to rankle Congress is not so much the pure politics of the judicial appointment process as the courts' attitude. It used to be that the courts would set the floor, but Congress got to add to constitutional rights, got to weigh in on the substance of constitutional provisions. And that seemed to be a nice trade-off that gave a role to both institutions. . . . But *Bush v. Gore* really has people in Congress starting to get scared that there really is one branch that is trying to be more than one of three.

GARRETT: But the cases that disturb me more are the ones where the Court is actually telling Congress how to make decisions, by telling

the most democratic branch how it is to constitute itself and how legislators are to find facts. These decisions appear to hold that Congress can't rely on things outside the formal record, and that they can't
rely on information obtained during interactions with constituents.
That strikes me as even more denigrating of Congress.

CROTTY: We are talking about the least democratic institution deciding the most important decision of the republic, the presidency. They
are getting much more arrogant in what they tell Congress. But, if
they are going to be a totally political instrument, and intrude in elections to make decisions, why not make the Supreme Court run in national elections? Then I would be satisfied, even if the guys I want
lose; at least I would have the feeling of legitimacy that I simply do
not have now.

These authors also express considerable concern that the rise of executive
power also threatens the Madisonian system of checks and balances. Daniel
Tichenor observes that at the national level the president frequently domi-
nates the panoply of interest groups, and his power is enhanced when foreign
policy concerns become predominant, as they have after September 11. Furthermore, on the state level, executive power is enhanced by recent impositions of term limits on legislators. Alan Rosenthal observes that term limits
free state governors from the constraints of electoral politics, while Nelson
Polsby argues that they also decrease the institutional resources of the legislatures. These authors tell a story of legislatures under attack.

Popular Participation

Madison regarded popular participation as "the primary safeguard of good government," but these essays raise two almost contradictory concerns. The symposium participants fear that there may be both too little and too much mass
involvement in American government.

Seeking a broadly participatory citizenry, the authors worry over the lack
of popular involvement and the increased public alienation from politics.
These trends are particularly evidenced in the decline of mass mobilization
in American political parties. William Crotty observes that even as they become stronger as organizations, better financed, and more programmatic, the
parties appear to be withering at the grass roots. A shared particular concern
is campaign finance, where the parties have become increasingly dependent
on contributions by the wealthy.

Generally agreeing that fuller participation is desirable, the authors are less consensual on the form or benefits of such participation. They debate whether individual participation in itself will improve American democracy, or whether structural change—in the parties, the electoral system, and the formal institutions—is more significant than individual agency. John Mark Hansen posits that while local activity enhances the self-esteem of individuals, it may be less efficacious than national action through impersonal interest groups. While Nancy Hirschmann argues that personal involvement is necessary to give a voice to all groups and to reflect their identities in political outcomes, Jane Junn warns that social inequalities are difficult to locate and eliminate and may actually be reinforced by a "meritocratic" society.

There are dangers, as well as benefits, in broadened participation. Madison certainly worried about participation, championing representation and an extensive republic as filters against the turmoils of direct democracy. The modern forms of these turmoils are teledemocracy, initiatives and referenda, and term limits, all criticized by these authors. Mass involvement could also create perils, especially in a time of crisis, if the nation accepts an expansion of government authority that threatens the liberties of individual citizens. The contemporary problem is the same as it has been throughout the American experience: "you must first enable the government to control the governed; and in the next place oblige it to control itself" (*The Federalist*, No. 51, 337).

Such diverse implications of popular participation are reflected in the dialogues among the authors.

MCWILLIAMS: You do have to have a great deal of face-to-face association or something like it to do what political participation was historically assigned to do, to tease us out of our private selves and make us more inclined to identify our welfare with that of others and with larger communities. To go to a public place under public circumstances gives you the opportunity for political friendship.

HANSEN: One can strengthen face-to-face interactions, which I agree do produce some very positive effects for the political system, elevating the political discussion and incorporating people into the political system. But at the same time I worry about that delegation to smaller collectivities, because there is also a long political history in the United States where those smaller collectivities inhibit, and in many cases prevent, the larger aims of majoritarian politics from coming true.

HOCHSCHILD: We know empirically that nonparticipants are disproportionately poor, less educated, more likely to be women, people of color, more likely to be whatever is on the bottom end of the justice scale. To the degree that nonparticipants are disproportionately losers in a whole bunch of other dimensions in society, to the degree that political mobilization by parties or something else would get them involved, would require greater accountability and greater responsiveness, then increased participation would increase justice.

HIRSCHMANN: We need to have multiple sites to think about achieving democracy. You can't just say we've got to go through the institutions of American politics *or* we have to go through interest groups *or* through identities. We have to do all of these. Then the issue becomes how do the various pieces fit together. I am not sure they always need to fit together in neat ways. One of the beauties of democracy is how messy it is, but it is also one of the unpleasant, frustrating things.

Liberty, Equality, and Citizenship

Both checks and balances and popular participation are designed not for their intrinsic benefits, but to advance other goals, particularly the American ideals of liberty and equality. The meaning of these abstract goals, however, remains contested.

The traditional meaning of liberty is "negative liberty," the absence of constraints on individuals from government, typified by the First Amendment to the Constitution, assuring freedom of speech and religion. Yet, as Nancy Hirschmann and Gordon Schochet recognize, freedom can also be restricted by social circumstances such as poverty and discrimination. State action may then be necessary to promote "positive liberty," the development of individuals' actual freedom through such means as welfare programs or antidiscrimination laws.

Liberty, though, is often seen in conflict with equality. Economic freedom, for example, will often result in vast differences in wealth among individuals. Government efforts to promote equality, as in affirmative action programs, limit some individuals' freedom to discriminate while promoting other persons' ability to develop their talents and expand their own liberty. In politics, the equal access of less wealthy voters to elected representatives may be limited by the advantages gained by the wealthy who use their freedom to contribute to candidates, anticipating privileged access, if not influence, in return.

Equality has been described as the defining premise of democracy, and Tocqueville saw it as the determining feature of American life. American history can be read as the progressive development of equality, including emancipation of the slaves, the empowerment of women, and the civil rights movements of the late twentieth century. These authors now see class inequality as the most serious threat to American equality as they compare its effects to previous discrimination.

HOCHSCHILD: Is it simply the case that we are substituting one form of inequality for another? Very crudely speaking, we've gotten rid of racial inequality and substituted class inequality. Is that all that we've done? Do we think that is actually an improvement to move to class or technological inequality rather than racial inequality?

MCWILLIAMS: In a sense it is better, because racial inequality strikes me as an injustice of such a fundamental level. Racial inequality is against common sense. The argument that the rich are superior to the poor is probably wrong, but it is not against common sense.

SCHOCHET: If we look at two groups in terms of their status and their position, and we can determine that one of them, on irrelevant grounds, is worse off than the other, then there is a burden upon us to remedy that situation. That is what justice requires. I think that is a principle that is at work in our society, but it is a principle that we are more willing to ignore than to enact. And among the few things that will enable us as a society, a society with a governing body, to effectuate that elimination of relative deprivation is shame, embarrassment. It is very difficult now for someone to stand up in a public place and defend the inherent inferiority of women. I think that is a good thing. It has taken a long time to get there, by all means, and it is not good that it took that long, but I think in that respect, the situation is better than it was before.

JUNN: I think those inequalities will grow rather than attenuate unless and until the disadvantaged start e-mailing and writing letters to their representatives. But, even then, those with more resources will simply find another way to get in and exert influence. Our imperative should be to help understand democracy's role in creating social and political structures that enhance equality, justice, and human dignity. If these indeed are our normative goals, then we need to be certain that participatory institutions and practices attenuate rather than encourage inequality.

To be realized, attractive principles require effective institutions, and both principles and institutions require insightful dialogue. The members of this symposium provide that insightful dialogue on the dynamics between relevant principles and successful institutions. They agree that politics is a noble and worthy enterprise, necessary for abler citizens and a fairer society. Using these ideas, leaders and citizens must now do the work to create a better America.

Part I

The Fundamental American Political Principles

USING AS A SET of lenses three basic principles of democracy—equality, participation, and liberty—the authors in this section assess the current state of national politics.

Jennifer L. Hochschild begins the discussion by applying James Madison's political philosophy to the contemporary United States. Relying primarily on national survey data, she finds some evidence for the traditional pluralist framework, based on the American "melting pot" and cross-cutting, overlapping social cleavages. In contrast, she finds considerable conflict along lines of ethnic and racial identity. The emerging resolution, she suggests, may be intergroup coalitions, in which ethnic identities are maintained but also become the foundation of a new Madisonian system of pragmatic and shifting alliances.

Wilson Carey McWilliams accepts Hochschild's application of Madison's theory, but he sees equality threatened in modern America. McWilliams finds the egalitarian expectations of the nation's founders undermined by extreme economic disparities that are likely to be further widened by developments in technology. Citizens are not connected to their government, and they believe they can control neither the economy nor political institutions. These trends signal a threat to the basic American principle of equality, which, McWilliams argues, can only be remediated by significant changes in American politics, from campaign finance reform to greater personal political participation.

John Mark Hansen considers the character of such participation in contemporary America. He finds participation increasingly separated from geographical place, as evidenced by the development of national interest groups without local affiliates, the separation of voter registration and balloting from local precincts, and the increasing importance of financial contributions in political action. This separation privatizes political involvement and risks the loss of social connections among citizens. At the same time, it may promote egalitarian ends, by empowering national democratic majorities.

Jane Junn examines participation of ethnic groups and social classes. She emphasizes that ethnicity and class are not self-evident classifications, but rather categories whose meaning is socially constructed and, as such, varies among individuals and groups. She speculates on the impact of large recent immigration on U.S. democratic participation. Examining rising levels of education, she expresses concern that these increases may not spur equal participation on the playing field of national politics, but may only reinforce status differences legitimized by an ideology of meritocracy.

Nancy J. Hirschmann turns the discussion to the third democratic principle, liberty, and takes up its interplay with social construction of identity and choice. Because choices are socially constructed, the achievement of liberty requires more than traditional "negative liberty," the removal of constraints on individual action. "Positive liberty" is also required, to enable all persons to define the choices available. Hirschmann illustrates her argument through analysis of current policy issues, particularly welfare reform, disability rights, and the treatment of battered women, and argues in favor of enhanced participation in decision making by disempowered groups.

Gordon Schochet examines the rhetorical uses of the concept of liberty, both historically and in modern usage. Although the principle of liberty is now universally accepted, its content remains ambiguous and contested. Tracing liberty's contemporary meaning to the English Civil War, Schochet examines its relationship to other basic democratic principles, particularly rights and equality. Rejecting the distinction between "negative" and "positive" liberty, he argues that the concept, properly understood, means the removal of restraints on individuals, whether derived from external or internal limits on free choice.

Chapter 1

Pluralism, Identity Politics, and Coalitions

Toward Madisonian Constitutionalism

JENNIFER L. HOCHSCHILD

> *How is it possible for there to exist over time a just and stable society of free and equal citizens, who remain profoundly divided by reasonable religious, philosophical, and moral doctrines?*
>
> —John Rawls, 1993

> *The best provision for a stable and free Gov't. is not a balance in the powers of the Gov't., tho' that is not to be neglected, but an equilibrium in the interests and passions of the Society itself.*
>
> —James Madison, 1792

JAMES MADISON THOUGHT he had an answer to Rawls's question, which lies at the core of democratic theory and constitutional design. Madison sought to create a political system that would control the "impulse" of "opinion, passion, or interest" by channeling citizens into relatively small factions spread across a wide territory and focused mainly on material interests. Arguably all of the separation of powers, checks and balances, veto points, layers of federalism, multiple systems of representation, and other features of American constitutional design that we were taught in high school were aimed at this kind of "equilibrium," which Madison thought could sustain Rawls's "just and stable society of free and equal citizens who remain profoundly divided."

Whether Madison's intent is to be honored or deplored is an issue that political analysts have debated since before the Constitution was ratified. This chapter sets aside that question for the narrower one of examining several ways in which the kinds of profound divisions that Madison feared and Rawls still fears—in this case, divisions according to racial and ethnic identity—play out within the American constitutional structure. Have they been balanced in an equilibrium of passions and interests? If not, could they be in the future—and how? And can such an equilibrium in fact create a just and stable society of free and equal citizens?

The analysis in this chapter simplifies several other enormously complicated literatures by asserting that there are three main trajectories for the politics of racial or ethnic identification within the American constitutional structure. The first is *pluralism,* understood as overlapping or even dissolving cleavages among people who mostly move away from the politics of passion and doctrines into the politics of interests. The second is *identity politics,* understood as separation or even increasing competition or hostility among people who understand their passions and interests mainly through their racial or ethnic identification. The third is *coalition politics,* in which identity-based groups seek to work together, rather than remaining separate or competing with one another, so that they can attain mutually shared interests.

In yet another simplification, this chapter moves quickly though some illustrative evidence for the persistence or growth of pluralism and identity politics in order to focus on several variants of coalition politics. The goal is to raise some questions about the kinds of coalition politics likely in the foreseeable future, with the purpose of circling back to a consideration of Madisonian constitutionalism and ultimately of the future of democratic politics in the United States.

Pluralism

Pluralism has at least as many meanings as users, and for present purposes not much is at stake in which definition one uses. The term is here intended mostly to invoke in more contemporary language Madison's notion of multiple, diffuse, interacting factions. Two meanings are especially common and relevant to the concerns of this chapter: the idea of the melting pot and the idea of overlapping cleavages.

The metaphor of the melting pot was popularized by Israel Zangwill in his execrable play, *The Melting Pot,* first performed in 1908. The protagonist is an immigrant Russian Jew who falls in love with an immigrant Russian Christian, only to discover that her father was the officer responsible for the pogrom that killed his family. After leaving her in horror, he returns, and they are reunited. Exalted by young love and the sight of the Statue of Liberty glow-ing in the sunset, David declares:

> It is the fires of God round His Crucible. There she lies, the great
> Melting-Pot—listen! . . . Ah, what a stirring and a seething! Celt and
> Latin, Slav and Teuton, Greek and Syrian, black and yellow. Yes, East
> and West, and North and South, . . . how the great Alchemist melts
> and fuses them with his purging flame! Here shall they all unite to
> build the Republic of Man and the Kingdom of God. . . . What is the
> glory of Rome and Jerusalem . . . compared with the glory of America,
> where all races and nations come to labour and look forward.

Writers from Hector St. John de Crévecoeur to John Jay, Herman Mel-ville, Theodore Roosevelt, and most recently Amitai Etzioni and Michael Barone (Etzioni 2001; Barone 2001) have all extolled the idea that immigrants come to the United States, lose their distinctive nationalities and cultures, and join together in creating a new nationality and culture that is uniquely American.[1] By now the metaphor is a cliché; an Internet search (using Ixquick.com) for the phrase produced, as its top five results, "The Melting Pot: Ultimate Candle info site," "The Melting Pot—Importers of Minidisc Walkmans," "The Melting Pot Restaurants—Fondue and Fine Dining," "Magickal Melting Pot—a guide to Wicca/Pagan beliefs and tools," and a se-ries in the *Washington Post* on "The Myth of the Melting Pot: America's Ra-cial and Ethnic Divides." But its very descent into advertising gimmickry suggests the phrase's resonance with many Americans. When asked if they think of themselves "mainly as a member of a particular ethnic, racial, or na-tionality group" or "mainly just an American," 90 percent of respondents to the 1994 General Social Survey (hereafter, GSS) chose the latter. That in-cluded not only 96 percent of non-Hispanic whites (hereafter Anglos), but also two-thirds of non-Hispanic blacks (hereafter blacks or African Ameri-cans), more than three-quarters of Hispanics, and nine-tenths of Native Americans.[2] Seventy percent of whites and 60 percent of blacks flatly agree that "the U.S. is a melting pot" (Gallup/CNN/ *USA Today* 1995).

Furthermore, a majority of Americans with clear opinions on the ques-tion believe that the United States *ought* to be a melting pot. On four surveys from 1994 to 2001, with a few small exceptions half to three-fifths thought it "better for America if different racial and ethnic groups . . . blend into the larger society as in the idea of a melting pot" rather than "maintain[ing] their distinct cultures." The proportions within each racial or ethnic group who agreed increased over the 1990s.[3]

The melting pot metaphor is thriving, at least rhetorically. One would need much more analysis, of course, to show how this ideal is actually practiced and who embraces it at a level deeper than a survey response. The point here is only to establish that it has real resonance among the public.

The other main form of pluralism—overlapping or cross-cutting cleavages—sounds almost as quaint, is the object of almost as much academic derision, and has almost as much resonance with the American public. The term received its definitive explication from Robert Dahl in 1967. Although citizens engage in serious conflicts, he argued, "these issues do not ordinarily polarize Americans into two exclusive and antagonistic camps. Indeed the pattern of disagreements in political attitudes and loyalties may itself actually inhibit polarization and encourage conciliation." This occurred for two reasons. "Differences in political attitudes, actions, and loyalties are not closely related to differences in region, social standing, occupation, and other socio-economic characteristics," and "differences in political attitudes and loyalties are not highly inter-related among themselves. . . . To overstate the point, every ally is sometimes an enemy and every enemy is sometimes an ally" (Dahl 1967, 338–39).

Was this ever the case? If so, is it still? According to one widely used measure of ideological and partisan polarization, cleavages among political elites were indeed overlapping through most of the period after World War II, but no longer: "the bipartisan consensus among elites (Congress in particular) about economic issues that characterized the 1960s gave way to the deep ideological divisions of the 1990s. . . . Previously orthogonal conflicts have disappeared or been incorporated into the conflicts over economic liberalism and conservatism. Most importantly, issues linked to race are now largely expressed as part of the main ideological division over redistribution" (McCarty, Poole, and Rosenthal 2003, 1–2).

But this argument is challenged (Heckman and Snyder 1997), and it is even less clear that the American public similarly lines up along a single ideological dimension or is becoming more polarized. The major presidential candidates' efforts in the past three elections to portray themselves as bipartisan cooperators suggest that campaign consultants do not think voters are increasingly polarized. The most systematic analysis of public opinion similarly finds little increase in polarization; only on the issue of abortion rights (and slightly, attitudes toward the poor), and only among Republican and Democratic party identifiers, did the extremes gain at the expense of the middle over the past thirty years (DiMaggio, Evans, and Bryson 1996).

The absence of polarization is not in itself sufficient to claim the presence of overlapping cleavages. But it is necessary. Another line of analysis comes closer to the claim of overlapping cleavages by showing at least two dimensions along which the American public is arrayed. One is distributive, following the basic left-right line that elites appear to be increasingly toeing. The other has been variously identified as social, moral, cultural, or religious. The most recent of these analyses distinguishes groups by moral and economic conservatism and finds that votes for candidates Bush and Gore must be understood in terms of both dimensions (Brady 2001; for earlier analyses, see Scammon and Wattenberg 1970; Gerring 1999). This too is not yet Dahlian pluralism, since we lack evidence of whether people sometimes vote in accord with their moral views and at other times vote differently, in accord with their economic views. We also lack good evidence about whether these dimensions are stably distinct over time, or whether one is superceding the other (as has perhaps occurred among political elites). But having at least two separate and politically salient dimensions along which people array themselves is another necessary if not sufficient condition for pluralistic cross-cutting cleavages.

The key question is whether partisanship or policy preferences line up with characteristics associated with identity politics more or less than they used to. The evidence shows a clear decline, then possibly a recent rise, in cleavages cutting across racial lines. There are, plausibly, three stages. From the 1940s through the early 1960s, the two parties' platforms, presidents and congressional delegations, and nonelective party activists were not sharply distinguishable in their views on racial issues. Race or gender had little impact on the structure of voters' beliefs or their party identification (Carmines and Stimson 1989). But from the 1960s through the 1990s, African Americans and women increasingly became Democrats, while whites and men inclined toward the Republicans. Party platforms, Congressional votes, views of party activists, and other indicators all changed dramatically so that one party became identified with racial liberalism and the other with racial conservatism (Carmines and Stimson 1989; National Election Studies 1998; McCarty et al. 2001). But racial and ethnic politics may again be shifting in a more pluralist direction. One analyst argues that even during the 1980s "racial attitudes had very little influence on party identification among . . . whites. Other issues, especially those involving the scope of the welfare state and national security, played a much larger role in driving many whites away from the Democratic party" (Abramowitz 1994, 1). Another set of researchers found, to their surprise, that as of 1990 racial or ethnic group consciousness had no impact on Americans' levels of political activity and that "there is considerable overlap in the issue concerns of Latinos, African-Americans, and Anglo-Whites" (Verba, Schlozman, and Brady 1995, 355–56, 247).

Some Republican party strategists are working to once again dissociate political parties from racial identification. "If we remain a party of all white Southerners we'll be a dead party by 2010," says one former Republican National Committee aide (quoted in Grann 1998, 12). The fantastically rapid increase and fairly rapid dispersion of Latino immigrants is mostly driving this new attentiveness to non-Anglos; after all, officials of both major parties have pointed out that "if Mr. Bush were to win the same percentage of minority voters in 2004 as he did last year, he would lose by three million votes" (Schmitt 2001).

Are these Republicans chasing a will-o'-the-wisp? Not necessarily, even among African Americans. Almost three in ten blacks now describe themselves as politically conservative and those numbers have risen slowly but steadily since the 1970s. An additional two-fifths are "moderate" ("Thinking by Ethnicity" 1998, 55; author's analyses of GSS and NES). Latino voters are an even more likely prospect over the long term. During the 1990s, up to two-fifths of Hispanics described themselves as conservative and another two-fifths were moderates. Fifteen to 25 percent identify as Republicans, and 10 to 40 percent more are Independents (depending on the survey and how one categorizes "leaners").[4]

Republican hopes are not yet close to being fulfilled, at least for blacks. Only 5 to 10 percent of African Americans identify as Republicans, a number that has not increased since the 1970s (NES and GSS); only 9 percent voted for George W. Bush in the 2000 presidential election. But a nontrivial number of black Republicans is not inconceivable in the future. One- to three-tenths of African Americans call themselves Independents, depending how the question is asked,[5] one in seven voted for President Reagan in 1984, and almost one in five voted for George Bush Sr. in 1988. Thus a recent series of headlines—"Democrats Fear Loss of Black Loyalty"; or "Blacks, Yes; Democrats, Maybe"; or "GOP Starts Minority Outreach" (Neal and Edsall 1998; "Blacks, Yes; Democrats, Maybe" 1998; Hallow 1997)—is not as foolish as it might first appear. If Republicans could occasionally attract a fifth of the black population, whether those with good jobs and high incomes who are edging into economic conservatism or those often with less education and lower incomes who espouse religious and moral conservatism, overlapping cleavages would begin to return.

Republicans have already attracted more than that level of Hispanic voters. Between three-tenths (*New York Times* exit poll) and four-tenths (*Los Angeles Times* exit poll) of Latinos voted for George W. Bush in the 2000 election, and at least a quarter have voted for the Republican presidential candidate in every presidential election since 1976, with one marginal exception (Connelly 2000).

Asian Americans split their votes even more; roughly 40 percent voted for George W. Bush and even higher percentages preferred his Republican predecessors in the previous two presidential elections. Almost a third call themselves conservative and more than a third, moderate; 20 to 35 percent identify as Republicans and 30 to 50 percent as Independents, depending on how the question is asked (GSS and NES; on Asian Americans, see Lien 2001).

A brief look at some important policy concerns gives further grounds for pluralist claims. There is decreasing, and sometimes very little, racial or ethnic disparity in preferences for governmental action on particular policy issues, so long as they are not associated with race in any explicit way. Across the four major racial and ethnic groups, we see greater disparity across issues than across groups in preferences for congressional action with regard to welfare or Medicare reform, budget balancing, and personal or corporate tax cuts. Affirmative action policy generates some group-level disparity, and abortion policy even more (*Washington Post* et al. 1995, 73–74). These are, of course, the policies that evoke the greatest passions and revolve least around material interests. But overall, the Madisonian structure largely obtains; Anglos, who would be the largest and therefore most dangerous faction if they held together, break up into smaller factions with different views on a variety of policy concerns, each of which can find allies across racial and ethnic lines.

In short, there are reasonable grounds for thinking that pluralism, defined as interlocking cleavages and even as a melting pot, reasonably describes some features of American politics. One would need to look at more understandings of pluralism as well as causal trajectories showing how pluralism takes hold and flourishes, even in an era of dramatic demographic change, in order to say much more about it. Here we should simply note its robustness before turning to its converse, identity politics.

Identity Politics

Identity politics has about as many definitions and nuances as pluralism, and here too this chapter can only suggest its contours. Proponents assert that membership in a group with deep cultural, psychological, normative, familial, and historical meaning—and sometimes with linguistic, religious, and geographical meaning as well—forms the essence of one's political persona. Identities usually involve a sense of having inherited or been chosen, rather than deliberately or rationally choosing to be of a particular race, gender, religion, etc. They usually include an intense commitment to keep the identity vital through many generations in the future. As Michael Sandel puts it, we are not "bound only by the ends and roles we choose for ourselves." Rather, we can "sometimes be obligated to fulfill certain ends we have not chosen—ends given . . . by our identities as members of families, peoples, cultures, or traditions" (Sandel 1994, 1768).

Identity politics understood in this strong way create one's interests, shape one's opinions, engage one's passions—but they are not reducible to interests, opinions, or passions. Above all, identity politics as used here implies a rejection of the classic liberal value of the right to be treated only or mostly as an individual without reference to ascriptive characteristics, in favor of the right to be treated as a person who is partly or largely defined by those ascriptive characteristics.

To claim that identity politics represents a totally new political stance would be silly. Many crucial events of American history, from the colonization of Massachusetts and Maryland through the civil rights movement, occurred because of clashes among people committed to particular identities. But identity politics is arguably now playing an unprecedentedly powerful role in peacetime national public life. Illustrations of this claim include assertions that challenges to bilingual education programs are attacks on Latinos, the social cachet now attached to recognition as a member of an Indian nation, the passionate demand for a multiracial category on the U.S. Census, and courts' use of the standard of the "reasonable woman," instead of the (presumably generic) "reasonable man" or "person." Not until 2000 did any conservative presidential candidate make "diversity" in his Cabinet a central campaign pledge. These are changes that would alarm Madison and the Dahl of "overlapping cleavages."

Identity politics rejects the melting pot in favor of celebrating difference. In this view, "universalism of the World War II era served to deracinate and to efface the varieties of humankind by using a too parochial construction of our common humanity, . . . [and] served to mask a cultural imperialism by which the NATO powers spread throughout the world their own peculiar standards for truth, justice, and spiritual perfection. . . . Universalism itself is too dangerous an ideal." Thus "our mission . . . is not to purge the old universalism of its corruptions but to renounce it as fatally flawed and to perfect instead the local and the particular, to live within the . . . unique civic, moral, and epistemic communities into which we are born, to devote ourselves to our ethnos."[6]

The precise nature of each group's identity-based claims is distinct and idiosyncratic. Chicanos, for example, rely heavily on history:

> Comparison to European immigrants . . . is . . . fallacious. . . . The
> presence of Mexicans in American society precedes immigration. . . .
> What is now the Southwest . . . is defined by an indelible Mexican
> stamp. This has allowed Mexican immigrants whether they came in

1950 or 1994 to join the heirs of Mexicans who lived in the region prior to 1848 in making what is in effect a primordial claim on the Southwest. Participating in this claim allows Mexican immigrants to develop a unique psychological relationship to American society, one which no other immigrants legitimately share (de la Garza 1994, 5–6).

More simply, as one student proclaimed on his T-shirt, "We didn't cross the border, the border crossed us." Thus Mexicans claimed coverage under the Voting Rights Act (which Congress granted) and affirmative action, *not* on the grounds of poverty or immigrant status or simple discrimination, but as compensation for the fact that "rights as codified in the Treaty of Guadalupe Hidalgo . . . had been systematically violated" (de la Garza 1994, 12).

Asian Americans also cite historical uniqueness, but perhaps a more powerful claim is social and cultural. In this view, the "American racial geometry" has two dimensions—superior/inferior, and similar/different. Whites have racialized Asians as superior to blacks though inferior to whites *and* as inassimilable and more different from whites than are blacks. This geometry appeared starkly in exclusionary immigration laws, restrictions on property ownership, and controls on naturalization (Kim 1999). Descendents of Japanese immigrants, but not of Germans or Italians, were interned in World War II; many Asian immigrants were made eligible for citizenship only in 1952, almost a century after African Americans were recognized as citizens in the Fourteenth Amendment. Almost all Asian Americans living outside an ethnic enclave can tell the anecdote of being asked when he or she came to the United States. Given this racial geometry, the president of the Korean Association of Southern California is not alone in proclaiming that "we'll never be white people no matter how long we've lived here. We cannot afford to live in America scattered and isolated. Only through unity can our people protect our rights and pass on a great legacy to our children" (Han Mo Koo 1979, quoted in Hing 1997, 229).

Identity-based claims among African Americans, of course, are extensive, complex, and well known; I will not attempt to summarize them here. One telling comment will serve as a placeholder for another huge literature. Rep. Eleanor Holmes Norton testified in the 1997 Congressional hearings on the possibility of a multiracial category on the U.S. Census. She, along with spokespeople for the NAACP and the National Council of La Raza, argued against the proposed category on the grounds that,

at one point, blacks thought they might mitigate the effects of being black by claiming something else in their heritage. "Oh, I am black, but I am also American Indian. . . . " Oh, it was so pitiful. About the only thing that American racism did for us is saying no, you are one or the other. . . . So I sit here as a light skin black woman and I sit here to tell you that I am black. That people who are my color in this country will always be treated as black. . . . We who are black have got to say, "look, we are people of color, and we are readily identified. Any discrimination against one of us is discrimination against another" (Norton 1997).

Madison's constitutional democracy is, for better or for worse, endangered by deep factionalism among large, mutually distinct racial or ethnic groups. But it faces an even deeper threat in the presence of a *majority* faction that "sacrifice[s] to its ruling passion or interest both the public good and the rights of other citizens." That threat focuses our attention on the identity politics of European Americans. Again, one quote will have to stand in for the growing literature on "whiteness" and the history of white domination and exclusion:

Through most of U.S. history, lawmakers pervasively and unapologetically structured U.S. citizenship in terms of illiberal and undemocratic racial, ethnic, and gender hierarchies. . . . Rather than stressing protection of individual rights for all in liberal fashion, or participation in common civic institutions in republican fashion, . . . restrictions on immigration, naturalization, and equal citizenship . . . manifested passionate beliefs that America was by rights a white nation, a Protestant nation, a nation in which true Americans were native-born men with Anglo-Saxon ancestors (Smith 1997, 1–3).

We return below to the subject of distortions in democratic practice caused by the presence of a white majority faction; for now, suffice it to say that identity politics is not the exclusive property of minorities protesting some feature of American political practice.

How much do ordinary, nonactivist Americans ascribe to identity politics? By setting up identity politics and pluralism as opposites, one can start to answer that question by examining the flip side of the survey data used above to demonstrate pluralism. This is conceptually and politically crude, but it is a useful starting point.

In 1994, almost three in ten blacks, almost two in ten Hispanics, and almost no Anglos thought of themselves as members of "some particular group" (rather than as just Americans) when asked to "think of social and political issues."[7] A year later a quarter of whites and more than a third of blacks disagreed that "the U.S. is a melting pot" (CNN/ USA Today 1995). In four surveys between 1994 and 2001, substantial minorities of those with clear opinions in all three of the largest groups agreed that racial and ethnic groups should maintain their distinct cultures (GSS 1994, 1996, 2000; Gallup Organization 2001, 1:23; see also Sears et al. 1999, 53–58). Identity politics does not predominate in surveys, but neither is it trivial.

The 1999 Latinos in America survey shows the complexity, or possibly volatility, of Americans' views about the relationship between pluralism and identity politics. About three-fifths of Latinos thought it "very important" for racial and ethnic groups to "change so that they blend into the larger society as in the idea of a melting pot." But in the next question, two-thirds *also* agreed that it is very important for ethnic groups to maintain distinct cultures. Similar results obtained for Anglos and, especially, African Americans (*Washington Post* et al. 1999; analyses by author). Respondents may have been confused, or this may be a dramatic case of "social desirability response set." But possibly Americans do not, in fact, see the melting pot and distinct identities as mutually conflicting; they may be enacting Horace Kallen's "democracy of nationalities."[8] This is an issue for further exploration, begun below in the discussion of coalitions.

A crucial question for Madisonian constitutionalism is whether identity-based groups are merely distinct from or are competitive with, even hostile to, one another. The former is bad enough from the perspective of *Federalist No. 10*, since it moves political dynamics far away from interactions among small, fluid, interest-based factions. But the latter is worse since it is likely to generate precisely the instability and contention that opponents of democracy continually warned of in the late eighteenth century. Again, this is a huge topic that this chapter can only touch on here, and it relies on survey data as a shorthand indicator of the complex analysis needed to sort all of this out.

Every survey finds that blacks see the most discrimination, both against themselves and others of their race and against other non-Anglos (especially Hispanics). But questions that ask for *rankings* of victimization from bias, not just overall levels of victimization, reveal a sharp racial/ethnic divide. The 1995 *Washington Post* survey, which was noted above to show more division across nonracial policy issues than across groups, shows a different pattern when questions explicitly address race. African Americans think that their group suffers the most discrimination by a huge margin; Latinos think their own group suffers just as much as, in their view, blacks do. All groups, including Asian Americans, agree that Asian Americans do not win that dubious honor. Here are the seeds of antagonistic identity politics, not only in the old form of blacks versus whites, but also in a new contest between blacks and Hispanics. This implies trouble for a Madisonian republic.

Responses from another survey sharpen the threat of enmity that always attends identity politics. Asked to identify groups other than their own with whom they feel the most, and the least, in common, respondents provide a striking pattern. Whites feel most in common with blacks, who feel least in common with whites (as well as with Asians). Blacks feel most in common with Latinos, who feel least in common with them. Asian Americans feel most in common with whites, who feel least in common with them. Latinos feel most in common with whites, who feel little in common with them.[9] Each group is chasing another which is running from it.

Even this quick overview shows that identity politics has enough vitality that it, like pluralism, cannot be dismissed as an organizing principle for understanding factions in contemporary American politics. That conclusion would dismay Madison. It need not dismay us, of course, and it in fact might gratify those who support the perspective of ethnic identity. Just how much they will feel gratified, and what the consequences of identity politics will be for the future of American democratic politics, depend on whether identity-based groups move toward competition or coalition.

Coalitions

Finding evidence of vibrant interracial or interethnic coalitions would be one way to reconcile the apparently contradictory findings that both pluralism and identity politics are flourishing. That is, people may act out of a strong sense of their own group identity, and express that identity in part by allying temporarily with others outside the group to pursue shared interests (which may themselves be closely linked to or distinct from identities). Identity politics provides the motivation; the practice generates a kind of pluralist interaction.

Identity-based coalitional politics, like pluralism and identity politics, can take many forms with various trajectories. Interracial or interethnic coalitions may be a transitional step between pure identity politics and a politics of multiple small, interest-based groups. Dahl usefully depicted sociologists' classic assimilationist theory through a political lens in *Who Governs?*, which "hypothesize[s] that an ethnic group passes through three stages on the way to political assimilation." First, almost every recent immigrant is poor or in the working class, and "ethnic identification color[s] his life, his relations with others, his attitudes toward himself and the world." Immigrants demonstrate a "high degree of political homogeneity. [Their] ethnic similarity is associated with similarity of political attitude, and there is a pronounced tendency toward voting alike." These people act as though they are engaged in self-conscious identity politics (even if they are not), in the sense that their opinions, passions, and interests all stem from their immersion in a particular ascriptive group.

In the second stage, group members begin to move out of identity politics and become more socially and economically heterogeneous. "Although the political homogeneity of the group declines . . . , even the middling segments retain a high sensitivity to their ethnic origins. Consequently an ethnic candidate who can avoid divisive socioeconomic issues is still able to activate strong sentiments of ethnic solidarity in all strata of his ethnic group." This is the stage of coalition politics—via electoral tickets balanced between an Irishman and an Italian, voting districts balanced between those with a majority of blacks and those with a majority of whites (or, more recently, Hispanics), or agreements among civic elites to let blacks run the schools and whites retain control of the downtown business district.

In the third stage of assimilation, descendents of immigrants are very heterogeneous socially and economically. "To these people, ethnic politics is often embarrassing or meaningless. Political attitudes and loyalties have become a function of socioeconomic characteristics. Members of the group display little political homogeneity. . . . The political effectiveness of a purely ethnic appeal is now negligible among the middling and upper strata" (Dahl 1961, 32–36; for later versions, see Waters 1990; Alba and Nee 1997). They have moved out of identity politics into pluralism, organizing their political life around fluid factions based on interests, or factions based on opinions and passions that cut across racial and ethnic lines.

Dahl argues that the politics of Germans, Irish, Italians, and Russian Jews in New Haven (and, by extension, other cities) followed this assimilationist trajectory. "Negroes" were still in the second stage in the late 1950s, but Dahl never suggests that they will not follow the same well-worn path.[10] If the argument about straight-line assimilation is correct, new Americans move *from* identity politics, *through* coalitional politics, *into* Madisonian interest-based politics, which are perhaps leavened by racially neutral opinions and passions.

Identity-based coalition politics might take a different form. Visionaries on the American left have promoted interracial working-class alliances ever since there were enough white laborers and free African Americans to make such an alliance imaginable. In their view, such coalitions are not a way station on the road to crosscutting cleavages or a melting pot; they are a means of gratifying interests and fulfilling moral commitments through the political resources generated by racial or ethnic identities. Lani Guinier and Gerald Torres, for example, seek to show "how racialized identities may be put to service to achieve social change through democratic renewal" by "build[ing] a progressive democratic movement led by people of color but joined by others." After all, those who have been raced as "losers" or as marginalized will often be among the first to see the pernicious effects of normalized inequality. . . . [They] will also be more motivated to understand those patterns of access to social power. As a result, those who have been marginalized or left out could be well-positioned to lead a movement for social justice that others will want to follow if they can frame that movement to speak to conditions of injustice that disfigure our social institutions more generally (Guinier and Torres 2002, 17).

A third type of coalition is a pragmatic interracial or interethnic alliance intended to enable small groups to win victory in a political system that rewards voting majorities and large influxes of resources. Their motto might be Benjamin Franklin's, "we must indeed all hang together, or, most assuredly, we shall all hang separately." Log-rolling coalitional leaders do not expect particular racial and ethnic groups always to ally with one another; that depends on whether interests consistently coincide and whether the groups can develop successful working relationships. Pragmatic or log-rolling coalitions are pluralism at the group rather than the individual level; identity-based factions come together for particular purposes and then separate when they judge that they will gain more by working with a different group on another issue.

Judging by citizens' expressed sentiments, there should be no difficulty in developing intergroup coalitions, especially of the pragmatic kind. At least 90 percent of all respondents to a 1994 survey are "willing to sit down with" members of the group with whom they feel least in common in order to "work out ways for you both to . . . get drug pushers out of the neighborhood," "help the schools teach kids what they really need to learn to succeed," or "protect each other's children from gangs and violence." Latinos were slightly less willing to ally than the other groups, but differences across racial or ethnic lines were small (National Conference 1994, appendices). Other survey responses hint at the possibility of progressive interracial alliances based on the shared status of disadvantage. In 1984 and again in 1996, four in five blacks agreed that an alliance of racial and ethnic minorities, poor people, and women "could decide how this country is run" (Jackson 1984; Tate 1996; analyses by author). Similarly, in 1993, more than half of blacks agreed that Latinos, Asian Americans, and "other disadvantaged groups are potentially good political allies for blacks." Three-fourths of black women agreed that their "fate is linked to that of women," and over half agreed to the same linkage when asked specifically about "white women" (Dawson, Brown, and Jackson 1993; analyses by author). At least twice as many members of all four groups in 2001 as in 1995 reported that "tensions between racial and ethnic groups have . . . decreased . . . during the last ten years" (*Washington Post* et al. 2001, 26).[11]

Perhaps more persuasively, we have no difficulty in finding examples of the three types of coalitions. Coalitional politics along the way to assimilation include,[12] for example, programs for transitional bilingual education in public schools, the traditional and still important balanced ticket for local elections, even former Secretary of the Interior James Watt's infamous boast that he had put together the perfect coal-leasing commission, comprised of "a black, a woman, two Jews, and a cripple."

Progressive coalitions have more cachet among academics, and here too successes can be found. Reading the same demographic projections as every one else, labor unions have begun to woo immigrant workers by expressing concern about immigrants' rights and support for amnesty for illegal immigrant workers. The dynamic here is perhaps similar to that of a few decades ago, when some unions promoted civil rights claims in order to recruit newly urbanized African Americans. After the federal courts ruled that affirmative action at state universities in Texas was illegal, legislators from poor rural Anglo districts, whose students had been largely excluded from the flagship universities, provided the margin of votes to pass the "10 percent solution" bill sponsored by blacks and Hispanics (Guinier and Torres 2002). The Industrial Areas Foundation sustains interracial cooperation to promote community development by "rel[ying] on its members' shared commitment to broad religious principles," by ensuring that its "issues originate from local consensus and thus are consensual, not divisive . . . [and] always framed in a race-neutral manner," and by permitting its organizers to "also serve . . . in other organizations or enterprises that address race- and neighborhood-specific issues" (W. J. Wilson 1999, 87; Warren 2001). In other words, racially- or ethnically-based groups provide the structure within which IAF activists emerge, but IAF itself carefully avoids racial claims or issues. It is a brilliant, and largely successful, strategy for creating progressive pluralism out of identity politics.

Finally, pragmatic log-rolling coalitions exemplify the cliché, "politics makes strange bedfellows." Black inner-city ministers provided the staunchest support for President George W. Bush's initiative to expand faith-based social services, while clergy from affluent white suburbs held back. Self-identified black nationalists have allied with white Republican mayors and conservative foundations to create publicly funded school voucher programs in Milwaukee and Cleveland. Some Chicano activists allied with Republicans and conservatives in California to abolish what they perceived to be a failed and stigmatizing program of bilingual education in public schools. Anglo libertarians have joined black nationalists to protest racial profiling and stringent controls on non-Anglo groups in the wake of the terrorist attack of September 11, 2001.

On balance, progressive coalitions have proved harder to sustain and less likely to succeed than assimilationist or pragmatic coalitions. Socialism and populism both foundered at the turn of the twentieth century at least partly because shared interests and ideologies were too weak to overcome ethnic conflicts (in the first case) or racial bias (in the second). African Americans and Hispanics have tried for decades to unite behind mayoral candidates in New York and Chicago; despite occasional successes (Harold Washington for two terms, David Dinkins for one), they have mostly failed. The reasons for failure varied: they were not able to institutionalize gains made in liberal administrations (note the dissolution of agencies created by New York's Mayor John Lindsay once he left office in 1973), or they could not agree on a single strong candidate (note the proposed candidacy of Herman Badillo in 1985), or the administration had so much internal dissension that allies deserted (note decline in Latino support for David Dinkins between his first and second campaigns), or they splintered once a charismatic leader no longer held them together (note the consequences of the death of Harold Washington). These two cities are not unique; moderate or conservative white politicians have recently proven more adept at appealing to nonwhite immigrants than have liberal black politicians. In Los Angeles, Gary, Philadelphia, as well as in New York and Chicago, white conservatives have won enough support from Latino (and other) voters to replace or defeat black liberal mayors.[13]

The structure of American politics (perhaps of all politics) gives a powerful incentive to develop coalitions with some opponents in order to win a fraction of what a group wants. Thus coalitional politics are not new; what might be new is a growing number and influence of coalitions in which the factions are organized around ascriptive identities rather than around individualistic opinions, passions, and interests. Such factions would be astonishing to Madison, but not as fearful as a more pure identity politics. Such factions can seem like a betrayal of what matters most or a reassuring step toward a safer political equilibrium, depending on whether one views them from the vantage point of identity politics or Dahlian pluralism.

Conclusion: Toward Madisonian Factionalism

Some analysts of contemporary American politics fear that the rising visibility of assertive racial or ethnic advocates is fragmenting at least the Democratic party (Gitlin 1995) and at most the whole polity (Schlesinger 1992; Bernstein 1994). They endorse instead, variously, class-based coalitions, melting-pot pluralism, or simply a focus on issues that really matter (Jacoby 1994). Whether their concerns are warranted depends on the trajectories of pluralism, identity politics, and the hybrids of coalitional politics. This analysis does not permit clear predictions; the structure of American racial and ethnic interactions is too complicated and the evidence is mixed or even flatly contradictory. More important, too many outcomes are contingent on personal and political choices not yet made and circumstances not yet faced. The analysis does, however, permit concluding with observations about the nature of Madisonian constitutionalism.

The American constitutional regime has not in fact, until recently, been very Madisonian. This seems an odd statement given scholars' increasing recognition of Madison's centrality in the constitutional framing of the United States. Nevertheless, American politics has been largely organized around the fact of white racial domination for most of our history. Majority factionalism, involving passions and opinions as well as self-interest, was *not* absent from the polity created by *Federalist No. 10*; rather, the whole constitutional structure was predicated on an unspoken assumption that only people with one identity could be political actors. They were propertied white men.

This fact is in some sense obvious to any student of American history, but its importance has been insufficiently recognized by most analysts of democracy in America.[14] A simple illustration of the point lies in James Q. Wilson's recent discussion of the four conditions that "have underlain the emergence and survival of our oldest democracies." The third was "*homogeneity*. . . . At the time democracy was being established, . . . [ethnic] diversity was so limited that it could be safely ignored. England was an Anglo-Saxon nation; America, during its founding period, was overwhelmingly English" (J. Q. Wilson 2000). But the United States was *not* overwhelmingly English in 1789 (and, in any case, well over half of its English inhabitants lacked the franchise); it simply practiced a form of identity politics that makes contemporary advocates look like pale surrogates.

During the succeeding two centuries, additional groups fought their way into the realm of legitimate political actors—first propertyless white men, then black men for a period, then white women, then Asian immigrants, then young adults, and finally black men and women. For the first time in history, Americans now live in a polity in which virtually all adult citizens can participate—thus eliminating the majority faction intrinsic to the first century and a half of American constitutionalism.[15] The right question then becomes, is American politics moving toward the kind of factionalism that Madison envisioned but never saw?

The question is surprisingly new. African Americans have been full members of the polity for barely a generation, about 15 percent of the time that the United States has been a constitutional republic. Asian immigrants have been allowed citizenship for barely two generations. Even now, the United States is not, and probably will never become, a colorblind nation with no racial or ethnic discrimination. But the political structure is now in place so that, for the first time in American history, members of all races and ethnicities can choose whether and how to move from identity politics to coalitions to pluralism, or in the other direction—as whites have been able to do for a long time. The recent growth of a vigorous national-level politics of identity, and its move into a variety of coalitional forms, means that Madison's constitutional aspiration is coming closer to reality. The future of democratic politics in the United States might now be brighter than it has been at any point in the past.

Chapter 2

Equality's Troubles

Madison in Modern America

WILSON CAREY MCWILLIAMS

In HER CHAPTER, Jennifer Hochschild describes an America that has made major gains in affording equal political access to hitherto disadvantaged groups. Our politics has achieved a broad measure of inclusiveness, offering a more general eligibility for civic membership. Identity politics is "robust," but so are the "overlapping cleavages of pluralism," and coalition politics, working to reconcile the two, edges our public life away from a politics of passion and doctrine and toward a politics of interests.

Our institutions, in other words, finally—after a history of damning exclusions and exceptions—seem to be delivering on James Madison's promise in *Federalist No. 10:* the diversities of a large republic virtually rule out government by any group coherent enough to "concert and carry into effect schemes of oppression" (Hamilton et al., 1961, 61); effective politics requires leaders, if not followers, to be open to pragmatic association with outsiders; comprehensive group claims are scaled down to realizable interests. If politics has lost some of its shine—if it seems less a grail and more a cooking pot— we are for that reason less reluctant to let others have a taste of the stew.

In this volume, Hochschild makes a compelling case, and not just with respect to the racial, ethnic, and gendered groups on which she focuses. Until very recently, evangelical Christianity was politically marginal, with only a partial exception for African American churches. In 1976, Jimmy Carter's born-again Protestantism was just this side of freakish for a good many voters outside the South, occasioning the notorious *Playboy* interview in which Carter sought to dispel the fear that he was a zealot. Now, of course, evangelicals are thunderously part of the political scene, a critical force in moving the political spectrum to the right, although—at least among their most visible leaders—subject to the republic's pragmatic imperatives (Hunter 1983, 1991).

Moreover, there has been remarkably little hostility to the latest wave of immigrants to the United States. After September 11, 2001, there was a predictable net decline in support for the rights of immigrants (exactly balanced by a net increase in trust for people of other races), as well as a rash of outrages against individuals or groups somehow imagined to be associated with terrorism. Nevertheless, while Attorney General Ashcroft's policies are bound to moderate any impulse toward celebration, there has been no significant public pressure for mass deportation, and the president has made gestures like visiting a mosque. Robert Putnam noted, regretfully, that it would have been out of the question for FDR to visit a Shinto shrine in 1942 (Putnam 2002, 22). And American anti-immigrant or anti-Muslim sentiments, so far, seem political small potatoes when compared with similar currents in Europe (Cowell 2002).

However, Hochschild's persuasive account of the tendency toward greater inclusiveness in American politics is at least loosely compatible with the tolerant America of Alan Wolfe's depiction, one in which there is little or no disposition to hurt others, but not much inclination to help them either (Wolfe 1998). Equality on such terms might prove to be thin gruel. Inclusion, though indispensable, is only a beginning: once erstwhile outsiders are included, how much equality do they find in American political life? If all the players are on the field, is the field itself level? And in relation to that issue, the answers are not so encouraging.

Begin with the obvious: economic inequality in America, already the greatest in the industrial world, is still on the ascent, and this, if it needs saying, was not Madison's vision. Not that he was a radical egalitarian: when, in the convention, Pinckney of South Carolina (cheerfully ignoring the slaves in his state and elsewhere), argued that Americans, burdened by "no distinctions of rank and very few of fortune," did not need so strong or so elaborate a national government, Madison responded that an increase in inequality was to be expected, and even valued, as a byproduct of an inclusive, commercial economy (Madison 1966, 186, 194–95, 375). But Madison also trusted that the laws—the Constitution's checks as well as the abolition, in the states, of primogeniture and entail—would deny permanency to wealth and keep it within bounds (Meyers 1981, 36, 406, 408).

At the moment, that hope seems pretty faint. In 1979, according to the

Congressional Budget Office, the top 1 percent of American families earned ten times as much as their middle-income compatriots; by 1997, they were earning twenty-three times as much (Krugman 2002a). Edward Wolff calculates that of the income gain between 1983 and 1998, 47 percent went to the upper 1 percent and 42 percent to the next 19 percent of Americans, leaving only 11 percent for the remaining 80 percent of the public (Wolff 2002). In 1999, Bill Gates's net worth was greater than that of the lowest 45 percent of his fellows (Hager, 1999).

Objectively, even the Clinton years have been described as "far less egalitarian than the . . . Reagan 'era of greed'" (Kotkin and Friedman 1998); in the current Bush administration, of course, ideology also marches in step with inegalitarian dynamics. And since economic inequality limits access to education as well as other opportunities, James Heckman contends that the accident of birth has never mattered more in determining life outcomes. This "market failure," Heckman argues, is structural in contemporary economics, moving Heckman, a libertarian, to call for intervention by public authority (cited in Stille 2001).

In one sense, this is only the latest, ironic chapter in modernity's egalitarian project. For ancient political thought and practice, the problem of political equality (putting aside, for the moment, differences of talent and virtue) was more or less defined by the fact of economic scarcity. Citizenship demanded reasonable well-being and independence; it required, in Hegel's famous formulation, the subordination of many in the interest of the freedom of some (Hegel 1956, 18). In Sparta, the ancient standard for rule by equals, *isokratia* was possible only because her helots, ruthlessly suppressed, attended to economic tasks. As Aristotle put it, only "if every tool could perform its own work when ordered"—if machines made machines—would "managers not need assistants or masters not need slaves," a possibility for storytellers and poets but not on the horizon of Hellenic politics (Aristotle 1977, 17). Barring a solution to the economic problem, civic equality was necessarily exclusive.

The dominant voices in modern political thought, by contrast, as part of the project for mastering nature, set as a goal the solution of the problem of production, seeing distantly the possibility of a thoroughly inclusive citizenship, one that potentially includes all peoples in an equality without boundaries.[1] Paradoxically, that supremely political aim—the goal of a political equality freed from economic constraints and necessities—makes politics broadly subordinate *to* economics, with production established as a rival, if not equivalent, to the claims of self-government (Wolin 2002, 571).

Modernization has evidently lessened—and is lessening—innumerable hardships and cruelties, and it deserves much of the credit for that inclusive equality that is Hochschild's subject (Jouvenel 1993, 16). But the success of the moderns in shattering the ancient basis of inequality has created regimes that are titanic in scale, bafflingly complex, and necessarily hierarchic. They are characterized by towering inequalities of power and, because they so radically specialize lives, they incline to emphasize difference rather than likeness. Devoted to equality in political doctrine, they are its enemies in all too much of political practice (Jouvenel 1993, 57–58, 139). We can hope to reduce this tension by political art, but it cannot be eliminated: it inheres in modern (and postmodern) politics.

There is altogether too much truth in the prophecy of Kurt Vonnegut's *Player Piano*. Visiting a future America alarmingly like our own, the shah of Bratpuhr asks, "Who owns these slaves we see all the way up from New York City." His State Department guide responds, patronizingly, that they are "not slaves . . . [but] Citizens, employed by the government. They have the same rights as other citizens—free speech, freedom of worship, the right to vote. Before the war, they worked in the Ilium works controlling machines, but now machines control themselves much better." The shah nods, referring to the people in question as "Takaru," which is translated as "slave." The State Department representative is outraged: "No Takaru," he tells the shah: "Cit-i-zen." And the shah responds, "Ahhh . . . Cit-i-zen . . . Takaru-citizen. Citizen-Takaru" (Vonnegut 1980, 18–19).[2]

The disparity between formal political equality and inequality in practice is especially marked in a colossus like the United States. The great majority of Americans recognize that government, if it is to deal at all adequately with the forces and dangers at large in the world, must match or outdo them in information and power and centralized authority (Barber 1998). They accept, too, that, in confronting lawlessness—terrorism, of course, but also all the dynamics that law fails to anticipate or master—government must itself have considerable freedom to act outside law (Broder 2001).[3]

Yet those necessities make government arcane, overwhelming and threatening, especially since experience tells us that it is morally suspect and sometimes inept (Rogin 1992; Hunter 2000).

Not many Americans see civic equality in public life: they encounter a two-tier politics in which government is dominated by money, by centralized and powerful interests, and by bureaucratic elites. The mass of citizens is likely to feel itself inadequate and relatively impotent. Whatever was true in the past, contemporary Americans have no strong sense of being linked to government by parties and associations: in 1999, a survey by the Council for Excellence in Government found that 64 percent of respondents described themselves as "distant and disconnected" in relation to government (Herbert 1999).

As Sheldon Wolin observes, it makes matters worse that, while the powers at government's command are titanic, politics seems more or less trivial (Wolin 2002, 564). Dominating in relation to individuals, government itself seems increasingly shaped by the forces of economic and technological change, seeking accommodation rather than rule. Worrying that government is "at worst responsible for the economic conditions that dominate their private lives," Lance Bennett writes, Americans are also coming to fear that it is "at best, of little use for remedying them" (Bennett 1998, 758; Inglehart 1998). In those terms, formal civic equality is bound to seem insubstantial, since the very idea of self-government is marginalized: in relation to any number of the great questions, immediate or impending, politics seems to be edging toward the irrelevant or the epiphenomenal.

This helps account for an otherwise curious aspect of contemporary inequality. Americans in growing numbers—45 percent as opposed to 25 percent during the Great Depression—say that they discern a fundamental conflict of interest between employees and employers. Yet this sense of a two-tier society, strong enough to trouble even Alan Greenspan, is not accompanied by any notable feelings of class outrage or solidarity. In part, of course, cold war anticommunism survives in the belief that any appeal to "class war" is taboo. More striking, however, is the conviction that employers are themselves simply responding to overmastering economic forces, caught up in the imperium of the market and globalization (Kotkin and Friedman 1998; Reich 1999; Bennett 1998, 751). This belief is reinforced by the fact that economic inequality—and the increasing centrality of money in politics—has tilted the terms of political debate sharply to the right (Krugman 2002a).

Still, it is hard to overlook the fact that we are not equally vulnerable to economic imperatives. Capital, situated in the virtual reality of the financial markets, finds it comparatively easy to move from one locale to another and to adapt its relationships and its organization to new conditions. Labor, by contrast, is more tied to place and to polity, its power constrained by the threat of low-wage competition from overseas or from immigrants, and relatively exposed to a "race to the bottom." As G. M. Tamás has observed, in practice globalization tends to mean "deregulation for capital, stringent regulation for labor" (Tamás 2000; Lowi 1998).

In the early days of the republic, informed opinion—paralleling ancient theorizing—was inclined to doubt that wage earners enjoyed the independence necessary for membership in a citizenry of equals. "In the general course of human nature," Hamilton wrote, "a power over a man's subsistence amounts to a power over his will" (Hamilton et al., 1961, 531). For many, this implied the need for property qualifications for voting; even for Jefferson, it indicated the desirability of a public dominated by small farmers, each largely able to live off the produce of his land.

As it became clear that more and more Americans would in fact be working for wages, Jefferson found a new ground for republican confidence: in the United States, he wrote John Adams in 1813, everyone who so chooses can be assured of finding a "satisfactory situation," an income sufficient to provide for "comfortable subsistence" and for old age (Jefferson 1944, 633). Jefferson was speaking of a decent competence, not affluence: that workers could reasonably *rely* on such socially adequate employment was what mattered, since that expectation made them relatively independent of any particular employer, as well as giving them an interest in civil order. Without that security, high salaries breed a bourgeois version of the courtier, assiduously currying favor with his superiors, especially by undermining his fellows.

Obviously, Jefferson's view of the conditions of employment in America was decidedly on the rosy side, but for much of our history, it had a significant basis in reality. By contrast, even before the recent economic slide, contemporary employees, well up the income scale, were confronted with an insecurity marked by terms like downsizing, outsourcing, and free agency and a workplace that tends to be "meaner," more competitive, and less civil (Grimsley 1998b; Uchitelle 1999). And that, as Jefferson would have warned us, is bad news for civic equality.

Of course, there are smoldering discontents. Market ideology, still ascendant, is past its prime, and even during the economic boom, anxiety and resentment stalked competitive euphoria (Pearlstein 2000). At its best moments, Paul Krugman writes, the new order has been "tolerated, but not loved" (Krugman 2000). Employers have learned to worry about "layoff rage" in all its many varieties, and in 2001, the Associated Press reported an increase in the public's support for labor in industrial disputes and a much more significant fall in its sympathy for management (Tahmineioglu 2001).[4] Part of the public force of the collapse of Enron, Krugman comments, is that it "reads like a leftist morality play," articulating and dramatizing the "gap between haves and have-nots": "wealthy executives make off with millions while ordinary workers lose their jobs and their life savings. After all that effort to convince people that the private sector can police itself, the most admired company in America turns out to have been a giant Ponzi scheme—and the most respected accounting firm turns out to have been an accomplice" (Krugman 2002b).

Middle- and working-class Americans have no shortage of economic worries and complaints; what they do not have is any clear conviction that government can make much of a difference or—if it can—that they have the power to affect it (Levison 2001). As Ronald Inglehart indicates, they are supportive of or reconciled to a great deal of economic inequality, seeing it as the price of liberty, but they seethe at indignities and evidences of disrespect, those violations of civic equality (cited from Stille 2001).

G. K. Chesterton located the moral center of American nationhood in the proposition that no one should aspire to be more than a citizen or endure to be anything less: as working Americans are at least half aware, that principle is at risk in the contemporary economy (Chesterton 1922, 16).

Marxists and liberal progressives agreed in the faith that new technologies and a solution to the problem of production, shattering old barriers and associated with a transforming "art of communication," would promote a new, expanded consciousness and a sense of solidarity (Dewey 1927, 184). That, in turn, would lead to a new capacity for collective action, a vastly increased human capacity to control life and the ascendancy of the political over government.[5]

Doubts about this vision have a long history, one reinforced by the failures and horrors of the late century; with reason, Wolin dismisses it as "fetishizing the future" (Wolin 2002, 566).[6] Still, there are some stirrings to encourage the old optimism, most notably in the revolution in information technology, much trumpeted as a revival of democratic hopes.

The Internet and associated wonders have shaken—and, here and there, shattered—old elites, especially since they have allowed entry at reasonably low cost. But they also create new hierarchies, especially given the pace of change: the public, struggling to catch up, masters a new skill only to find that it has been made virtually obsolete by some new development familiar only to the masters of technique (Ellul 1964, 208–18). Differences in aptitude, in understanding, and in using the new technologies—the "digital divide" in its various forms—dwarf those associated with transforming innovations like the automobile and television, which look, in retrospect, remarkably egalitarian. And this hierarchy of expertise only emphasizes our increasing vulnerability to intrusion, technology's increasing victory over privacy as a social fact (Powers 1998; Rosen 2000).

At best, the new technologies tend to drown us in information, promoting the ability to relate to that information (and any relationships that go with it) quickly and superficially (Grimsley 1998a). The new media also exert only a very limited claim on our bodies and the erotic dimension of our souls, so it is not surprising that Norman Nie sees them promoting a "lonelier crowd" (cited in Markoff 2000). Moreover, with the waning of the sense of novelty, users of the new technology—given the inevitable constraint of time—develop routines, visiting only a few familiar Web sites, tending toward a fragmented audience and more concentrated power (Harmon 2001). Increasingly specialized, the Internet's version of a public is effectively privatized, attending to the likeminded (Sunstein 2001).

So far, citizens are not experiencing much in the way of active ability to control public life; theories that emphasize "social construction" are, in the contemporary context, largely wishful thinking. For that matter, citizens have only a peripheral sense of themselves as members of a public: Tocqueville was right to argue that as the power of government expands, individual political and social involvement contracts, so that the logic of mass democratic politics—left to itself—does not point to the triumph of the political but to the retreat into small social circles and an ever more radical individualism (Tocqueville 1980, 2:98–99, 215–16).

For Tocqueville, much of this was a cautionary tale, and so it can be for us. In the present, democracy and civic equality may be "receding," as Wolin says, but his language reminds us that they are not utterly lost (Wolin 2002, 9). We are not compelled to leave mass democracy to its own worst tendencies: democratic forms and institutions still matter—not least in promoting the more inclusive citizenship that Hochschild describes. Despite the privatizing impetus in American life and culture, the vast majority of Americans know that government, with all its faults, is still to some extent accountable and that their voices, however whispery, are more likely to be heard in public councils than in private boardrooms or terrorist cabals. Government, as we have been forcibly reminded, is our best (and some would say our only) hope of treating with the powers of the time on anything like terms of equality.

It is no surprise that trust in government surged after September 11, 2001, or that the change was particularly marked among the heretofore disenchanted young (Putnam 2002, 20–21; Apple 2001; Donohue 2001). But that trust in and enthusiasm for government did not itself draw us into public life. Putnam found some increase (about 6–7 percent) in various forms of episodic volunteering but no change at all in organizational membership and only a minute increase (1–5 percent) in attendance at church or political meetings. People were much more likely to watch TV (an increase of about 16 percent) but were less likely to ask friends to drop by (Putnam 2002, 22). The public's instinct, in other words, was to hunker down at home and, in politics, to follow a sort of pragmatic Machiavellianism that relied on the president to get the job done.

Still, as Putnam remarks, there was a window of opportunity, the terrible moment when Americans recognized that the destruction of the World Trade

Center touched all classes and all ethnicities: tragedy dramatized the fact of political community. It offered the president a rare opportunity to strengthen civic solidarity, but the administration let it slip by. If the World Trade Center reminded us of our commonalities, the president's zeal for aiding commercial airlines, combined with his indifference to workers laid off by those companies, pointed very graphically to the differences in our destinies and our powers. At his most heroic, President Bush did not ask us for public spirit and service; he told us to pursue private goods, to hug our children, and, like good consumers, to visit the mall (Rich 2001). Now, of course, the early mood is passing into memory, just as the flags on homes and cars are fading and frayed.

For the agenda of civic equality, that lost chance is to be regretted desperately, since inclusiveness needs to be supported by a citizenry better linked to government and better able to hold it accountable. The program, of course, is a familiar litany: we need to do whatever we can to strengthen the art and habit of association, especially the face-to-face gatherings that possess what Tocqueville called "the power of meeting"—the ability to enlist our bodies and sentiments as well as our minds and to afford us a species of public dignity (Tocqueville 1980, 1:192, 2:110).

Another caution: citizenship and civic equality are resources that grow greater with use, but—like exercise—only if we are prompted and prodded to begin: public policy can empower us only if, in large measure, it leaves us to endure the consequences of what we do (Tocqueville 1980, 2:105). The failures of the reform tradition—ignoring, for the moment, its numerous successes— were and are chiefly due to its desire to do too much and its unwillingness to endure human flaws (Whitlock 1925, 204; Mackenzie 1996).

One reform, however, has high priority. We need to be relieved of the burden of *Buckley v. Valeo* (424 U.S. 1 [1976]), with its argument that the political expenditure of money is speech entitled to the protection of the First Amendment. The escalating weight of money gives an oligarchic tilt to our politics, reinforcing public suspicion that the game is rigged, that public life only masks "government of the moneyed, by the moneyed and for the moneyed" (Buffett 2000).

The Court's decision, among other flaws, slights the right of Congress to protect, as far as possible, an *equal* freedom of speech. After all, if money is speech, it is not clear why bribery is not entitled to constitutional guarantees: the affront of bribery is precisely that it silently introduces into the sphere of civic equality the inequalities of private life.

As that suggests, moreover, we have every need to rethink the relationship between economics and democracy (Bowles and Gintis 1999; Jouvenel

1993, 409–10). Aristotle points out that democratic forms are compatible with an oligarchic regime in which a majority of the comparatively well-off discount the claims of a poorer minority. The heart of democracy, Aristotle argues, is not rule by the many, but a democratic idea of justice, the conviction that a life freely given—something that all have an equal power to offer—is the greatest and most deserving contribution to the public good (Aristotle 1977, 207–13). Where economics is a ruling standard, by contrast, it operates as an essentially oligarchic measure of justice even where the intent is democratic, since it regards the most valuable contribution as an addition to wealth.[7] There are altogether too many tendencies in that direction in American politics: think only of President Bush's defense of his various tax reductions, that since the rich pay the most taxes, they deserve to get the most back (Krueger 2001; Madrick 2001). Still, we know better, even if it takes desolating experience to remind us: remembering September 11, we do not honor those who lost the most wealth, but those who gave their lives.

American democracy will need to continue fighting the battle for inclusion, but it also has every need to insist on democratic standards of sacrifice and service, reaffirming Lincoln's proclamation of a republic dedicated to the principle of equality.

Chapter 3

The Majoritarian Impulse and the Declining Significance of Place

JOHN MARK HANSEN

POLITICAL PARTICIPATION IS Janus-faced. It is simultaneously an instrument with which citizens influence government and an academy in which democracy develops citizens. In examining political participation we look both forward to its effects on the political system and back to its effects on the political community.

Democratic participation in the United States has reached an interesting state of affairs, one that is likely to carry forward into the new century. It is most accurately characterized as a detachment of political activity from place. People write checks rather than engage in associations; people support rather than participate in election campaigns; people vote at home, or where and whenever it is convenient, rather than at precinct polling stations. More and more, in both collective action and individual action, in both electoral politics and governmental politics, political participation does not take place in any particular place.

The main purpose of this chapter is to explore some of the implications of political participation increasingly detached from place. On one side, detachment from place is detachment from the social contexts that support participation and teach citizenship. On the other hand, detachment from place is also detachment from the local and insular in favor of the national and programmatic. Indeed, of the several motives that have brought us to the state of affairs of participation detached from place, the most important and intriguing is the quintessentially democratic impulse of majoritarianism. Political participation is increasingly separated from place in part because politics, intentionally, is increasingly liberated from place.

Political Participation Detached from Place

Political participation in the United States has long been set deeply in place. The political system itself privileges place in defining political communities. Federalism imparts a substantial—if in many ways arbitrary—political reality to subnational territories, to the extent that the concept of "national" citizenship was slow to develop (Keyssar 2000). The use of place of residence as the foundation for representation and the prevalence of single-member representative districts together link government leaders to constituencies defined by place (Rehfeld 2001). Finally, centuries of local responsibility for such important public functions as policing and schooling necessarily situate much public decision making in specific places. In the United States, and probably particularly in the United States, politics takes place in particular places and, accordingly, so does political participation. Indeed, such is the importance of place that Speaker of the House Tip O'Neill could claim that "all politics is local."

Over the last few decades of the twentieth century, however, the connection between political participation and place has begun to erode. In some important instances, political involvement has come to be detached from the particulars of place.

The detachment from place is probably most pronounced in mass participation in collective action. Theda Skocpol and her collaborators in the Civic Engagement Project have made an exhaustive study of the universe of large American voluntary associations, identifying all that have enrolled as much as 1 percent of the population since the Civil War, forty-six in all. The formation of large mass-membership organizations, they find, occurred substantially in two waves, one—the larger—around the turn of the century, the other immediately after World War II (Skocpol 1999a, 1999b; Skocpol, Ganz, and Munson 2000).

More strikingly, they find that the structure of associations has undergone a marked change in the course of the last century. Early-century organizations were almost invariably federal in structure. They had national offices and local chapters, and they often had intermediate organizations as well, most often at the state level. Late-century organizations, in contrast, were more often unitary, lacking local chapters and intermediate structure. In both instances, Skocpol stresses, the impetus for organization was more prominently top-down than bottom-up: organization began at the national level and spread downward. But early in the century, organizers fanned out from national headquarters to encourage the creation and support of local affiliates. Late in the century, organizers went to the countryside to solicit memberships. Thus, where once the predominant pattern of large voluntary associations was membership in local affiliates of national organizations, the new pattern was membership in national organizations directly (Skocpol 1999b).

The findings of the Civic Engagement Project dovetail with observations about the formation of new lobbying groups in recent times. Famously, recruitment into the citizens group Common Cause began with a full-page advertisement in the *New York Times*. Equally, the prototypical vehicle of the religious right, the Moral Majority, solicited its initial membership with advertisements in Sunday newspaper supplements like *Parade*. Jeffrey Berry has documented the extraordinary degree to which membership in the hallmark political organizations of the era, public interest groups, is based upon financial contribution rather than face-to-face interaction. To be sure, there are exceptions on both the left and the right: Ralph Nader's Public Interest Research Group invested in chapters on college campuses, and Pat Robertson's Christian Coalition nestled into the congregations of the charismatic denominations. But compared to earlier times, and not only a century ago, associational involvement appears increasingly to have become a connection to an office in Washington rather than a membership in a local affiliate of a national federation. More and more, participation in voluntary associations—particularly in organizations whose agendas are "causes"—seems to be detached from place (Berry 1999a; Skocpol 1999b).

The same might be said of participation in other kinds of collective action. Taking a long view, electoral campaigns a century ago were collective action set in place in a sense that no longer holds true today. Political party organizations mustered campaign workers whose public-sector jobs depended upon their candidates' successes. Campaigns sponsored rallies not only to entertain voters but also to involve them (for example, McGerr 1986).

More recently, and of greater immediacy to this discussion, campaign organizations have substituted national professionals for local volunteers. Particularly in campaigns for federal office, but increasingly in campaigns for state and municipal offices as well, candidates hire professional staff and consultants to perform campaign tasks that once were the domain of local volunteers, such as mailings, canvasses, and phone banks. It is difficult to tell whether campaigns have given up on volunteers because they prefer to use professionals or whether they need to use professionals because volunteers have given up on campaigns. But it is clear that participation in elections is more likely than before to be the detached activity of an individual, in turning out to vote or in making a donation, rather than cooperative involvement in the collective efforts of a campaign. Given the territorial mode of representation that prevails in the United States—surely a robust feature of the political system—election campaigns cannot be divorced entirely from place. But in their form of organization, campaigns seem less and less to be "of a place."

The detachment of political participation from place is more extensive than a simple decline in engagement in collective action. Even in the more individualistic types of political participation, there are discernable tendencies toward participation that is not dependent upon place. Consider voter turnout. Territorial representation ties voters to place in a very direct way: citizens are represented in national, state, and local government (almost) entirely on the basis of their place of residence. Accordingly, the vast majority of Americans vote on election day in their designated precinct.

Over the past two decades, however, the experiential connection between voting and place has begun to erode. The trend began in the 1970s with the liberalization of access to absentee ballots in California. In the 1980s, Texas and other states began to experiment with "early" voting: registrants were allowed to cast a ballot at any time during a period of several days leading up to Election Day. Finally, in the 1990s, drawing on a decade's experience, Oregon went the furthest, implementing balloting by mail in statewide contests. Now, twenty-six states with 45 percent of the voting age citizen population allow people to vote other than on Election Day and other than in their home precincts (Hansen 2002).

The expansion of access to the new forms of balloting may just have barely broken the connection between the act of voting and the physical precinct, but new technologies may make possible a future in which voter turnout need hardly be connected to place at all. A round of reform studies after the 2000 presidential election converged on several key policy ideas, prominently recommendations for statewide voter registries and direct-recording electronic (DRE, or "ATM-style") balloting technologies (National Commission on Federal Election Reform 2002; Constitution Project 2001; National Task Force on Election Reform 2001). For the most part, the recommendations envisioned purposes other than the liberation of voting from home precincts. But the innovations could ultimately serve such purpose. Statewide registries with real-time access in polling stations could allow poll workers to make instant verification of the enrollment of any resident of the state. Moreover, DRE devices with preloaded ballots could make it possible to custom assemble ballots with all of the right offices and all the right propositions for any voters, no matter their home precincts, anywhere in a state. Put together, electronic balloting technologies and statewide registries could free voters from the need to vote at the precinct nearest their residences. They could vote near work, near school, near errands, and not only near home. Even retaining geographic representation, new technologies might further detach participation in voting from place. Voters could still be represented according to place, but they would not be tied to voting in place.

Last, consider participation through monetary contributions to political parties or candidates, a form of political activity that seems to have risen in importance in politics if not in the extent of donor bases.[1] Financial participation in politics is unique in its fungibility: its transferability—it may be moved; its temporality—it may be banked; and its form—it may readily be converted to other, more specific political resources. Monetary contributions permit citizens to participate in campaigns without their physical presence. And indeed, in many congressional elections, a majority of campaign money comes from sources outside of the state. Contributing money to candidates and parties in election campaigns, like "checkbook" participation in voluntary associations, is quintessentially a placeless form of popular participation (Sorauf 1992).

In sum, over several decades, but especially in the past thirty years, political participation has become increasingly detached from place. Voluntary associations less often have local chapters, and membership more often takes the form of a financial donation. Election campaigns less often rely upon volunteers for campaign services but more often call upon citizens for monetary contributions. Even in voting, the form of participation most closely tethered by institutional requirements to place, participation takes place less often in a common place.

If the state of affairs in political involvement is an increasing separation from the specifics of place, what are the implications? What does detachment from place mean for our understanding of the emergent nature of political participation in America? And what are the consequences for participation and for its place in the conduct of American democracy?

Let me venture two possibilities. They are consistent each with the other, and they relate each to the other in interesting ways, because one looks back from participation and the other looks forward. Looking back, we might say, political participation that is detached from place is political participation that is privatized. Looking forward, it seems, political involvement that is detached from place is political involvement that is nationalized.

The Privatization of Political Participation

From one perspective, tracing activism back, the detachment of political participation from place amounts to the privatization of involvement in politics. When group membership is a monetary gift rather than an appearance in a meeting, when campaign activity is receipt of a call from a professional phone bank rather than participation in a rally, when voting is an errand to the courthouse or a chore at home rather than a gathering at the polling station, political involvement is no longer a social enterprise but an individual endeavor, undertaken in private rather than performed in public.

Political participation that is privatized raises several significant issues. First, what is the normative psychology of a privatized political participation; that is, how do citizens understand what they are doing when they participate in politics? One strand of normative political theory, which traces back to John Stuart Mill, extols popular participation in government not for the effects of its exercise on policy outcomes but for the effects of its experience on the self-understanding of the participants themselves (Pateman 1970). On one hand, the argument goes, participation in politics produces a heightened sense of efficacy, a personal sense of ability to influence government, a proposition for which there is evidence (Finkel 1985). Whether this effect depends upon a social process of participation is unclear, but it may. On the other hand, and more to the direct point, participation in politics produces an enlightened conception of citizenship, a sense that democracy is a joint enterprise, that participants act not only "for me" but "for us" (Nie, Junn, and Stehlik-Barry 1996). By this line of the argument, the sociability of political participation is a key element in the achievement of a sympathetic understanding of a citizen's relationship to fellow citizens. A citizen understands others, a citizen understands democracy, by participating together with others in democracy's essential rituals. A placeless politics undermines the sense of common democratic purpose (see McWilliams, this volume).

Concerns of this kind most certainly animate the near-universal condemnation of such recent innovations as voting by mail and unrestricted absentee balloting by the many election reform commissions that formed after the 2000 election (National Commission on Federal Election Reform 2002; Constitution Project 2001; National Task Force on Election Reform 2001; Committee for the Study of the American Electorate 2001). In their view, citizens learn democracy from joining together in its exercise. Accordingly, if the outlets for democratic participation are privatized, the fabric of mutual engagement that supports self-government begins to unravel.

Much of the current distress over "America's declining social capital" shares in these concerns. An essential part of "social capital," as Robert Putnam defines it, is social trust, a belief by individuals that their neighbors, colleagues, and fellow citizens can be counted upon to perform their part of the social contract. Putnam catalogs decades of removal from multiple aspects of American social life: less involvement in politics, less involvement in recreational clubs, less entertainment of others in homes, and on and on. Of particular interest to Putnam is Americans' withdrawal from activities that are grounded in immediate communities, in places. Interactions in local communities, more intimate, more familiar, more recurrent, give people opportunities to work together with fellow citizens, to take their measure, and to come to trust them. By Putnam's argument, political participation that is privatized and removed from place fails to replenish society's stock of social capital (Putnam 2000).

Political participation that is removed from place also endangers the capacity to overcome social divisions, a point emphasized by Skocpol. Precisely because of their grounding in local communities, she finds, federated membership organizations reach deeper into the social hierarchy, bridging differences of occupation, class, and condition (Skocpol 1999a; see also Hochschild's and Junn's chapters in this volume). Even as participation in federated associations reinforces the particular interests of the organization, it transcends the interests of the individual because of the collective nature of their objectives, it transcends the interests of the class because of the inclusive character of their membership, and it transcends the interests of the locale because of the national focus of their political efforts. Collective action that opens out from place creates a moral psychology that finds common purpose above the particularities of self, class, and even locale.

What is the effect of a placeless, privatized political participation on the degree to which political involvement finds encouragement? A mountain of evidence finds that integration into places fosters political involvement. Even holding economic resources constant, people who are better integrated into places are more likely to participate than people whose roots are more shallow. Homeowners turn out to vote and participate more in other ways than renters. Churchgoers move in politics more than the unchurched. People who live and work in the same community throw themselves into more political activities than compatriots who commute between bedroom community and workplace community. People integrated into work communities through union membership are more involved in politics than people who lack organizational ties to coworkers (see, among others, Huckfeldt 1979; Wolfinger and Rosenstone 1980; Rosenstone and Hansen 1993; Verba, Schlozman, and Brady 1995; and Gimpel 1999). If the options for collective political action and individual political action are increasingly detached from place, political participation can hardly enjoy the support of place.

That political participation is so often dependent upon place is plainly the result of the web of social and solidaristic rewards that social interaction in well-integrated communities provides. From the standpoint of narrow instrumental self-interest, political involvement of any kind is seldom a paying proposition. Rather, much is motivated by the social approbation received for having undertaken "responsible" and "public-spirited" action, conveyed in regular and intimate interactions with others whose opinion matters. Robert Huckfeldt and John Sprague have gone furthest in documenting the degree to which political participation responds to the expectations of the people around us, people who are most often accessible because of place (Huckfeldt 1979; Huckfeldt and Sprague 1992; see also Lazarsfeld, Berelson, and Gaudet 1948; Berelson, Lazarsfeld, and McPhee 1954; Weatherford 1982).

But other evidence points in the same direction. Sidney Verba, Kay Schlozman, and Henry Brady find that the most private form of political involvement, monetary contributions to political campaigns, was also the least satisfying to the participants. Contributors were much less likely than other participants to believe that their activity had made a difference in politics, despite their more affluent economic profile and despite the popular understanding of the efficacy of money in politics (Schlozman, Verba, and Brady 1999). Numerous others have observed the startlingly low rates of membership renewal in the new citizens groups, organizations that by and large lack the supportive infrastructure of local chapters. Annual rates of membership renewal in such groups struggle to stay above half. In the course of their "experiential search," most group members find too little satisfaction to keep them involved, even in the minimal activity of financial contribution (Rothenberg 1988; Johnson 1998). Political activity that is detached from place is also detached from the social interactions that support much involvement in politics.

Privatized and placeless options for political involvement may also present fewer or less attractive options for political mobilization, at a time when mobilization is a central institutional challenge (see Crotty, this volume). At an extreme, a participatory repertoire that was entirely private would virtually preclude mobilization by candidates, parties, groups, and activists. Atomized individuals detached from social settings would simply be too difficult to identify and notify. The increasingly placeless political involvement that is our subject is not as radically privatized as that.

Still, it may be privatized enough to matter. Elsewhere I have wondered about the extent to which new procedures of voting, like voting by mail and early voting, might discourage voter mobilization efforts, by raising their cost in spreading efforts over multiple days, in the case of early voting, or by undermining their raison d'être, helping to move voters from home and work to the polls, in the case of voting by mail (Hansen 2002). But the questions go further. If opportunities for political participation are detached from the social context of place, it will be harder for political elites to contact potential participants, because much contact occurs through social networks. Likewise, mobilization efforts will be less efficacious, because much participation occurs when mobilizers' calls to action set social processes of encouragement into motion (Huckfeldt and Sprague 1992; Rosenstone and Hansen 1993; Brady, Schlozman, and Verba 1999; Oliver 1996). Finally, mobilizers will know that much less about their targets, and their aims in mobilization will be that much narrower. As is well known, mailing lists of contributors to causes have considerable commercial value, and contributors to one purpose are routinely approached for contributions to other purposes (Schlozman and Tierney 1986). But that is all. Without the broader knowledge that the social infrastructure provides, a privatized and placeless routine of political participation has little likelihood of being mobilized to wider activity or broader purpose.

Political participation detached from place, in sum, is political participation detached from social context, and detachment from context has consequences. It threatens citizen involvement in politics by separating activity from the social connections that encourage participation and from the social networks through which elites mobilize participation. It puts civic values at risk by removing citizens from the social interactions that educate participants in the opportunities and obligations of democratic citizenship. Looking back from participation, at its effect on participants, political participation detached from place is tied part and parcel with the detachment of Americans from political involvement.

The Nationalization of Political Participation

Looking forward from political participation, at its effects on politics, a contrasting picture emerges. Political participation that is detached from place is not only wrenched from its social context, it is also liberated from the parochialism of place. Political participation detached from place has been a key component of a nationalization of politics in pursuit of common and inclusive interests and broad and coherent principles. It has allowed political participation to flow across borders, enabling citizens to pursue causes in other places.

The detachment of political participation from place, that is, may not be an accident. The detachment of political participation from place may, in part, be a consequence of postwar "cause" politics, which on both the left and the right demanded the nationalization of politics and political participation. In important ways, political participation detached from place has furthered majoritarian impulses, or at least impulses that have professed themselves majoritarian.

Certainly, a nationalization of politics was viewed as desirable in many quarters. In the fifties and sixties, for example, many of the leading figures of our discipline earnestly sought a politics that breached political boundaries in pursuit of broader, majoritarian objectives. Grant McConnell described broad public purposes subverted by narrow interests that dominated decision making in particular places, a problem he characterized, in a phrase, as "small constituencies." Theodore J. Lowi depicted a new "public philosophy" that failed to plan and failed to achieve justice because it "parcel[ed] out to private parties the power to make public policy." Finally, in the most celebrated analysis, E. E. Schattschneider characterized democratic politics as a fight, the outcome of which will be determined by the "scope of conflict." Narrow interests will be advantaged by conflict that was "privatized," restricted to the involvement of the parties most immediately involved. Broad interests will be better served by conflict that was "socialized," extended through democratic appeals for support from the larger political community. Despite their differences in ideological perspective and despite their disagreements over the nature of the solution—for Schattschneider to strengthen political parties, for McConnell to strengthen the presidency, and for Lowi to strengthen the commitment to "democratic formalism" in the national legislature—all three advocated a brand of democratic politics that would advantage national and majoritarian interests over local and parochial concerns (McConnell 1966; Lowi 1979; Schattschneider 1960).[2]

The prototype for a new majoritarian politics motivated by a cause to overcome an entrenched local power structure was the civil rights movement, a textbook instance of the socialization of conflict. According to Michael Lipsky, its strategy of nonviolent confrontation was a considered attempt to reach and mobilize third parties—blacks and liberal whites outside the South—with appeals to their egalitarian conscience. The movement used the undeniable drama of confrontation to attract the attention of the mass media, especially television, and it allowed the obvious courage of the demonstrators in the face of appalling violence to activate the broader national public (Lipsky 1968). To be sure, the civil rights movement was grounded in the social networks of African Americans in the particular places of the South. But it needed, and got, a political participation that was detached from place, to bring political pressures across political borders into the South. The strategy of nonviolent confrontation mobilized financial support, both from individuals and from foundations, from outside the region.[3] As important, it mobilized political sympathy for the cause. The movement confronted repressive power situated within a locale that could only be defeated by the mobilization of political participation from without.

In the use of nationalized participation in pursuit of a cause, citizens groups follow and extend the civil rights movement's strategy. According to the Civic Engagement Project, they are strikingly different from their associational forebears. They are much less likely to have local affiliates. They are much more likely to have an explicit political purpose, a cause, and a headquarters in Washington (Skocpol 1999b). From the start, the public interest groups functioned chiefly as staff organizations, and, in fact, a number depended upon the presence of a visible and charismatic leader, like Ralph Nader or Archibald Cox. The policies they pursued moved them toward a conception of broad cause rather than narrow interest. The environmental lobbies, for instance, sought to use the regulatory power of the federal government to address environmental externalities, which are supralocal by definition. Advocacy for government reform, moral values, and social justice is likewise broad in conception. With these objectives, accordingly, they offer to members a chance to subscribe to a cause through a financial donation rather than to participate in a task through a local affiliate. The "interests" they represent are not concentrated in place, where affiliates might be located, but rather diffuse and encompassing. With the cause-oriented associations, the means corresponded to the nature of the ends. In pursuit of majoritarian, national political goals, they mobilized placeless, expressive political involvement.[4]

The mode of financial support for the citizens lobbies surely also encouraged the detachment of participation in associations from place. As Jack Walker first emphasized, a sizable proportion of public interest groups solve their collective action dilemmas by recourse to the donations of patrons, be they individuals, foundations, or governments (Walker 1983; Berry 1977). For individual and foundation patrons, the motivation for subsidy is often a principled, ideological commitment to the group's cause. Patronage itself commits groups to broad purposes. Moreover, with patrons' continuing help, the new organizations do not depend upon membership to the same extent. They do not need a deep commitment from members to pay for the organization, they do not need involvement from members to set purposes; instead, they need members to show the breadth of support for the cause. In some respects, patronage may even necessitate the confinement of membership to subscription and the detachment of participation from place. Membership activism is a distraction, even a threat, when the central organizational purposes are already determined by leaders and patrons. For the promotion of the cause, it is to the best if members select in and out of the group on the basis of its purposes.

The majoritarian impetus toward nationalization of political participation has also played itself out in election campaigns. Political boundaries prevent citizens from holding *all* of their governors—or even a significant fraction— accountable at the ballot box. Any particular citizen can use his vote as an instrument of retribution and reward in just one state and one congressional district, not in the 49 other senatorial constituencies and the 434 other House constituencies. Moreover, as a practical matter, political boundaries prevent citizens from offering their labors to election campaigns that are very far from their places of residence.[5] Nevertheless, the laws Congress passes apply equally to all.[6]

The institutional inaccessibility of most of American government to majoritarian politics certainly spurred the search for devices through which political participation might be nationalized, at least in its effects. McConnell's desire to strengthen the only officer of American government who is accountable to all of the people, the president, was one such proposal. Schattschneider's idea to bolster the only institutions that link the fates of government officials across offices and across places, political parties, was another. Checkbook participation in elections, through financial contributions to political parties and candidates, is still a third—and the only one available directly to individuals (Sorauf 1988). Even if contributors are not qualified to vote in elections elsewhere, they can participate in trying to persuade those who can.

It cannot plausibly be claimed, of course, that the current finance law was designed at its creation to extend the opportunity to participate in campaigns to the mass citizenry throughout the land. The 1971 Federal Election Campaign Act and its 1974 Amendments did not obviously have the effect of unleashing mass involvement in campaign finance. Although recent trends in the proportions of campaign contributors are subject to conflicting evidence, it is clear that the greatest changes—toward expansion of participation—occurred in the 1950s, well before the law (Rosenstone and Hansen 1993, 61; Schlozman, Verba, and Brady 1999). Rather, the current campaign finance regulatory regime responded largely to concerns about the increasingly prominent but murky role of money in federal elections and (in the case of the much tougher 1974 law) the financial abuses perpetrated by the Nixon campaign in the 1972 election.

The campaign finance system, however, did make possible a nationalization of political participation in elections, even if that was not the intention. The 1974 law significantly broadened the legal campaign resource pool to which election campaigns had access: for the first time, it allowed firms and industries that did business with the federal government to make donations to candidates for federal office. Once FECA opened the gates, resources flowed more freely into campaigns. FECA lowered the marginal cost of campaign dollars, making it relatively cheaper to hire professionals to perform tasks that once were the province of volunteers. Thus, campaigns increasingly needed subscribers to causes rather than campaign workers. Causes motivated individual donations, and donations purchased campaign services (Jacobson 1985).

Further, the desire to strengthen majoritarian institutions did play a subsequent role in the design of the campaign finance system. The Federal Election Campaign Act, and especially the 1974 Amendments, once understood, strengthened the position of partisan organs like the congressional and senatorial campaign committees vis-à-vis candidates. By inserting parties between contributors and candidates, the idea went, office seekers were made less beholden personally to contributors and made more responsive personally to party programs. In addition, the Federal Election Campaign Act Amendments of 1979 exempted contributions to state and local political parties for "party building" activities, creating one part of the category now notorious as "soft money." Although critically characterized in retrospect as nothing but a laundering device for corrupting campaign cash, the exemption for party building activities "was ostensibly to help those parties find a role in an increasingly national and centralized campaign politics" (Sorauf 1992, 149 and chap. 4; Drew 1983; Bibby 1999). In terms of the aims they pursued, the reforms seem to have succeeded. After decades of political scientists' laments about the increasing irrelevance of political parties in elections, the literature of the 1990s was the story of the increasing robustness of political party organizations in American politics (Broder 1972; Sundquist 1982; Crotty 1984; Wattenberg 1990; Herrnson 1988). And whether for this or other reasons, there has been a surge of party discipline in the House of Representatives and even, astoundingly, in the more individualistic Senate (Rohde 1991).[7]

In addition, many private political organizations put the opportunities of the campaign finance system to the service of broad, programmatic objectives. The most obvious activities were on the political right. In the 1970s, the fundraising consultant Richard A. Viguerie perfected the use of direct-mail solicitations on behalf of conservative causes and candidates, building an enormous mailing list on the initial base of the roster of the Young Americans for Freedom. The secret of his success, Viguerie once commented, was "believ[ing] there were millions who, if given the opportunity, would be interested in contributing." As a result of the attention conservatives have given to the mobilization of mass participation in campaign finance, conservative candidates and causes had—and continue to have—a much broader popular base of financial contributors than liberal candidates and causes (Sabato 1983, 161; Drew 1983; Jacobson 1985).[8]

The conservative movement not only worked to broaden the mass base of participation in campaign finance, it also directed the resources toward a national program. The financing enabled conservatives to pursue their cause across political boundaries, to put their ideological case before voters in states across the nation. In many cases, they were very successful. In 1980, for instance, the National Conservative Political Action Committee (NCPAC), led by Terry Dolan, used "independent expenditures" to support conservative Republican challengers to six liberal Democratic senators. NCPAC made the case to the voters of California, Idaho, Indiana, Iowa, South Dakota, and Washington that their senators had policy views that were too liberal. Although other factors probably played the major role in all the races, NCPAC's candidates won four of the six, contributing to the surprising GOP takeover of the Senate in that year. Checkbook participation enabled the conservative strategy of nationalization of electoral politics.

The causes the conservatives pursued through nationalized participation in election campaigns were really little different in scope from the causes liberals pursued through nationalized participation in citizens groups.[9] Republicans characterized the Democrats as the party of parochial "special" interests that resisted popular majorities. They sought to nationalize elections on questions of major importance, like the size of government. The apogee of the conservative campaign to nationalize elections, of course, was Newt Gingrich's "Contract with America," which led the way to Republican control of the House of Representatives for the first time in a generation. It could be held up as a paragon in any number of paeans to responsible party government. The possibilities inherent in a nationalized form of political participation dovetailed with the conservative strategy for assuming power on the national level (Pomper 1999; Bibby 1999; Herrnson and Dwyre 1999; Jacobson 1985; Reichley 1985).

The increasing detachment of political participation from place, then, has accompanied an increasing nationalization of political participation. Placeless forms of political participation facilitated the pursuit of encompassing causes, mostly liberal, in associational politics. Equally, placeless forms of political participation facilitated the pursuit of encompassing causes, mostly conservative, in electoral politics. The great irony, of course, is that democratic (in the sense of majoritarian) ends worked at cross-purposes to democratic (in the sense of inclusive) means.

Looking Ahead

Although often said, it is never certain that the past is prologue. Such is the nature of human rationality that an understanding of the social world sometimes feeds back into its reform. The detachment of political participation from place arose from the decisions of both citizens and their leaders. It was unintended in some ways but intended in others. Perhaps the new bipartisan concern with the detachment of individuals from society, with "the collapse of American community," might redirect policy attention toward the promotion of political involvement that is more firmly attached to place.

Or perhaps there are too many forces that work in the opposite direction, toward the further detachment of political participation from place. Such recent innovations as unrestricted absentee voting and voting by mail have been advanced to serve the convenience of voters and to encourage their involvement, two considerations that are not likely to diminish in importance. As technologies like statewide voter registration and electronic balloting eventually remove the necessity that voters present themselves physically in their residential precincts, they also make possible even greater convenience for voters. Tracing out the possibilities even further (perhaps well beyond the bound of practical likelihood), new technologies of voter participation even undermine the practical justification for geographic representation (Rehfeld 2001). To be sure, the situation of representation in place is deeply ingrained in the American political tradition, not least in constitutional federalism. But already large numbers of people have substantial and direct interest in places other than their sites of legal residence, and there is no reason to believe that community of residence is necessarily more central to political interests than any other. Some 24 percent of the workforce, for instance, works outside the county of residence, about 4 percent out of state.[10] And, already, the ever-shifting constituency boundaries necessary to guarantee voter equality render representation more and more an abstraction and less and less a relationship.

Or perhaps there are just too many considerations that conflict. The detachment of political participation from place and its attendant detachment from social context have raised concern, even alarm, in many quarters. We would probably agree that forms of participation that inculcate democratic values and promote citizen involvement ought not to be weakened. And we would probably all worry when the primary vehicle for a nationalized politics that transcends the parochialisms of place is money, the political resource that of all the political resources is the most unevenly distributed (Schlozman, Verba, and Brady 1999; Rosenstone and Hansen 1993; Skocpol 1999b).

But we may not be able to have matters both ways, both to strengthen support for political participation through place and to strengthen a nationalized majoritarian politics that transcends place. If political participation set in a particular place is just an idle exercise, to be overridden by decisions reached above, broad popular involvement in democratic processes may well be difficult to sustain. But if it is not an empty exercise, if participation set in place is to matter, then how and when are majorities to rule?

Political participation that is detached from place may well be worse for democratic participation, but if it overcomes the particularism of place, it is not necessarily worse for democracy. The object of political participation is not just to develop citizens but also to produce policies that serve national majorities. Participation detached from place may make it harder for people to develop as citizens, but it may also make it easier for citizens to have clear and coherent choices as voters.[11] The future of democratic participation depends not only upon who is its subject but also, crucially, upon what is its object.

Chapter 4

The Future of
Democratic Participation

The Significance of Immigration,
Race, and Class

JANE JUNN

Dᴇᴄʟɪɴɪɴɢ ʀᴀᴛᴇs ᴏꜰ ᴠᴏᴛɪɴɢ and participation have recently become something of an obsession among analysts of U.S. politics. These negative trends
in civic engagement have been interpreted as signaling a demobilized and apa-
thetic electorate, an evasive and unresponsive government, or perhaps both.
Various theories attempt to explore this participatory anemia: weakened political parties and civic associations fail to mobilize like they once did; corruption and political scandals make politics seem uglier today than in earlier
decades; even television and working mothers have been identified as culprits.
The nationalization of the political spectacle, covered on network news and
driven by an inside-the-beltway mentality, and the privatization of politics,
best exemplified by the influence of PAC money and political consultants willing to switch allegiance at the drop of a check, are interpreted as further evidence of the ill health of the American democracy.

Yet the story of participatory decline is complex, and some of the factors
thought to attenuate activity are either identified erroneously or behave in a
contradictory fashion. For instance, political parties are in many ways stronger
today than a quarter-century ago (see Crotty, this volume), and while political
scandals of late are perhaps more lascivious than in the past, politicians in
the United States have never acted nor been portrayed as paragons of moral
virtue. Further complicating matters is the observation of seemingly paradoxical
trends in antecedents to political activity and participation itself. Education—

what Philip Converse (1972) described as the universal solvent because it is always the strongest predictor of activity—has increased dramatically over the past quarter century during exactly the time participation has declined. Likewise, substantial growth in the nonwhite minority population in the United States has not been accompanied by political mobilizations similar to the organization of ethnic immigrants in the early twentieth century or race-based activity during the civil rights movement.

Renewed interest in the quantity and character of civic engagement is a welcome trend, not only so that better sense can be made of changes over time, but also because the contours of participation—a critical mechanism of representation linking citizens and leaders—are an important starting point for an evaluation of the existence of liberty and equality in American democracy. A focus on the future of democratic participation leads to this central question: how level is the playing field among the potential participants?

Concern about the context and amount of participation animate many of the chapters in this volume. Indeed, this essay originates in John Mark Hansen's analysis of the declining significance of place for participation and the possibility of better policy alternatives resulting from national majoritarian impulses. Furthermore, before we can advocate that more participation is desirable for democracy, particularly at the local community level, we need to consider, as Nancy Hirschmann urges, the significance of social context in constructing the incentives and opportunities for political activity. Participation may not be beneficial for particular groups of potential participants. On a different tack, Jennifer Hochschild's project to reconcile pluralism and identity politics suggests that participation has recently facilitated the possibility of a true Madisonian constitutionalism. Her contention that individuals from groups previously marginalized and discriminated against have now "fought their way into the realm of legitimate political actors" (this volume, 27), suggests a bright future for equality. In response, Wilson Carey McWilliams wisely cautions us to consider how satisfied we are with an equality that, while allowing players onto the field, might nevertheless tilt that field in favor of some at the expense of others. To use another metaphor, have we a hearty stew of strong liberty and equality, or is it a thin gruel? (McWilliams, this volume, 30).

This chapter focuses on the increasing significance of immigration, race, and class for future democratic participation in the United States. The basic premise is that we need to develop better analytical tools to measure individual-level variables such as race and class, as well as better strategies to conceptualize their significance for participation. The argument raises three issues. First, what classifications of race and ethnicity are relevant to political participation, and how can such categorization be made? Here, we need to recognize and better account for the interplay between race as a social structural context and ethnicity as an affective identity. Second, what aspects of the social and political context interact with race to influence political activity? While having few concrete answers to this question, I suggest we need to better understand the circumstances wherein a racial or ethnic identification becomes relevant for political action. Third, in what ways do the assumptions brought to the design and conduct of research, as well as the interpretation of findings, influence conclusions about the significance of race and class to political participation in the United States? Here, I quarrel with a widely held and mostly implicit epistemological perspective among students of political behavior that assumes an equality of individual agency.

Immigration and the Significance of Race for Political Participation

Questions about race and political participation in the United States are becoming increasingly salient as foreign immigration dramatically alters the demographic composition of American society. In 2000, one in ten residents of the United States was a foreign-born immigrant, and more than three-quarters of these new entrants to the U.S. political system came from sending countries in Latin America, the Caribbean, Asia, and Africa. Together with their first-generation offspring, this is the highest proportion of immigrants and their children since the last great wave of immigration in the early twentieth century. The combination of foreign migration to the United States and higher birth rates among minorities has resulted in a remarkably diverse population, with nearly one-third of Americans classified as something other than "white." What are the consequences of this diversity for politics in America? More specifically, what is the future of democratic participation amidst this diversity?

Not since the critical elections of the New Deal realignment has the American populace appeared so ethnically diverse. The proportion of residents born outside of the United States has grown steadily to more than 10 percent of the population from its midcentury low point, and the absolute number of new entrants to the U.S. political system, totaling 28.4 million foreign born in 2000, rivals the pace of immigration in the late nineteenth and early twentieth centuries, when between 500,000 and 1 million immigrants entered the country each year. Immigration policy shows no imminent signs of retreat to the restrictive policies set forth by the Johnson-Reed Immigration Act of 1924 (which traces some of its more insidious roots to the Chinese Exclusion Law of 1882 and the activities of the Dillingham Commission between 1907 and

1911). While some political rhetoric and recent ballot initiatives in California echo President Calvin Coolidge's restrictionist message of an "America for Americans," the continued demand for willing and able workers from abroad foreshadows a continuation of the relatively open immigration policy of the past two decades.[1]

A number of politically relevant parallels can be drawn between the pattern of ethnic diversity at the turn of the last century and today's situation of a multiethnic polity: Like their earlier counterparts, today's immigrants to the United States come from a wide variety of foreign countries. While the largest number of late-nineteenth and early-twentieth-century immigrants came from sending countries in Europe and disembarked in New York City, new citizens from Asian and North American locations also entered through western states and U.S. territories. Like immigrants today, this earlier generation of newcomers spoke languages other than English, came from poor or modest economic backgrounds, often lived in urban ethnic enclaves, were younger than the average native-born American, and, on average, had larger families. Then, as now, some raised questions about their ability to assimilate to American politics and culture.[2] While the earlier immigrants from Germany, Ireland, Italy, and eastern Europe were slow to naturalize, the eventual strategic mobilization of these new citizens by ethnic organizations and the urban political machines of their era created lasting political consequences for politics in the United States.[3] As time passed, later generations moved out of the enclaves, married members of competing ethnic groups, retained some culinary and holiday rituals, but lost the language and identities of their grandparents' home country. The mixtures of Irish, German, Italian, and East European were eventually amalgamated to simply "white" (Alba 1990; Waters 1990). This combination of social and political assimilation contributed to an altered understanding of the racial category of "white." Slowly and grudgingly, the once-undesirable immigrants—the Irish, Italians, and Jews—were given and adopted the racial identity of "whiteness."[4]

Race and ethnicity have always been an important story in the study of political participation, particularly during the period in which the power of urban political machines and political parties were built on coalitions of ethnic voting blocs. Yet as these earlier ethnic identities among voters began to fade, research on the significance of race for political participation began to concentrate more of its attention on the differences in political behavior between whites and African Americans. Coinciding with the widespread use of the large-sample survey, this line of inquiry produced important findings, particularly with regard to African Americans. Most studies showed that while African Americans were less likely to take part in a range of political activities, their rates of participation were actually higher than what would be predicted given their relatively low socioeconomic status.[5] In addition to resources, mobilization by religious organizations and black candidates for office has been particularly effective in increasing political participation among African Americans (Tate 1993; Harris 1994; Bobo and Gilliam 1990).

Analyses of political participation among Latinos similarly highlights the importance of social and economic resources.[6] However, Latinos are substantially less likely than non-Hispanic whites and African Americans to participate, even when their level of socioeconomic status is taken into account; studies of regional populations in Texas and California found similar results (see Calvo and Rosenstone 1989; de la Garza 1995; de la Garza and DeSipio 1999; DeSipio 1996; F. C. Garcia 1988, 1997; Leighley and Vedlitz 2000; Junn 1999; Montoya 1996; Verba et al. 1993).

Work on Asian American political participation is more rare, with a few studies based on state samples, mostly from California. The data show that there is a great deal of variation in political activity among Asian Americans based on generation of immigration, ethnic background, and, to a lesser extent, socioeconomic status (see Lien 1994, 1997; Tam 1995; Lee 1998; Uhlaner, Cain, and Kiewiet 1989). In addition to research on minority political behavior using quantitative survey data, there are also a number of studies utilizing data from in-depth interviews of small populations of activists, as well as historical accounts of participatory action by groups of minority Americans.[7] A growing body of research among political scientists uses multiple methodologies to study immigrant political participation.[8]

Two conclusions follow from the research on race and political participation. The more in-depth, qualitative analyses demonstrate the critical effects of economic, social, and political contexts on the ability and willingness of African Americans, Latinos, and Asian Americans to participate in political activities. The findings from quantitative studies based on survey data reiterate the importance of individual-level resources, particularly education and other indicators of social standing, for political participation. With few exceptions, the story of the significance of race for political participation reveals that the social and economic resources (or SES, for socioeconomic status) play the dominant role. Data demonstrate repeatedly that those more highly educated and those with more substantial economic resources participate in politics at higher rates than those with less formal education and more modest incomes. With respect to explaining political participation among minority Americans, the SES model has also proved useful; once higher levels of education and family wealth among whites have been accounted for, African Americans and Latinos have been found to participate at or near the same rates as their more economically and educationally advantaged white counterparts.

Yet despite its perceived success, the SES model suffers from several significant problems. First, while it identifies the individual-level factors related to political activity, the model says little about what exactly makes education and income such powerful predictors of participation.[9] Second, and more damaging to its logic, is the fact that the model yields predictions about political behavior in the wrong direction over time. What has famously been described by Richard Brody (1978) as the "puzzle of participation," is the expectation of the SES model that participation should grow over time, with rising education and income, but in fact we have seen a decline in electoral activity. Inconsistent with the model's prediction, political engagement has not followed the upward trajectory of socioeconomic status; voting, campaign work, and other forms of engagement in electoral politics have declined or remained constant while average levels of formal education have increased dramatically over time.[10] Finally, there is a problem in any positive reaction: the finding that differences in political activity with whites either disappear or recede significantly once disparities in resources are considered. Making whites and minorities look like one another statistically disguises substantial differences in social and political resources. It is an odd way to find optimism. The statistical technique creates an imaginary society where everyone is well educated and wealthy, one that would be impossible in the current American democratic system. The hierarchical configuration of democratic-capitalist values, structures, and the institutions that support them—including education—are in no imminent danger of extinction. Notwithstanding these difficulties, the implications of the SES model have been interpreted by fans of liberal democracy as encouraging. Potential participants in the polity can and should be brought into the political system by increasing their reserve of social and economic resources.

CATEGORIZING BY RACE

In considering the significance of race for political participation, we must first decide how to categorize people into groups. Over the past few decades, the most common approach has been a simple binary classification of black or white, and when there are a sufficient number of Latinos, adding a third measure for that racial grouping. This simple division is harder to justify as the U.S. population has become increasingly diverse.

Nearly one-third of the population considers itself something other than white, and less than half of those, in turn, identify as black. Similar to the complex reconstruction of the category of whiteness in the early twentieth century, the category of "blackness" is undergoing its own shifts as a result of international migration to the United States from the Caribbean, the African continent, and, to a lesser degree, South America. In 1996, more than 15 percent of the foreign-born residents in the United States came from a sending country in the Caribbean or Africa. Most Africans identify themselves as black, but Cubans and Dominicans of African and mixed descent, for example, might feel equally comfortable with the classification of Latino. Sociologist Mary Waters (1999) has researched black racial identities among immigrants. Tracing generations of black West Indian immigrants in New York City, Waters finds that while these immigrants initially find success in a relatively smooth transition into the American economic structure, their children begin to lose positive West Indian cultural values through erosion by persistent and blatant racial discrimination against blacks in American society. The intricate interplay Waters reveals between race as a social-structural context and ethnicity as an affective identity demonstrates the complexity of the task of sorting out these classifications.

Further complicating the task is the fact that the categories of race and ethnicity are not mutually exclusive. For instance, in the Census 2000 long form, respondents are allowed to select more than one category of "race" to describe themselves: "White; Black, African American or Negro; American Indian or Alaskan Native; Asian Indian; Chinese; Filipino; Japanese; Korean; Vietnamese; Other Asian; Native Hawaiian; Guamanian or Chamorro; Samoan; Other Pacific Islander; or Some other race." The question preceding the race item asks if the person is "Spanish/Hispanic/Latino," with the following categories: "Mexican, Mexican American or Chicano; Puerto Rican; Cuban; or other Spanish/Hispanic/Latino." A few questions later, respondents are asked for a verbatim response to their "ancestry or ethnic origin," which includes examples such as "African American; Cambodian; Cape Verdean; Dominican; French Canadian; Haitian; Italian; Jamaican; Korean; Lebanese; Mexican; Nigerian; Norwegian; Polish; Taiwanese; Ukrainian." If you are now even more unsure about the distinctions between "race" and "ethnicity," you are not alone. The U.S. Census Bureau itself faces political challenges from a number of ideologically—and ethnically—diverse groups regarding the way it will use the Census 2000 data to identify minority populations, a decision of particular significance to the practice of race-conscious legislative districting.

The intricacies of racial and ethnic classification extend still further and encompass resistance to categorization into wider racial groups when subjective identities are in conflict with more objective racial categories, or when diverse racial and ethnic backgrounds require multiple hyphens. For instance, Cubans may chafe at being grouped with Mexicans, third-generation Chicanos may take exception to classification with new immigrant populations from Central America. Alternatively, some minority Americans may refuse an ethnic or racial label, preferring a "white honorific" instead.[11] There are others—for example, ethnic Chinese who are native to former African slave colonies such as Jamaica, whose subjective identification is black Caribbean—who have even more complex identifications (Rogers 2000). Finally, how are we to classify the rapidly growing group of multiethnic Americans, whose parents come from different racial and ethnic backgrounds? Popular news magazines, such as *Newsweek,* are asking these questions and showing the faces of native-born Americans with such racial and ethnic backgrounds as "Trinidadian-Sicilian; German Jewish-Korean; African American-German-Native American; Polish-African American-Puerto Rican; and Lebanese-Dominican-Haitian-Spanish."[12] The steadily increasing rate of intermarriage (particularly among Latinos and whites and Asians and whites) foreshadows more growth in the set of hyphenated racial and ethnic categories.

While this degree of variation and malleability can be bewildering, it also provides fertile ground from which a robust set of politically relevant classifications for race and ethnicity can grow. The diversity of categories indicates the degree to which such groupings are social constructions, created and maintained by individuals alone, and together in society (Omi and Winant 1994). From the perspective of studying the significance of race for political participation, political science needs to construct categories for analysis that are both relevant to the people themselves and signify the group's location within the political structure. In other words, a racial and ethnic classification that is salient to political action is one that must be contingent upon both affective ascription and identification, as well as the categorical boundaries imposed and maintained by the social order. A. L. Epstein describes the latter as negative identity and uses the example of the social category of *mischling,* in which "elements of negative identity are nearly always present where ethnic groups occupy a position of inferiority or marginality within a dominance hierarchy. Abundant evidence is to be found in colonial situations, but it is no less characteristic, though in varying degree, of minority groups in modern states: it has contributed importantly to the identity of American Blacks" (Epstein 1978, 102).[13]

Categories of racial and ethnic identity are therefore most fruitfully understood as the interplay of both internal (ascriptive positive identity) and external forces (negative identity). Using evidence from his fieldwork in the United States and New Guinea, Epstein argues that this framework is explicitly defined in structural terms.

Ethnicity quickly becomes intimately interwoven with questions of hierarchy, stratification, and the pursuit of political interests. In these circumstances, the categories quickly become 'social facts' in the Durkheimian sense, increasingly taking on a life of their own, from which it may be extremely difficult for the individual to escape. Identity, as I have suggested, always involves a measure of choice, but here it operates within severe constraints, though these may vary in their intensity as between different groups. (Epstein 1978, 109)

Nevertheless, these categories need not be durable to be useful; rather, their definition and composition should accurately reflect the social circumstances at the time of the analysis. By way of example, the reason behind the virtual disappearance of contemporary scholarship on the Irish vote is the same reason why Irish identity in the United States today is most often recognized during what has become a celebratory holiday in March and signified with a "Kiss Me, I'm Irish!" button. Being Irish no longer signals one's place at the bottom of the social and political hierarchy, nor does the subjective identification carry with it as substantial a political meaning. Classifications of race and ethnicity that are relevant to political participation should reflect the social structural forces at play.

THE STRUCTURAL CONTEXT
A parallel challenge for political science is to specify a set of measures that capture the structural opportunities and constraints within which Americans conduct politics. What are the aspects of the social and political context that interact with race to influence political activity, and how might we measure them?

Scholarship in social science provides ample evidence of the racial biases in American political institutions, jurisprudence, and public policies such as welfare (for example, Lieberman 1998; Skocpol 1995; Smith 1997; see also Hirschmann, this volume). While scholars disagree as to the scope of the bias and the intention of the policymakers who created the policies and institutions that continue to structure government in America today, they concur that race has played a major role in American political development and that minority citizens have usually been on the short end of the stick. While much research on citizen participation in the political behavior tradition is mindful of this legacy, the emphasis on individual-level survey data often leads analysts to see individuals in social isolation. To deal with this problem, we need both to generate better measures of the social and political context and to provide better explanations for the impact of these structural indicators. Some excellent research moves in this direction. In their analysis of participatory activity among minority residents of Texas, Jan Leighley and Arnold Vedlitz demonstrate the significance of psychological resources, social connectedness, group identity and consciousness, and group conflict in addition to resources for minority participation (Leighley and Vedlitz 1999). While not explicitly a structural argument, they include indicators of the structural constraints and relevant opportunities. Burns, Schlozman, and Verba (2001) on gender and political activity provide a second example. They analyze the effect of home and family environment on women's participation, but, more important, they consider what being a woman means to her place in society, including non-political institutions. Explicitly integrating the structural constraints for individuals within politically relevant groups, they attempt to demonstrate the linkages between individuals, institutional contexts, and the eventual participatory consequences. Eric Oliver (2001) offers a third example in his work on the effect of suburbanization on civic engagement.

This research moves us in the right direction in three important ways: by proposing and testing varieties of inferential models of activity, theorizing about and then operationalizing the mechanisms by which structural inequalities constrain individuals in subordinate groups through institutional context, and marrying aggregate-level data of the local political region with individual-level data. Together, it demonstrates that a focus on the nexus between institutions, context, and individual behavior illuminates the significance of race for political participation. We can make more progress if we shift our attention to uncovering how particular institutional and structural contexts present systematically different opportunities and constraints for political activity for people classified by race.

CLARIFYING ASSUMPTIONS AND EVALUATING NORMATIVE CONSEQUENCES

Such innovative research will go a long way toward clarifying analytic assumptions and to working out the normative consequences that result. Yet even with the innovations and the progress made in recognizing the importance of context for participation, the 800-pound gorilla representing the logic of the SES model still remains. SES is the gorilla because it always eats up (or sits on, depending on one's version of the analogy) the biggest chunk of variance in models predicting participatory behavior. In this regard, no one—not even those who identify and analyze the importance of identity-based mobilization, or structures of local government—can avoid the gorilla in their empirical results. The fact that the gorilla is always there is uncontroversial; rather, what is at issue is the interpretation of the relevance of his omnipresence.

The consistency of the findings about the significance of SES has contributed to a more reflexive rather than purposive response. It has helped turn what should be an explicit assumption about individual agency—the independent effects of personal attributes—into an implicit premise. The common assumption about the equality of individual agency is best exemplified in models that include separate controls for race and class. A companion assumption is one about representation; that more participatory input from citizens means that there will be more responsiveness from political representatives. These are reasonable assumptions, but they are only assumptions, which individual-level data on political behavior do not necessarily validate. The more significant problem, however, arises when these two assumptions are bundled with a particularly popular normative perspective about democracy that advocates more political activity. This combination encourages conclusions from the findings about the significance of race for political participation that may be contradictory at best and, at worst, counter to the interests of minority populations.

The equality of individual agency assumption is something we want to believe; it is an attractive notion that one more year of education will garner the same increase in political engagement for whites as for blacks. But if structural constraints create unequal contexts for opportunity among racial groups, the assumption becomes much more problematic. The representation assumption presents the same problem. If it is the case, both objectively and subjectively, that a black man's letter to his congressman receives the same attention and action as the white man's, then this assumption is justifiable. But if there is something systematic in the political process that makes the campaign contribution from the Asian American worth less than the same dollar amount from a white American, we can be less sure about this assumption, and we need to find ways to account for the interaction between race and representative responsiveness.

Finally, it is worth reconsidering, within the context of what we know about the significance of race for political participation, one of the more enduring normative positions—that more participation is good. More political participation is usually considered to be a good thing, particularly during a period in history when democracy has few ideological rivals. We advocate more political activity—that is, more liberal democracy in the form of expanded expression of voice and deliberation among citizens—as a procedural and substantive solution for distributional inequities in social and political goods. Increasing political activity among those traditionally disadvantaged and politically underrepresented, we claim, can help create public policies that take their interests into account as well as empower those previously disenfranchised to take political stands in order to develop and forward their interests. Because minorities tend to participate in politics at comparatively lower rates, these groups have become the target for calls for political activity through naturalization and voter registration drives.

Such well-intentioned campaigns seek greater equality in political outcomes by making the electorate more descriptively representative of the population at large. We infer that policies beneficial to those previously disenfranchised are most likely to be adopted when the face of the electorate mirrors the face of the polity. Conversely, undesirable political outcomes are inferred as resulting from the lack of political activity among those whose interests are at stake. Given relatively modest rates of political activity among minorities, what falls under scrutiny is change among the individuals who supposedly influence the institutions and process of democratic government, rather than the institutions and practices themselves. The analytic emphasis on the individual-level subject has trained the focus for change on the nonparticipant rather than a more critical examination of the structure and institutions of democracy in which agency operates.

But we might relax the assumption that the political process—the democratic culture, practice, and institutions of democracy—provides equality of agency for all regardless of race or some other politically relevant category. Then the comparatively low rates of participatory activity among minority Americans can be interpreted in another way, as an indicator of structural inequalities. The analytic strategy of questioning the assumption asks us to consider the location of the significance of race for political participation as more complicated than a dichotomy between structure and agency. It suggests that the location will be somewhere between the ends of the continuum from the debilitating determinism of a system continually reenacting domination, to the unwarranted optimism of unencumbered agency. To the question of "Were they pushed or did they jump?" (perhaps more appropriately for participation, "Were they held back or did they sit out?"), studies of citizen participation have too often answered from the agency end of the continuum.

The Significance of Class and Education for Political Participation

Class affects political participation through multiple causal processes. Rather than a uniform influence, class has more than one type of effect on political activity. What role does it play for political participation, and how does it provide both opportunities for political action as well as barriers to individual agency?

A widespread expectation is that increasing levels of the antecedents to participation, particularly education, should drive a commensurate rise in political activity and a diminution in observed patterns of participatory inequality. While many more Americans are better educated today than they were a quarter century ago, this increase has not produced more political engagement in the aggregate, despite the fact that the strength of the relationship between education and participation has remained strong and positive at the individual level. To some, this is paradoxical, for the trend over time goes directly counter to the expectation generated from models identifying formal educational attainment as the most powerful antecedent to political activity. From another perspective, however, the very same data that pinpoint the critical importance of education to political outcomes such as participation simultaneously identify education as one of the main mechanisms driving the maintenance of "durable inequalities" in antecedents to political activity.[14] To the extent that indicators of socioeconomic status such as education reflect class, then the expectation of more political engagement with more education is unwarranted.[15]

RECONSIDERING EDUCATION: LOCATING STRUCTURE AND AGENCY
A consistent refrain in the vast literature concerning education in America is that it is good—good for democracy, for employment, for social mobility, for building strong communities, and for democratic values. For the most part, the scholarly research implies a system now open to all, but still with fewer opportunities for minorities and the poor. Education is most often viewed as a resource that, when fairly distributed, can provide equal opportunities for individuals in society to succeed. Scholars can easily be drawn into the claim that more education is better, not only for its normative appeal but also because of the sheer quantity of evidence that supports the notion that education positively contributes to many important individual-level outcomes.

Over the past half century in the United States, social scientists have presented highly consistent empirical findings demonstrating a strong and positive relationship between level of formal educational attainment and political, economic, and social phenomena. The better educated vote more, have higher-paying jobs, and are more socially active in their communities than those individuals with less education. Extending these findings suggests that more education will help the disenfranchised to participate in politics, the unemployed to get jobs, and the socially disconnected to engage with their communities. Moreover, historians have most often characterized public education in the United States as a democratizing force, where schooling enhances opportunities for all (for example, Cremin 1961).

The school desegregation decision in *Brown* and the civil rights movement expanded access and eliminated many racial barriers to public and higher education, improving the lives of many minority and poor Americans. More-over, more education is valued because of its societal consequences, including enhanced political knowledge, worker productivity, and social trust. In so do-ing, more education creates "human capital" and "social capital," which are considered beneficial for both individuals and society at large. This positive bias toward more education manifests a strong and pervasive liberal demo-cratic philosophy among scholars, who conceive of education as an equaliz-ing force and as a powerful producer of individual agency.

Early educational theorists of the American democratic school, notably John Dewey, argued that formal education ought to have developmental as well as integrative and egalitarian effects (Dewey 1916). The expectation that education would enhance achievement—that is, what goes on inside the minds of students—is perhaps best exemplified today by the preoccupation of edu-cators with student test scores (Ravitch and Finn 1988). Economists, most recently within the human capital school of labor economists, concur with the developmental imperative of education, arguing that its greatest signifi-cance is the stimulating effect of education on the knowledge, skills, income, and productivity of workers. Indeed, labor economists have identified formal education and training as the most important investment one can make in human capital (Becker 1993; Schultz 1971; Mincer 1974). Political scientists and sociologists also identify as the primary causal influence behind increased participation, interest in politics, and adherence to democratic values.

This praise of education, however, is at odds with a seemingly divergent conclusion that places education among the most powerful stratifiers in mod-ern postindustrial society. The very same data that pinpoint the critical im-portance of education to social, political, and economic outcomes and inform the position that more education is good also simultaneously identify educa-tion as the main mechanism driving the maintenance of inequality and hier-archy where outcomes are scarce. In these instances, rather than adding aggregate value to society and economy, more education may have either no positive effect on enhancing equality or, instead, have a negative effect.

More education in American society over the past quarter century has not produced a commensurate rise in many social, economic, and political out-comes. For example, citizen political participation in various forms of volun-tary activity has remained steady, and voting has declined precipitously; the nation's stock of social capital is by some accounts dangerously low; and real income has remained stagnant despite the aggregate increases in education. At the same time, education is more important than ever as a prerequisite for getting a job that pays well. Labor economists demonstrate that a student who invests in a college education will reap rewards in future income that far offset the cost of obtaining the degree. However, as more people have become better educated, the labor market has also become increasingly stratified, leaving those without the requisite educational credentials even further behind. At a time in which nearly one-quarter of the U.S. population is college educated, we also have an unprecedented unequal distribution of wealth accompanied by growing disparity between rich and poor.

Echoing the economics research, sociological studies of social mobility, status attainment, and stratification point to the strong relationship between years of education and occupational position. The common theoretical strands in this work are the meritocratic and functional theories of social stratification that posit that formal education provides individuals with the skills necessary for performing the tasks of occupations (Blau and Duncan 1967; Sewell and Hauser 1975; Sewell, Hauser, and Featherman 1976). Within this tradition, measures of intelligence have been identified as a critical intervening variable of status attainment, though strong critiques of meritocratic theories have also been articulated.[16] In short, a meritocratic approach implies that individuals with more education are smarter and better qualified and therefore deserve to occupy higher positions in the occupational and social hierarchy. The role of education in status attainment has also been interpreted as the result of the organization of society around educational credentials. Instead of acting as an agent of change on the mind of the individual, more education and degrees simply convey information about past performance or a preexisting advantaged status, rather than adding further ability (Collins 1979).

Other scholars have questioned the efficacy of formal education as presently constituted for the positive development of cognitive ability, noting the lack of a relationship (except at the extreme margins) between standard measures of intelligence and educational attainment. In their influential work on the relationship between education and economy in the United States, Bowles and Gintis (1976) highlight the strong and positive relationship between family wealth and level of schooling. By juxtaposing this set of findings, they suggest that it is not those who go to school who get smarter, but rather, it is the rich who are better able to go further in school and who then get certified as being smarter and better qualified.

This perspective provides another way to look at education as an individual-level resource. While formal education may indeed encourage the development of cognitive ability, it may also be that these skills are far less relevant to securing one's place in the hierarchy of American life. Instead, the importance of education to stratification may be the role it plays as a powerful socialization device, teaching students who are successful and who progress through educational institutions to also become initiated into the hierarchical norms of commerce, politics, and social life (Bourdieu 1987, 1989, 1990). In short, education may be a particularly effective means of reproducing cultural, political, and economic practices. Most students in higher education succeed by developing analytic and communications styles consistent with those rewarded in the marketplace of jobs in the United States. This may be precisely what the human capital economists are after—educated workers who can assimilate easily into the workforce. As one of the primary mechanisms behind social stratification, education can also be conceived as exactly the opposite of an equalizing force. Instead, at the macrosocietal level, education may reproduce and legitimate structural inequalities that in turn drive vast disparities in wealth and nurture the persistence of the dominance of the in-group to the systematic disadvantage of out-groups.[17]

How can education be understood simultaneously as both an equalizing force and a stratification mechanism? Education may be positive and empowering at the individual level yet, at the macrosocietal level, education may at the very same time have negative consequences and debilitating effects for those at the bottom of the social, economic, and political hierarchy. If we acknowledge that educational institutions both function within and are products of the American democratic-capitalist system, then the revelation that education is at once a potential equalizing as well as stratifying mechanism is a predictable redundancy rather than a contradiction requiring explanation. Education both enables and restricts; it is a location for the development of both individual agency and structural constraint.

The value of the resources conveyed upon individuals by educational attainment must be considered in relation to the level of resources held by others. The value of education to political participation must be compared to what everyone else has, so that more education in the aggregate does not necessarily improve conditions at either the macrosocietal level or the individual level. Instead, more education only shifts the baseline upward; if the pace of gains by disadvantaged groups does not keep up with the growth in education by advantaged groups, the former fall further behind even as they are making progress in level of educational attainment in an absolute sense.

Far from a simple theoretical exercise, this situation reflects the current reality of more rapid gains in education by the advantaged over African Americans and Latinos, who continue to operate at a distinct educational disadvantage (Murphy 1990). The gap in educational attainment between whites and Asians on the one hand, and African Americans and Latinos on the other, remains and, since the 1980s, is once again increasing. These conclusions about the collective outcomes of education are sobering for minorities and the poor, who have more to lose from the educational progress of advantaged groups.

Disadvantaged groups stay that way not only by virtue of their relatively low placement in the educational hierarchy, but also because the legitimacy of this unequal structure is propagated in part by American educational institutions themselves. Rather than sitting outside of the political, economic, and social structures that reinforce inequality and domination, education is a part of it. Education plays two important roles in the maintenance of an ideology of meritocracy in the United States. In its sorting function, formal education confers certification, degrees, and other scarce outcomes that places those with what are defined as the best credentials at the top of the hierarchy. In its role as a powerful socializer, education also teaches the ideology of meritocracy, by grading on normal curves and assuring those who finish on the right tail that they deserve to succeed. The second role is a critical mechanism, reliably reproducing the ideology that maintains positions of power for those at the top who benefit from the system as it already exists. When outcomes are positional or scarce—when not everyone can be rich and not everyone can be granted admission into a top school—the liberal democratic ideology must have an answer to its production of unequal outcomes. Merit can be used as a justification for inequality of outcomes in a system where the rules are supposed to be fair.

This discussion of education as a location for the development of both individual agency as well as structural constraint provides a reminder, gentle if unpleasant, that policies that seek to redress the consequences of political inequality cannot assume that providing more resources for competition in an unequal system will eliminate the inequality (Jencks 1992). To the extent that education contributes to the maintenance of social stratification—sorting those with high attainment and credentials to the top and those with less toward the bottom, while at the same time reproducing an ideology of meritocracy—it cannot also be expected to dismantle the hierarchy.

The Future of Democratic Participation

Recognizing the contingent meanings of race within the contemporary social context of the United States is an important first step toward understanding how classifications by race are relevant to citizen activity. Many of the factors we identify as positive contributors to political activity may have multiple and sometimes contradictory influences on participation. Durable inequalities in social and political structures that are located in antecedents to participation can easily be misperceived exclusively as settings for the enhancement of individual agency rather than simultaneously as a negative constraint on action. Clearly, race and education serve as markers of inferior or superior positions in social, economic, and political hierarchies, yet to make inferential progress, we need to do more than demonstrate descriptively that these inequalities exist. Instead, analyses must combine a more explicit structural theory of systematic contextual influences on individual agency, along with creative efforts to measure this context. Those efforts will add to our ability to understand just how level the playing field is for potential participants in U.S. politics.

The demands of a democracy in which participation can be meaningfully linked to liberty and equality is one where simply being allowed on the field is not enough. The lifting of racially motivated institutional barriers to political activity does not in itself create a set of procedures that will guarantee fair play. Rather, a determination of the extent to which the field is level is both complex and far from certain. Not only must the character of political procedures be considered when assessing the nature of the game, but so should the set of factors that promote individual activity. An effort to examine more carefully the presupposition of equality of agency among individuals will be very valuable in clarifying the normative consequences of conclusions about the significance of race and class for democratic participation. While it has long been recognized that participants bring different skills and motivations to politics, democratic institutions and practices should attempt to attenuate rather than exaggerate these tendencies. Myriad forces continue to tip the field in one direction, such as the use of technology to mobilize more efficiently those on the advantaged side of the "digital divide." Democratic government should mitigate these tendencies, and it will be better armed to do so with the aid of analyses identifying practices that exacerbate inequality. Through changes in both agency and structure, the future of democratic participation can be brighter.

Chapter 5

The Future of Liberty
in American Democratic Politics?

Or the Future of Democracy
for the Politics of Liberty?

NANCY J. HIRSCHMANN

IN THE MOST WRENCHING way, the events of September 11, 2001, raise fundamental questions about liberty in democratic politics.

We can find one easy and straightforward response: a key purpose of democracy is to protect individual liberty. The attacks on the World Trade Center
and the Pentagon were characterized by President George W. Bush as "an attack on freedom" against one of the world's historically most successful democracies. And the military campaign launched in response was aptly (if
ambiguously) named Operation Enduring Freedom. Certainly the thousands
of people who died in these attacks were, in part, casualties of the United
States' open borders and respect for individual liberties. This respect is an important feature of liberal democracy, but it has made employing antiterrorist
measures difficult. And the societies that presumably breed this terrorism strike
most Westerners as highly antidemocratic, marked more by absolutism, ex-
tremism, and intolerance than by the liberal democratic values of openness,
exchange of views, and mutual respect.

But in the aftermath of September 11, democracy can also be seen as an
enemy of freedom. What John Stuart Mill and Alexis de Tocqueville called
the "tyranny of the majority," which mindlessly follows convention—or perhaps mass hysteria—is clearly evident at U.S. airports, where middle-class
America is positively relieved to have its luggage ransacked and shoes X-rayed,
as well as to see racial profiling proceed, as long as Arab Americans are targeted

rather than African Americans. Supposedly in the name of "the majority," and of preserving our democratic freedoms, individual liberties have been abridged in the justice system, through such measures as secret detentions, permission for prison guards to listen to conversations between some prisoners and their attorneys, and efforts to replace criminal trials with military tribunals for suspected terrorists. Increased FBI wiretapping authority, military control of information available to the press, and vague scare-tactic warnings of future terrorist attacks undermine key liberal democratic values concerning privacy and freedom of information.

Those who have raised questions about these actions have been chastised as unpatriotic, disloyal, and self-serving, suggesting that a deeper threat to liberty in the aftermath of September 11 may lie in the psychology of Americans. Liberty is jeopardized not just by the pointlessness of many of the new rules regarding security and immigration and the racism with which they are frequently enacted. It is even more seriously endangered by the mindless enthusiasm with which Americans have embraced these new surveillance strategies in the interest of feeling "safer," even though no actual increase in safety has been demonstrated. Fear, not a real concern for freedom, is motivating both the new policies and citizens' attitudes toward them. Such a psychology threatens to transform, and possibly undermine, the democratic ethos in the contemporary United States. For as Benjamin Franklin said, "They that can give up essential liberty to obtain a little temporary safety deserve neither liberty nor safety" (Franklin 1759). These events thus compel us to consider carefully the meaning and practice of democracy.

The Politics of Freedom

Political theory may offer us some broader perspective on these events and their deeper significance for the relationship between freedom and democracy. As the critical arm of political science, political theorists have long sounded cautionary alarms about the state of freedom in liberal democracy. At least since C. B. Macpherson (1962), theorists have been suspicious of Enlightenment claims of natural freedom and equality supposedly sitting at the heart of democratic theory, let alone democratic politics, and have argued that the kind of "democracy" that the modern Enlightenment theorists advocated promoted a particular kind of freedom for a particular subset of citizens. Macpherson maintained that the freedom being promoted by the forms of democracy advocated by Enlightenment theorists such as Locke was freedom only for the propertied classes and came at the expense of unfreedom and oppression for the poor: "freedom" was economic freedom for those who were already in possession of substantial amounts of property. This economic freedom was often cast in terms of political freedom and put in terms of the political language of rights; and, indeed, some of those rights were to intangible ideals such as freedom of religion. But as scholars such as Gordon Schochet (2000), James Tully (1980), and Richard Ashcraft (1986) have shown, property was also a key principle, and never far away from those other, less tangible ideals.[1]

Other leftist critics further developed Macpherson's argument by pointing out that freedom was a value not for democracy per se, but for liberalism; that was why the liberal democracies that emerged from Enlightenment thinking were "democratic" only for those who already had wealth and power (Pateman 1985). Feminist and critical race theorists pushed further to maintain that the conception of freedom underwriting most contemporary theories of democracy involved freedom not only for people of a particular class, but of a particular gender and race as well. Some of these theorists, dating back to Mary Astell and Mary Wollstonecraft, argued that liberalism actually contradicted itself thereby; as Astell put it with her inimitable scorn, "*If all Men are born free,* how is it that all Women are born slaves?" (Astell 1996, 18; see also Wollstonecraft 1982).[2] They maintained that liberal democracy needed to be more consistent and extend its conception of freedom to (white) women. Others maintained that the poor and men and women of color could similarly be encompassed by extending liberalism's categories of natural freedom and equality to make it more genuinely universal.

Still others, by contrast, maintained that liberalism, being the problem, could not be part of the solution, and that freedom and equality for historically excluded groups required an altogether different understanding of democracy (Fanon 1968, Young 1990). For true democracy required giving primacy to equality; freedom could emerge only indirectly and secondarily, through equal access and power. Participatory democracy, direct democracy, and socialist democracy were all seen as political forms that decentered freedom in its classic liberal form and reconstituted freedom as the embodiment of political participation. And so-called communist societies of the latter half of the twentieth century, claiming to follow Marx, seemed to reject freedom altogether as bourgeois illusion and instead claimed to give equality, or community, or production, greater importance (even if most people now believe that they failed even in that).[3]

If freedom is a bourgeois illusion, that might suggest an equally straightforward, though decidedly depressing, answer to the question of the future of liberty in democratic politics: none whatsoever. But Marx did in fact value freedom and predicted its actualization through communism and the withered-away state. He considered systematic and institutional phenomena, particularly capitalism, to be significant barriers to freedom. After the restrictions of capitalist exploitation have been removed, individuals will be free to express their natures and do as they wish, fishing in the morning, hunting in the afternoon, and philosophizing in the evening. "Only in community" formed once the division of labor is ended "is personal freedom possible," because then the "individual" has "the means of cultivating his gifts in all directions" (Marx 1978, 197). Perhaps unintentionally following Marx in this regard, feminist and critical race theorists at least tacitly argue for either expanding existing conceptions of freedom and applying them more consistently to historically excluded groups such as women, racial minorities, gays, and the disabled, or reconceptualizing freedom altogether to accommodate them.[4] Even those who reject rights as the foundation of freedom argue that what enables white men to utilize rights is their ability to systematically oppress white women, the poor, and men and women of color (Brown 1995; Cornell 1999; Mills 1997). If such oppression is wrong, then freedom has to be at least an implicit goal of such critics.

Thus, notwithstanding the critique of liberalism and the tension between its language of natural freedom and equality, and its practical denial of freedom to large segments of the population, freedom is a core feature of democratic politics. It is a core goal of all historically excluded groups, who identify themselves as victims of "oppression" (ending which, by definition, requires some form of "liberation"), and all of whom advocate equalization of power in democratic terms. Indeed, the importance of democratic equality to these groups' struggles for freedom suggests that, rather than asking about the future of liberty for democratic politics, we should be concerned with the future of democracy for the politics of freedom.

Freedom, as John Rawls (1999) said about justice, *is* political, not metaphysical. That is, it is not some essential state that we are naturally born into, as the social contract theorists would have us believe. Rather, it is constructed by and through power. When people make claims of oppression and unfreedom, they are making claims about the unfair use of power. In some cases, this power is individualized, such as when a burglar ties me up while he robs my house. In many cases, though, power is systematized through social structures, laws, institutions, practices, customs, and even sociolinguistic categories. Critical race theory, postmodern theory, and feminist theory have all argued that power is not simply what one person does to another, but is exercised in and through social practices and linguistic forms that create meaning: we are "socially constructed" by and through relations of power (Butler 1990; Foucault 1990). The idea of social construction says that who I am and what I want are not natural, but the product of social, cultural, and historical forces and contexts. Social forms and institutions, cultural practices, family configurations, gender, race, and class structure, language, and epistemology all shape individuals, who in turn shape these social formations. Such contexts are what makes meaning possible; and meaning makes "reality."

We do not need elaborate theories to see the reality of social construction, however. In 1896 the U.S. Supreme Court, in *Plessy v. Ferguson*, made that argument when it postulated that racism cannot operate without a conceptual category of racial difference. Plessy's one-eighth African heritage, not his behavior, dress, or even physical appearance, resulted in his being barred from the "white" railroad car in which he wanted to sit. Justice Brown (just before declaring Louisiana's "separate but equal" laws constitutionally valid) denied that "the reputation of belonging to the dominant race, in this instance the white race, is 'property;'" rather, it constitutes a conceptual category of sociolinguistic usage. The conductor's "power to assign [passengers] to a particular coach," he said, "obviously implies the power to determine to which race the passenger belongs, as well as the power to determine who, under the laws of the particular state, is to be deemed a white, and who a colored, person" (163 U.S. 537, at 549). And he noted that whether Plessy should be considered white or "colored" was up for grabs (163 U.S. at 552). Foucault could not have put it any better. Yet such assignment to race was fundamental to the practice of segregation, which, as Justice Harlen noted in his dissent, "interferes with the personal freedom of citizens," an interference that derives from the systematic power that racism gives to whites (163 U.S. 557, at 559). Freedom, or its lack, is a function of the power to define and to put those definitions into practice.

Defining Freedom: A Matter of Domination

The problem with defining freedom, however, is that the word is used in conflicting, at times contradictory, ways by different people in different contexts. The dominant conception of freedom that underwrites the liberal form of democracy centers on an absence of external constraints or "interference," what Isaiah Berlin (1969) called "negative liberty." Berlin focused specifically on obstacles that are intentionally and purposefully placed—say, if a woman of color is held back from a professional promotion which she wants, and for which she is qualified, unless she sleeps with her boss. As Berlin put it, "By being free in this sense I mean not being interfered with by others. The wider the area of non-interference, the wider my freedom" (Berlin 1969, 123).

This is the major conception of freedom that underwrites Enlightenment versions of liberal democracy, though the fact that individuals' freedoms can conflict means that such noninterference can never be absolute. Hence, Locke defined liberty in terms of leaving other people alone to do what they want, within "the bounds of the laws of nature," which restricted individuals' desires to kill or injure others except in self defense; to take more than they could use; or to violate the dictates of reason (Locke 1960, 347). Mill most fully expressed this principle of "equal liberty," stating explicitly that only harm to others, specifically to their liberty, could ever justify interference with one's freedom—whether by other individuals or by the state—to do what one wants (Mill 1992).

But this deceptively simple understanding of freedom—not being prevented from doing what one wants by intentional agents—masks complications concerning the individual, social, and political conditions of "prevention" (and, conversely, "ability") as well as the nature of desire, or "what I want." It is necessary to recognize that the conditions for preventing people from doing, or enabling them to do, something they want to do are rarely limitable to the individuals themselves. Such limitations and abilities are constructed by power, prejudice, or just plain shortsightedness. For instance, it used to be thought that paraplegics were not "unfree" to enter public buildings that required entrants to climb stairs or navigate public sidewalks, they were only "unable" to do so. That is, nobody was actually stopping them; only their personal, individual disability prevented them. Eventually, because someone had the bright idea of substituting ramps for stairs and putting sloping depressions into curbs, the realm of the possible shifted as well as common views of social responsibility: stairs became not a "natural" function of building architecture, but a barrier to people in wheelchairs. Accordingly, we have come to recognize the rights of the disabled to wheelchair accessibility, and laws guide the construction of new buildings that benefit from public funding (Oliver and Barnes 1998).

The notion of being "unable" to do something, and being "restrained" from doing it, then, has shifted in terms of the social context in which we find ourselves. The disability rights movement—along with the feminist movement and the civil rights movement—has identified certain physical customs like stairs, or social practices like segregation, once seen as natural or inevitable parts of the social landscape, as "barriers" to freedom. Such successes are testimony to increasing democratization, the expansion of the identity of "citizen" to include the perspectives of those previously discounted: women, blacks, and the disabled, to name a few.

The other part of the standard definition of freedom—"what I want"— seems intuitively more individualistic and even "natural," but it is equally subject to historical and social analysis. The negative liberty myth of the rugged and abstract individual whose desires simply come to him has given way to the recognition that desire, and the subjects that feel and express desires, are "socially constructed." That is, differences in desires among individuals in different social settings can be attributed to a significant degree to those settings. Islamic women who feel naked without the chador and Western women who feel naked without their makeup are equally the products of their cultures, which are in turn constituted by relations of power. Similarly, men who want their dinners ready as soon as they get home from work may be expressing "natural" desires based on hunger and fatigue, but these desires also stem from socially constructed norms of gendered power and privilege that dictate the terms of the sexual division of labor within the patriarchal nuclear family. Desire is both individual and social, "natural" and constructed.

Recognizing the complexity of both desire and ability (or interference) leads us to the conclusion that negative liberty is not the only conception of freedom that underwrites liberal democracy. Another strand of freedom, what Berlin called "positive liberty," also plays a significant role. The concept of positive liberty adds two features to negative liberty's correct, but incomplete, understanding of liberty as the absence of interference. First, it includes the psychological, or "inner" factors of desire, will, and self-understanding that negative liberty's emphasis on external barriers and interference by others leaves out. If, for instance, a woman's husband beats her up to prevent her from leaving the house, most people would agree that he interferes with her liberty. But what if he only threatens to hit her if she tries to leave? What if such a threat produces, not fear, but shock and surprise, so that she does what he tells her because she is stunned by his behavior and is trying to fit it into her previous understanding of him? Or what if he convinces her that she actually deserves the abuse so she gives up wanting to leave (Barnett and LaViolette 1993)? Her spouse's ability to affect and manipulate her perceptions, feelings, and desires prevents her from formulating the "what I want" part of freedom as much as the "ability" part.

As Philip Pettit argues, freedom can be inhibited through domination rather than interference, and the republican ideal of "nondomination" supercedes the classically liberal negative liberty ideal of "noninterference." For people may be restricted in their liberty even when no apparent interference is being exercised, such as when a wife who was once hit by her husband structures her behavior around avoidance and fear of being hit again, even though the violence has not recurred (Pettit 1999). Pettit's conception of freedom as "nondomination" rather than "noninterference" makes an important contribution to our understanding of liberty as a function of power.

Domination does more than actively prevent people from doing what they want; it determines the options that are available to people. And the availability of options, as Elster (1983) suggests, affects desire by causing us to "adapt" our preferences.

Thus, the concept of domination is important to the future of liberty because of the ways in which power socially constructs individual subjectivity, desire, and choice. Choice is central to freedom, and negative liberty theory is correct that choices must be made by individuals by and for themselves; nobody can force battered women to leave their abusers, or "out" closeted lesbians or gays, or prevent poor people from having children, without grossly violating their freedom. But choice is a complex process, involving a mixture of the external factors that negative liberty focuses on and the internal factors that positive liberty highlights. Because "choosing selves" are located in particular political and economic contexts, the activity of choice-making is itself a social process and therefore necessarily involves positive liberty elements of community and social relationships.

This points to the other way in which positive liberty supplements negative liberty, namely its recognition of social conditions and systemic structures, like poverty, or racism, or patriarchy, as barriers to freedom. Domination is not something that individuals can sustain all on their own; structures and systems are essential. An abusive husband can sustain power over his wife only with the complicity of police who do not arrest, courts that do not convict, and clergy who urge endurance and reconciliation. An abused woman would have greater liberty to leave the marriage if employment discrimination, gender-biased pay differentials, and sexual harassment did not make single motherhood economically unviable for many women. The controlling of women by men is greatly facilitated by general social norms of gender that make women responsible for the success or failure of relationships, even when they are the victims of abuse (Hirschmann 2003, chap. 4).

Thus, domination affects three different aspects of freedom. First, it sets the parameters for what choices are available: for instance, can African Americans attend public universities? Are women promoted to executive positions? Can gays get married or adopt children? Do paraplegics have wheelchair access to public buildings? Systems of power and inequality shape and construct cultural and legal norms that determine what options are available to which people.

Second, those options encode expectations of freedom and desires that are self-fulfilling; domination, by affecting the creation of choice, affects the construction of desire. For instance, sexism may not only prevent women from being hired to agenda-setting positions in government or business, it may also prevent them from even wanting to pursue such positions. Similarly, if economic advancement is an unlikely reward for sticking with a low-paying job, as is the case for many single mothers in "workfare" programs, then the motivation to keep plugging away is severely reduced; yet the individual is seen as lazy or unreliable instead of rational (Williams 1987, 156).

Third, domination affects the understanding of what counts as a choice. That is, not just the choices or options available, not just what different kinds of individuals want in different kinds of contexts, but the very meaning of the concept of "choice" itself is defined and articulated differently in different contexts that are marked by power and inequality. For instance, poverty discourses that blame the poor for being lazy are constructed from the perspective of class power and privilege and are made possible only by blinding ourselves to the reality of poverty: the deplorable conditions of inner-city public schools, for instance, that produce poorly educated children who are ill-equipped to compete in the labor market (Kozol 1991). Accordingly, people may be seen as making a choice when they have been forced in a particular direction, such as when it is assumed that a battered woman who stays with her abuser because she cannot support her children on her own does not mind being beaten.

If domination results in a structural variability of freedom, those with more power have greater choice than those with less power: whites more than blacks, men more than women, rich more than poor. The future of freedom lies in the equalization of this power. Freedom requires equalizing participation in the processes that create our options. Focusing on domination reveals that freedom cannot be simply about making choices within existing contexts; it has to be about having a say in defining the context, and thereby the choices, in the first place. It shifts the central question from "what do I want" to "why do I want it," and it shifts the central goal of freedom from "doing what I want" or "making choices" to "defining what the choices are." Although making choices is necessary for freedom, it is not sufficient.

Women, for instance, make choices all the time: they decide to have children or not, to work for wages or not, to stay with violent men or not. But they make these choices within constrained parameters, under conditions over which they often have little say. They do not get to construct the options because they do not participate in defining the context within which options are defined. At best, they only get to choose among the limited range of options that male-defined power has set for them. So, for instance, battered women can choose to hide from their abusers in a temporary shelter, abandoning their homes, possessions, and possibly their children, or they can choose to remain and continue to be victimized (Mahoney 1994). They are "free to choose," but such choices hardly make them free.

None of us usually gets to define our options fully, it might be pointed out; we all have to make choices among available options. I may want to fly off the roof of my house, but gravity complicates the effort. I may want to live to be 110, but there is only so much that medical science can do to keep me alive. But focusing on the issue of domination has two important consequences. First, it directs us to focus on *equalizing* power. Equalizing access to the social construction of choice does not mean that every individual will get to choose the options she would ideally want. But it does require a relative *equality* in the power to do so: if you can set the options, then so should I. You should not have greater power simply because of your race, gender, class, or, indeed, almost any other social difference.[5] The liberal principle of equal liberty that Locke and Mill propounded recognized that the freedom to do what I want must synchronize with others' conflicting wants. That they resolved this tension in ways that have come to favor the powerful in terms of gender, race, and class does not invalidate their initial ideal. But that is why the future of liberty lies in democracy: democracy is the political form that most readily deals with the problem of equal liberty.

Second, focusing on domination emphasizes the ways in which the construction of choice is often not an individual process. Particular groups or classes of people categorized by gender, class, and race systematically have considerably more power than others to determine what the options are. For instance, because the overwhelming majority of politicians and legislators in the United States are economically privileged white men, this group of people has a disproportionate power to affect, if not control, what options are available to the rest of us. They thereby influence the desires of citizens who are forced to adapt their preferences to those options, and they control the discursive accounts of desire and option to define when, how, and under what conditions choices are made.

The Social Construction of Freedom: The Case of PRWORA

Welfare policy is an excellent case in point to illustrate these arguments about freedom, domination, and social constructivism.[6] The Personal Responsibility Work Opportunity Reconciliation Act (PRWORA) of 1996 ended "welfare as we knew it" by dismantling the Aid to Families with Dependent Children (AFDC) program and replacing it with Temporary Assistance to Needy Families (TANF). It denationalized welfare by turning funding over to states in the form of block grants along with a great deal of discretion to construct welfare programs and policies and to decide how payments would be made and under what conditions. PRWORA set some broad parameters with which states had to comply, however, particularly time limits and work requirements (Orloff 2001).

States have instituted various approaches within those parameters; in some states, after only two months of receiving benefits, regardless of the age of their children, recipients must engage in community service labor; others have extended the period in which recipients may receive benefits before engaging in work. Still other states have created exceptions for work requirements, and some have allowed certain kinds of educational training to fulfill the work requirement for a limited period of time. Additional PRWORA provisions and state policies establish long-range goals for family structure and reproduction, such as the reduction of abortion and out-of-wedlock births, increasing rates of marriage by structuring benefits to favor married couples, "family caps" on benefit increases after the second child, mandatory child support, and cooperation by recipients in locating noncustodial parents.

If the goal of welfare reform was to reduce the welfare rolls and save money, then PRWORA was a success, for most states have reported significant declines in welfare participation. But if it was to give the poor the resources they need to attain permanent independence, then it was a failure, for rates of poverty have not significantly decreased and by some measures have noticeably increased over the past several years (Bernstein 2001; Kilborn 2001; Kilborn and Clemetson 2002). Such failure will worsen with TANF's reauthorization. The Bush administration has proposed that more work be required from recipients, but without employment supports, such as childcare, transportation, or education. Such policy puts incredible pressures on poor families, requiring more of them to enter the workforce—at a time when unemployment is considerably higher than it was when PRWORA was originally enacted—and without giving them the resources they need to make work possible. President Bush instead proposed $300 million for "strengthening marriage" and almost doubled funding for abstinence education (to $73 million).

Domination and freedom were at the heart of these policy initiatives in several ways. The most obvious was that welfare reform sought explicitly to restrict the freedom of recipients, who are seen as lazy and irresponsible. Moreover, the measures were designed to change not just recipients' behavior but also their attitudes about work, public assistance, and themselves: in other words, to shape their desires, their choices, their very subjectivity. Indeed, conservative Republicans actively sought to reconstruct the character of welfare recipients, as the discourse of dependency that engulfed welfare reform made clear: AFDC had *made* the poor dependent on welfare "handouts," producing a "cycle of poverty" wherein children raised on public assistance grew up expecting continued public assistance as a way of life and never learning the Protestant work ethic. The problem was not lack of opportunities, it was laziness and dependency, which not only kept adults out of the workplace but also kept their children out of school so that they would never develop the skills they needed to enter the labor market. The rubric of "personal responsibility" in the bill's title emphasized the need for welfare recipients to "get off the dole" and be active contributors to the economy and civil society. And since AFDC had undermined their ability to see the benefits to themselves of working, and how public assistance had robbed them of their dignity and self-respect, they had to be forced off assistance and into work: to borrow from Rousseau, they had to be "forced to be free."

Such constructions of welfare, operating from the perspectives of privilege, express forms of domination, for they misrepresent the reality of lived experience. They produce ideological distortions of need, situation, and choice and thereby silence the voices of the poor single mothers whom PRWORA targeted. The Institute for Women's Policy Research has repeatedly demonstrated that most welfare recipients are on public assistance for less than two years and have already made valiant attempts to engage in wage labor, often alternating between work and assistance, or combining benefits with wages (Hartmann and Yi 2001; Spalter-Roth and Hartmann 1994). But this reality of welfare rarely gets recognized, for conservative constructions of welfare recipients impose abstract imaginings based on prejudice and ideology rather than addressing the real needs of the poor. In the process, the power of domination turns these distortions into reality.

Consider, for instance, the trope of the "cheating" welfare mother, the welfare "queen," which peppered much of the rhetoric justifying reform (Albiston and Nielsen 1995; Murray 1994). The majority of welfare recipients do not cheat; the stereotype is just that, a stereotype. Anyone who could imagine getting rich off of welfare has never lived on public assistance with three children to support. Indeed, so far from cheating are most welfare mothers that they do not even take advantage of exemptions from work requirements such as the Family Violence Option, which allows victims of abuse to delay entering the labor market (Tolman and Rosen 2001; Lein et al. 2001). But beliefs that most welfare recipients are fraudulent "queens" fed into the construction of welfare policy to keep payments so small that some people were actually forced to cheat by working under a false social security number or by failing to report support from family members. "Public Aid forces you into deceit and dishonesty," as one welfare recipient put it, "things you normally would not think of doing" (Edin 1991, 469–70).

Domination is thus at work in welfare reform to limit freedom in the three ways earlier discussed. The ideological misrepresentation of reality produces material effects on the options that are available to welfare recipients, and such options require recipients to make choices that superficially seem to fulfill the misrepresentation. Ideology materializes itself into truth. This truth in turn affects the very subjectivity of recipients and their power to participate in the discourse. That is, it not only interferes with individuals' abilities to do what they want; it impacts on those wants themselves and on individuals' ability to define and represent who they are and what they want. Hence, although all of the women Kathryn Edin interviewed who "cheated" on welfare saw themselves not as frauds, but as strong mothers who were doing what they had to do to feed their kids, they also reported feelings of shame, depression, and lack of self-worth, suggesting that at some level they could not avoid buying into the dominant construction of themselves as cheats.

Similarly, Karen Seccombe shows that even though women declare that they themselves are hard workers and are struggling to fulfill welfare requirements and make a better life for their children without public assistance, they simultaneously claim to know lots of other women who do cheat, who fulfill the stereotype of the lazy welfare queen (Seccombe 1999). Such claims may be an effective way for these women to present themselves to the interviewer or their case worker in a positive light; by acknowledging the "reality" of the dominant discourse, their claims to be "different" gain greater legitimacy. But at the same time, such efforts further reinforce the dominant construction of welfare subjects and thereby of themselves. The ways in which their identity and choices are constructed by larger discursive frameworks and material options shape how they themselves participate in making choices and how they see themselves as choosing subjects. Though they may make choices within the existing framework, they do not get to participate in shaping and defining that framework; they do not participate in constructing the options and hence their own desires and subjectivity.

Women, of course, are not the only targets of welfare policy's attempt to socially engineer the subjectivity and self-conceptions of the poor. Although for the past two decades the problem of welfare has been blamed on immoral women who, fueled by the woman's liberation movement, had promiscuous sex without worrying about marriage, experts are now beginning to blame men for the "epidemic" of children born out of wedlock. The House Ways and Means Committee's hearings on "welfare and marriage issues," for instance, described men as "promiscuous, their paternity casual, their commitment to families weak" (Popenoe 2001). These allegedly unreliable, unfaithful, and exploitative men may be the new target for explaining the "pathology" of welfare dependency.

The policies that emerge from such discourses, which construct poverty as an individual pathology, are antidemocratic because they fail to attend to the voices of those most affected. The Ways and Means hearings did not take testimony from poor single mothers, after all, nor from poor single men. To the relief of feminists, it did hear testimony from Edin, who pointed out that the reason that the women she interviewed shunned marriage was the inability of poor men, and particularly men of color, to obtain steady employment (Edin 2001). But her testimony was not acknowledged by policy makers, whose proposals to strengthen marriage consist of classes for couples rather than employment supports and better economic opportunities for women or men. It is much easier—and probably cheaper—to blame character than to recognize the systematic unfairness, sexism, and racism of capitalist free-market economics.

These discourses also affect freedom, however; because choice is individualized, responsibility is individualized, and individuals can be blamed for their own lack of freedom. The failure of welfare reform to provide what welfare recipients need—good jobs, adequate benefits, sufficient salary scales to encourage persistence, as well as employment supports such as national health care, child care, and transportation—presents institutional barriers to the ability of poor people, and particularly to poor single mothers, to realize a life plan and pursue it.

The Future of Democracy, the Future of Freedom

PRWORA represented a failure of democracy as much as a failure to protect freedom, and the two failures are intertwined. Public policy is rarely formulated by, or even from the perspective of, the poor or women, the two groups most centrally affected by PRWORA. The poor, and particularly poor single mothers, were seen as the problem, not part of the solution, and so were, for the most part, excluded from participation. But if we are truly concerned about the future of liberty, they must be part of the solution, they must be included in the democratic process of constructing policies that in turn construct them as democratic citizens. Increasing freedom for nondominant groups like women or racial minorities or the poor requires increasing their ability to participate in the processes that set the terms for choice, desire, and subjectivity.

Feminists are quick to point out that governments are overwhelmingly male and that this feature makes it easier for them to create policies that ignore women's real needs. Similarly, calls for more legislators of color stem from fundamental beliefs that the interests of people of color often get subverted by white politicians. Such identity politics views are often presented simplistically and reductively, but the point they raise is legitimate. For instance,

Kathleen Casey and Susan J. Carroll (2001) have shown that Republican women in the U.S. House and Senate had a noticeable impact on the welfare reform bill of 1996, making it less harsh, more flexible, and more "woman friendly." Those female legislators were obviously not poor, but their being women sensitized them to the difficulties of being working mothers. Including poor people in Congress is a logical impossibility, but it is possible to include poor people in various aspects of the legislative process.

Such inclusion might have produced policies that better addressed the real needs of the poor rather than the punitive measures that resulted from the Republican Right's ideological constructions. When writing his Contract with America, Newt Gingrich did not go into the housing projects to ask what residents needed to change their lives; he did not talk to women waiting in line at the welfare office. When writing PRWORA, Republicans did not engage in the kind of data gathering that Edin (1991) conducted with her interviews of women on AFDC in Chicago (see also Edin and Lein 1997). Admittedly, advocacy groups such as the Coalition for Human Needs and the Center for Law and Social Policy did seek to represent the voice of the poor by emphasizing the need to eliminate the lifetime five-year limit for families who are working but need supplemental support, or to exempt families from work requirements who faced significant obstacles such as domestic violence, mental illness, or drug abuse and to increase educational opportunities by repealing federal caps on educational training. That they have not succeeded in getting these provisions into welfare policy does not mean that democracy has failed. After all, democracy inevitably involves some people winning and some people losing.

But that is why it is so important to attend to questions of power and domination in determining freedom. Domination exists when some groups consistently and repeatedly win because they have greater social resources while others consistently lose, and when those wins and losses reinforce the unequal balance of power that ensures the winners keep winning and the losers keep losing. As Edin's Ways and Means testimony suggests, it is not enough for "participation" that you get to talk; those with decision-making power have to listen. That is one key reason why identity politics advocates seek to diversify the makeup of legislative and policy-making bodies to reflect populations more accurately. It is easier to hear someone when you share some common ground.

But democratic politics entails more than conventional political participation. The ways that domination works are much more systemic than could be undone by simply electing a few women or African Americans to Congress. Meaningful participation in the formal political process also requires "participation" in broader and less well-defined social processes (see Junn, this volume). For instance, if higher levels of education are associated with higher levels of voter participation, perhaps that is because education provides individuals with a set of capabilities that enhances their powers to act on the world around them; it influences their sense of themselves as effective agents. Similarly, that class is a correlate of formal political participation suggests that economic resources provide middle- and upper-class individuals with a sense of power and control over their lives and environment that the poor do not have. And whiteness, in a society marked by racism and white privilege, will similarly enhance an individual's self-perception as a person whose opinions matter, who can make an effective difference in her immediate world and possibly the larger world as well.

All of these features point to the ways in which "participation" is not simply showing up at the voting booth and pulling a lever, or passing out campaign literature, or even passing laws. Such forms of participation are "outcomes," but freedom requires us to consider the forms of participation that affect "inputs," namely subjectivity and desire. It involves a much broader network of social factors and activities that affect our understandings of ourselves as actors, either efficacious or nonefficacious, in the social and political arena.

Freedom thus requires expanding the arenas of participation that are considered "political." Empowering excluded groups and individuals to participate in the processes that define choice means redefining not just the overtly political institutions of government such as bureaucratic agencies and elected bodies that pass laws and implement social policy. It also involves the broad redefinition of social institutions such as families, schools, clubs, political parties, social organizations, as well as overarching social categories of identity and meaning such as race, gender, and class.

For example, as Susan Okin (1989) suggests, decisions within the family over how money is spent are political, and they clearly affect women's efficacy and self-perceptions. Having equal say in those decisions enhances women's freedom by giving them more control over their lives. Of course, while participation within the family is necessary, it is not sufficient; calling family discussions "political" does not mean women need not partake in traditional public arenas. Having an equal say in the decisions over how household income is spent makes a woman freer than if she has no say; but having a say in formulating public policy that equalizes credit for women, and that eliminates gender discrimination and differential pay scales, also makes women freer, in part because it is bound to strengthen women's bargaining position within the family (Nussbaum 2000; Sen 1999).

Economic participation is an important starting point for equalizing participation. As political scientists have long known, class has a strong relationship to participation, and economic resources now determine a great deal of freedom in most of the world. That is why welfare so clearly illustrates the problems of freedom. Ending poverty and increasing the poor's economic opportunities—goals of equality and equal liberty—were not the goals of welfare reform at all; rather, the goal was reducing federal expenditures. Such an outcome, whatever its possible virtues, can hardly be seen as democratic in terms of freedom, for the negative freedom of reduced taxation of the middle class trumped the positive freedom of the poor to develop skills and life plans. As Anne Phillips notes, a focus on political equality without attention to the systemic structure of economic inequality is deluded at best, a "confidence trick" at worst (Phillips 1999, 6).

Obviously, however, enabling women, racial minorities, and the poor to participate more actively in policy making is not a simple matter. After all, law and public policy, precisely because they constitute such a powerful terrain for the social construction of options, desires, and subjectivity, have produced the very people that need to participate. Even AFDC, by failing to help the poor out of poverty, and through the surveillance techniques it established, helped disempower many welfare recipients by catching them in a cycle of powerlessness. In this respect, conservative Republicans were decidedly, if only partially, correct.

But to say that historically disadvantaged peoples like the poor or women should participate in policy making is not to say that they should—or can—determine it by themselves. For if the conditions of oppression have produced the very subjectivities that undermine genuine change, then the existing power dynamics may simply be replicated. The inclusion of "excluded others," therefore, cannot be a final goal or ending point. But it is an important starting point. They should be *included* in the process of policy creation, they should be contributing authors and not merely solitary objects, for their experiences provide insights that cannot (normally) be attained by privileged lawmakers. Understanding the role of domination in freedom allows us to see the ways in which structures of power and privilege operate systematically to favor and empower certain groups of people over others, to give some people a larger number of options than others, and thereby to create different understandings of individual subjectivity, choice, and freedom. Ending domination is key to freedom, and democratic participation in the construction of public policies that set the terms for choice is key to ending domination.

The notion of domination thus suggests that the future of liberty in democratic politics is, in a sense, what it has always been: the heart and soul. But at the same time, it is also the wrong question. Perhaps we should be asking about the future of democratic politics for liberty. Democracy, in this reading, is central to freedom, for it can facilitate the broader participation in social structures and processes that is key to freedom as the nondomination that Pettit (2001) urges. Democracy is the only political form that can do so. It can ensure that excluded groups, such as the poor, white women, and men and women of color, play an equal role with economically privileged white men in constructing discursive meanings and their material expression and in setting forth principles by which contexts can be evaluated.

In mainstream political theory and political science, freedom is the foundation for democracy, because freedom is conceived of as a state, a condition, or quality that individuals achieve, and that requires individuals to be situated vis-à-vis state power in positions of identifiable authorization as voters, holders of civil rights, as candidates, and holders of political office. By contrast, my suggestion here is that democracy must be the foundation for freedom, because freedom is something that is created and constructed through social relations of power.

Democracy involves much more than voting or rights. Rather, by considering democratic politics in the context of freedom, domination, and social constructivism, we can see that democratic politics involves much broader social powers and structures that involve the creation, interpretation, and definition of who we are. This means that equalizing participation in social forces that create and determine the contexts in which options are defined and choices are made is essential to freedom. As long as people are not full and equal participants in creating the contexts in, by, and through which options are formulated and made available, desires are formulated, and choices are defined—the three ways in which domination affects freedom—they are not full citizens within democratic politics, and they are not free.

To recognize the contributions of positive liberty does not entail a rejection of negative liberty. Rather, it suggests the need to think of the two interactively and interdependently rather than as a dichotomy. Each model suggests important ideas about the meaning of freedom, so we must include both in our understanding of the concept and practice of liberty. Indeed, it may be accurate to say that positive liberty *is* the future of negative liberty; for realizing the negative liberty definition of freedom, being able to do what I want without interference, requires us to create and maintain social structures that equalize power in the processes of creating the contexts that construct us as desiring, choosing individuals. Equalizing power will require radical changes not only in traditional governmental institutions but also in all kinds of social relations and institutions, such as the workplace, schools, and the family. If we can do that, then freedom may have a future after all.

Chapter 6

The Rhetoric of Democratic Liberty

GORDON SCHOCHET

> The fundamental sense of freedom is freedom from chains,
> from imprisonment, from enslavement by others. The rest is
> extension of this sense or else metaphor. To strive to be free
> is to seek to remove obstacles; to struggle for personal
> freedom is to seek to curb interference, exploitation,
> enslavement by men whose ends are theirs, not one's own.
> Freedom, at least in its political sense, is co-terminus with
> the absence of bullying or domination.
> —Isaiah Berlin, 1969

> The state has a duty, not merely to liberate its citizens
> from . . . personal exploitation and dependence, but to
> prevent its own agents, dressed in a little brief authority,
> from behaving arbitrarily in the course of imposing the rules
> that govern our common life.
> —Quentin Skinner, 1998

LIBERTY IS ONE of the most important and—in one form or another—persistent notions in the political vocabulary of the West. Especially in times of crisis and conflict, our freedom is a central part of the incorporating and integrating story we tell ourselves and the rest of the world about who we are and what defines us. To see its future, we must first understand its past. That is the subject of this chapter.

We all believe in freedom and are dedicated to its preservation, but after more than two thousand years of discussion, we still do not agree about what being free or being "a free people" means. Countless books and essays—extolling the virtues of freedom, explaining its nature, calling for its extension or contraction, debating its value and even its existence, contesting whether this or that alleged instance of freedom is "real"—have not done the job. Indeed, the job cannot be done, for freedom has acquired multiple meanings because of its importance and long history. And its inherent imprecision is also the source of much of its continuing vitality.

This essay is a contribution to that protracted discussion, presented not in the vain hope of finally bringing it to an end, but with the more humble ambition of clarifying some of the stakes. It deals with liberty or freedom— used interchangeably and conceived along the lines suggested in the two passages quoted above—in the modern democratic state.[1]

The following arguments, like the politics and history from which they derive, are not altogether compatible. The most important are:

- Liberty functions primarily as a rhetorical or ideological concept and is, therefore, difficult to define and implement.
- The concept of liberty has attracted both more acceptance and more controversy over recent centuries.
- Despite its varying, abstract, and sometimes conflicting meanings, liberty is very close to the notion of "rights," a concept that has more determinate meanings and lends itself to political implementation.
- Liberty is a fundamental part of modern notions of constitutionalism, the "rule of law," and equality.
- All liberty is about the absence of restraints or impediments (or the removal of obstacles) that we tend to associate with so-called negative liberty.

Implicit in these arguments is an insistence that much of what is significant as well as vexing about liberty can be understood by knowing something about its "conceptual history."

The Rhetoric of Liberty

Whatever its diverse meanings over the last two millennia and whatever the contexts, liberty has always *functioned* ideologically and rhetorically. It is an evaluative—or what philosophers have called an "appraising"—term, generally carrying a positive connotation. Only rarely has *liberty* been invoked negatively—usually in attacks on liberalism or democracy—and even those usages are often directed at specific accounts of liberty. In recent years, however, there have been almost no *governmental* objections to liberty; there is instead a virtual worldwide agreement among public officials about the desirability of achieving or preserving something called liberty, even though there is no consensus about its meaning or how it can be implemented. Criticisms of liberty have come from theorists and philosophers, not politicians.

To say that freedom is significantly rhetorical and ideological is not to denigrate either the concept or its use, but to suggest its ambiguous, contentious, often tendentious, and contestable meaning, status, and function. Beliefs and values are fundamental parts of the cement that holds cultures together; for the Europeanized societies of the modern world, the commitment to some notion of freedom is at the very basis of their dominant belief systems. In the rhetorical world created by the United Nations and its Universal Declaration of Human Rights, almost all political systems at least pay lip service to the value of freedom. Few overtly attack it, and none would argue that political bullying or slavery are legitimate, that public officials are entitled to act arbitrarily, or that freedom in general is bad for people.

What is put into practice, however, is quite another matter. Some states sanction slavery, and others engage in racial, sexual, religious, and political oppression. In response, the United States occasionally condemns abuses of freedom by other nations in the name of fundamental human rights. Some non-Western states insist that freedom is a cultural notion that is not applicable to them, while others insist that they are preparing their people for it. People on both sides of substantial political disputes—Muslims and Hindus in India, or Palestinians and Israelis in the Middle East, or Protestants and Catholics in Northern Ireland—claim the mantle of liberty to defend their policies. What these claims have in common is the quest for autonomy, the belief in a people's entitlement to be left alone—not interfered with—to pursue their own objectives. For some, this means having their own relatively closed societies, states in which they are governed by people like themselves; for others, it means being permitted to coexist with other cultures in a single society. Some fear contamination, others persecution. And when the fears are strong enough, all are willing to kill to preserve their own freedoms.

These latter claims manifest a kind of cultural anxiety, an inward-looking selfishness, often voiced in calls for freedom: freedom is something people want *for* themselves to protect them *from* the intrusions of others. The cultural assertion of a right or entitlement to be free is often a response to oppression and, at the extremes, can lead to "separatism" or territorial secession. In this selfish form, freedom is generally intolerant of—or, at best, indifferent toward—what would be the corresponding entitlements of others. It might also be hostile and view all other cultures as enemies that should be destroyed. These demands are undertaken in pursuit of freedom, but it is a freedom not compatible with democratic tolerance.

Within a culture, members of persecuted, anxious minorities also might seek freedom out of something resembling envy—which is still self-interested—rather than selfishness alone. Envy begins with an other-regarding perspective; it asks why someone is treated differently from someone else: What is it about you that entitles you to this preferred status or treatment that is denied to me? So construed, envy tends toward democratic principles of equality and tolerance.

Furthermore, the egalitarianism of envy shifts the burden of justification from the proponent of equality to the defender of privilege. It does not call for a full or robust conception of equality—which, given the vast differences among people, is virtually impossible to sustain. Rather, it requires a pragmatic and context-specific defense of a particular inequality, one that points to the ways in which differences among people are *relevant* to the political distribution of benefits, burdens, and statuses. However modest, such claims result in a form of equality grounded in the actual features of human beings, the concrete facts of their lives, and the ways of life adopted by the communities in which they live, not abstract, metaphysical beliefs about their essential natures that would effectively erase their differences. The preservation of differences within the population of a single society ultimately gives rise to a spirit of tolerance and forbearance. So long as one is persuaded that the differential treatment is not unfair or unjust—in part because it is based on appropriate criteria—and one does not feel deprived, what might otherwise be envy will give way to toleration. Explicit in the openness of such a society is the acceptance of differing and even competing conceptions of freedom.

It is this consequential imprecision of liberty that gives it ideological importance: in the diverse, pluralistic, multicultural societies that characterize much of the modern world, it would be impossible to have a precise sustaining belief that all accepted. Furthermore, this inherently indeterminate understanding of freedom means that there will be occasional contests about its implementation and actualization. These contests will be conducted rhetorically in the first instance. That is the nature of ideology and of ideological disagreement. That discussion, with its internal flexibility, is also an important part of what holds a pluralistic society together.

Historical Sources of Freedom

The very idea of political liberty has changed (and sometimes evolved) over time. It has been attached to and used to characterize different practices and institutions but is not itself institutionally identifiable, unlike its conceptual cousins, rights and property. Rather, liberty undergirds and is implicated in most of the practices of democratic society. Moreover, liberty does not have a stable, consistent, or consensual meaning. For these reasons, the historical origins of the concept cannot be determined. There is not even a conjectural, let alone discoverable, moment at which freedom became a significant political concept. But even if there were, there would be no reason other than antiquarian curiosity to search for it.

It *is* possible, however, to construct the history of the *idea* of freedom and to identify occasions when it assumed a new or renewed importance in political discourse. This history illustrates both the tentative and tenuous nature of freedom and the circumstances under which it has been championed or threatened. It also reveals the frequency with which freedom is invoked in ideological arguments that aim to justify policies and advance programs that others may see as having little to do with the cause of liberty. Furthermore, this history demonstrates the differences among various conceptions of freedom and liberty and helps us appreciate how much outmoded or undesirable conceptual baggage our modern notion carries. In those terms, we might see why freedom and liberty are so often puzzling and even troublesome concepts.

THE ENGLISH CIVIL WAR AND AFTER

Libertas—meaning *inter alia*, "nondomination" (Pettit 1997),[2] as well as the entitlement and ability to act—was an important notion for the ancient Greeks and Romans (Wirszubski 1968; Brunt 1988, chap. 6). This republican or neo-Roman understanding of liberty continued to appear in Western history in various contexts until the eighteenth century (Skinner 1998). But by the 1640s, in the context of the English Civil War, the modern notion of political liberty as an entitlement of individuals and a bulwark against governmental excesses began to replace the older conception. It did so as part of a shift in the understanding of constitutionalism (that will be discussed below) that was itself a response to the conflicts between Parliament and the Crown about the meaning and control of what was called the "fundamental law" (Gough 1955, chaps. 5–8).

The ideological and political disputes of the English Civil War, and the short-lived Parliamentary victory, set the stage for subsequent changes that are central to the emergence of political liberty. The modern understanding of liberty developed then is inseparable from the parallel emergence of an individualistic conception of the political world. That conception, with roots in the Protestant Reformation, the new science and epistemology of the age, and opposition to the absolutist pretensions of rulers, was itself just beginning to emerge in the seventeenth century.

In politics, this individualism would ultimately be manifest in an expansion of participating membership in the political community, which was in turn a consequence of an alteration of the meaning of *person*. This latter transformation is evident in an unusually strong attack on slavery that appeared in a London newspaper of 1737:

> I suppose it will readily be granted, that *all* Mankind are equally *free born*; and this *Natural Freedom* is with great Reason highly *valued* by the whole *human* race. And I think no one Individual of the Species, who may be deemed a *Moral Agent*, can at anytime, on any Pretense whatsoever, consistent with Justice, without his or her own voluntary Consent, be deprived of this *Natural Right*, excepting only those who by their *Crimes* have *forfeited* their *Liberty*. . . .
>
> But what Right have those *Europeans*, who carry on the Trade upon *Negroes*, thus to degrade human Nature, and treat them in the same manner as they treat the *Brutes that perish!* Are not those unhappy *Africans* in the same Rank of Beings with those who enslave them? Or, do they weakly imagine, that the Tincture of the Skin makes an essential Difference between the Blacks and other Men? These *Negroes* never forfeited their *Liberty*, and cou'd never have injured their *cruel Lords* if they had left them to their *Natural Rights*, unmolested in their *native Country*. . . . have not the *Negroes* as much Right (if it were in their Power) to invade *England*, and carry away, by force, Men, Women, and Children, and make them Slaves in a foreign Country, or to come and purchase Slaves here, as any of the English have thus to deal with them? (*The Old Whig* 1737–38, 1)

The radicalism of this plea—far greater in its sweep than the later U.S. Declaration of Independence—is not yet a call for equal *political* rights and liberties. That was still many years off; when it did come, it would initially be based on just this sort of natural egalitarianism. Subsequent developments included equal entitlements of women to the natural liberties and rights enjoyed by men, removal of religious qualifications for office-holding in England, disestablishment of state churches, elimination of the property requirement for the franchise, constitutional outlawry of slavery in the United States, and women's suffrage movements on both sides of the English-speaking Atlantic. All were derived from the same principles as this 1737 attack on slavery: fundamental human equality. Once that was granted, all that remained—empirically difficult even if theoretically straightforward—was determining who belonged to the category "human" and then agreeing on their legal and political attributes and entitlements.

Making those determinations is still incomplete. On the one hand, appeals to merit and economic achievement, which often mask prejudices, stand opposed to liberty- and justice-based calls for the more equitable distribution of the benefits and burdens of social and political life. On the other hand, animal rights advocates, seeking to extend liberty and rights protections to nonhumans, attack the "speciesism" that deprives animals of some of the same entitlements and considerations that are accorded humans.[3]

LIBERTY AND CONSTITUTIONALISM

Among the lingering effects of the English Civil War was the emergence of a new and distinctly modern conception of constitutionalism as a formal and systematic means of defining and imposing limits on governmental actions. This new conception reflected a shift in the early-modern period, away from the traditional conception of the constitution as a presumption about the informal conformity of government to the *constituent* parts or components of its polity (from the Latin *constituere*, "to constitute") and the nature of its people, to one rooted in formal and specific rules for the structure and operation of government.

The various *Agreement[s] of the People* devised by the Levellers before the Regicide, the 1653 Instrument of Government that defined Cromwell's Protectorate, James Harrington's *Rota*, and John Milton's *Readie and Easie Way to Establish a Free Commonwealth* (both published in 1660), all presaged the American Constitution in their formalism and conceptions of limited government. The principal limits on the English government were the ancient and fundamental liberties of the people that had been abused by King Charles I, and the operating presumption was that explicitly incorporating those liberties into the constitution would help prevent such abuses in the future.

This shift to modern constitutionalism and the rule of law was itself part of a reorientation of the central concerns of English politics. The dominant, traditional conception was rooted in the (civic) virtue of the members of political community; it ultimately gave way—although it did not disappear—to a model that looked to their *interests*. The contrast is between "humanistic" and "juridical" ways of conceiving the political world (Schochet 1994).

The virtue-based view of politics was appropriate to a homogeneous (by pretension if not actual accomplishment) and stratified society in which participating political membership was restricted and members of lower economic and social orders accepted their relatively devalued statuses. Freedom was not a proper goal for people who, for the common good as well as for their own benefit, needed instruction and restraint. At least that was the image that the political, religious, and literary elites attempted to convey. By the 1640s, however, England was well on its way to becoming a pluralistic, conflict-ridden, class-divided, religiously fragmented society. It could no longer be held together by papering over those growing differences through moralistic appeals to a humanistic common good and sense of virtue. Both of these appeals were oppressive and left little room for free choice or actions that differed from the announced good of the society.

The heart of this imposition was the officially established Church of England and its intolerance of other religious beliefs and practices, especially those of other Protestant denominations. Accordingly, the first of the new freedoms sought in England was religious liberty, the arguments for which began as requests for the *grant* of toleration but soon became an insistence on the *right* of people to follow their own religious consciences. The vehicle for these reforms was to be the law, an institution that, partially because of its inherent formalism, is much better suited to the governing of a pluralistic society than are declarations issued by a king or church official.

The story of the movement from "virtue" to "interest"—from humanism to legalism—was in part a consequence of the growing importance of lawyers in English politics and of their eventual domination of Parliament. This lawyerly perspective imposed upon the Anglophone world a conceptual vocabulary that continues to characterize its politics and is one of the marks of the transformation of the sixteenth-century English commonweal into a modern state. That vocabulary prominently features such familiar common-law notions as "interest," "obligation," "property," and, fundamentally, "rights" and "freedom." Missing were such notions as "honor," "counsel," "prudence," and especially "virtue" that characterized the humanistic vocabulary. "Freedom," or "liberty," was present in both vocabularies, but in the juridical context, it was stripped of it associations with republicanism and virtue, coming recognizably close to the negative liberty of modernity.

In the rhetorical world of the common law, freedom initially suggested the *removal* of restraints and obstacles and granted *exemptions* from restrictions, which made it a privilege attached to specific statuses. It was not yet an inherent or natural entitlement. That addition would soon come in the constitutionalist response to the absolutist claims of Charles I and his apologists, but it was not conceivable in the humanistic conception of liberty. Modern freedom is the product of the meeting of traditional constitutionalism and republican liberty in the England of the 1640s. The association of "freedom" with "rights" and the general tendency to conceive of them in terms of one another has continued ever since.[4]

Liberty and freedom were certainly not newly minted in the 1640s, when the relations between king and Parliament finally broke down. What the Civil War debates initially contributed was a highly politicized understanding of liberty that was radically individualized and rooted in *nature*. Freedom was no longer to be regarded as a "privilege" contingent upon one's status or dependent upon the largess of a political superior who might withdraw it. Instead, it was increasingly seen as an entitlement or right (Schochet 1992b). As Jefferson would later put it, "governments are instituted among men" precisely to secure "life, liberty, and the pursuit of happiness."[5] The notion that there were natural liberties that preceded and determined the establishment of political authority would prove to be an altogether new and, especially from perspective of rulers, unsettling conception of governance.

Who was the best guardian of the people's liberties? In the 1640s, Parliament, as the representative of the people, claimed the title and tried Charles I for treason, usurpation, and violating the limited power that had been entrusted to him *"For the good and benefit of the People"* (*Charge of the Commons* 1648, 3). To no avail, Charles I repeated his oft-made claim that he was responsible "to God first, and my People next, for the preservation of their lives, Liberties, and Estates," and said that he was not answerable to an illegally constituted tribunal (*King Charles His Tryal* 1649, 11). Nearly 150 years later, James Madison would also ask, "Who are the best keepers of the people's liberty?" And his reply was, "The people themselves. The sacred trust can be no where so safe as it is in the hands most interested in preserving it." "What a perversion of the natural order of things!" he added, "to make *power* the primary and central object of the social system, and *Liberty* but its satellite" (Madison 1792, 532, 533).

THE GROWTH OF FREEDOM

Overcoming many obstacles, freedom has increased over the past 350 years, partially realizing the Enlightenment's optimistic faith in the continuing improvement of the human condition. The larger sweep of history shows a gradual but evident expansion of social and political membership through the inclusion of previously marginalized or excluded groups of people. Like all politics, the extension of rights and liberty has hardly been consistent or without setbacks and reversals. It has usually been slow and often insufficient; it has almost always been accomplished grudgingly and as a result of calculations about the best interests of the political system or state rather than because of the triumph of righteous principle over undesirable practices (Moore 1966, 413–52; Schochet 1992a, 1992b; Drake and McCubbins 1998, esp. 1–12; Schmale 1996; and Tilly 1998b); and it has certainly not been the inevitable working out of anything like an historical purpose or divine plan. Whatever the values of this process, "democratization" or "liberalization" has not been without its costs and critics (see, for the former, Dahl 1998, 50–57, and for the latter, Drake and McCubbins 1998).[6]

Problems of Liberty

The development of freedom is substantively difficult, as the historical record demonstrates. And this history also illuminates the problems in the very concept of liberty. We now turn to their consideration.

IMPERFECT FREEDOM

All politics—democratic or authoritarian, bourgeois or radical—is inherently about the official resolution of conflicts that are not self-resolved satisfactorily and are of substantially wider significance than the immediate concerns of the conflicting parties.[7] Whatever else it is, politics is a matter of power tempered by legitimacy, and democratic legitimacy requires that power be exercised with as much impartiality and neutrality as possible.[8] The state is thus something of an arbitrator that can enforce its decisions. Ideally, parties to the resolved conflict should feel that the resolution was right even if not necessarily good for them from the narrow perspectives of their interests. This is the baseline, and it is necessarily *imperfectionist;* it means that politics is a legitimate way of ensuring that the members of the society will not destroy one another because of their freedoms and their differences, with the very important proviso that the political process itself cannot become a disguised forum for bringing about that destruction.

None of this would matter in a society that was sufficiently homogeneous to avoid the differences and conflicts that have characterized Western societies since the Reformation. Modern freedom and the constitutionalism in which it is embedded are direct consequences of the fragile diversity of religious beliefs and the various pluralisms spawned by the Reformation and the secular, territorial state.[9] Thus, guarantees of nondestruction must include the preservation of what John Stuart Mill and Alexis de Tocqueville identified as minority rights, a principle that simply applies toleration and freedom of conscience to politics more broadly conceived. There is a further and equally important proviso—and difficulty: that religious matters, for the most part, remain self-contained. This posture is virtually impossible for people who feel implicated in the salvation of others or responsible for the general moral well-being of their societies. Such people are incapable of participating in the tolerance and procedural consensus required by membership in a pluralistic society committed to maximal political freedom.

The modern, democratic state was functionally constituted to replace political perfectionists of this sort, and they still present that state with some of its greatest problems. Whether they are in power and attempt to impose their views on others, or in the minority and feel deeply threatened by the requirements of toleration, such perfectionists will be unhappy with the full measure of liberty that democracy promises. One of the most important tasks facing modern, pluralistic states is to persuade detractors inside and out that diversity is unavoidable in practice, that freedom is valuable and precious, and that cooperation, tolerance, and forbearance are pragmatic virtues.

Contrary to the aspirations of political perfectionists, it cannot be the job of the democratic state in a pluralistic society to make its citizens moral—to bring their beliefs and behaviors into conformity with some substantive standard of ethical rightness—either for their own good or for the general benefit of society. The pluralistic state sees its task as the provision and protection of a nonpolitical space in which people may attempt to make themselves moral. Behind perfectionism and the positive liberty on which it depends is a religious-like commitment to the notion that moral error is never a mark of freedom: no one in full command of his or her faculties would willingly embrace the social equivalent of sin. To do so is a sign of weakness or error that keeps one from acting freely, and it is the responsibility of the state to save people from themselves. Democratic pluralism, on the contrary, carries with it the right and freedom to be wrong, precisely because one person's error is another person's truth. Freedom can be difficult and sometimes even unpleasant for some, but it cannot be transformed into a quest for rightness.

FREEDOM AND GOVERNMENT

Liberty is not an individual attribute but a political status involving government. The principle of freedom is one of starting points of constitutionalism: the task of government is to preserve and protect liberty and to ensure that it is equitably distributed. Here, it is helpful to distinguish between recognized liberties and granted liberties.[10] Recognized liberties, as the name suggests, are those that already exist but either do not enjoy full legal protection until they are enacted into law or impose conditions or limits on what is legally permissible. Granted liberties are those that governments create or bestow as means of improving the conditions of some or all the members of the political community. They can be granted as remedies for inequities or as special privileges, but in either case, they would not exist without positive governmental action.

The general presumptions behind recognized liberties are that people are free to do whatever is not prohibited—which is almost a truism, but a very important one—and that they have the right to act in various ways without fearing the interference of the state. The protection of religious freedom in the First Amendment to the Constitution is an obvious example of a recognized liberty. But the very notion of recognized liberty rests upon a contentious, if not dubious, metaphysical presumption, that rights and freedoms exist prior to government. Without some such notion, however, it is very difficult to defend the general proposition that the protection of liberty is one of the primary ends that government should serve.

The rule-of-law constitutionalist claim is that freedom is a limit on government—that is, that governmental actions that contravene liberty are not simply objectionable but are actually illegal. Determination of the proper extent as well as of improper encroachments on liberty are necessarily matters of negotiation and rhetorical construction. Governments in these terms are supposed to *recognize* the prepolitical liberties of their citizens, to put them into practice, and to protect them. However, from the perspective of the government and its law—a perspective that suggests a strong form of legal positivism—there can be no functional or operational difference between recognized and granted liberties: they are both granted. Once freedoms that are claimed on extralegal and prepolitical grounds have been enacted into law, the metaphysics that may have influenced or even prompted their "recognition" is irrelevant.

The connection between liberty and government is fundamental to American democracy. Every schoolchild is taught that the quest for liberty was the driving force behind our nation's dual foundings—when the Pilgrims fled England in search of religious freedom and again in 1776 when the violations of "Life, Liberty, and the pursuit of Happiness" became grounds for the Revolution. From Patrick Henry and Thomas Jefferson, through the preamble to the Constitution and the *National Anthem* and numerous patriotic songs, to Martin Luther King and popular music of the late twentieth century,[11] liberty and freedom have been mainstays of our national belief system.

Democracy and liberty can be separated theoretically, however, as the non- and often antidemocratic *Federalist* shows in its invocation of liberty in the name of republicanism. Nonetheless, it would now be impossible to proclaim or defend democracy without at the same time appealing to liberty. We need only recall the cries of hypocrisy that greeted Sukarno's announcement of "guided democracy" as the description of his government of Indonesia and the uniform agreement that this new concept was a thinly veiled euphemism to cover his dictatorship. Similarly, Rousseau's assertion that some citizens of his social contract state would be "forced to be free" has led many commentators to question his commitments both to democracy and to freedom. Whatever else it is, democracy is a system of government built upon and dedicated to the liberty—or freedom—of its members.[12]

As the *Federalist* suggests, a commitment to freedom precedes democracy, but, at the same time, liberty is one of the ends served by democratic governments. The essence of democracy—participatory self-government—is no better expressed than by Lincoln's invocation: "of, by, and for the people." Since the seventeenth century, the presumption has increasingly been that a self-governing people is a free people and that only a free people can be truly self-governing. Thus, the democratic commitment to self-government is simultaneously a commitment to liberty. Historically, as the categories of person and citizen expanded, these democratic commitments manifested an important egalitarian tendency that called for the removal of unwarranted and irrelevant obstacles to full and equal participation.

FREEDOM AND EQUALITY

Full liberty of citizenship and personal participation amounts to radical political egalitarianism, yet it does not necessarily lead to social and economic equality. The commitment is to the removal of politically *unjust* inequalities—that is, those inequalities that are avoidable and function as obstacles to political equality (and render some citizens politically less free than others). The remedies may call for the redistribution of some social benefits and burdens by increasing the opportunities of some relatively less well-off members at the expense of others who enjoy greater opportunities.

But governmental democracy cannot consistently be radically egalitarian. A nation such as the United States, whose geography is expansive and diverse, and whose population is culturally and economically heterogeneous as well as large, cannot be fully participatory, which is what generalized political equality would require. Instead, elected but responsible officials make political decisions based on their subjective principles and interests, pragmatic judgments, and concern for the general welfare of the nation—all presumably informed by their commitments to freedom and the discernable preferences of the population. The free participation of the citizens, according to the old-fashioned Madisonian view, is the primary means of determining the paramount interests and concerns in society and their relative intensity. For this determination to be reliable, the "people" must have unfettered access to relevant information—a free press, in the widest sense—and sufficient leisure both to become informed and to participate—freedom from burdens that would inhibit functioning citizenship. Ideally, democratic participation is individually time-consuming and socially expensive, rather more, in fact, than most democracies have been able to support.

Even with broad participation, no democracy can expect that all its members share in approving of or identifying with its substantive policies. At some point, decisions will frustrate the concerns and interests of some citizens and will therefore limit some of their liberties. In consequence, they may experience a coercion that is destructive of the claims of liberty and feel "resentment"

(Bernard Williams 2001, 18). Similarly, rules that permanently exclude a class of residents from citizenship are presumptively illegitimate violations of liberty. Restrictions on immigration and requirements for nationalization do not fall into this category, nor do differential standards for citizens and aliens. But permanent bans to citizenship for legal resident-aliens, or native-born members of specific racial, religious, ethnic groups, or gender are illegitimate, as are economic bars to fully participating citizenship.

Freedom has always functioned as aspiration and ideology. It is a term that is not easily rendered operational nor attached unambiguously to institutions and practices, and its extent cannot be measured with anything more accurate than rhetoric and feelings. It is one of the most illusive and contestable concepts in our political vocabulary, contestable in the senses both that there are conflicts about its meaning and struggles over its possession. But we cannot get along without it. We are committed to the belief that it is virtually constitutive of what we take ourselves to be and that there is something inherently problematic about the unequal distribution or contraction of liberty. On the surface, this presents a puzzle for attempts to analyze democratic politics, for liberty and freedom are irreducibly ideological terms that demand concrete implementation. And the relationship of "theory to practice" is notoriously difficult to determine.[13] These problems are particularly evident in modern usage.

Negative and Positive Liberty

Much of the way we conceive freedom today is derived from Isaiah Berlin's *Two Concepts of Liberty*. In that not-so-long but venerated tradition of English-speaking discussions of freedom and liberty that stretches back to John Stuart Mill, *Two Concepts* is one of the benchmarks,[14] and we cannot avoid its terminology, however vague and problematic.

Berlin made a famous distinction between "positive" and "negative" liberty. He was disdainful of "positive liberty," seeing it as a fraudulent misappropriation of the vocabulary of freedom. Although it can be argued that positive liberty is valuable as an indicator of the importance of desire and internal dispositions to the structure of freedom (see Hirschmann, this volume),[15] it is doubtful that a separate concept of freedom is necessary to make these points. Liberty can be most satisfactorily conceived as the absence of restraints or obstacles, or as Berlin's "negative liberty." In fact, all liberty is properly seen as "negative."

"Positive liberty" is not separately about liberty at all, but is about being "self-willed," or, in Berlin's own words, it "derives from the wish on part of the individual to be his own master" (Berlin 1969, 131). That "wish" may indicate an individual's belief or feeling that she is not in control of her own life. What is required is an expansion of Berlin's original conception of negative liberty to incorporate some of the psychological dimensions of positive liberty. The difficulty, it is often alleged, is that "liberalism," to which negative liberty is held to be foundational, is wedded to the externalities of actions and institutions and so can neither account for nor adequately comprehend psychological categories.

Being self-willed is not irrelevant to freedom: I am hardly free in any meaningful sense just because I am physically able to act in ways that others have determined for me, but which have nothing to do with my own choices and values. Freedom is far more complex than Hobbes believed it was, simply the absence of *external* impediments to action (Hobbes 1651 [1991], chap. 20). Freedom is necessarily about the absence of internal as well as external obstacles, not just to action but to choice as well, and about the ability to act or refrain from acting in ways that one has chosen. The impediments include, beyond the obvious material deprivations that hinder action, ignorance of one's (potential) options, subtle discriminations, and even various psychological problems. The test for freedom, however, is not whether one actually acts in a particular way but, rather, whether one *would* do so without coercion or intimidation. In other words, there is first a psychological and material test about knowledge, choice, and fear followed by a more overtly social and political test about actual ability.

The criticisms of negative liberty seem to presuppose and build upon the Hobbesian model and its claims to preserve *choice* of any kind as the operational manifestation of freedom, even choices that are unpleasant or are the result of coercion. For Hobbes, complying with a highwayman's demand for "your money or your life" constituted a valid exercise of freedom. He could make this claim because he maintained that coercion did not defeat freedom. Hobbes was insistent on this point, but his theory is deeply flawed and simply unworkable in its own terms (Schochet 1990). Contrary to Hobbes, coercion defeats freedom by constraining individuals to act in ways other than they would have acted in its absence.

We would not say that a slave "chooses" to surrender freedom by refusing to run away, especially if a runaway faces the possibility of being severely punished or even being put to death if he is caught. Despite Hobbes, choice cannot be made to function that way, as many of the critics of negative liberty realize. A sensible response would say simply that Hobbes was wrong on this point and then attempt to reconstitute his model.[16] An important place to start is with the rejection of his insistence that the impediments that hinder freedom must be imposed from without.

With the exception of Hobbes, no one has ever advocated a notion of negative liberty independent of the value of being self-determined, of being able to formulate and act upon one's own cogent desires and life plans. Berlin understood this liberal tradition, but he ultimately ignored it, inviting the widespread but simplistic understanding of his analysis. Liberalism's critics have accepted what amounts to his distortion, and, with him, they have read back into the liberal theorists they attack the impoverished conception of liberty that these theorists, in fact, only propounded as part and parcel of some concept of self-actualization (see, for example, Unger 1975; George 1993; and Garvey 1996).[17] On the readings of their critics, liberal theorists look naive if not downright silly, and it is no wonder that this so-called liberalism—which, in fact, has never existed except in the minds of its enemies—suffers such theoretical disrepute.

One might say, then—to address the question asked by one of the foremost of those detractors, Ronald Beiner (1992), "What's the matter with liberalism?"—that the fault is the lazy scholarship of its critics, followed by the conceptual capitulation of its friends. Too often today those who defend the grand, but not necessarily consistent, tradition of liberty, rights, constitutionalism, justice, and even equality as they have occurred in the history of liberalism allow their opponents to define the terms of debate and, in consequence, find themselves supporting principles that have never been articulated. Like most traditions, liberalism is a pastiche, concocted by advocates and critics alike in order to impose a unity on the past and to guide the present and future (see Schochet 2003). It is not inherently consistent, nor does it speak with one voice.

The specific difficulty here is not unlike the more familiar one that notoriously plagues John Stuart Mill's *On Liberty,* the problematic separation of preventable *harm* to the external or physical self, which can be prohibited, and *offense* to the values of the internal self, which cannot. In both cases, what is at issue is classic mind-body dualism. Need we surrender either the liberal tradition or its conception of liberty in order to accommodate what we now accept, the significant relationship between our interior and exterior lives?

Negative liberty and part of positive liberty can be combined into a single notion of freedom that can be conceptualized, in accord with "ordinary" usage, to mean the absence of restraints.[18] Whatever limits desires and choices and renders people incapable of having what William James termed "live options" would qualify as a restraint on freedom. Freedom has to begin with the ability of people to conceive their own ends and desires and, beyond that, must include their capacities to pursue those objectives.

This is the point at which the rhetorical issues become crucial, for freedom and liberty are normative or evaluative concepts and are almost always used positively. In order to be understood, freedom must be contextualized in terms of what an agent is or ought to be free to do and the costs of removing the obstacles that stand in the way of other conceivably greater freedoms. This will require judgments about policies if it is to advance beyond assertions and accusations. Thus the notions of "free" held by "freedom loving" peoples by themselves contribute very little to our modern understandings that associate freedom with individual rights (see Skinner 1984, 203). Cicero—echoed by Machiavelli—claimed that the only way of ensuring personal freedom is for people to be "slaves to the public interest" (*De Officis* I, x, 31, quoted by Skinner 1984, 214). Modern liberalism rejects this part of the classical vision, asserting instead that citizens need not be active, frequent participants so much as they must constantly function as watchdogs over their officials, ever ready to call them to account, to question the regulations they adopt, and to demand explanations for their actions. Representative government carries with it, as a direct consequence of the popular freedom on which it rests, the responsibility and accountability of representatives to their constituents.

But all this must be seen in the further context of the social science truism—which would be utterly trivial if it were not so often forgotten by proponents of "positive" as well as "negative" liberty—that in varying degrees we are shaped by our environments. We are not and cannot be "free agents" in the uncompromisingly strong sense that is implicitly presumed by virtually all freedom-talk and held up as a standard by which social and political practices are to be judged. This is not an argument for determinism so much as it is an insistence that we recognize what we already know and acknowledge about other aspects of our social and conceptual lives, that we are surrounded *and constrained* by numerous inescapable "variables" or "givens" that we have not created and which we have limited powers to alter.[19] The shorthand for all this, of course, is society, which includes structures, practices, and institutions as well as ideology and social beliefs and values, and its theoretical recognition is a form of social (or sociological) realism.

From a political perspective, what we need to remember is that parts of this entire apparatus are often subject to the control and manipulation of others, which means that some of the restrictions on our freedoms are sometimes intentionally imposed. Opponents of the liberal—or "individualist"—conception of freedom, at least since Marx and continuing through contemporary "communitarians," have used this notion of society and its partially "conventional" nature as the basis of their attacks (for example, Beiner 1992; Sandel 1996).[20] And they naively write as if it were possible to eliminate restraints altogether and to create a world in which people are universally autonomous and utterly self-willed and, at the same time, other-regarding.

But no matter how freedom is conceived, choice is its central manifestation. Coercion—forcing someone to act in a way that she has not chosen—is the antithesis of freedom, even if the person would have made that choice had she been given the option. The absence of choice or of the ability to choose is the denial of freedom. As Hirschmann says, "Choices must be made by individuals by and for themselves; nobody can force battered women to leave their abusers or 'out' closet lesbians or gays without grossly violating their freedom. But because 'choosing selves' are located in particular contexts of relationships in which power and production occur, the activity of choice making is itself a social process" (this volume, p. 80). This expanded understanding of freedom carries with it the mandate that we consider all the background conditions for the appearance and exercise of freedom, not just those external impediments that seem to stand in the way of its realization.

When we move from the philosophy to the *politics* of freedom in democratic society, we are immediately confronted by an apparent conflict with the principle of equality in the distribution of burdens and benefits of social living. Antiliberals generally would have us believe that liberty is the enemy of democratic equality and that the expansion of one person's liberty and entitlements can only come at the expense of someone else.[21] But a proper understanding of liberty and equality sees them as capable of working in much closer alliance. Many of the inegalitarian practices of our society are also antidemocratic denials of liberty, derived from social constructions that categorize individuals unfairly and structure the contexts of their desires.

What is not sufficiently clear, however, is the relationship of "desires" to "social construction," to "free will," and to what used to be called the problem of "false consciousness." At what point and according to what standard do we determine that individuals are truly the authors of their own desires? When, to revert to the language of positive liberty, am I genuinely self-willed, and when do I merely think that I am? Indoctrination and imposition are among the primary characteristics of all societies; at the relatively low level of individual desires and life plans, it is difficult to make that determination without the aid of intensive psychological analysis.

One of the most important issues facing contemporary constitutional democracies has to do with the extent to which they should be in the business of attending to the psychological needs of their citizens. To the extent that psychological disabilities lead to unwarranted, unjust, and politically relevant inequalities among citizens, it is presumptively appropriate for the state to seek and perhaps provide remedies. On the other hand, the received understanding of the principle of freedom seems to require that states remain indifferent to personal psychology, especially in light of the difficulty of distinguishing between what amounts to foolish choices and those that are the result of disturbed mental states. But until the larger question of freedom as including the absence of internal impediments is properly addressed, this problem will not be resolved.

On the societal level, liberty and equality are joined, not competitive. The history of liberty has been the story of its greater distribution in accord with the demands of equality. *Liberty* then should be understood as a substantive principle and *equality* as a distributive one. In other words, *liberty* tells us what to distribute and *equality* tells us to whom it should go. The grounds are always "social justice," and the criteria are what W. G. Runciman, in an early sociological application of Rawlsian "justice as fairness," called "relative deprivation" (Runciman 1966). The task of the equality—or distributive—principle is to determine when the criteria that have led to differential distribution are inappropriate, when the "relative deprivations" are unwarranted—that is, to identify "unjust" distributions. It follows, positively as well as negatively, that not everyone is entitled to the same kinds or degrees of liberty. Some people, under some specifiable circumstances and for specified reasons, will *legitimately* have more or less than others. But where the unequal distributions are determined to be "unjust," official programs may be instituted to *remedy*— with the goal of eliminating—them.

The Rhetorical Future of Liberty

Liberty will surely be invoked in future policy disputes. Hirschmann (this volume) has shown how the concept is deeply involved in welfare reform and the treatment accorded battered women. The rhetoric of freedom sounds even more broadly today than in the past. Taxation limits the liberty of consumer choice, while social security benefits increase the life choices of the elderly. Compulsory schooling limits the autonomy of children, while it increases their ability to define their choices as adults. The left champions access to abortion as enhancing the liberty of women, while the right champions access to firearms as enhancing the liberty of gun owners. Indeed, virtually every current policy issue has significant implications for the meaning of liberty.

Freedom is especially invoked in the United States in times of crisis, reminding the American people that what they share is more important than what divides them. During the Cold War, America was the leader of the "free world." In the aftermath of the September 11 attacks on the World Trade Center and the Pentagon, President George W. Bush explained, "America was targeted for attack because we're the brightest beacon for freedom and opportunity in the world." And he concluded by saying, "Yet, we go forward to defend freedom and all that is good and just in our world." On November 9, 2001—the anniversary of the fall of the Berlin Wall—issuing a proclamation for World Freedom Day, he said, "During the Cold War, freedom and authoritarianism clashed. Countries and entire regions suffered under repressive ideologies that sought to trample human dignity. Today, freedom is again threatened." And at the end of that speech, he declared: "On World Freedom Day, we also honor those who, at this moment, fight for freedom half a world away. On September 11, freedom was attacked, but liberty and justice will prevail. Like the fall of the Berlin Wall and the defeat of totalitarianism in Central and Eastern Europe, freedom will triumph in this war against terrorism."

All the while, however, Arab and other Muslim residents of the United States—citizens as well as aliens—were being detained for questioning, upon no apparent ground other than their ethnic and religious identities, and plans were being formulated for the use of military tribunals rather than civil courts to try captured Afghan fighters. The intellectual community was divided, but most of our citizens were apparently willing to extend freedom to only *some* of the inhabitants of the land, virtually recasting the inscription on the Liberty Bell in order to protect what the president had identified as our "liberties." Thus, an early NPR–Kaiser Family Foundation–Kennedy School poll reported that "the vast majority of Americans are willing to forgo some civil liberties to fight terrorism and that they trust the government to do the right thing in carrying out the fight."[22]

Liberty will continue to be prominent in our rhetoric, but its practice is less secure. The "rule of law" as well as modern "constitutionalism," its conceptual and political twin, are the principal means by which liberty is protected from governmental impositions, just as they are the means by which new liberties are created and old ones extended. Together, they are the most fundamental components of our democratic heritage; to surrender even this small bit of liberty is to attack the rule of law. The larger story of liberty is one of expansion, not contraction, which is what Benedetto Croce meant when he called history "the story of liberty" (Croce 1941). But that does not mean that liberty is sacrosanct and politically immunized against interference. The same contentious, aggressive forces that have been responsible for the extension of liberty are necessary to protect it from its enemies, by exercising that "eternal vigilance" that is its cost. Liberty is vital to our culture: *whatever it might mean* and however *contestable* its surrounding practices may be, its larger history shows that it needs to be nurtured, taught, and defended.

Part II

The Practices of American Democratic Institutions

IN THIS SECTION, contributors examine the institutions that embody the fundamental political principles of liberty, equality, and participation. The primary concern of these six chapters is the dynamic effects of our current institutions on the future of American democratic politics.

Nelson Polsby initiates the discussion by tracing the simultaneous growth of federal executive power and the concomitant expansion of the legislature. He argues that Congress and most state legislatures are robust institutions, not severely threatened by their corresponding executives nor by the "less proximate annoyances" of teledemocracy, the increased use of initiatives, and term limits. Polsby is confident that American legislative institutions will continue their historic achievement—to adapt to changing politics effectively, even if slowly.

Alan Rosenthal is less sanguine about the current state of American legislatures. He finds them challenged by two critical changes in American political culture—democratization of both legislatures themselves and their environment, and the disaffection of the public and a diminution of public support. Rosenthal argues that the combination of these trends negatively affects legislatures more than executives. As a result, he predicts that legislatures will be unable to maintain their coequal status.

Elizabeth Garrett uses *Bush v. Gore*—the lawsuit that capped the 2000 presidential election contest—to explore "how contempt for politics endangers democratic governance and diminishes the vitality of Congress." Observing that the Electoral Count Act provided Congress with an *ex ante* framework—a stable, neutral, preexisting set of rules for electoral dispute resolution—she argues that an overreaching Supreme Court did the country a tremendous disservice. The Court's "disdain for the political branches," she concludes, will have both short-term and long-term negative effects on the institutional balance of power.

Milton Heumann and Lance Cassak take a historical approach and find *Bush v. Gore* to be "something of a worst-case scenario." They observe that current law does not fully guide Congress's substantive decision in resolving a disputed presidential election. Noting that the decisional possibilities range from "high-politics" to pure logrolling, they ask What should have been Congress's decision rule in resolving the electoral dispute? Turning to the future, they consider the likely impact of the Court's decision on the canon of constitutional law, as well as the possible effects of the Court's decision on its future reputation.

William Crotty turns his attention to political parties as the key intermediary between the American people and its government. Using three criteria to assess the current performance of American political parties—representativeness, accountability, and participation—Crotty reaches a mixed judgment. American parties, he argues, are fairly representative, somewhat accountable, but poor performers in the mobilization of the electorate. With these findings, Crotty links together the key themes of this volume and concludes that the future of American democratic politics depends "on the ability of the parties to promote increased public participation."

Daniel Tichenor picks up on Crotty's concern for citizen-government linkage but approaches it from the perspective of the presidency and interest groups, the other vital intermediary institution of American democracy. He maps a theoretical framework of their relationships, illustrated by four case studies. In considering the interaction of the chief executive with interest groups, he finds that fragmented government power—as it was designed to do—still frustrates dramatic political change. With that observation, Tichenor closes the circle of the symposium as he returns our attention to Madison's constitutional framework.

Chapter 7

The Future of Legislatures in Democratic Politics

NELSON W. POLSBY

A DISCUSSION OF THE FUTURE of legislatures in democratic politics requires a few preliminary words about the idea of the future, which, in the first place, takes up an indeterminate amount of time (see Kahn 1975). Thus we must ask: Do we want a model of the future that is reliable for the next three or four days, as would be necessary for a television weather forecast? Do we want to talk about the next year or few years, in which we can guess that, on average, the winters will be cold and the summers will be hot? Do we want to be able to talk about the social equivalent of El Niño, whose effects spread themselves across several seasons? Or, on a somewhat grander scale, should we be thinking about global warming?

There are, after all, serious policy choices to be made at each scale of futurology: whether or not to take an umbrella to work, whether to invest in a new set of snow tires, how high a priority we should give to the control of greenhouse gasses. Tomorrow morning belongs to the future, and so does the next generation, and so does the long run, at which point, as John Maynard Keynes comfortably assured us, we are all dead.

The next interesting fact about the future is that it arrives packaged as a cocktail, or combination, or configuration, or manifold of historical events. This contrasts with the fact that our most reliable knowledge is almost entirely of the disaggregated variety in which we can aspire with reasonable confidence to talk about how one variable, usually known as a cause, relates to another variable, an effect. The truly remarkable capacities of human beings to produce interesting knowledge of this sort in very large quantities, often bundled ingeniously into models and theories and arguments and paradigms and sometimes into whole disciplines, gives us the impression that the future is more intellectually tractable and less surprising than it frequently proves on arrival to be. These considerations underpin my fundamental solidarity with the late, great Casey Stengel, or whoever it was, who said, "I never make predictions, especially about the future."

Legislatures

But we can discuss legislatures, which are, as I shall attempt to argue, probably here to stay. What are legislatures, after all, but social organizations taking a particular range of forms and performing a particular portfolio of functions within a constitutional order (see Polsby 1975)?

All societies—indeed most social organizations of any sort—need entities performing the tasks associated with lawmaking, or legislating, but of course not all such organizations have specialized entities we would recognize as legislatures. There are many societies in human history in which lawmaking proceeded by decree. We can exclude these from consideration, since they are not democracies. Likewise, rubber-stamp legislatures that exist primarily to give the appearance of legitimacy to the acts of authoritarian regimes need not trouble us further. We all know, more or less, what a legislature is. My working definition is this: it is a multimembered body that meets to do its business, that deliberates and discusses matters in a more or less orderly way, and the votes of its constituent members determine outcomes. These outcomes presumably consist of rules that are supposed to apply to the behavior of some population and these rules have a high probability of being enforced, meaning that some sort of sanctions are available to give effect to them.

All modern democratic nation-states have legislatures, and these are embedded in systems displaying several varieties, as contemporary political science tends to sort them out. For a while, we were working with two basic systems, or regime types: parliaments, in which all elected officeholders, both executive and legislative, are members, and the so-called presidential systems, in which the chief executive is elected separately from other elected officials. Now political scientists seem to feel the need for a third category, semipresidential, originally invented to take account of the French Fifth Republic but now used to cover other nations (Austria, Finland, Poland, Portugal, and a few others) in which important responsibilities are distributed between separately elected presidents, on the one hand, and, on the other, prime ministers who are accountable in the first instance to elected parliaments and are themselves members of the parliament (see Linz and Valenzuela 1994; Roper 2002).

Students of legislatures need slightly different categories, in which the main distinction is between systems in which most constitutional powers are vested in a single body and those in which powers are separated. The original structural distinction between the two styles of modern democracy is that in one case the leadership of the executive branch of government is directly constituted by members of the legislative body and in the other case the legislative body is a separate entity with no overlap in members with leaders of the executive. For simplicity's sake, we can refer to legislative entities more or less following the Westminster model and those following the American model.

If we confronted a group of intelligent visitors from Mars and asked the Martians which basic design conferred more power on the legislature, they would probably pick the Westminster model, where executives arise out of the parliament. And they would be wrong. So out of deference to that conclusion, let us impose one further distinction on the population of democratic legislatures and ask about the probability that a legislative body will act in such a way as to change the substance of the proposals that it is asked to process. If that probability is low, what we probably have, as a matter of historical fact, is an arena on the Westminster model—a talking shop that questions and criticizes the government but does not itself govern. If the probability is high, we have a transformative legislature, of which the U.S. Congress is the most conspicuous example (Polsby 1975, esp. 277–301).

The claim that arenas contribute significantly to democratic governance is a serious one, not trivially supported by the fact that nations that have such parliaments are in fact without doubt frequently democracies. Why this should be the case requires a look—perhaps more than a look—at the party systems that actually determine the identities of people who form the government and make public policy and the electoral processes that underpin the party systems—as students of the United Kingdom from Lewis Namier to the present day have done (Namier 1929; Epstein 1967). How these processes originally evolved from the primeval ooze of the Middle Ages, the standoffs and compromises and arms control agreements and economic developments that created estates of the realm, and taxes, and tax-limitation schemes, and the web of rights and responsibilities such as Magna Carta that in due course acted to civilize the stratification system of the UK—is a very complicated story. It is less complicated to see how this system traveled around the world, basically with the British navy. From a no doubt simple-minded perspective, it seems something of a miracle that a system with the structural properties of the British parliamentary system, with its weak and incompetent parliament, should sustain democratic government in a number of nations, as it undoubtedly does today.

A subsidiary miracle of less consequence is that for most of the last century this historically anomalous structure that muddled up from the Middle

Ages has been almost universally regarded by Americans who have thought about such matters as the supreme example of how to organize and run a modern democracy. This heresy is only uttered as an aside, as a way of paying tribute to New Jersey's Woodrow Wilson, who did so much to jump-start this sentiment in the world of American political science (Wilson 1885).

Tributes aside, it will be best to devote most of this essay to worrying a bit about the future of strong transformative legislatures with independent responsibilities for public policy, such as are found in most U.S. state capitals and in Washington, D.C. These are, on the whole, quite healthy institutions and therefore do not face particularly clouded futures. Two reasons support this view: First, the growth of executive powers, the force in the political system most frequently identified as a proximate threat to legislatures, is in fact not particularly threatening. Second, legislatures have the means for combating the effects of less proximate annoyances that lurk on the horizon, although it is not certain that they will muster the will to do so in all cases. These lurking annoyances are teledemocracy, so-called, the spread of initiatives, and term limits.

Legislatures and Executives

We begin with a story about the growth of executive power, embodied in a short historical sketch of what happened to the national government, mainly as a result of World War II. In response to the administrative requirements of a society mobilized for total war, we had the rapid growth of what it might be reasonable to call a presidential branch of government, separate and distinct from the executive branch, under the direct control of the president (see Somers 1950; Hart 1987; Dickinson 1996). The conclusion of the war did not shrink the presidency back to its prewar shape. Fears of a postwar recession and the expansion of America's worldwide responsibilities precluded this reversion. Instead, the managerial responsibilities of the president expanded, illustrated by the creation of a Council of Economic Advisors, a Central Intelligence Agency, and a Department of Defense. It soon also included the capture by the presidency of executive agencies—notably the Bureau of the Budget, now the Office of Management and Budget (OMB)—that once provided more or less neutrally competent ad hoc service to the legislative branch. This development diminished the overall influence of the so-called permanent government, the executive branch. But did it hurt Congress? Not for long.

Starting with the Johnson administration and accelerating with the Nixon presidency, a great many of the underlying facts and numbers on which day-to-day legislating depends, and which used to be supplied routinely to Congress by the executive branch, became subject to presidential political spin. Mistrust of the presidency, known in Johnson's day as a "credibility gap," began to develop on Capitol Hill along a broad front, and not only with respect to the Vietnam War. Shortly, Congress felt the need for its own access to information and completely changed its pattern of staffing.

The sheer numbers are staggering (Ornstein, Mann, and Malbin 1987, 135–59; for commentary, see Malbin 1980 and Hart 1987). Two entirely new congressional agencies were created: the Office of Technology Assessment in 1972 and the Congressional Budget Office (CBO) in 1975. The CBO in particular had an almost immediate impact. Staffed by nearly two hundred economists and other professionals, the CBO's budget estimates quickly developed a reputation for realism that overshadowed the increasingly partisan and massaged numbers of the OMB. Very soon it became a commonplace Washington practice to conduct bipartisan or nonpartisan discussions of live economic issues using Congressional Budget Office, not Office of Management and Budget, numbers.

Between 1960 and 1980, the staff of the Congressional Research Service of the Library of Congress was increased fourfold; the numbers of employees assigned to the House and the Senate, to individual members and to committees, jumped comparably. By 1985, roughly 25,000 staff members worked for Congress. This includes only the Congressional Research Service component for the Library of Congress and only a third of the General Accounting Office employees who work directly for Congress. In 1957, 2,441 staff were employed by House members and 1,115 by senators; by 1985 those numbers had turned into 7,528 and 4,097, respectively. In 1960, 440 staff were employed by House standing committees and 470 by Senate standing committees. In 1985 those numbers had become 2,009 and 1,080, respectively. The growth in a couple of short decades was remarkable. The growth in another measure is even more remarkable: In the forty years from 1946 to 1986, while the consumer price index rose 450.8 percent, appropriations to the legislative branch rose 2,859.3 percent (Ornstein, Mann and Malbin 1987, 140).

An inspection of the year-to-year figures shows double digits in the growth of congressional appropriations after Lyndon Johnson's 1964 landslide, continuing right through the Nixon era. There is no sure way to quantify the attitudes of mistrust that appear to have caused these figures to lift off the planet earth when and as they did, but it is possible to speculate about the causes of the creation of a legislative bureaucracy after so many years in which the legislative branch found it possible to live comfortably with a comparatively thin roster of professional staff. Loss of comity with the executive branch, driven by the development of a greatly augmented presidential branch of government, is by far the most plausible explanation (see Jones 1982, 133–48, 379–408).[1]

Under the old dispensation what congressional staff were professional at was looking after the political needs of members, mixed in, in exceptional cases like the House Appropriations Committee, with some attention to oversight of the executive (Macmahon 1943a, 1943b). On the whole, service on congressional staff did not require much interest in or competence at public policy analysis, much less political innovation. Expertise came with long years on the job rather than as the result of professional training.

Today, while the numbers of professionals employed by Congress has burgeoned, their average age has shrunk, and they now come to Capitol Hill with professional credentials (for a profile of congressional staff, see Fox and Hammond 1977; see also Cohen 1987; for the earlier story, see Rogers 1941). Many more of them—not just in absolute numbers, but also as a proportion of the whole—focus on policy and on promoting their employers' interests through the advocacy or adoption of public policy positions. This is most noticeable in the Senate, where individual senators are stretched so thin by the multiple responsibilities of committee work that it is largely impossible for them personally to keep track of everything. Their staff members do it for them, and in the process not infrequently engage in sophisticated forms of political entrepreneurship in their principals' behalf. Sometimes it is a part of a staff member's duties not only to seize and promote a policy position or to make or adopt an issue in behalf of his or her principal, but also as a part of the exercise to engage the interest and approval of the principal as well (see Price 1972, esp. 329–31; Pertschuk 1982, 26–28; and Malbin 1980).

Staff members with these extraordinary opportunities to affect public policy tend not to devote their lives to congressional service as so many of their predecessors did, but to job hop around the policy subcommunities on which they are making a mark. So not only are congressional staff different today in their sheer numbers, they are different also in the ways in which they define their jobs, different in their training, and different in their career expectations. Collectively, they far more resemble their counterparts in the political entourages of the presidential appointees who run the federal agencies of downtown Washington than they do preceding generations of staff members on Capitol Hill. They have brought increased capability, overall, to Congress to deal substantively with policy, and they have done much to provide a link between Congress and the increasingly specialized and professionalized worlds of policy makers, policy advisors, lawyers, and foundation, university, and think tank personnel who make up the various policy subcommunities of

Washington and throughout the United States. There was a time—not long ago—when Congress, and congressional staff, stood aloof from the communications networks maintained by these policy subcommunities (see Polsby 1970). This is no longer true.

So, for a period of time, Congress put up with deceptive budgeting practices and other flimflam by Presidents Johnson and Nixon, but after a while they acted decisively to protect their own interests. They hired their own professional staff and competed with reasonable success with the augmented, sometimes imperial presidency for influence over governmental policy making. Of course, sometimes this created stalemates and what some people took to calling gridlock in national policy making. Or we might call it checks and balances.

We may like congressional influence or we may deplore it—or both, depending on the issue and the occasion. The central point is that the ordinary operations of the American government at the national level, and even important trends in these operations tending to strengthen the president have not, so far, taken Congress out of the picture.

Regrettably, some of the reforms pressed on Congress by Speaker Newt Gingrich in the heady, early days of his so-called revolution may have had less happy consequences. It was a self-inflicted wound when Congress abolished the Office of Technology Assessment and slashed so-called outsider groups that had augmented the information available to members.[2] These moves were bound to weaken the capacities of Congress to make independent judgments on public policy.

So the fact that Congress has it within its power to sustain itself even when confronted by a strong and active president and by complicated world conditions does not mean that it will use its power to do so, and not the opposite. But twenty years before the Gingrich revolution Congress sought professional help in policy making and built professionalism into the legislative branch on a bipartisan basis. Something similar happened in a great many of the state legislatures in the latter half of the twentieth century. Much of it was stimulated by the very creative California Speaker Jess Unruh.[3] This work demonstrated that a constitutionally independent legislature can in general take care of itself and its needs. What it must guard against are trends tending to limit its independence and its competence.

Threatening Trends

There are, in the United States, a few such trends that might harm American legislatures. On the whole, they have not yet done so, but they bear watching: term limits, the initiative, and electronic voting.

Electronic voting simply harnesses—to use a horse-and-buggy expression—modern technology for the purpose of eliciting popular sentiment on political issues (Becker and Slaton 2000). Presumably one would not have to wait for an election day to tap into this sentiment; in principle this could be an ongoing means for settling issues as they arise. If we wait for Election Day, we have an initiative, or a referendum. What could be more democratic? Here are some of the problems.

In the first place, who gets to pick the issues that are settled in this way? How do we pick the people who pick the issues? Is it good enough to say that anybody rich enough to afford to hire a team to collect the signatures of voters as they wander about shopping malls is entitled to set the political agenda as a substitute for the elected officials of a state legislature?

The problem is not just picking issues, it is framing issues (Tversky and Kahneman 1974). Enough is now known about public opinion polling—of which teledemocracy and initiatives are fancy examples—to know that how a question is asked can predispose respondents to answer in varying ways (Schuman 1981). An all-time favorite example of this was the 1974 poll that asked whether Richard Nixon should be impeached. Overwhelmingly, respondents said no. The same poll asked if he should be charged with misconduct and removed from office, and of course an equally impressive majority said yes. As Ellis (2002, 77) says: "Ask people whether they support spending for the 'poor' and their responses are far more favorable than if they are asked about spending on 'welfare.' Similarly, people have a much more negative reaction to the term 'preferential treatment' than they do to 'affirmative action.' Most people agree that a terminally ill person should be helped by a physician to 'die with dignity' but far fewer support 'physician-assisted suicide.'"

In California, with Oregon the most referendum-prone of all the American states, it is quite common for initiatives that get on the ballot (and California has very long ballots), and are even approved of by the voters, to be thrown out later by the state supreme court as unconstitutionally vague, confusing, or mutually contradictory—in short, they are defectively worded (see Ellis 2002; Broder 2000).

Presumably technical glitches of this sort can be warded off by some mandatory prescreening device. In Oregon, the state attorney general is required to write ballot titles. These are appealable to the state supreme court, which frequently ends up writing the summaries and arguments pro and con that go on the ballot (Ellis 2002, 149). But there is also the very substantial problem—not a technical problem but a political one in states that are less careful about prescreening—of purposely deceptive wording. Mass electorates, as compared to legislatures, are easy prey to such practices, and initiatives readily go on the ballots that feature, as Richard Ellis says, "poorly designed policies, obscene amounts of money, highly technical measures, unanticipated consequences, and confused voters" (2002, 2).

What electronic voting cannot possibly do is provide for a deliberative process prior to voting. Well, an advocate might say, what about public discussion, forums, newspaper editorials, and so forth? Doesn't that count as deliberation? No doubt sometimes it would. And sometimes it might even be better and more disinterested than the sorts of deliberation that sometimes goes on in legislatures. But mostly not. It is worth contemplating what deliberation contributes to a decision-making process.

Deliberation is what presumably happens when alternative courses of action are publicly compared before one alternative is settled on. Deliberation provides an institutionalized opportunity to think about alternatives, to imagine different combinations of outcomes, different payoff schedules, different side-payments, different details than may be embodied in any single alternative that may originally have entered the conversation. It gives decision makers an opportunity to conduct thought experiments and to test their preferences against an array of possibilities that themselves can arise as the result of the deliberative process. Going through a deliberative process can increase the confidence of actors that they have chosen wisely and not neglected considerations they ought to have taken into account. And if this process is public, as in a legislative debate, that confidence can be spread more widely.

Legislatures, being entities that sponsor face-to-face interaction prior to voting, are capable of fostering deliberation; automated systems of voting are not. If alternatives are cut-and-dried and well formulated in advance, there may be little or no need for deliberation. But for that population of decisions where alternatives are not well worked out in advance, a deliberative process may make the differences between competent and incompetent handling of an issue.

The growth of nondeliberative decision making constitutes an alternative to decision making by legislatures that can usually be counted on to be a grossly inferior alternative. The existence of technological capacity capable of wiring up large numbers of people constitutes a standing temptation to avail ourselves of this mechanism even if policy options are inadequately explored and only a small number of voters actually vote. From the standpoint of sustaining the influence and the capacities of a legislative body, it is not a good idea.

Much the same can be said of old-fashioned initiatives, voting in the regular way by showing up at a polling place at stated intervals but for items that ordinarily would be processed by a legislative body. This is a device that intentionally weakens the authority of legislatures; historically the initiative and referendum were brought into being expressly for this purpose. Obviously, if a legislature is being superseded or overruled or bypassed on important matters of public policy, the incentives to serve there diminish. If the legislature itself has the power to put initiatives on the ballot, the temptation to pass the buck on difficult issues arises, and that too weakens legislatures in the exercise of their powers.

Finally, there are term limits, a fad that seems to have run its course but which was quite popular in the early 1990s and did change a fair number of state legislatures. The threat this gimmick posed to Congress was removed when the Supreme Court declared it unconstitutional (*U.S. Term Limits, Inc. v. Thornton* 1995).[4] Political scientists have been watching the results of term limits on the state level, where the first generation of term limited legislators has begun to disappear (Carey, Niemi, and Powell 1998; Little and Peery 2000; Thompson and Moncrief 2000).

It looks as if those of us who anticipated that it would weaken the legislatures were right. Some observers, in response, say so what? Many legislatures were never all that powerful or important anyhow. Other observers say: good!—that's what term limits were intended to do. Weakening legislatures means no career legislators, who therefore remain close to the people and do not aggrandize themselves at public expense (Petracca and Smith 1990; Petracca 1996 and 1998; Elhuage 1998).

Actually, it appears not to work that way. Under term limits politicians may not legally entrench themselves in particular legislative positions, but they cannot be prevented from playing musical chairs. So many of them have found ways, as individuals, to cope with term limits and still piece together political careers. A more serious threat is that term limits harm legislatures as corporate entities because they cause them to lose institutional memory and influence overall in the policy-making process. And it is the consequences for legislatures, not for individual legislators, that ought to concern us most (Polsby 1993).

When a legislature is afflicted by term limits, its power as an independent entity in its political system suffers. Who gains? That depends: perhaps legislative staff, perhaps executives, perhaps bureaucrats, perhaps lobbyists. The immediate beneficiaries are governors. Sometimes lobbyists become more powerful, at least those lobbyists capable of supplying substantive information to legislators and supporting them with campaign resources. Sometimes administrative bureaucracies gain influence. The professional capacities of legislatures to process issues and render independent judgments always suffer (Kousser 2002). All of these other actors can mobilize expertise and can reap the benefits of experience, which term-limited legislators are precluded from doing.

Experience in the rather complicated work of being a member of a transformative legislature really does increase the effectiveness of individual members and improves the collective product. One would think that this proposition would appeal to common sense. In virtually all sorts of work, experience enhances effectiveness. The issues that regularly come before legislatures are not all straightforward. Some require technical mastery. Others require understanding of political cross-currents of various sorts. Many require deliberation, the consideration of claims and counterclaims in a setting in which members do not work alone but in work groups, affording the opportunity to communicate back and forth and exchange information: committees, subcommittees, task forces, caucuses of varying sizes and shapes. Conscientious members—and in a transformative legislature there are incentives to be conscientious—strive not merely to decide whether to vote up or down on the final passage of bills but also to seek to understand, and also sometimes to contribute to, the substance of measures that the entire body must consider. There are alternative possibilities that need to be explored, amendments to be weighed, and bargains to be struck as the legislature moves toward the enactment of public policy.

This is all serious work. It is perfectly true that members of Congress, for example, being ultimately responsible only to electorates in their home districts, have great leeway in the extent to which they apply themselves to legislative tasks. Some specialize narrowly. Some seek publicity rather than the rewards of substantive mastery. Some are lazy and some are untalented. But many work at legislating. As a body, Congress accepts more substantive responsibility entailing the independent weighing of alternatives than any legislature on the face of the earth. Hence term limits were a dire threat to Congress more than any other legislature, but they also threaten any legislature that seeks to approximate congressional levels of performance, as more and more seek to do. Despite the inevitable unevenness in the talents of members, such legislatures organize to do business, mobilize energies, and produce a work product deserving of respect. Moreover, they do so while accepting the meaningful constraint that members must as individuals stand regularly for elections in which they submit themselves to the judgment of constituents who quite frequently have no idea what the job of the member actually is or how well their member does it.

Members cheerfully accept this constraint and work as best they can to convince their constituents to return them to office with, on the whole, notable success. Indeed if they were not successful, term limits would scarcely be necessary. But members are generally popular with their constituents, even when legislatures as a body are not. It is the legislature as a body that would be harmed most by term limits if term limits were constitutional and enacted. Individual members can for the most part take care of themselves. But what term limits threaten is the collective enterprises that exercise strong and sometimes detailed influence on policy making, by arbitrarily amputating—along with the time servers—members who have learned how to legislate effectively. And these bodies, legislatures, are the governmental entities most readily exposed to popular access.

Arranging to banish knowledgeable, skilled, and experienced members on a regular basis can scarcely be good for any institution with serious work to do. And this is especially true in view of the fact that willy-nilly, the work must be done. But with term limits it is done by less experienced and knowledgeable legislators who, deprived of the option of a legislative career, are bound to be less willing to invest personally in the mastery of policy.

The relationship of term-limited legislators with interest groups is especially problematic. Consider what it takes for a legislator to gather up resources in order to run for public office in the first place. Consider what provision legislators must make for themselves if they know they must exit at a certain time. In aggregate, the more entering and exiting, the more dependence upon interest groups. And, with less experience on the job, dependence also increases.

In most parts of the United States, in order to enter a legislature, a prospective member must self-start. This requires putting together sufficient resources to run and usually requires at least some alliances with like-minded interest groups in the constituency. Once a member is in office for a while, the interest groups usually need the member more than the member needs any particular interest group. Term limits guarantee a steady flow of more new members and hence create more opportunities for the initial dependency of members on interest groups. This dependency arises at the start of a member's service.

Even greater dependency would occur toward the end of a legislator's tenure. Term-limited members must then worry about what comes next. They cannot, after all, be prevented from seeking gainful employment of any sort. For many departing members, cordial relations with interest groups can provide leads into life after their membership terminates. Able members may distinguish themselves in the evenhanded performance of their work and thus commend themselves to future employers who do regular business with the legislature. Similar opportunities will unavoidably also exist for the less scrupulous.

So both at the beginning and the end of a member's legislative career the member is unusually susceptible to interest group influence. To shrink the distance between these two points creates a bonanza for outside interests properly organized to take advantage of it, as more and more would be bound to do. Inexperience at legislative work for members new on the job provides yet a third toehold for interest groups who can supply knowledge about issues and make up for the ignorance of the newly arrived.

So the idea that term-limit advocates sometimes express that term limits act to emancipate legislatures from interest groups is dubious; indeed, more likely exactly the opposite is the case. It remains to be said that a dependent, relatively ignorant, inexperienced, and weak legislature is not a good thing. Ordinary Americans need the access to their government at national and state levels that strong legislatures can provide. And, as experience shows, strong legislatures can deal perfectly well with strong executives.

Representation remains a significant task of democratic legislatures in large-scale, modern societies. We know that in the last half century a real revolution in the representative process was peacefully visited upon American legislatures by a line of cases brought before the Supreme Court.[5] Could we have predicted this? Certainly not in detail. We could watch the demography of the United States change as Americans streamed off farms and into cities, and later into suburbs, over a fifty-year period.[6] We could have guessed that there would be a lag—a substantial lag—between the redistribution of the population and the effective reflection of that redistribution in the balance of power in state legislatures and Congress. But no body of theory exists that could have predicted the actual course of events. The same is true of equally momentous changes affecting the civil rights, and the representation, of racial minorities.[7]

Extrapolating from these historical landmarks, can we confidently expect American legislatures to continue to adapt as new challenges arise? We can say that overall American institutions have proved to be remarkably adaptive, but not in any hurry. All of these events are really best seen as a gigantic set of projective tests. Optimists will read a rosy future filled with further occasions for democratization. Pessimists will remember generation-long roadblocks, lynchings, poll taxes, filibusters, and other delays (Salamon and Van Evera 1973a, 1973b; Kernell 1973). It would take a braver and better-informed scholar to attempt to adjudicate between these equally plausible constructions of American history and therefore of the future of legislatures.

Chapter 8

Legislative Politics

Institutional Democracy and Public Disaffection

ALAN ROSENTHAL

PREDICTING THE FUTURE of legislatures is a job for the foolhardy. As far as American legislatures are concerned, it is difficult enough to predict the past. The present, let alone the future, of the United States House and Senate and the ninety-nine legislative bodies in the fifty states will vary from one body to another. Nevertheless, we will risk generalization while allowing for exceptions. As for the future, the best we can do is try to get a handle on present tendencies and project ahead cautiously.

In trying to determine whether legislatures can adapt to what is ahead, Nelson Polsby's backward look in chapter 7 makes good sense: "We can say that overall American institutions have proved to be remarkably adaptive, but not in any hurry." That's about it. Like "The Little Engine That Could," the children's classic about the indomitable train that made it over the mountain, American legislatures will also make it. Puff puff, chug chug, they too will continue to deliver the goods. After all, they have done so for more than two hundred years, so why should they stop now?

Legislatures play a major institutional role in American democracy, performing three major functions: furnishing representation to people; providing processes for making laws and allocating resources; and balancing the power of the executive (Rosenthal 1998b). The U.S. Congress and state legislatures all perform these functions, and they will continue to do so, but probably not in quite the same way as in the past.

Polsby sees three major challenges to legislatures in the years ahead: term limits, the initiative, and electronic voting. These challenges, I suggest, all stem from the democratization of both legislatures and the environment in which they exist, an important recent trend. That trend has been accompanied by another important recent trend, the disaffection of the public and a diminution of public support.

It may appear contradictory, but even as voting participation has declined, the role of the public has increased. Simultaneously, the boundedness of the legislature has been reduced; the institution and its processes are much more permeable than they used to be (Rosenthal 1998a). The public is not undifferentiated, however. It is expressed in partisan terms as Democratic supporters or Republican supporters. It is also expressed in group terms, as members of the various special interests that have legislative agendas. Thus, the publics that account for democratization are primarily ones that are organized and mobilized. Sometimes—as virtual publics—they are even manufactured. Legislatures are less able, and less inclined, to resist these publics.

One might think that the democratization of legislative institutions and processes would have been welcomed by Americans. But this is not the case, and legislatures have lost the support of both the more- and the less-involved citizenry (Cooper 1999). Public disaffection, not with the abstract principles of democracy, but with the actual practices of representative democracy, as exhibited by Congress and state legislatures, is widespread (Hibbing and Theiss-Morse 1995). The most obvious manifestation of disaffection is term limits, which were adopted for state legislators by electorates voting on ballot initiatives in nineteen states and by legislatures pressured by electorates in two others.

If democratization and disaffection persist, the functioning of legislatures will change. Democratization will strengthen legislative performance representing constituencies, but it will make legislative performance of lawmaking less substantive, less deliberative, and more contentious. Most important, the ability of legislatures to balance the executive will suffer.

How Legislative Representation Works

To see how legislatures function and the ways in which they are being affected by democratization and disaffection, it is necessary to start by examining those who are represented—the *demos* of democracy. Americans or Californians or New Jerseyans have many different opinions, but fewer opinions on politics and public policy than is generally believed or implied by responses on opinion polls. Americans do have values and interests, and ones that are affected by politics and government. For the most part, however, people do not directly engage in the political process, nor do they want to engage in it (Hibbing and Theiss-Morse 2002). Their involvement tends to be limited to voting in elections, affiliating with a political party, and belonging to one or several interest groups.

Many of the policy views Americans hold are at a general level and provide little guidance to policy makers. People agree on the need for better education for children, improved highways, safer streets, and so forth. But such agreement breaks down when the question becomes how to reach common objectives. Such questions, of course, are exactly what policy makers have to figure out. Will vouchers help? More mass transit or additional highway lanes? Gun control or the legalization of concealed weapons? On these issues and at these levels, people disagree. And at more specific levels—at levels where legislators ply their trade—they disagree more.

Indeed, there is much greater disagreement in our nation and individual states than Americans believe or want to believe. The tendency is for people to associate with people of similar backgrounds, values, and interests and, thus, to assume a consensus that does not actually exist. Even the rally-around-the-flag response to September 11 has been dissipating, as the objectives of the war on terrorism become murkier and domestic issues rise in importance (Rosenthal et al. 2003).

The absence of consensus is not surprising in a diverse nation (or diverse state), where people can be expected to have different values and interests. Disagreement on issues is manifested in national and state polls and was nicely captured in a series that appeared in USA Today in mid-February 2002. On the basis of a poll by the newspaper, CNN, and Gallup, a national "values gap" emerged. Americans, according to the report, are divided over issues related to values, such as gay rights, the death penalty, guns, abortion, and the role of government. In addition to a national survey, two communities were specifically polled: Montclair, New Jersey, which in 2000 voted for Al Gore, and Franklin, Tennessee, which voted for George W. Bush in that election. People in both Montclair and Franklin generally agreed on the issues, but Montclair agreed in one direction, Franklin in the other direction. Naturally, people in each of these communities assumed greater consensus than existed in the nation overall.

Americans agree on generalities but not on specifics, and they divide on issues involving values. They are also contradictory and inconsistent in setting priorities. It is not unusual for citizens to choose options that appear to preclude one another. For example, they want an expansion in services, but they also want a reduction in taxes. They think that both objectives are attainable, if only waste is eliminated. Waste, of course, consists of government personnel who deliver services and programs that an individual respondent doesn't care about. "My program is not waste," we strongly believe; "It is their program that is unnecessary," we believe almost as strongly. However general, divided, inconsistent, and contradictory people's views may be, Americans do get represented. Not everyone's view—if they even have a view—is adopted, but everyone's view gets expressed in the processes by which legislatures decide on laws and budgets. Representation occurs in three distinct, but overlapping, ways.

The first, and most obvious, way in which people receive representation is by those they elect to Congress and state legislatures. Legislators take the job of representing their constituency most seriously. The ways in which they connect—through casework, projects, making the rounds of their district, and so forth—are probably more important than the extent to which they represent constituency policy views (Rosenthal 1998a). But the views of constituents are always taken into account. On the most visible issues, representatives have an idea of where the constituency stands, at least for the most part. And where they themselves stand on these issues normally is where they believe most of their constituents stand. Cognitive dissonance is the exception. When representatives think of constituency views, they think mainly of the views of their political supporters—usually Democrats or Republicans, and also their supporters as organized into political interest groups.

On the many less visible issues, where constituency views on an issue appear to be held by only a few constituents—some organized on one side, the others organized on the other—representation is a different matter. Even then, constituency counts. Whatever the issue, the legislator will ask—explicitly or implicitly—what does it do for or against my constituency and what will my position on it do for or against me in my constituency? Indeed, it is fair to say that constituency matters to the legislator more than anything else; often, however, constituency is not really in play as a factor because an issue has little or no resonance in the district.

The second way in which people receive representation—one that overlaps with the first—is through the political parties with whom they affiliate (see Crotty, this volume). Regardless of the party of the legislators from their districts, people's values, interests, and opinions are also expressed by the Democratic Party on the one hand or the Republican Party on the other, or sometimes by both. To whatever extent parties have declined or changed, they remain key agencies in the political system. Citizens still affiliate with them, strongly or not so strongly. Only about one out of five people is strictly independent, without leanings in one direction or the other. Many of those who share ethnic identifications, religious preferences, and economic standing tend to be either Democratic or Republican.

Because their support is about equally divided, the parties are extraordinarily competitive today, both at the national and state levels. Candidates from both parties have a chance to win the presidency or a statewide election in just about every state. While nine out of ten seats in the U.S. House are relatively safe for Republicans or Democrats, either party has a chance to win control of the entire House. Of the ninety-nine legislative chambers in the fifty states, about 60 percent are competitive: each party has won control during recent years and/or each has a chance to win control in the period immediately ahead. Although their techniques have changed, the parties as parties are highly active in elections—at national, state, and district levels—raising and allocating funds, adopting strategies, and executing campaigns.

Finally, Democratic and Republican officeholders in Congress and state legislatures differ in their policy preferences and priorities. They differ, among other things, on the overall role of government, governmental regulation, and spending and taxation. They differ in ways that are generally in line with the values and interests of those people and groups that support them. In Congress, and in just about every state, it matters a lot whether Democrats or Republicans have control.

The third way—which overlaps the first two—in which people are represented is through interest groups (Baumgartner and Leech 1998). Seven out of ten Americans belong to one interest group or another, four out of ten belong to several groups. And, whether we recognize it or not, the political views of each and every one of us is represented by some of the thousands of groups in existence. Whether these groups are organized by profession, occupation, trade, company, issue area, or by an alternative classification, they are significant participants in the legislative process. They seek change or work to protect the status quo, they try to gain ground at the expense of their competitors, and they attempt to advantage their interests on matters of budget and tax policy.

One of the most notable features of the political landscape is the proliferation of interest groups in recent times. As documented in the *Encyclopedia of Associations*, the number of such groups has quadrupled since about 1960. And as Clive Thomas and Ronald Hrebenar (1999a, 34) conclude on the basis of their continuing study at the state level: "There are more groups representing more people across the 50 states today than ever before." According to one estimate the number had tripled from 1975 to 1990. At state capitals alone, there are roughly 45,000 lobbyists working on behalf of thousands of groups (Rosenthal 2001, 1–6).

Changes in the System

The representational system described above is highly democratic. But the system is lately becoming even more democratic. Legislatures are more representative than they used to be, particularly in the descriptive sense of representation. More women, African Americans, and Latinos and fewer attorneys are members. The processes are more transparent and the members more accessible than previously. Legislators reach out to their constituencies, and constituents are encouraged to reach in. A new standard of conduct has emerged, that of appearance. How legislatures and legislators appear in the public eye is now a serious concern (Rosenthal 1998a).

Most important, power in Congress and state legislatures is more dispersed today than it used to be. Strong leadership is the exception, not the rule. Information and staff are more broadly dispersed. Members are less willing to follow the leader, and leaders—even more than in the past—have to figure out where their members want to go and help them get there. Strong leaders—such as the Speakers in the Georgia, Illinois, Massachusetts, and New York Houses—still exist, but they, too, have to serve the interests of a majority of members. Leaders in the seventeen states that currently have term limits are further diminished. They have had little preparation for leadership roles and only short tenure in them. Members know that leaders are on their way out, so members do not have to be concerned with the future benefits leaders may or may not bestow on them.

Internal democratization has been accompanied by a more democratic environment of the legislature and a growing sensitivity of legislatures and legislators to the publics they represent. Their inclination is to be as responsive as possible, if there is anything out there tending in one direction rather than another. When their constituents give no signals, or when signals are unclear or mixed, responsiveness is a frustrating business. Ironically, perhaps, the public role today is greater, despite the fact that most Americans are disinterested, uninformed, and disengaged and voting turnout is disappointingly low. That is because, for legislators, the public—which is defined more specifically as the constituency, the group, or the electorate—is more important in lawmaking than ever before.

The public's heightened presence in the legislative process is not manifested through public opinion polls, because rarely are polls conducted at the congressional or legislative district level. National polls count for little in the states, and state polls count for little in legislative districts. Polling at the state and district level tends to be restricted to the campaign season and to targeted districts. Otherwise, poll data at an extra-constituency level tend to reinforce what legislators already suspect about public opinion on key issues. If polls have any effect, it is probably to sound a cautionary note rather than a rallying cry. When significant percentages take an opposing position on a measure, legislators become alerted; yet, similar percentages endorsing a proposal do not produce a surge of support. Such data, like any information that favors one side or the other, are used in public debate to support a given position.

Statewide opinion can have a significant effect on legislative lawmaking, but only when it reflects what legislators already believe to be a public mandate. The best contemporary example of such a mandate is that of opposing tax increases. Particularly when such expressions of public opinion are reinforced by real-world examples of retribution at the polls, legislators react as if a mandate exists. And indeed it does. New Jersey Governor James Florio's 1990 income- and sales-tax package, it is commonly believed, resulted in the Democrats losing the governorship for eight years and the legislature for ten. More than a decade later, having won back the office of governor and having gained control of the assembly and a tie in the senate, Democrats remain income- and sales-tax averse. Few elected public officials in Congress or state legislatures today want to risk increasing taxes, except for levies on cigarettes, possibly gas, and—if there is no other way—business. But income and sales taxes are off the political table just about everywhere but Massachusetts and Tennessee.

Technology today affords public opinion the ability to have more targeted impact at the legislative district level. Lawrence K. Grossman, in a recent study, offered the prospect of people sitting at home or at work, able to use telecomputer terminals, microprocessors, and computer-driven keypads, pushing the buttons to tell their legislators how they as citizens would vote on issues before the legislature (Grossman 1995). It is within the realm of technological possibility for people to vote in "advisory referendums" on the same issues that face their legislators on the floor or in committee. And such votes can be allocated electronically to districts where these voters reside. Legislators could know how some of their constituents would have voted on a specific measure. They would have to think hard about voting in opposition to referenda that ran in the other direction, especially since they could anticipate television or radio ads or direct mail with the message and evidence that they acted against the wishes of their constituency.

In his 1992 presidential campaign Ross Perot advanced the idea of electronic plebecites. More recently, Dick Morris, in his book *Vote.com* wrote that direct electronic democracy was both inevitable and desirable. If the nation and the states move further away from reliance on the judgment of legislators, the losers will be those institutions that have been main intermediaries between government and its citizens, particularly political parties and civic associations. The techies refer to this phenomenon as "disintermediation," the cutting out of the middleman (Rosenthal et al., 2003).

Existing technologies have not yet been harnessed for the continuing issue referenda mentioned above. If they were, political interest groups would have their work cut out for them. They would raise appeals, through issue campaigns, so that their interests would prevail in any referendum. Their lobbying, thus, would be indirect—aimed at people who, by registering their views, would impress their legislators. Indirect lobbying of this kind is not entirely new. Today political interest groups not only express views on behalf of their members; they mobilize members and appeal to broader publics as well. Without the campaigns of organized interests, representatives would have even more difficulty figuring out where their constituents stood on many of the issues with which the legislature deals. Interest groups drive the process, and increasingly their modus operandi involves the mobilization of grassroots and beyond.

Lobbying used to be an "inside game," pretty much restricted to interest-group agents and key legislators, or even a larger number of legislators. Now, the "outside game" is also important (Kollman 1998). Participation has expanded substantially, not on all issues but on the high-stakes ones (Thomas and Hrebenar 1999b). Participation may be less spontaneous and more manipulated by issue and media campaigns, but it is the way in which the values, interests, and opinions of contemporary publics tend to get expressed nowadays.

The most direct means of public involvement on issues is through the initiative, a means of bypassing legislative decision making and allowing groups to appeal directly to the public for votes. The initiative bypass exists in twenty-four states (although in one, Illinois, it is much abridged), but it is a significant alternative to the legislature in only about half a dozen states. In the period 1990–2001, for example, seventy-five initiatives were voted on by the electorate in Oregon, sixty-six by the electorate in California, forty-four in Colorado, and thirty-nine in Washington (Rosenthal et al., 2003). The initiative process not only threatens legislative control of policy, it also threatens legislative control of the legislative process itself. It is significant that of the twenty-one states that adopted term limits for legislators, all but two did so through the initiative, and in one of the two (Utah) the legislature did so only under threat of a more draconian initiative.

Whatever the role of the electorate in the initiative process, individual politicians (including governors and legislators) and interest groups are the initiators and mobilizers. They set the agenda, collect the signatures, devise the strategies, and frame and conduct the issue campaigns. Voters get to choose, but political entrepreneurs and organized interests determine the choices they have and what these choices mean (Ellis 2002).

Lawmaking by means of the initiative brings totally different values to the process than does lawmaking by the legislature. Issues are decided separately, not in relation to one another. A media campaign usually substitutes for deliberation. One side wins, the other loses. Compromise is not possible; consensus rarely is built. Accountability is lacking (Magleby 1984). The initiative also plays an intimidating role in the legislative process. In states where initiatives are possible, their threat sometimes persuades the legislature to act on its own—whether it wants to or not—in order to head off a more undesirable measure.

Public participation—of sorts—in the legislative process is on the rise, not only in states that make use of the initiative, but in other states as well, and particularly in the larger ones. This is partly because constituents today are more likely to contact their representatives about issues and about ideas they may have for legislation. Legislatures and legislators provide greater access; they make it as easy as possible for constituents to contact their representatives. When legislators have staff and/or offices in the districts, most notably as members of Congress do, even more contact tends to be generated.

As John Mark Hansen writes in chapter 3, it is a kind of participation different from what democratic theorists have in mind. Most of the time when constituents address their representatives about issues, they have been mobilized by the efforts of organized interest groups engaged in some type of issue campaign. During the past thirty or so years, direct lobbying has been supplemented by indirect lobbying, whereby efforts outside the legislature are designed to support those inside the legislature (Kollman 1998). Since the successes of the environmental and consumer movements, grassroots lobbying has come to be a technique that no group can entirely ignore. In the words of a Maryland lobbyist, "The old politics don't work anymore, you have to get back home where it really hurts." In a grassroots campaign, members of a group, who are also constituents, tell their representatives directly how a measure will affect them instead of the lobbyist doing it. Currently, just about every group with a legislative program tries to develop the capacity to mobilize grassroots of some sort. Such campaigns, while more frequent than they used to be, are still the exception; they occur on high-stakes matters where an inside strategy alone cannot be counted on to suffice.

Beyond grassroots, which focus on members and fellow travelers, are media, public relations, and advertising, which are employed in even broader campaigns. These campaigns—known in the trade as "message politics"—are designed to project a client's issues and image favorably to both the public and public officials. The intermediate target here is the public at large, or targeted segments of the public, but the objective is to persuade legislators that a group or a position has considerable support. Citizen and advocacy groups rely heavily on the media to persuade legislators of the popularity of their cause; business and industry also resort to public relations and media campaigns. Equally as important are "institutional advertising" or "issue advocacy" by groups that undertake continuing public relations campaigns to promote their political objectives. The alcohol-beverage industry, health-care organizations, pharmaceutical companies, and teachers associations exemplify groups that are engaged in long-term campaigns to change how the public, and consequently how legislators, think about them.

Democratization pertains not only to how legislatures relate to their publics and how interest groups relate to legislatures. It also involves political parties. The legislative parties are more electorally sensitive nowadays, in part because in Washington, D.C., and in most states the environment is so competitive. Their electoral sensitivity does not mean, as William Crotty notes in chapter 11, that they mobilize partisans or that people flock to participate as members of parties. Most people simply do not want to be directly involved in politics, not in party activities or any others (Hibbing and Theiss-Morse 2002). Rather, political parties, in order to win votes, are quite responsive to what people appear to want. Despite the fact that the overwhelming majority of members of the U.S. House and majorities of state legislators are in districts that are relatively safe for their party, they still run scared. They may be challenged in a primary or lightning can strike them in a general election. Even if individual legislators feel safe, the legislative parties do not.

At one time, several degrees separated the legislative process from election campaigns, although partisan politics was never absent from the process. Today the legislative process and the election campaigns are almost intertwined; that is, the campaign is conducted by the legislative parties inside the legislature, as well as by the candidates, parties, and groups outside. Legislative party leaders see one of their major responsibilities to be getting their members elected and winning or maintaining control of their chamber. In most states where the parties compete, they raise and allocate funds to their party's incumbents and challengers. They help members from targeted districts by appointing them to key committees, giving them popular legislation to sponsor, and providing them with extra bacon to take home to their districts (Rosenthal 1998a, 168–99).

Decision making on controversial issues before the legislature (including nearly always the budget) nowadays is characterized by three principal activities. The first is policy related—debate and deliberation on the merits of the issue. This is much of what goes on in the legislative process (Bessette 1994). The second is enactment related—discussion and execution of a strategy by which successive majorities can be won at stages of the process. This includes negotiation, tradeoffs, payments, and compromise. The third is electorally related—discussion and execution of a strategy, where positions are tailored to take into account the likely reaction of voters. This goes on as measures are shaped and reshaped. The first two activities probably have not changed much in intensity, but the third activity appears to be more important today than it used to be. Thus, democratization has resulted in a public or publics that are more relevant to the lawmaking process. Whether the public role is direct or indirect, it matters. Meanwhile, the autonomy or wiggle room of legislatures is reduced and the mobilizing role of interest groups is increased.

Public Disaffection

Increased legislative responsiveness and greater opportunities for public participation have not, however, resulted in increased support for American legislatures. In part, this is because involvement in politics is not what citizens want. September 11 may have revived trust in government, but not in politics. People still have a negative view of the nitty-gritty practices of democracy. They do not understand why legislatures are so conflict-ridden, and they attribute it to the machinations of political parties and special interests, not to the fact that rank-and-file citizens disagree. They are impatient with deliberation, which they think drags on much too long. And they reject compromise as selling out one's principles, even though it is the way that majorities in a legislature get built. They are cynical about the motivations and integrity of legislators, despite the fact that the large majority of legislators have public-service objectives and adhere to standards of conduct that are higher than they used to be. They are upset by the influence of special interest groups, although they are really not very special, since most people belong to one or more of these groups. Indeed, a large percentage of Americans would even bar lobbyists from the legislative process, disregarding free speech rights and the role of advocacy in a democratic political system (Hibbing and Theiss-Morse 2002).

The ways in which Americans view legislatures should occasion no surprise. Legislative institutions and processes are difficult to grasp and even more difficult to appreciate. Moreover, since Watergate and Vietnam, environmental forces have contributed substantially to negative orientations. The media stress the negative, and the more negative, the better for the media's business. Investigative reporting is in vogue, and the more sensational, sordid, and scandalous a story, the better it sells. Political campaigns focus not only on what is wrong with the opposition, but also on what is wrong with the system. Incumbents, as well as challengers, run against the legislature. Issue campaigns also lay blame on the system, since an enemy is needed if troops are to be mobilized. No one is ever happy with what comes out of the legislature. Losers, of course, are dissatisfied; winners think they deserve even more than they got. And when both sides come out ahead, neither is content—the system is at fault (Cooper 1999; Rosenthal et al. 2003, 14–30).

Public disaffection, more than any other factor, accounts for the success of initiatives that proposed term limits in the states. In voting for term limits citizens of California, Colorado, Arizona, and the other states were not trying to get rid of their own legislators. Public opinion polls and reelection rates of incumbents indicate that people are happy with their own. It is the others that they want periodically removed from office. (Similarly, while people oppose special interest groups, they do not regard groups with which they are affiliated as special interests.) Only in two states—Mississippi and North Dakota—did people reject term limits when they were on the ballot.

Term limits may not be as popular today as they were in the 1990s, but when a very modest liberalization of the term limits provision was placed by the legislature on the California ballot in March 2002, it was decisively defeated. Chances are that if Americans voted on term limits in each of the states today, they would pass in an overwhelming majority of places. It is unlikely, however, that absent the popular initiative, legislatures themselves will adopt or put term limits on the ballot.

What Consequences Are Likely?

The combination of democratization on the one hand and disaffection on the other can be expected to have an impact on the functioning of the legislature. As far as representation is concerned, ties to constituents and to interest groups that are constituency based will be strengthened. Or, to use sociologist David Riesman's formulation, legislatures will be more "other directed" and less "inner directed." As far as lawmaking is concerned, electoral factors will continue to weigh heavily on the larger issues and interest group pressures will continue to count on the smaller issues. The merits of a case will not be unimportant, but the politics of issues will gain in weight. But probably the main effects of institutional democratization and public disaffection will be on how the legislature performs its third major function, that of balancing the power of the executive.

Ordinarily, the executive has an advantage over the legislature. As much as any other legislative body, Congress has maintained reasonable coequality with the president, but state legislatures, with only a few exceptions, have labored in the shadow of dominant executives. During the 1970s and 1980s, as a result of a period of legislative modernization, state legislatures made considerable progress enhancing their institutional capacity and also their ability to check and balance executive power. Since then, however, the executive advantage has again grown.

Greater dispersion of power within the legislature makes it tougher for these representative institutions to hold their ground. State legislators require strong leaders, if their interests are to be adequately represented in dealings with a governor. Leaders not only help the legislature (the chamber or the legislative majority party) arrive at a position, they are the ones who can best defend and advance such a position with the executive. Weaker leadership affords governors better opportunity to deal, not with the senate or house collectively, but with members one-on-one. Facing members individually, the governor's resources are most persuasive and the ability of a legislature to stand its ground most threatened.

Weaker leadership is harmful to the legislative institution in another way. By virtue of their tenure and responsibilities, leaders are the ones who feel the strongest commitment to the legislature as an institution. Individual members are devoted to their constituencies, their agendas, and their careers. Only a few have time or energy left for institutional concerns. Leaders, however, develop commitment over time and recognize that one of their jobs is that of maintaining the well-being of their institution. Term-limited and weaker leaders are less disposed to concern themselves with the needs of an institution; they have to busy themselves with more practical matters.

Democratization no doubt has effects on the executive, but such effects are marginal only. The executive branch is a pyramid, hierarchically organized, with the president or governor at the top. The executive speaks with one voice, the legislature with as many voices as there are members. At best, the legislature can speak as a chorus composed of a majority in each chamber. Democratization makes it more difficult for legislatures to resolve conflicts, while the executive is little affected in this respect. Today's legislatures are highly permeable; executives are still relatively insulated. Despite presidential-interest group relations analyzed by Daniel Tichenor in chapter 12, access to the president or to a governor is far more limited than access to members of Congress or of state legislatures. Chief executives are lobbied, but usually indirectly; legislators are lobbied directly, indirectly, and any which way. Expert and bureaucratic values can—and do—play a greater role in an executive's policy decisions than in legislative decisions.

Executives tend to be more removed than legislatures not only from public pressures but also from electoral considerations. In Congress and all but six states, elections for the legislature are held every two years. Elections for president and for governor in all but two states are held every four years. Legislators in thirty-three states are not term-limited, so their sensitivity to what voters like or dislike never subsides. And even in the seventeen states with term limits (except for Nebraska), although members in their last terms may be unconstrained by the fear of voter sanctions, the legislative parties are heavily invested in the forthcoming election.

While the senate and house are both continuing bodies, the executive is not. The president and forty governors are term-limited to two four-year terms (except in Vermont, where the governor may have three two-year terms). In the last year or two of their first term, with an eye to a second term, governors pay heed to electoral currents. If they are reelected, during their final term or essentially during half their administration, term-limited governors need not worry about punishment at the hands of the electorate. And there is no executive party, comparable to the legislative party, to do the worrying instead. The governor walks away from office; the legislature remains.

Disaffection also is hitting the legislature harder than the executive. Executives nearly always top legislatures in approval ratings on public opinion polls. Presidents and governors have a distinct advantage, because they have a face. They are human and tangible. Legislatures are institutions, with no faces as far as the public is concerned. They are abstract and remote. As was mentioned above, although people like their own legislator, because he or she has an identity; it is easy for them to dislike what they don't know and can't really imagine. The president and governor, in contrast, stand on their own; they are thought of and judged as individuals, not as a faceless executive branch. The presidency or the office of governor does not suffer if an incumbent happens to be unpopular. Chief executives, moreover, have the bully pulpit at their disposal. They can present themselves to the public in their own terms and on their own issues. They have a chance to shape opinion. There is little way that legislatures will be able to match executives in presenting either themselves or their issues.

It is ironic that increasing democratization threatens to diminish the power of the most democratic of the three branches of government. It is ironic also that the public is most disaffected with the most democratic branch. If democratization and disaffection persist, which they are likely to do, the ability of the legislature to balance the power of the executive will be in jeopardy. The result likely will be a more dominant executive, and the functioning of representative democracy will change. Those legislatures, which in past years managed to attain coequal status will not be able to maintain it; they will revert back to greater reliance on the executive for policy and budgetary leadership. Yet—weaker, but enduring—the legislature will still be able to chug along. And chug it will.

Chapter 9

The Impact of *Bush v. Gore* on Future Democratic Politics

ELIZABETH GARRETT

THE SUPREME COURT'S decision to end the election contest between George W. Bush and Al Gore generated two kinds of reactions among scholars and other commentators. First, there was widespread belief that because it avoided having any election dispute decided by the United States Congress, the Supreme Court's intervention into the 2000 election saved the country from a constitutional crisis or, at the least, a disruptive descent into political chaos.

Not surprisingly, those who support the outcome in *Bush v. Gore* laud the Court for working so hard to avoid a disaster. For example, Richard Posner argues that had the Court refused to expend its reputational capital to bring the contest to an end, "it might have invited comparison to Nero fiddling while Rome burned" (Posner 2001a, 54). It is startling, however, to hear scholars who disdain the Court's reasoning also adopt this alarmist perspective as a way to reconcile themselves to the decision. In terms that resonate with Judge Posner's, Cass Sunstein, a critic of *Bush v. Gore*, describes congressional involvement as very likely to have resulted in a "genuine constitutional crisis" (Sunstein 2001a, 218) and concludes that the judicial decision "brought a chaotic situation to an abrupt end" (221). Both scholars appear to view Congress bleakly.

The second theme dominating the commentaries focuses primarily on the effects of *Bush v. Gore* on the reputation of the Supreme Court. A debate has raged about whether the Court's intervention will do permanent damage to its reputation among the public and members of the legal and political communities. The dissenting justices are partly responsible for this focus. Justice Stevens warned that the final decision "can only lend credence to the most cynical appraisal of the work of judges throughout the land . . . The identity of the loser [in the long run] is perfectly clear. It is the Nation's confidence in the judge as an impartial guardian of the rule of law" (*Bush v. Gore* 531 U.S. 98, 128–29 [2000]). Justice Breyer invited comparisons to the long-term reputational hit suffered by the Court because of the *Dred Scott* decision when he described the opinion in *Bush v. Gore* as risking a "self-inflicted wound" (158).

Most legal commentators have taken their cue from the dissenters and focused on determining the effect of the decision on the judiciary. In a particularly shrill and admittedly *ad hominem* attack on the five justices in the majority, Alan Dershowitz claims that their votes "reflected . . . the partisan quest for immediate political victory. In so voting, they shamed themselves and the Court on which they serve, and they defiled their places in history" (Dershowitz 2001, 4). Bruce Ackerman states that the Court has so "betrayed the nation's trust in the rule of law" that it has "called its fundamental legitimacy into question" (Ackerman 2001, 48). Others, however, have concluded that these concerns are overstated and that any tarnishing of the Court's reputation will be short-lived and minor (Klarman 2001). As Jack Balkin concludes: "The Supreme Court has often misbehaved and squandered its political capital foolishly. It has done some very unjust and wicked things in the course of its history, and yet people still continue to respect and admire it. If the Court survived *Dred Scott v. Sandford,* it can certainly survive this" (Balkin 2001, 1453).

The larger and more troubling issue, however, is the future of congressional legitimacy. The institution that is tarnished by both the judicial intervention in the election and the overheated rhetoric following the decision is the United States Congress, the main arena for democratic politics in the federal government. The widespread acceptance—by commentators, scholars, and perhaps the public—that a legislative resolution of the election would have caused a presidential succession crisis serious enough to threaten the stability of American democracy suggests a profound distrust of Congress. In turn, this distrust further increases the alienation of the public toward its elected lawmakers. Ultimately, it undermines the ability of democratic institutions to handle the country's most important questions in a transparent and accountable way.

This chapter discusses how contempt for politics endangers democratic governance and diminishes the vitality of Congress. Increasingly, we try to avoid politics and partisanship when we grapple with the most difficult problems facing the country, working to move decisions into a more dignified and antiseptic realm, like the judiciary. This chapter argues that this reaction is inappropriate, although some disappointment with rampant partisanship and excessive rhetoric in Congress is understandable.

The better response to the extremes of political behavior would be to structure politics so that partisanship and opportunistic behavior are channeled and somewhat reduced. In some cases, including resolving contested presidential elections, Congress can shape politics by adopting ex ante frameworks to structure decision making and restrain self-interested behavior. This chapter describes the framework that would have shaped congressional involvement in the 2000 presidential election—the *Electoral Count Act, U.S. Code,* Title 3, secs. 1–18[1]—and also considers an ex ante framework that is more frequently used in the modern Congress—the congressional budget process. Analyzing these two ex ante frameworks allows us to identify conditions that seem hospitable to the enactment of such structures.

Developing framework legislation is a costly activity for Congress because it requires legislators to develop information about future problems and reach agreement about procedures to resolve such problems. In addition, lawmakers must be willing to incur significant opportunity costs, spending time and energy constructing framework legislation, rather than responding to constituents' immediate demands for substantive programs. Judicial intervention, such as *Bush v. Gore,* that renders framework legislation superfluous will discourage members of Congress from developing these relatively neutral procedures in the first place, leaving the legislature ill-equipped to address some difficult issues and therefore more vulnerable to attacks on the way it discharges its deliberative and lawmaking functions.

Bush v. Gore *and the Distaste for Politics*

The public has held Congress and its members in low esteem for some time; *Bush v. Gore* cannot be blamed for the legislature's poor reputation. The growth of powerful grassroots groups supporting term limits for federal legislators, gift and travel restrictions on Congress members and their staffs, campaign finance reform laws, and regulation of lobbying activities reflect widespread public distrust of elected officials. Congress is seen as a flawed institution, dominated by wealthy special interests and characterized by strategic behavior as members seek personal and political advantage without sufficient attention to the public good. Recent episodes, from the partisan and innuendo-laced Clinton impeachment proceedings, to the unsavory picture of Congressman Gary Condit frolicking with a series of naive interns, to the access that money seems to have bought for Enron and its executives, to the expulsion after felony conviction of Congressman James Traficant, have not helped Congress's reputation. But these events have only confirmed what people have already suspected—that the institution is degraded and perhaps irreparably broken.

Congress, among all political institutions, has long been viewed with the most dissatisfaction by the public, a dissatisfaction, depending on the group, occasionally bordering on hatred (Hibbing and Theiss-Morse 1995, 33–36).

In their book *Congress as Public Enemy*, political scientists John Hibbing and Elizabeth Theiss-Morse explain why the public so detests Congress. They find that people dislike Congress in large measure because they dislike many of the inherent characteristics of political discussion and democratic deliberation. Constitutional provisions and other rules have created a deliberative body characterized by procedures that are designed to slow things down—but the public prefers rapid action on salient matters. Representatives and senators represent geographic constituencies, and the electoral connection is designed to make them react to the wishes of their constituents—but the public denounces special interest deals and pork barrel projects. Committees and other places of political deliberation are structured to make deal-making and debate public so that lawmakers can be held accountable for their actions—but the public is uncomfortable with disagreement, compromise, and logrolling because these activities can appear unprincipled.

Hibbing and Theiss-Morse found that dissatisfaction with Congress was not limited to the general public, which might not be expected to fully appreciate the benefits of proceduralism and other superficially unattractive traits of democratic politics. Political elites also disapprove of Congress and its members. Although they are more tolerant of debate, deliberation, and compromise, elites are also more familiar with the flaws of the federal legislature, including "representationally skewed procedures." Even though they appreciate the "need for possibly raucous debate and unsatisfying compromises in a democracy," they prefer the more civilized debate and decision making that occur in the unitary executive or in the Supreme Court because these more closely resemble the kind of discourse to which they are accustomed (Hibbing and Theiss-Morse 1995, 144).

The combination of public disgust and elite discomfort leaves Congress the most vulnerable of all the federal governance institutions, and *Bush v. Gore* further weakens the power and prestige of Congress. When judges work hard to keep a case away from elected representatives, their contempt for Congress is palpable. The justices fed this perception by aggressively issuing decisions even when there was no need for intervention, a circumstance that made them appear desperate to avoid congressional decision making.

Take for example the unanimous decision in *Bush v. Palm Beach County Canvassing Board* (531 U.S. 70 [2000]), the case first brought to the Court by George W. Bush to challenge the Florida Supreme Court's postponement of the date of certification of vote totals. The best decision for the Court at this stage was to dismiss the petition for certiorari as improvidently granted and issue no opinion on the matter. By the time of the oral argument, it was clear that the additional votes that had been counted because of the delay in certification had not changed the outcome of the vote in Florida. Bush remained the winner. Although he had lost 393 votes in his certified total, it was not clear whether this fact would make a difference in the long run. If it did matter in a subsequent election contest (because the certified vote totals might be given a presumption of correctness that votes found in subsequent recounts would not), courts could then address the issue. But the Court did not choose this minimalist route; instead, it issued a 9–0 per curiam decision, full of heavy-handed and ultimately inaccurate hints about the justices' views on the substantive issues.

Furthermore, several aspects of the decisions rendered in the final challenge before the Supreme Court reflect intense judicial distrust of Congress's ability to solve this controversy. A divided Court was so afraid of the democratic process that it halted the recount, even though allowing the count to go forward might well have eliminated any need for judicial involvement. So far, Governor Bush had won every count and recount. It is possible he would have continued to win after another recount, or that the Florida state judge might have imposed standards that would have satisfied, or at least ameliorated, the equal protection concerns articulated by seven justices.

Justice Antonin Scalia, in an unusual separate opinion concurring in the stay of the recount, defended stopping the recount at this early juncture: "Count first, and rule upon legality afterwards, is not a recipe for producing election results that have the public acceptance *democratic stability* requires" (*Bush v. Gore* 531 U.S. 1046 [2000]; emphasis added). This statement about the requirements for democratic stability, apparently a product of Scalia's political intuition, is unconvincing.

In some election disputes, recounts occur as part of the proceedings, and then the courts or Congress determines whether the information provided by the recounts justifies accepting the new vote totals or retaining the certified totals. For example, in a case similar to *Bush v. Gore*, because its final resolution also lay appropriately with the legislative branch, the Supreme Court allowed a state-run recount in a contested Senate election even though the Senate retained the ultimate authority to decide whether to include the recounted ballots (*Roudebush v. Hartke* 405 U.S. 15 [1972]). If the Court was concerned that the recounts were flawed, then it could have required the state institutions to set forth rules to govern the hand counts,[2] beginning a process that would have then allowed Congress ultimately to determine how to use the information in resolving the election controversy.

The Court's conviction that maintaining democratic stability required suppressing information and imposing order is a theme of this episode, and it is more generally a theme in the Court's recent jurisprudence on the political process. In two essays situating *Bush v. Gore* in a larger context, Richard Pildes argues that the Court's decision to intervene in the way that it did resulted in part from what he calls "cultural" factors that have shaped the justices' view of democracy and politics (Pildes 2001, 2002). In addition to the opinions in *Bush v. Gore*, he analyzes the opinions in the case striking down the blanket primary (*California Democratic Party v. Jones* 530 U.S. 567 [2000]), the case allowing states to prohibit fusion candidacies (*Timmons v. Twin Cities Area New Party* 520 U.S. 351 [1997]), and the case permitting organizers of publicly sponsored debates to exclude some candidates who appear on the ballot (*Arkansas Educational Television Commission v. Forbes* 523 U.S. 666 [1998]).

Pildes argues that the five justices in the majority in *Bush v. Gore*, as well as justices in other cases, are driven by a fear that too much politics and too much room for experimentation with different governance structures may destabilize democracy. This cultural perspective is responsible for a view of democracy as requiring "order, stability, and channeled, constrained forms of engagement" and as threatened by "wide-open competition that may appear tumultuous, partisan, or worse" (Pildes 2001, 160). Contrasting the Court's preference for order and the public's dissatisfaction with many facets of the existing political system, Pildes concludes that "the Court has invalidated experiments with new forms of democracy while refusing to require that the system be open to emerging sources of challenge . . . The Court has done so because it believes, or fears, or assumes that American democracy requires judicial constraint to ensure that stability and order are maintained" (Pildes 2002, 186).

Another related line of recent cases forcefully demonstrates the Supreme Court's "fundamental and complete distrust of the [federal] legislative process" (Buzbee and Schapiro 2001, 137). In *Board of Trustees of the University of Alabama v. Garrett* (531 U.S. 356 [2001]), the Court reviewed the state of the legislative record supporting the enactment of the Americans with Disabilities Act to determine if the empirical basis of the legislation was sufficient to find that Congress abrogated the states' immunity under the Eleventh Amendment.[3] The Court held Congress to an evidentiary standard more appropriately applied to a court or an administrative agency, discounting the varied mechanisms through which legislators gather facts, reach conclusions, and deliberate about important issues. The majority did not factor into its analysis the democratic pedigree of Congress, nor did it discuss whether the fact that legislators are frequently elected, in sharp contrast to federal judges or agency administrators, should have some bearing on how congressional process is assessed. In contrast, the dissent in *Garrett*, written by Justice Breyer and joined by the other three dissenters in *Bush v. Gore*, includes an appendix providing a more nuanced view of the legislative materials informed by a realistic view of congressional practices (531 U.S. 389–423).

In "Dissing Congress," an aptly named article that assesses this new trend in the Supreme Court's jurisprudence, Ruth Colker and James Brudney argue that legislative record review treats "the federal legislative process as akin to agency or lower court decision-making; in doing so, the Court has undermined Congress's ability to decide for itself how and whether to create a record in support of pending legislation" (Colker and Brudney 2001, 83). Certainly, like *Bush v. Gore*, these cases demonstrate a lack of respect for Congress and a clear preference for more orderly and formal decision making than is currently the norm for the legislative process.

The justices' belief that the country was at the brink of political chaos, if not an outright crisis, may have driven the final decision in *Bush v. Gore*, but it is baffling because it ignores the calm reality during the weeks between the election and the final Supreme Court opinion. Chief Justice Wells of the Florida Supreme Court has described his relief when he looked out the window of his office at the crowds gathering before oral arguments and noticed street performers, families, and even a skunk trained to do back flips. Unlike other instances in American history where the presidential election ended in a dispute, no armed forces were gathering. Nor was the country at a critical historical juncture, as it was in 1876 when it faced rebuilding part of the country in the wake of a civil war.

Would a crisis have developed if the controversy had lingered on and required congressional involvement to resolve disputes, say, between two slates of electors? A descent into chaos seems only a remote possibility, in part because of the Electoral Count Act, framework legislation designed to provide a series of default rules to influence congressional decision making and to ensure a president is selected. The act's drafters explicitly rejected the notion that congressional involvement was tantamount to a political crisis, even though they drafted and debated the act when the problems of the Hayes-Tilden election of 1876 were fresh in their minds.

The provisions of the Electoral Count Act reveal that its drafters understood that Congress might be asked to resolve a politically chaotic situation; their solution was not to avoid politics altogether by punting the decision to the courts. Instead, the "consistent and prevailing view of Congress" was that "it is within the power of the political branches, not the Supreme Court, to resolve such disputes" (Barkow 2002, 291–92). The sponsor of the act, Senator Sherman, explained why he had rejected the option of relying on the Court to end presidential election disputes: "It would be a very grave fault indeed and a very serious objection to refer a political question in which the people of the country were aroused, about which their feelings were excited, to this great tribunal . . . It would tend to bring that court into public odium of one or the other of the two great parties" (U.S. Senate, Sherman, 1886).

In short, the only "crisis" that was looming was congressional involvement itself, which apparently was sufficient for the doomsday pronouncements of the Court and the commentators. Of course, had the 2000 dispute reached Congress, some of the rhetoric, debate, and compromise would surely have appeared extreme and unreasonable, even with the backdrop of the Electoral Count Act. That is part of the political process, and through deliberation and discussion, such views are often rejected. The debate would not have resembled the formal interactions in the Supreme Court, and only a small part of the legislative discussion would have risen to the intellectual level of some of the repartee between justices and advocates. But, the activity of the political branches is not supposed to look or sound like a Supreme Court argument, and the election of the president is a political act that should remain in the political sphere when possible. The dismay that some commentators express when confronted with legislative debate and political wrangling is unfortunate. Not only does it have elements of elitism, but it also reinforces the increasing alienation of the people from their elected representatives.

A judicial, academic, and popular culture that abhors the rough-and-tumble of politics is also partly responsible for another tendency in the legislative branch: a preference for mechanisms that hide political discussions and decision making from public view so that important policies appear to be the product of calm bipartisan consensus rather than of energetic give-and-take among partisans. Such a tendency to hide politics was evident in the wake of the September 11 catastrophe, although politics-as-usual began to reappear in the first months of 2002. In the days and weeks immediately after the attacks on the World Trade Center and the Pentagon, congressional leaders worked to avoid all public debate and disagreement as they negotiated a series of bills dealing with issues related to the terrorist attacks. Three bills were enacted quickly,[4] without committee involvement and with virtually no discussion on the floor. Instead, the White House proposed language, and the so-called Big Four—Speaker Dennis Hastert, House Minority Leader Richard Gephardt, Senate Majority Leader Tom Daschle, and Senate Minority Leader Trent Lott—would reach a deal on behalf of Congress (Cohen 2001, 3000–3001).[5] Although this system allowed quick legislative action (which even in an emergency may or may not be a virtue), it denied drafters the expertise of committees and the accountability of public debate and deliberation.

Moreover, the laws that emerged from this process are hardly models of thoughtful or careful policymaking. For example, the supplemental appropriations bill appropriated $40 billion in one paragraph, allowing the president wide discretion to allocate $10 billion for several broad purposes relating to combating terrorism, ensuring domestic and national security, and rebuilding public facilities and transportation systems. An additional $10 billion could be allocated to those purposes as the president saw fit, but only after the Office of Management and Budget submitted a report to Congress detailing his decisions. The final $20 billion could not be obligated without further directions from Congress in subsequent legislation that would follow an official amended budget request by the president (Parks 2001, 2465–67). Interestingly, the strings that Congress attached to half of the appropriated money have allowed the legislature to reassert its traditional oversight role with respect to appropriations, demonstrating that lawmakers anticipated a return to typical political interactions within a short time after the terrorist attacks.

The generally low esteem in which Congress is held by the public, coupled with signals by elites that the legislative branch cannot be trusted to handle important and possibly divisive issues, makes it easier for those who want to pursue their own objectives to equate partisanship and unbridled political discourse with un-American conduct. It becomes easy to attack the delay that is inherent in legislative deliberation as unpatriotic foot-dragging during wartime. For example, in testimony before the Senate Judiciary Committee in December 2001, Attorney General John Ashcroft attacked his opponents: "To those Americans who . . . scare peace-loving people with phantoms of lost liberty, my message is this: Your tactics only aid terrorists, for they erode our national unity and diminish our resolve. They give ammunition to America's enemies" (Senate Judiciary Committee 2001). Of course, these tactics are always available during a national crisis—but they are more likely to succeed in an environment already permeated with antagonism toward Congress and skepticism of lawmakers' motives and competence.

In the end, low expectations of members of Congress may become a self-fulfilling prophecy as fewer qualified people seek the office and those who do have little incentive to transcend the public's perception of them. We would do much better in a variety of circumstances, including the resolution of contested presidential elections, not to rely on nonelected officials to save us *from* politics but to rely on the most democratically accountable branch of government to save us *by* politics (Garrett 2001b, 54). If the decision of the legislature is unjustified or irrational or if the behavior of politicians is inconsistent with citizens' preferences, voters have recourse at the next election to make their views known forcefully. Even if it is not as robust a threat as some would like, it is more effective than any recourse we possess when we believe that the Court has entered the political fray in an unseemly and counterproductive way. Dismay with politicians, justified in part by some recent legislative behavior, should not lead us to avoid or hide politics; rather, lawmakers should search for ways to structure and improve political discourse, restraining some of the raw politics, providing transparency to discussions, and improving the quality of information for lawmakers and voters.

In some instances, Congress has adopted procedures and rules designed to serve precisely that goal—to improve politics. The 2000 presidential election and the effort by so many to deny Congress any role in it are distressing in part because Congress already had in place a framework designed to structure politics, restrain partisanship, and enhance decision making in just such circumstances. After assessing this framework legislation, this chapter provides more general conclusions about such techniques that promise to improve the operation of the legislative branch. These conclusions will also be informed by a modern example of framework legislation, the congressional budget process. This far-reaching and detailed framework was first adopted in 1974 to shape congressional decision making and affect the relationship between the legislature and the executive with respect to budgeting decisions, and it has been modified, expanded, and institutionalized in subsequent decades.

The Electoral Count Act and Other Ex Ante Frameworks

Rules that shape decision making are seldom neutral in their effects; in many cases, the selection of one procedure rather than another will significantly affect and sometimes determine which outcomes will emerge.[6] Once an issue becomes concrete enough for participants to be fully aware of their interests, they will work to choose rules that advance their substantive goals. This was among the concerns in the Florida contest, when political actors formulated rules about hand recounts in an environment of apparently good information about the kind of ballot errors that had occurred and how they had affected Vice President Gore and Governor Bush. It is one of the reasons that some commentators have accused the Supreme Court of partisanship; it delivered its opinion, adopted an expanded understanding of equal protection, and refused to provide a remedy for the constitutional violation when it had nearly perfect information about how its ruling would affect the combatants in the 2000 presidential election. In contrast, if procedures can be specified before it is clear what issues will be considered and how participants will be affected, then the rules can be designed to further longer-term, more public-regarding objectives.

Because decision makers act behind a partial veil of ignorance when they adopt *ex ante* procedural frameworks, their incentive to behave in self-interested ways is impeded (Fitts 1990; Vermeule 2001). To be successful, a partial veil of ignorance must make parties uncertain about their interests in the future when the framework legislation will be applied. Uncertainty can exist, for example, when the framework will not apply for some time to any particular decision, and the drafters either will no longer be in power or do not know what their positions will be when the framework is actually triggered. This type of uncertainty reduced self-interested behavior in the adoption of the Electoral Count Act. The act was intentionally designed to provide a structure for debate, deliberation, and decision making in order to avoid what was seen as nakedly self-interested behavior on the part of decision makers during the disputed Hayes-Tilden election of 1876.

The *ad hoc* procedures to select a president devised in 1876–77 did not result in a full-blown constitutional crisis even though the country then was much more vulnerable to succession disputes than it was in 2000.[7] Yet there was widespread dissatisfaction at the time with the performance of Congress and the Electoral Commission created specially to resolve the controversy. Examples of manipulation of the process by lawmakers are legion, including attempts by politicians to bribe the certifying boards of the three southern states with contested electoral votes (Harrison 2000, 714). Accusations of partisanship had long been leveled at the commission, including some justices who were members. Justice Breyer alludes to these charges in his dissent in *Bush v. Gore* as proof of the majority's folly in deciding the 2000 election (531 U.S. 98, 156–58).

Thus, policymakers acting in the shadow of Hayes-Tilden became convinced of the necessity of framework legislation because they believed that ad hoc solutions devised without a veil of ignorance would allow legislators the opportunity to give full rein to their self-interests and partisan objectives. One of the primary difficulties in 1876–77 was that Congress established its solution, the Electoral Commission, after the election dispute had arisen and when the stakes were clear and concrete. Each decision about procedure or substance was suffused with partisanship because supporters of both Hayes and Tilden worked to advance only their candidates' interests. In the aftermath of that controversy, legislators sought to avoid a repeat by specifying *ex ante* the procedures that would channel political behavior in future contests.

The preference for using rules determined before a particular contest ensues is reflected in the provisions of the Electoral Count Act. Section 5, the safe harbor provision, gives special weight to "laws enacted prior to the day fixed for the appointment of the electors."[8] The other main provision of the

Electoral Count Act, section 15, provides a series of default rules for both houses to rely on when actually counting the ballots cast by the Electoral College. It works together with the safe harbor provision to encourage states to determine contests relatively quickly after the election, but it also provides rules to apply if a contest lingers past section 5's deadline. Because of their experience in the Hayes-Tilden contest with the electors of Florida, Louisiana, and South Carolina, the drafters anticipated a dispute that would involve two or more slates of electors being sent from one state. Section 15 provides that each house will independently consider this problem and make a decision; if the two bodies split, then the winning slate is the one bearing the governor's signature.

Virtually no framework legislation can be designed to deal with all contingencies because drafters cannot perfectly foresee the future. Had Congress played a role in the 2000 presidential election contest, it would have discovered some of the gaps in the Electoral Count Act, and it might well have spent time in the 107th or 108th Congress working on amendments to plug some of the holes.

There are a variety of gaps in the relatively detailed provisions of the Electoral Count Act. For example, the default rule favoring the slate officially endorsed by the governor might have proved problematic in the 2000 election contest. Had the state processes been allowed to continue, it was certainly possible that the Democratic electors would have won after a court-ordered recount. It is also possible that the governor would have refused to withdraw the first slate of Republican electors that he had already sent to Washington, D.C., even at the risk of being held in contempt by the state supreme court. Finally, the state legislature could have ordered Governor Jeb Bush not to comply with the court order and to maintain his certification of the Republican electors.

Under these circumstances, which slate of electors would have been considered as "the electors whose appointment shall have been certified by the executive of the state" (3 USC 15), the final decision rule provided in the act in case the House and Senate cannot agree after an objection has been lodged? This gap in the act is probably the result of a failure to anticipate this particular scenario (including the very unlikely reality that the governor in question is the brother of one of the presidential candidates), together with a desire to pick a default rule that vests power in a state entity. This latter decision was driven both by federalism and by the concern that a Congress that chose the president would be able to exert an unhealthy influence over him in the future (U.S. House of Representatives, Dibble, 1886, 45–46). Doubtless there are other gaps in the Electoral Count Act that might be the product of imperfect information and might have been the focus for change had Congress been forced to use the framework. For example, the role of the vice president in the Senate's deliberations and votes is somewhat murky and yet extremely important because it is likely that the vice president will be a candidate in some presidential contests. The authors of the Electoral Count Act were aware of this possibility, and thus the act's relative silence on the role of the president of the Senate probably indicates that he has no enhanced role in these circumstances (U.S. House of Representatives, Dibble, 1886, 45–46; Adams, 1886, 52). Other gaps in the Electoral Count Act are the result of doubts about how far the act could go constitutionally in influencing internal state electoral processes. And some gaps are intentional because the drafters wanted to preserve a domain for partisanship and politics, albeit in a more structured setting, or because they could not agree on a solution for problems they anticipated.[9]

The Electoral Count Act thus illustrates some of the limitations of framework legislation. *Ex ante* rules must be constructed when drafters have incomplete information about the circumstances in which they will be applied. A partial veil of ignorance hides not only the information relevant to discerning self-interest, but it also denies drafters a great deal of helpful information necessary for precise tailoring (Vermeule 2001). Thus, *ex ante* procedures are often vague and open textured, relative to rules adopted when more complete data is available. In all cases of procedural choice, institutions must resolve a tension between the need to guard against strategic behavior through use of a partial veil of ignorance and the competing need to obtain specific information necessary to draft detailed rules. The greater the specificity that is possible while still allowing drafters to operate behind the partial veil of ignorance, the greater the likelihood that such rules will reduce self-interested behavior in future deliberation and decision making. However, the same information that permits drafters to craft more detailed framework legislation may also enable them to discern their self-interest and to act strategically.

Although framework legislation is more likely to be successful when there will be a delay between the drafting of the rules and their application, a lengthy delay may also reduce the chance that legislators are willing to spend the time and effort required to construct fairly detailed procedures. If the event that will require the framework legislation is far in the future, and may well be faced by different lawmakers than those considering adopting *ex ante* procedures, legislators may decide that the opportunity costs are not outweighed by any benefit to them. Even if they expect to benefit from the framework legislation, these future benefits will be discounted and then compared to the immediate costs of forgoing opportunities to work on other legislation. Thus, the delay necessary for a partial veil of ignorance not only makes it harder to construct specific rules, but it also makes it more unlikely lawmakers will be willing to spend time on the matter.

A final tension arises from the need for specificity to avoid opportunism in the future and the competing need for flexibility to take account of unforeseen developments in the future. Not only may circumstances change so that framework legislation no longer provides an appropriate structure for decision making, but new interests may develop that were not considered as possibilities when the procedures were drafted. Those who draft *ex ante* procedures will try to anticipate all their likely positions when the substantive decisions must be made, but they have little incentive to consider parties who are unrepresented at the time the rules are devised. Interests may be unrepresented either because they do not exist at the time and are not anticipated or because they are not powerful enough to participate in the negotiations. Framework legislation inevitably provides some flexibility for future application because drafters are aware that they lack perfect foresight, and sometimes this flexibility will allow new interests to meaningfully participate in future decisions.

All these tensions must be resolved as the legislature drafts, debates, and occasionally adopts framework legislation. In some cases, *ex ante* guidelines remain so general that all the key decisions are postponed until after a controversy arises and the benefits of framework legislation are lost. The Supreme Court's decision in *Bush v. Gore* provides a telling example of the pitfalls of relying on a very general *ex ante* decision rule. Although the Constitution's equal protection guarantee was adopted long before the presidential dispute in 2000, it is so open textured and vague that virtually all the specification occurs when it is applied to particular cases. As an *ex ante* framework, it is essentially all gap to be filled in the future.

In other cases, probably including the Electoral Count Act, the tensions are partly resolved so that the framework is fairly well specified, but gaps are not entirely eliminated. Gaps remain not only because drafters lack the information required to craft a solution, but also because they do not want to eliminate all opportunity for partisanship and political decision making in the future. Such a decision to permit some room for *ex post* negotiations and strategic behavior at the time the framework is interpreted does not necessarily result in a destabilizing situation. The framework acts to channel the partisanship and make particular issues salient even if politicians would prefer to ignore them.

John Harrison provides an example of opportunistic political behavior that could have occurred in the 2000 contest notwithstanding the restraint of the act (Harrison 2000, 708–9). Because the new Congress determines election disputes (albeit with the old vice president as president of the Senate), Senate Republicans might have declined to seat Jean Carnahan, who was appointed after her dead husband "won" the election in Missouri. They could have referred her credentials to a special committee to investigate whether her appointment was the appropriate way for the governor to deal with this unusual circumstance. Such a decision would have allowed Republicans a one-vote majority in the Senate and avoided the possibility that Gore would be able to break a tie if voting fell strictly along party lines. The Senate is the sole judge of its members' qualifications; thus, Republicans could have increased their margin by refusing to seat Carnahan and accepting instead the candidate coming in second in the Missouri race, Republican John Ashcroft.

Perhaps the commentators' alarm about crisis and their failure to take solace from the presence of framework legislation stem from their awareness that statutory frameworks can be ignored or repealed once a real controversy arises. During the debate on the Electoral Count Act more than one hundred years ago, some opponents of the proposal argued that nothing—not even an *ex ante* framework—could restrain Congress from giving in to "political prejudices or its political bias" in the context of a presidential contest (U.S. House of Representatives, Browne, 1884, 5079).

Congress certainly could have ignored the Electoral Count Act, perhaps justifying any departure by raising plausible arguments that key provisions are unconstitutional. For instance, many have questioned whether the default rule favoring the slate of electors certified by the governor is consistent with Article II, which delegates the power of determining the manner of choosing electors to state legislatures (Greene 2001; Posner 2001b). Although constitutional issues might have been raised merely to give legislators cover for a decision to ignore the *ex ante* framework, this strategic behavior might have prompted some sincere and serious consideration of the act's constitutional implications. Such deliberation is not necessarily a bad result because the act's constitutionality is unlikely to be considered by any other institution.

The assertion that anything could have occurred in Congress and that members would have acted purely strategically is, however, simply not credible. Given the visibility and importance of the issue and its relatively straightforward nature, any congressional decision to discard the *ex ante* framework would have been made transparently, after public debate, and in a way that would have allowed the public to hold members accountable. As Howard Gillman characterizes the congressional debate and decision that the country was denied, it would have been "precisely the sort of high political moment, and hard political decision, that it was designed to be" (Gillman 2001, 194).

Salience and the relative simplicity of the Electoral Count Act framework
would have made it costly for members to ignore or repeal the procedures.
Sustained public attention would have produced the threat of an electoral
backlash if members appeared to be exchanging neutral rules determined in
advance of a conflict for rules devised to further the fortunes of particular
candidates.

It thus seems likely that Congress would have retained all or part of the
act, which would have provided order in the debate. Although lawmakers
could have replaced the Electoral Count Act with new procedures, those rules
would have been tainted because their drafters would have been seen as self-
interested partisans acting to further the fortunes of either candidate. Thus,
any ad hoc rules would have been less binding in a practical sense and less
legitimate than the 1887 procedures, even if the latter posed some serious constitutional questions. In short, legislators would probably have followed the
Electoral Count Act's provisions because it would have been in their interest
to do so.

The Uses of Framework Legislation

The presidential contest and the Electoral Count Act allow us to think about
the larger questions of when Congress should consider adopting framework
legislation to structure politics and when it is likely to do so. Drawing on the
act as well as the more ubiquitous, influential, and typical federal congressional budget process, we can specify five conditions that provide an environment favorable to such legislative procedures. These two examples of
framework legislation meet all five conditions, but they do so in different ways
that demonstrate the varied circumstances under which *ex ante* procedures
might improve congressional deliberation and decision making. The first three
conditions are necessary ones for the development of fairly detailed framework legislation. The fourth and fifth conditions may be required before members of Congress are willing to accept the costs of an *ex ante* framework.
Agreeing to the constraints of such a framework is attractive to politicians
only when the benefits are substantial enough to justify giving up opportunities in the future. The last two conditions describe some circumstances in
which the benefits of *ex ante* frameworks usually exceed their costs.

First, Congress must face a discrete problem, such as how to resolve a contested presidential election or how to cope with burgeoning federal deficits.
Often such a problem will arise as the result of a particular episode that makes
the problem salient to lawmakers and to the public. The Hayes-Tilden election elevated the issue of presidential succession to the top of the legislative

agenda. The Nixon impoundment battle prompted Congress to adopt the first congressional budget act in 1974, and the massive federal deficits of the early 1980s convinced members to accept draconian (and unrealistic) deficit targets and budget enforcement by sequestration in the Gramm-Rudman-Hollings Act (*Balanced Budget and Emergency Deficit Control Act of 1985*). An impending budget train wreck in 1990 resulted in a budget summit that produced the current Budget Enforcement Act procedures, with spending caps, pay-as-you-go requirements, sequestration, and congressional enforcement of budget rules through supermajority voting requirements.

Second, Congress must have the means to develop enough information about the problem and possible contingencies so it can construct a relatively specific framework that will constrain opportunistic and self-interested behavior when the rules are triggered. This requirement implicates tensions discussed above, because the more information Congress has, the less opaque the partial veil of ignorance and the more possible that procedural choices will be driven by self-interest rather than by principle. Nonetheless, enough information about contingencies and possible environments in which the procedural framework will be applied is necessary in order for Congress to include enough detail so that it will successfully constrain opportunism. This second condition is related to the first because information is more likely to be developed when the problem that lawmakers will face is discrete, although not all discrete problems permit lawmakers to pursue a strategy of *ex ante* procedures because other conditions will not be satisfied.

Third, drafters must be uncertain about their future interests and positions with respect to the problem, even in the face of enough information to allow the design of a relatively detailed framework. The partial veil of ignorance relevant to the Electoral Count Act was particularly opaque; the politicians involved in drafting and enacting the act knew they were unlikely to face a contested presidential election again during their careers. Thus, they were constraining the behavior of their successors, and probably of successors far into the future who would be dealing with a presidential election contest long after those who passed the act had retired or died.

Had the 107th Congress been forced to grapple with the act to resolve contests of the 2000 election, any subsequent evaluation of the act and proposals for improvement or gap filling would also have occurred behind a true veil of ignorance. Although small disputes about electors occur with relative frequency, they seldom make any difference in election outcomes and thus do not trigger showdowns in Congress. For this reason, again, it is very unlikely that the current members of Congress would have anticipated that they or anyone they knew would face another election like the one in 2000.

The congressional budget process illustrates a different kind of uncertainty that can result in a partial veil of ignorance sufficient to allow lawmakers to agree to a far-reaching framework. The congressional budget framework is adopted before any particular spending or taxing decisions are made and is applied for several years in the future in order to facilitate macro-budgetary goals such as smaller federal deficits or better priority setting (Garrett 1998b). Some interest groups may seek to enact subsidies in some years and to block enactment of subsidies for competitors in other years. Or they may hope to repeal laws in the short term but to protect some laws from repeal in the long term. They may not know if they will be seeking government support through appropriations, entitlement programs, or tax expenditures. A particular set of rules may advance their objectives in some cases but hinder them in others. Uncertainty exists because the parties are repeat players whose interests are likely to change over time and thus are more likely to favor relatively neutral procedures that do not skew outcomes consistently in one direction.

One problem with the current budget process is that the *ex ante* framework tends to expire every five or so years, so the amount of uncertainty for players is reduced. Political actors need only have an idea of their likely positions in the next few fiscal years to have a good idea of which rules will benefit them and which will harm them. A more permanent *ex ante* budget framework is probably undesirable, however, because economic conditions change with relative speed and require a reconfiguration of the decisional rules. Certainly the congressional budget process has led to substantial modifications over time, such as replacing deficit caps with spending caps or extending fiscal discipline past discretionary funds to include tax expenditures and changes in entitlement programs (Garrett 1998a). Nonetheless, the strong presumption in the budget context is that the basic design of the system will remain in place, as it has since at least 1990, and this norm increases the *de facto* durability of the framework and allows for some partial veil of ignorance that works to minimize the effects of self-interest.

Fourth, *ex ante* frameworks are attractive in policy arenas where stalemate or inaction is unacceptable. In those cases, members may be more willing to forgo political advantage and opportunities for partisanship because they know that in the end they will have to compromise and decide on a course of action. Policy leaders are aware that extreme partisanship in such cases will make the inevitable deal more difficult to sell to constituents and to rank-and-file members and that the electoral consequences of the bargain may be more serious. If compromise must occur ultimately, then a framework that structures the deliberation and decision making, tones down the rhetoric, and channels political behavior is in virtually everyone's interest.

Both frameworks considered here fit this description. The country must have a president to avoid a true constitutional crisis; gridlock here is unacceptable. At other similar points in U.S. history, indecision would not only have paralyzed the government but also threatened to leave resolution of the succession question to violent means. Similarly, but less dramatically, the country must have a budget each year. Inaction in the appropriations process leads to shutdowns of at least part of the government and fiscal crises that may have widespread economic effects.

Fifth, *ex ante* frameworks are most likely to be adopted when members anticipate that the substantive decision will elicit extreme opportunism, partisanship, or widespread defection from overarching goals that a majority has decided to pursue. Both examples of framework legislation reflect this characteristic. A presidential election is the prototypical example of a decision where participants can be expected to seek every opportunity to advance their candidate's causes and undermine his opponent's position. Such was the case in 1800 and in 1876. Partisanship is appropriate in this context; after all, electing a president is a political act. Rational lawmakers might still prefer a structure that channels partisanship and provides a more neutral framework for decision making because it will increase the legitimacy of the decision in the eyes of the public and it will allow Congress members to interact more productively on subsequent legislation in the days following the presidential selection.

The budget arena is another area where opportunism and defection can be expected, particularly if there is consensus on a large macrobudgetary objective, like reducing the deficit, which must be implemented in a series of actions through a decentralized body. The *ex ante* framework serves as a coordinating mechanism to help Congress avoid a classic—and inevitable—collective action problem (Cogan 1994, 26–27).

Legislators who believe that the public interest is best served by reduced federal spending—apparently the consensus since at least 1985 through the beginning of the short period of budget surpluses—know that in the absence of coordination, most of their colleagues will not resist the temptation to spend, nor would it be rational for them to do so. The cost of government programs is spread among millions of taxpayers, while the benefits of federal spending can be concentrated on a few who will reward their benefactors with votes and campaign contributions. This dynamic of dispersed costs to pay for targeted benefits often leads to grateful and energized beneficiaries without affecting those who foot the bill significantly enough to rouse them to political action. Even if taxpayers decide to exact an electoral price from politicians who impose costs on them, voters are likely to hold all lawmakers responsible for increased taxes or a higher deficit—not just the big spenders—because government programs are seldom linked closely to funding mechanisms. Defection from the collective objective is the rational course of action, and thus opportunism pervades this area of decision making. The framework of the budget process is the mechanism used in the last twenty-five years to restrain strategic behavior, at least as much as possible.

Conclusion

The threat posed to democratic politics by *Bush v. Gore* is (at least) twofold. First, the contempt for political decision making and for Congress itself that was manifested by the five justices in the majority increases the alienation of the public from Congress and their distrust of lawmakers. *Bush v. Gore* is not an outlier, unfortunately, in the Court's jurisprudence; several other recent cases, in particular those applying a strict level of scrutiny to the legislative record supporting some federal laws, also show a strong distaste for the congressional process. The Court's disdain for the political branches has translated into an increased willingness to treat Congress, the most democratically accountable branch, as though it were an administrative agency or a lower court subject to aggressive judicial review not only of substantive outcomes but also of the process through which decisions were reached. This approach evinces a distrust of the ability of Congress to collect facts, solicit diverse perspectives and expert opinions, discuss difficult issues, and reach acceptable solutions. It is also based on a naive view of the way Congress works and thus slights the institutional strengths of a branch that consists of elected and accountable members.

Second, judicial intervention such as occurred in the 2000 election is likely to discourage Congress from developing procedures that might improve the political realm and provide structure to democratic dialogue and governance, even when conditions would otherwise favor this *ex ante* strategy. Designing framework legislation is costly. Lawmakers will be unwilling to invest time and energy if they expect that the Court will frequently short-circuit the democratic process and impose a decision. Judicial and public contempt for democratic institutions discourages politicians from working to improve political deliberation and decision making, thereby resulting in lawmaking that feeds the distrust and strengthens the tendency to avoid or hide politics when we are faced with decisions crucial to the future of the country. Only if judges and others become more convinced of the robust nature of democracy will they be willing to act so as to invigorate, not marginalize, the political system.

Chapter 10

The Supreme Court
and *Bush v. Gore*

Resolving Electoral Disputes in a Democracy

MILTON HEUMANN
LANCE CASSAK

In December 2000, with the presidential election of the previous month at an impasse over Florida's electoral votes, the Supreme Court took, heard, and decided *Bush v. Gore* (2000). By doing so it effectively decided the election. Perhaps not surprisingly, that decision garnered a tremendous amount of attention and an enormous scholarly reaction.[1] Most of the assessments of the case, particularly by legal academics and constitutional scholars, focused on the litigants' constitutional law arguments and the Court's legal reasoning. Some of these efforts sought to assess the motivations of the justices, the mechanics of state election law, and the fit of the decision into democratic culture.

One theme that deserves more analysis is institutional competence: which institution *should* have resolved the election impasse? Separate and apart from the doctrinal merits of *Bush v. Gore*, one can argue (and some have) that the Court should never have taken the case in the first place, that Congress was the appropriate forum to resolve the dispute.[2] In this volume, Elizabeth Garrett argues that Congress, rather than the Court, should have resolved the 2000 election. We pick up on that theme and ask what members of Congress can or should consider when they are called on to resolve disputed or deadlocked elections. In deciding the selection of the president in such a situation, can Congress rely on the conventional considerations of legislative decision making? We turn to the historical record for guidance. We also address institutional competence by taking up the Court's perspective by asking, first, whether *Bush v. Gore* harmed the Court's reputation. Then we ask whether—notwithstanding the sharp criticism the decision has attracted—*Bush v. Gore* may ultimately be viewed in a more favorable light, in the same way that some earlier high-profile cases that initially drew harsh criticism have, *Brown v. Board of Education* (1954) being the most prominent example.

The Proper Forum

Garrett argues that democracy would have been better served if Congress—the quintessentially democratic institution—had settled the issue. The process might have been complicated but given what Garrett terms an *ex ante* framework—preexisting rules for tackling election challenges—not chaotic. As a result of the Electoral Count Act of 1887—passed after the disputed Hayes-Tilden election of 1876—a specific mechanism was in place to guide Congressional resolution of the 2000 election.

Although Congress had rules in place to address the dispute, defenders of the Court's decision stress that it "spared" the country a costly and inevitable clash—a messy, ugly, and perhaps devastating battle. Such a confrontation, critics suggest, would have induced the worst imaginable manifestations of political deal making, and of power substituting for "right" (see, for example, Posner 2001 and Sunstein 2001). Garrett, by contrast, first argues that the preexisting rules would have channeled the contest in predetermined directions.[3] Congress would not have been writing upon the blank slate conjured by skeptics. She draws a particular analogy to the legislative budgetary process, one that on its surface might appear to invite much dispute and contention but for which similar *ex ante* procedures serve to cabin excess and deadlock to allow reasoned compromises and decisions. Second, Garrett argues that even if the process was a bit sloppy, it would have been good for democracy to have an open, political resolution as opposed to the inherently elite, nondemocratic nature of Court decision making. The relative transparency of congressional debate is much more consistent with democratic principles than is the secrecy of deliberations by unelected justices.

Despite the claim in the majority opinion that the Court *had* to resolve the issues in *Bush v. Gore*,[4] we agree with Garrett: it did not; the resolution of the Florida dispute could have been left to Congress. The fact, however, that the Court's decision is not particularly well crafted and smacks of a partisan and result-oriented approach is not by itself an argument that Congress should handle the dispute. The case still must be made that Congress is competent to do so, and the case must be reconciled with the concern that Congress is simply too messy a place for this kind of debate, and that the appearance—if not the reality—of partisanship in resolving a presidential electoral dispute would do irreparable harm to public expectations of impartiality in the electoral system. This concern invokes memories of the Clinton impeachment hearings, where presumptively political mechanisms yielded clear partisan results.

The conclusion that Congress could and should have handled the issue raises a number of significant issues. The first part of our approach turns to history.

Some Lessons from History: 1800, 1824, 1876

Congress has a record of three resolved electoral disputes. Historian James Sharp noted that "there is some evidence that the Founders had expected that, after the universally popular Washington had left the presidency, the House would frequently be called upon to elect the president after the electoral college had screened the candidates" (1993, 252). While it has not been called upon "frequently," the House of Representatives has been in a position of deciding the outcome of an election three times: in 1800, 1824, and 1876.

The election of 1800, in which Thomas Jefferson and Aaron Burr received the same number of electoral votes, may generally be viewed as the cleanest of the three elections. Still, it was marked by political rumors, threats, and machinations from Election Day to February 1801, when the House of Representatives selected Jefferson as president. Jefferson and his supporters feared that the Federalists would try to push Aaron Burr—whom they considered much less principled generally and less devoted to Republican principles—through the House. There was also talk that the Federalists might try to block filling the presidency altogether.[5] Joanne Freeman describes the pressures facing House members:

> This jumble of suspicions and expectations—partisan, regional,
> personal, ideological—was at the heart of the subsequent controversy
> over the tie between Jefferson and Burr. Forced to take a stand with
> their votes, congressmen found themselves torn between conflicting
> aspects of their public identity. Voting along partisan lines might do a
> disservice to one's region; voting along regional lines could endanger
> the Union; and either of those paths could damage one's public career.
> There was no single correct course of action, but a poor choice could
> bring dishonor, defeat and disunion. In the end, most men remained
> true to partisan demands. Republicans voted for Jefferson and
> Federalists withheld enough votes to allow him to win. But resolution

came only after six days of conflict, questions, persuasion and suspicion (2001, 244).

In the context of institutional electoral frameworks, it is worth noting that the election of 1800 was at least part of the force behind passage of the Twelfth Amendment.[6]

In 1824, the failure of any of the five candidates running for president to win a majority of the electoral votes again threw the election into the House of Representatives. Despite the fact that Andrew Jackson won the popular vote, the presidency went to John Quincy Adams, after Henry Clay pledged his support. Clay subsequently became the secretary of state in the Adams administration, and the results of the 1824 election were widely and strongly criticized as the result of a "corrupt bargain" between Adams and Clay, tainting the Adams presidency.[7]

The 1876 dispute—how to allocate electoral votes in three states, including Florida—was decided not strictly by Congress but by a commission composed of members from both houses of Congress and some members of the Supreme Court. As did the House before, the commission split along party lines. Despite strong evidence that Samuel Tilden had earned at least some of the contested electoral votes, the result was to hand all of them to Rutherford B. Hayes, supposedly as part of another backroom bargain to end Reconstruction. The dismay over this turn of events resulted in the passage, a decade later, of the Electoral Count Act, an *ex ante* framework specifically created to provide guidance to Congress should such a dispute arise again.[8]

One should be careful not to make too much out of the historical record. Three prior case studies is a small sample from which to work in any event, and for each of the cases, there were large forces or concerns at work that might influence or qualify any lessons that we try to learn from them. For the election of 1800, for example, concerns about intrigue, instability, and even civil war certainly predated and existed independently of any action taken by the House of Representatives (Sharp 1993; Freeman 2001). Moreover, it was certainly more important that the election was the first transition of power between rival political parties—a circumstance that generated considerable concern at the time and something not even foreseen or planned for by the framers—than that the Federalists may have plotted a number of moves to deny Jefferson the election.

Nonetheless, two themes emerge from a review of these three disputed elections. First, the political machinations were not debates solely about "high" politics—that is, discussions of broad and grand political principles.[9] Rather, entangled in the congressional debates were considerations of partisanship and individual self-interest. Indeed, that is the exact indictment of the "corrupt" bargain of 1824. In this regard, the debacle of 1876 may arguably have been the most free of self-interest and partisanship of the three disputes. Democrats may have sacrificed the election in an effort to unify the country after the Civil War and Reconstruction, rather than seeking pure partisan gain. Second, such political machinations were not well tolerated by the institution itself, or the broader population. After the 1824 election, some congressmen proposed a resolution to remove such disputes from the House of Representatives (Currie 1997, 338). While that proposal did not pass, similar efforts in 1876 did result in the passage of the Electoral Count Act, an *ex ante* framework specifically designed to structure electoral dispute resolution.

How Should Congress Decide?

The Electoral Count Act does place responsibility for resolving electoral disputes in Congress. Congress considered delegating the task to the Supreme Court but decided against it.[10] That, by itself, may be enough to settle the issue. Moreover, the election of a president is a political event, and the Electoral Count Act does envision a political decision. Still, questions remain.

When Congress is called on to resolve a disputed presidential election, what—exactly—should it do? After all, the election of a president is fundamentally a political act. Is it Congress's responsibility to resolve the dispute about the election in the "right" or accurate way, or are there other considerations that Congress should entertain? Is the whole notion of the Electoral Count Act time-bound, the product of an era—before the "Imperial Presidency"—when Congress was in its ascendancy and it was natural to look to Congress first to solve problems (Keller 1977, 299–307; Rothman 1966)? Or did Congress, in reinforcing and structuring the Constitution's allocation of the task to itself, have something else in mind?[11]

To flesh out these critical inquiries, we pose the following hypothetical situation. Borrowing a scenario from Cass Sunstein (2001a, 216–18), assume that the Supreme Court had declined to take the case or to issue a final dispositive ruling and that, following the recount ordered by the Florida Supreme Court, Florida sent two slates of electors to Congress: one for Vice President Gore and one for Governor Bush. Now suppose you are a member of Congress, from a heavily Republican district, participating in the resolution of the electoral dispute. Suppose further that based on the best available credible evidence, you believe that more Florida voters intended to vote for Gore than Bush. Under these circumstances, which, if any, of the following defines your options or responsibility?

- to decide in accordance with the result you think Florida law dictates;
- to decide in accordance with what you think actually happened in Florida;
- to vote for the person you think would be the best president, regardless of what happened in Florida or in the popular vote;
- to vote for Bush, despite the fact that you think Gore actually won Florida and would be the better president (since with a Republican House and the tie-breaking vote in an evenly divided Senate in the hands of the vice president, you believe it would be easier to push through the Republican agenda with Bush in the White House);
- to commit to Bush despite the fact that you think Gore actually won Florida and would be the better president, because you and your fellow Republican colleagues have spent the last eight years trying to take the White House back from the Democrats and you would rather be shot than squander that opportunity;
- to commit to Bush, despite the fact that you think Gore actually won Florida and would be the better president (out of concern that 80 percent of your constituents want that result and to do otherwise would endanger your own reelection);
- to commit to one candidate or the other in exchange for promises of support from colleagues for controversial legislation you intend to propose that currently does not have sufficient votes to pass;
- to commit to Bush, despite the fact that you think Gore actually won Florida and would be the better president (because you see a cabinet position or ambassadorship to some exotic locale in the offing).

We could go on, but the question is clear: What exactly should Congress consider in resolving the dispute? The options range from the ridiculous to the sublime. While it is clearly dubious to trade your vote to secure a cabinet position or ambassadorship, is it necessary or reasonable to think in terms of deciding which slate would be recognized under Florida law, or even to re-construct voters' intentions?

For guidance, we turn first to section 15 of the Electoral Count Act governing how Congress should count electoral votes. The section contains language that *might* be read as requiring Congress to determine who actually won the electoral votes—that is, who would have been awarded the electors under Florida state law.[12] While the section is intended as an *ex ante* procedure to guard against a wayward Congress, the statute provides no clear guidance as to what Congress is supposed to consider in determining who has been appointed an elector under state law. On the one hand, it might present to Congress the same issues of state law taken up at the Florida and U.S. Supreme Courts. On the other hand, it might point to the candidate who, purely as a factual matter, received the most popular votes. Unfortunately, as the 2000 election demonstrates, determining which electors are legally authorized to represent the state is not necessarily the same as determining factually who got the most votes.[13]

If, under the act, all that Congress is supposed to do is resolve the same election law issues that the Court did, or merely count votes, we think that lessens Congress's claim that it alone is responsible to make the determination. Analyzing the matter from either the legal or factual perspective is problematic. The resolution of Florida election law caused difficulty for sixteen justices from the U.S. and Florida Supreme Courts; the prospect of hundreds of legislators wrestling with the same legal questions is mind-boggling. Similarly, while Congress certainly has the competence to perform fact-finding, the type of factual questions posed in this matter are more akin to adjudicative facts than legislative facts—not the type in which Congress can claim any special competence, let alone expertise.[14]

Moreover, if Congress is simply to revisit the same questions of state law that the courts grappled with, then where is the politics? As Garrett suggests, the constitutional relegation of the decision to Congress is presumed to have injected a political element into the equation. It is counterconstitutional to sidestep that assignment on the charge that it will result in mere politics. It is not at all clear that Congress is to be allowed to consider either only the legal issues or who actually got the most votes. Electing a president is essentially a political act and the decision entrusted to Congress seems undeniably to have a political component. Our current political culture may have an affinity for judicial resolutions, but this decision—Congress's decision—was intended to be political. To be sure, legislative history, specifically the oft-quoted remarks of Senator Sherman, suggests that it would be unwise to leave such "political" questions to the Supreme Court. "Congress clearly concluded," writes Samuel Issacharoff, "that such decisions would have an inevitable political cast and should therefore be kept clearly confined within the political branches" (Sunstein and Epstein 2001, 72, 160).

Assuming that this decision was intended to be political, we are still left with the key question: What should Congress consider? Returning to our hypothetical situation, the third option—a determination of who would actually make the best president—may be closest to what the framers had in mind. That option is consistent with the civic high-mindedness of the republican ideology often attributed to many statesmen of the founding era.[15] Perhaps most important, it is similar to what presidential electors, at least as originally conceived, were supposed to do. That criterion—which candidate would make the better president—qualifies for principled decision making.[16]

Would any of the other considerations we have suggested make a similar claim to principle, the idea behind "high politics"? Perhaps a decision based on which candidate one believes would further the policy goals in the best interest of the nation? And trading a vote for one candidate for support on a bill he intends to introduce raises even more questions. What about voting in a way to please constituents, with at least one benefit being a smoother road to reelection? People are likely to come down on both sides of that question.

While the answer is unsettled, a vote for president in this setting is not the same as any other vote a legislator has to make in the course of his or her tenure. Even allowing that the decision is in some measure a political decision, it is not clear how the "political" facet of it gets limited or whether it even *should* be limited. Though some consensus on what political considerations would be appropriate would help, the election dispute resolution of 2000 failed to offer any consensus.

Another way to assess the Court's capacity considers the reasoning of the opinion the Court ultimately delivered. Despite the very harsh criticism the opinion received from constitutional scholars,[17] we consider now whether the Court's decision will someday emerge as a meaningful part of the canon of constitutional law.

Bush v. Gore, *the Opinion*

Both critics and supporters of the decision agree that we should be thankful that the Supreme Court does not usually take only four days to decide and write opinions![18] The election dispute of 2000 presented both a complex factual scenario and novel issues of law; further, it involved the parsing of state election statutes that were well suited for ordinary elections but out of place in extraordinary situations, as well as the application of the Equal Protection Clause to statutory standards in a manner that the courts had not previously operated. These factors presented themselves in a highly partisan, pressurized situation with tremendous stakes, compounded by rabid media pressing for answers. Even had the Court taken weeks or months to consider the matter, the case would have presented a challenging setting in which to craft a well-reasoned and persuasive opinion. By trying to resolve the complicated legal issues and negotiate the tenuous factual terrain in a matter of days—with time "running out" as it were—the Court virtually guaranteed a weak, hasty, and ill-prepared decision.

Nonetheless, we are not as entirely dismissive of a role for the Court in election disputes as Garrett appears to be. Perhaps it is the triumph of hope over experience, but we think that the Court *might* have made a real contribution and done precisely what its few supporters claim it did—that is, bring a well-reasoned and principled resolution to a difficult situation. If the Court would have produced a unanimous well-reasoned opinion, then even the Gore supporters would have had to concede it was a principled resolution of the problem.[19] Although a few proponents of the opinion believe it was decided correctly (or at least legitimately) (Greene 2001), most commentators have not been persuaded. Even many of those who applaud the Court's intervention, or like the result, believe the opinion was lacking in crucial aspects of its reasoning.[20]

The same criticism, however, could be leveled at many Supreme Court decisions, including some of the most famous. Like *Bush v. Gore*, *Brown v. Board of Education* (1954) provoked serious criticism when it was first issued,[21] not only by southerners who thought the Court was threatening a cherished way of life but also by a respected constitutional scholar, Herbert Wechsler (1959). The analogy is striking: Wechsler liked the result in *Brown* but not the manner by which the Court reached its conclusion. Other landmark decisions, such as *Roe v. Wade* (1973) and *Miranda v. Arizona* (1966) have also drawn strong criticism and provoked controversy over the reasoning expressed in the opinions, even by those who otherwise prefer the practical results of the opinion.[22] Of course, neither *Roe* nor *Miranda* has come to be as widely accepted as the decision in *Brown*, but both cases continue to be good law and show a remarkable resiliency in the face of recent, unsuccessful efforts to overturn them.[23]

To analyze the decision's staying power, we identify several key points. At the heart of the complaints about the Court's reasoning is its treatment of the equal protection clause, which forms the basis of the majority's ruling. It is here that the criticism that the decision was based as much, if not more, on the justice's political sentiments as their legal views most resonates. The Court's consideration of equal protection was inconsistent and incompletely explained. The first time certiorari was sought, the Court refused to take up the equal protection argument; a week later, it decided that there might in fact be equal protection concerns with the Florida results. It raised the issue in a way that most scholars posit deviated significantly from prior equal protection doctrine. As Sunstein put it, "nothing in the Court's previous decisions [applying equal protection principles in the context of elections] suggested that constitutional questions would be raised by this kind of equality. The cases that the Court invoked on behalf of the equal protection holding . . . were entirely far afield" (Sunstein and Epstein 2001, 213; for a similar position, see Karlan in Rakove 2001).

The Court's decision was "unprecedented" in a number of different ways and on a number of levels. Most fundamental, the Court had never used a violation of equal protection to decide a specific election before. Also, the Court had developed a large body of law on the race-conscious drawing of congressional districts to further the "one man, one vote" principles developed in the reapportionment cases and had also used equal protection law to assess efforts like the poll tax and literacy requirements to exclude classes or groups of voters. But here the Court was applying equal protection principles to strike down different standards for recounting ballots. Never before had the Court used the Equal Protection Clause to police the "nuts and bolts" of elections—that is, the procedures and mechanisms used generally in voting (Hasen 2001, 377).[24]

Of course, simply because the Court's use of the Equal Protection Clause was unprecedented does not mean that that is necessarily a bad thing. But the selective manner in which the Court used equal protection principles has drawn criticism. For some the problem was not the violation the Court identified, it was the remedy—stopping the recount—that the Court chose. For others, the problem was also that the Court did not carry the analysis far enough to cover the many other features of the Florida vote that also ran afoul of equal protection principles as the Court had applied them in this case (McConnell and Issacharoff essays in Sunstein and Epstein 2001; Rubenfeld in Ackerman 2002; Tushnet 2001; and Balkin 2001).

Aside from the majority's equal protection analysis, other aspects of the case cast doubt on the decision as a purely principled rendering of the law unrelated to the political context in which the Court was dealing and are likely to invite skepticism in the future as well. David Strauss (Sunstein and Epstein 2001), Gillman (2001), and Balkin (2001) discuss some of these aspects of the case, although for different reasons. As Justice Scalia described it, in a very unusual opinion in support of the grant of certiorari, the decision to grant a stay was necessary to protect the legitimacy of a Bush presidency, should he eventually prevail. Why should this political effect concern the Court?

Another point of analysis focuses on how the Court's handling of the issues subverted the Court's reputation for protecting states' rights from encroachments by the federal government. That imperative—previously cherished by the conservative majority—now second-guessed a Florida court's interpretations of state law, finding violations of an obscure federal statute that few, if any, had ever heard of before.

Another consideration is the political background of the decision—such as the often-repeated and widely circulated rumors that Chief Justice Rehnquist and Justice O'Connor wanted to retire but were waiting for a Republican president to determine their successors, and Justice Scalia's spring 2000 remark that he was voting for Bush because he wanted to be chief justice and would resign if Gore won. Given these rumors and comments, one can understand at least the perception that something other than a disinterested legal analysis motivated the Court ("Campaign 2000 Roundup" 2000; Gillman 2001, 188).

Finally, there is perhaps the most vexing point of all: the 5–4 split along ideological lines. *Bush v. Gore* stands as the prime example of the problem of a controversial decision by a divided court gaining acceptance.

None of those features of the decision presents an insurmountable hurdle if the Court had crafted a well-reasoned decision. But that was not the case. Moreover, the Court itself does not want posterity to make too much of the decision—the majority specifically warned us that it is deciding *this* case only, based on the unique facts involved (531 U.S. at 109).

Two other considerations speak to whether *Bush v. Gore* will have a lasting positive influence or will remain saddled with criticism. First, whatever one thinks of the results and reasoning in cases such as *Brown, Roe,* and *Miranda,* they do involve claims such as equal protection of the laws, and fundamental rights, in which the judiciary has a well-established role. One may not like the decision in *Roe,* for example, and may think that the Court created that particular right to privacy owing to its own policy preferences, but delineation of the right to privacy had been something the Court had been dealing with for a while. Moreover, most people believe that the determination of constitutionally protected rights is the job of the judiciary. Likewise, in *Miranda,* one might think the Court went too far in "handcuffing" the police, but few—if any—would contend that the Court should have no role in assessing police tactics against protected Fifth Amendment rights.

In *Bush v. Gore* the Court entered an arena—that of political elections—that it seems to understand much less well. Since the Court was apparently not interested in announcing any sweeping changes to or broad reaffirmation of basic rights such as equal protection, the Court's basic effect if not its main intent was to decide the deadlocked election. At least, that political focus became the reported story.[25]

Even if the majority did not *intend* to create any lasting doctrinal legacy, the decision may have long-term effects unintended by the justices. Even if the Court did not want its equal protection ruling to extend beyond the particular facts of the case, the decision may yet alter, and perhaps revolutionize, election law if aggressive litigants and lower federal courts seek to capitalize on the decision's equal protection analysis. Alternatively, the long-term influence might be nondoctrinal but may manifest in the relationship between the Court and the other branches of the government. This is especially true for Congress, the body responsible for rendering advice and consenting on all federal judicial nominations.[26]

Was the Supreme Court Harmed?

Our concern turns to the impact of *Bush v. Gore* on the Court's reputation and legitimacy. An oft-repeated refrain—a cautionary flag—to the Court is to "stay out of the political thicket." Deciding whether to decide is one of the Court's most important institutional determinations. Justice Felix Frankfurter best expressed this dynamic in his now-classic dissent in *Baker v. Carr*:

> Disregard of inherent limits in the effective exercise of the Court's "judicial power" not only presages the futility of judicial intervention in the essentially political conflict of forces by which the relation between population and representation has time out of mind been and now is determined. It may well impair the Court's position as the ultimate organ of "the supreme Law of the Land" in that vast range of legal problems, often strongly entangled in popular feeling, on which this Court must pronounce. The Court's authority—possessed of neither the purse nor the sword—ultimately rests on sustained public confidence in its moral sanction. Such feeling must be nourished by the Court's complete detachment in fact and appearance, from political entanglements and by abstention from injecting itself into the clash of political forces in political settlements. (1962, 267)

With neither purse nor sword, the Court's only real resource is its legitimacy. To use a financial metaphor, this legitimacy is the Court's capital, to be used prudently and sparingly. Shortly before the Court handed down its decision, Gerald Gunther urged it not to decide the case, on the basis that any decision would threaten its "institutional legitimacy." However, Gunther continued, if the Court did rule on the case it should offer a clear and unanimous decision, because anything less would threaten the Court's legitimacy (2000). The Court, Alexander Hamilton wrote in *The Federalist*, No. 78, has only its legitimacy, and it must guard it carefully. Historically, the Court has avoided most major political issues, and when it did decide high-profile cases, it heeded Chief Justice John Marshall's advice that unanimity is desired, if not essential—especially to make the ruling more palatable to the general public.[27]

The decision in *Bush v. Gore* is in direct opposition to these axioms. Not only did the Court not decline the case, but it reached out to make a decision that could have easily been left to the Florida courts, the Florida legislature, and the Congress. And in hastily settling the matter, the justices offered the worst of all kinds of decisions—a 5–4 judgment, filled with the most vitriolic dissents imaginable.

In acting as it did, then, according to conventional wisdom, the Court should have suffered a severe blow to its legitimacy. By jumping into the political fray, rendering a split decision, and dramatically revealing that certain justices felt the Court had sacrificed its objectivity to partisan gains, the Court's "self-inflicted wound" should have been at least temporarily debilitating. It does not appear, however, that it was.

In a careful study of post–*Bush v. Gore* public attitudes toward the Court, political scientists found no support for the hypothesis that the Court sacrificed its legitimacy by deciding the way it did (Gibson, Caldeira, and Spense 2001). Despite the axioms of constitutional law, and despite conventional social science literature, the data—at least that which we have thus far—do not provide any evidence that the Court's legitimacy was weakened. We speculate now on "why the dog didn't bark."

There are six possible explanations:

1. *Too little time:* It is possible that the predictions about loss of legitimacy are correct but will only be evident over time. It is not that specific decisions do not affect support—it is just that it takes time for these effects to reflect in opinion polls (Easton 1965).[28] This may be true regardless of whether the opinion of the general public or of political elites is measured. To illustrate, while it is difficult to envision George W. Bush lashing out at the Court for having decided the case as it did, one might easily imagine that Congress might find ways to retaliate. Nelson Polsby suggests that Congress has done so through its handling of subsequent judicial nominations (see the introduction to this volume).[29]

2. *Supreme Court legitimacy:* It may be that the Court has ample stored legitimacy to survive the loss occasioned by *Bush v. Gore*. In other words, while *Bush v. Gore* was a threat to the legitimacy of the Court, the reservoir of diffuse legitimacy the Court possesses simply "trumps" a short-term diminution of the Court's authority.

3. *Low saliency decision:* This hypothesis suggests that despite the elite/media attention paid to the decision, most of the public neither knew nor cared much about the decision. Much research shows that the public

has very little knowledge about the Supreme Court and its decisions. Despite the academic ballyhoo surrounding *Bush v. Gore,* it is quite possible that when the dust settled, knowledge of the specifics of the Court's decision was not widespread.

4. *The triumph of finality:* It is possible that the protracted situation in Florida taxed citizens' patience and respect for the political process and that dragging out the decision would have had huge societal costs. Ending the process, therefore, had an intrinsic value that inured to the benefit of the Court as the intervening institution.

5. *A decision without a difference:* It may be that since at least some recounts made it clear that Bush would have won, what the Court did really made no difference. In other words, it is not unreasonable to consider that ultimately the outcry may have been much ado about nothing.

6. *September 11:* Within ten months, the tragic events of September 11 dominated the country's interest. It may be that the terrorist attacks substantially displaced public concern (and perhaps anger) with the decision and rendered the fuss inconsequential.[30] In the months following the attacks, President Bush's approval ratings soared, and the country rallied around its leader during this time of crisis. Further, at least for awhile, criticism of the administration was muted—seemingly in an attempt to demonstrate solidarity and national resolve—and Al Gore, the losing litigant, was careful to pledge his support for the president's war on terrorism.

The eventual impact of the case will remain unclear for some years. We will need to wait, probably for new cases, new justices, and even the next presidential election dispute.

Concluding Thoughts

We conclude with three overarching questions and observations about the electoral nightmare of 2000. First, Garrett argues forcefully that democracy would have been better served by congressional resolution of the dispute. Others reach this same conclusion but stress the costs of the Court acting. While we join in criticizing the Court's action, we do not expect congressional orderliness. Garrett and others believe that Congress would have muddled through, probably, but not necessarily, in an admirable way. What if Congress's muddling hadn't been admirable? Regardless of normative concerns and relative responsibility arguments, we are left wondering whether the Court under these circumstances should have avoided swimming, apparently hypocritically, in political waters.

Second, it is now commonplace to note that the Court is sometimes legal, sometimes political. Only the naive would paint a picture of justices being driven exclusively by legal doctrine; that straw man has collapsed, if he ever stood at all. Nonetheless, some have pointed to the unique ability of the Court to "rationalize" its decisions by grounding them in legal analysis (Cox 1976, 108–18). Perhaps in *Bush v. Gore* the Court failed even in this effort to make a minimally persuasive case for legal principle. And if the rationalizing test was not met, then perhaps, once again, an argument for congressional resolution, even if partisan in nature, can be made.

Finally, there is the question of procedural justice (Tyler 1992; 2000, 117–25). Mostly concerned with trial courts, this notion argues for the importance of consumer participation in the dispute resolution process. A sense of participation leads to more favorable evaluations of the fairness of the process, to some extent independent of the outcome of the procedure. Process matters to the individual. In *Bush v. Gore*, the fairness problem is appreciably raised in the context of democratic principles. Which mode of resolution is fairer? Which is more democratic? Or better for the system? Which is most consistent with particular institutional responsibilities? Would the public have had greater participation through a congressional decision than it did through the Court? If so, is this sense of the fairness of the process an important ingredient of a democracy, something that should have been weighed by the Supreme Court?

To date, we have not yet seen the costs of the Court action demonstrated. Professor Garrett details what she thinks the benefits of congressional action would have been. In this chapter, we speculate why the costs have not yet materialized, what the other costs of the Court action might be, and why Congress, even if less of an attractive alternative than portrayed in the Garrett study, might still be a better alternative for promoting democratic values. Yet, we remain puzzled because the worst of the consequences from what actually happened have not been realized, and so while we speculate about what would have been better, the worst of what might have been has not been. Will it be? This remains to be seen.

In the end, *Bush v. Gore* represents something of a worst-case scenario, even without ultimate costs to the Court itself. However the issues are characterized, the Court ultimately decided the election, knew what it was doing, and issued a divided opinion that failed to articulate or reinforce any larger, broadly agreed-upon persuasive principles. Whatever criticism one wants to level at the Florida Supreme Court—either in terms of partisanship or judicial craftsmanship—all it did was keep the clock running, leaving the final decision to the voters. It did not try to decide the election. The same cannot be said for the U.S. Supreme Court, which stopped the clock and ended the game. And if that was all it was going to do, the resolution by the Court was no better than, and arguably was *worse* than, leaving the decision to Congress, an action that might have yielded a more principled, even if political, decision.

In conclusion, we wonder whether all of this matters. We think it does, although not for the reason that most commentators have identified. We are not certain whether the justices acted for purely partisan reasons, despite the evidence frequently cited. What concerns us more is that the Court's treatment of *Bush v. Gore* represents a kind of institutional arrogance in which it insists it has the last word on everything (Kramer 2001). And that is an attitude this Court has demonstrated before, also in derogation of Congress. In that regard, the dangers posed by *Bush v. Gore* may well extend beyond the once-in-a-lifetime situation presented in the election of 2000.

Chapter 11

Democratic Ends and Political Parties in America

WILLIAM CROTTY

CONTESTATION AND PARTICIPATION are the keys to the democratic process.[1] As an intermediary agency, political parties are the exemplary vehicles of contestation and participation. They forge the most vital and, simultaneously, the most vulnerable link between the mass electorate and the governing elite.

Democratic party systems build on the conflicts and cleavages natural to any social grouping. To win control of government, parties mobilize and promote these divisions and facilitate the peaceful resolution of conflict. Contestation exists both among and within parties. As an organization, each political party is a complex institution—a series of overlapping, intersecting, and even independent associations. In their search for power, parties promote participation. They mobilize mass support and articulate popular demands. In so doing, they contribute to a legitimization of government while serving as the bond between public preferences and elite decisions.

The vital importance of political parties to democratic government is underlined by recent efforts of many nations to mold truly open and representative political systems. Those efforts—many of them painful—involve experimentation with forms of party organizations and electoral arrangements best suited to the history, culture, and major divisions in the society. As it did in the United States, the willingness to engage in that experimentation provides a basic indicator of the centrality of parties to the democratic process.

While vital, parties are also vulnerable. Ethnic, religious, regional, economic, cultural, class, tribal, and geographic fault lines may all be building blocks of representative systems. These same divisions, however, may also constitute a source of political immobilization, even of political warfare. Nonetheless, all emerging democracies make efforts to implement party systems.

When they fail to channel contending interests into this mechanism of peaceful resolution, conflict can be catastrophic, as exemplified in the Balkans, Haiti, Somalia, and other nascent democracies.

As these nations illustrate, a party system and competitive popular elections are necessary but not sufficient for a democracy that truly works. An effective democratic system requires that contestants both win *and lose* elections, and that the losing party peacefully deliver control of the machinery of government to the winning party. In a working democracy, the competition of parties will achieve three vital democratic dynamics. First, those chosen for public office will reflect the preferences and demography of their constituents. Second, once in office, elites' actions will be guided by the need to answer—electorally or otherwise—to those who put them there. Third, electoral competition will enable the entire citizenry, constituting the brute force of politics, to maintain power through active involvement in the political process.

These dynamics suggest three criteria to assess the performance and contributions of these vital and vulnerable democratic agents. *Representativeness* appraises the extent to which parties actually reflect and promote the interests of their constituents. *Accountability* measures the extent to which they hold those in power responsible for their actions and election promises, most fundamentally, through elections. And, *participation* judges the mobilization capacity of the parties and the degree to which they include the mass public in the political decision-making process.

This chapter assesses the record of the American democratic party system on these criteria. Overall, the American party system does well in its representative function, has a mixed record of accountability, and does poorly in terms of the mobilization of participation. This deficiency significantly affects the problems of American democracy discussed in other chapters of this volume.

Representativeness

We begin with an examination of representativeness, the degree to which the parties and their elites reflect the views and composition of the citizenry. We focus on the ties to, and the changes in, the parties' relationship to the broader electorate and the extent to which party elites reflect the concerns and social characteristics of the party membership.

THE PARTIES' ROOTS IN THE ELECTORATE

According to the theory of "party-decline," the parties have suffered a diminished capacity to influence voter decision making by structuring the political world. Earlier studies showed political party identification to be the principal factor influencing voter decision making. More recent studies have questioned the primacy of the parties' influence, emphasizing instead the role of campaign issues and personal appeals in a candidate-centered political environment. The major shift appears to have taken place in the late 1960s and early 1970s.

Walter Dean Burnham has been particularly influential in assessing changes in the American electorate. In his seminal book, *Critical Elections and the Mainstream of American Politics* (1970), he analyzed the "dealignment" of the electorate from the parties, the increasing independence of voters in deciding on candidates, and the decreasing impact of the party on the electoral decision.

Other studies (Popkin 1994; Jackson and Crotty 2001; Dalton 2002) have demonstrated substantial fluctuation and decline in party identification over the decades. There has been an increase in the number of independents; party images are less positive and less compelling for voters; and split-ticket voting has become an election staple. The changes in party relevance are directly correlated with demographic factors, such as age—dealignment tendencies increase as one systematically moves toward younger voting groups. In itself, this cannot be a happy omen for party proponents.

In the contemporary context, the party works as a service agency for candidates seeking political office; candidate-centered campaigns now dominate contemporary politics. It is not that political parties disappear, but their impact on voting decisions and mass attraction has been threatened. Voters may well see political parties as less relevant in shaping electoral decisions. "Most voters now view parties as a convenience rather than as a necessity," Martin Wattenberg argues, so that "the key question is not whether political parties can survive in an atmosphere of dealignment, but rather whether they can still perform many of their key functions" (1991, 32).

The thesis of party decline, however, is disputed. Warren Miller and Merrill Shanks (1996) argued for the continuing importance of party identification as the standard for structuring voter decision making. They contended that events associated with the late 1960s and the early 1970s—Vietnam, Watergate, political assassinations, the civil rights revolution, counterculture demonstrations—affected the young in particular. This generational effect has had a lasting impact on the intensity of this age group's ties to the parties. The impact of these events was less pronounced on the older generations (see also Lawrence, 2001).

"The young reacted to the events of the period more sharply and possibly even more permanently than did the older cohorts," argues Miller. "It was the refusal and delay of the young in accepting partisan ties, *not the lasting rejection of the loyalties once held by their elders*, that produced the indicators of dealignment in the mid–1970s." But, later, these same groups "experienced a dramatic increase in both the incidence and the intensity of partisan sentiments," resulting in renewed partisanship (Miller 1994, 109; emphasis added).

Overall, while partisan identification has declined, it is still significant, and possibly even of increasing significance for those who vote. But, the parties are still deficient in their representation of all citizens. The parties do not reach out as systematically or as effectively as they might to organize or draw into the electorate the less politically sophisticated nonvoters and to many minority groups (Bartels 2000b).

While substantial disagreement exists as to the extent of partisan dealignment and its consequences, this discussion pales in comparison to efforts to explain the future directions of party loyalties in the electorate. A realignment of the New Deal party system, one that would reinvigorate the parties and position them as a force of primary relevance in contemporary politics, has long been anticipated. Although the parties' bases of support have changed greatly since the 1960s, none of these changes mobilized significant groups in the apolitical strata of the electorate or fundamentally altered the parties' demographic composition. The concept of realignment is irrelevant to the practice of contemporary politics.

PARTY ELITES AND THE PARTY BASE:
DEMOGRAPHIC AND ISSUE REPRESENTATION

If parties are still representative, who and what do they represent? We examine the congruence of issue positions and social group characteristics (age, region, religion, gender, income, and occupation) among political party leaders and followers (Crotty, Jackson, and Miller 1999; Miller 1987; Miller and Jennings 1986; Kirkpatrick 1976; McClosky et al. 1960; Lerner et al. 1996). Research consistently indicates several major tendencies:

1. There are significant differences on issue positions between the parties' elites and party identifiers. Compared to the rank and file, Democratic leaders are more liberal and support stronger government action in relation to social concerns. Similarly, Republican elites are considerably more conservative, emphasizing private initiatives and a restricted government role.

2. The followers of each party evidence the same differences, although the leaders are more intensely committed in their views than those at the parties' base. The parties' elites are also more consistent in their issue preferences over time than their parties' mass followers. At both levels, the parties are stable in their policy positions.

3. Particular social groups are overrepresented in party leadership positions. Their overrepresentation directly reflects the coalitions the parties appeal to in elections.

The Republican Party elites are generally more consistently in tune and closer to their party's base than are the Democrats, and the range of consent/dissent within the Republican Party is narrower than for the Democrats. On the other hand, the Democratic Party's coalition is broader and more heterogeneous than is the Republican Party's, a contributing factor to the poorer fit between mass and elites on policy.

A gender gap appears in the two parties' positioning on policies of direct relevance to women. Democratic leaders, in particular, as well as their followers, are far stronger in their commitment to women's rights than are the Republican leaders or followers. Underlining the difference, Democratic Party followers are even stronger in their support of these policies than is the Republican leadership.

In terms of demographic characteristics, Democratic national convention delegates are, on average, younger, better educated, and more "white" than party identifiers in the electorate—whites are overrepresented given the party's base, blacks underrepresented. There are no significant differences in relation to gender, one result of the reform movement of the early 1970s.

In turn, the Republican delegates, in contrast to their party identifiers, are younger and better educated (90 percent had attended college). No significant differences in relation to gender or regional representation were found, and in terms of race, the delegates had more minority representation than was found in the mass party's ranks (although both groupings had low levels of minority leadership, 9 percent and 5 percent respectively).

Regional differences are evident, reflecting the transformation of southern party loyalties—once solidly Democratic—to an equally strong commitment to the Republican Party. This is true for presidential and, increasingly, for congressional elections as well (Bullock and Rozell 1998). The Republican Party's leadership mirrors its growing reliance on southern support, exemplified by the emergence of Newt Gingrich as leader of the House Republicans in the 1990s and Trent Lott of Mississippi as the party leader in the Senate. For the first time in history, southerners constitute a majority of the Republican's House membership. The southern wing of the Democratic Party, in contrast, is underrepresented in its leadership structure.

A broad index of policy views and demographic characteristics shows that Republican elites are closer to their mass base on both policy and demography than are the Democrats (Crotty et al. 1999). There is a striking consistency in policy commitment and the opposing directions taken by the two parties over the years, despite changes in the political climate and leadership.

Overall, the parties do offer competing and consistent policy choices to the voting public. In an age when many might choose not to believe it, political parties do make a difference. As would be expected, the parties' leadership is more ideological, and more issue-sensitive, than the party's electoral base, which is more centrist. Republicans and Democrats mobilize different constituencies and offer the electorate contrasting ideologies and issue programs.

Taken as a whole, the parties appear to fulfill their representative roles remarkably well. While not to the extent they once did, they do affect the electorate's decision making, and their positioning in this regard has improved since the 1970s. As the views of the parties' elites demonstrate, they do offer meaningful choices on fundamental political issues. And elites do share common values and policy positions with the parties' base, and in greater depth, precision, and intensity. The parties do represent the opinion of their constituencies. Thus the American party system satisfies a basic requirement of democratic government.

Accountability

Accountability asks, *to whom are the parties responsible?* This criterion can be examined by looking at the parties' role in policy making—most particularly in Congress—and in the funding of campaigns. The key questions are, how well do the parties mobilize support—or opposition—in Congress for party programs or for presidential agendas? From whom do they receive the bulk of the funds needed for election to office? Does party finance distort, or reaffirm, a sense of accountability to a mass citizenry?

POLICIES, PARTIES, AND LEGISLATIVE SUPPORT PATTERNS

The cohesion and political loyalties of parties in Congress provide reasonable indicators of their accountability.[2] Among the most helpful of these indicators are the presidential support and party unity scores for the two parties. Presidential support scores measure votes for the issues on which the president took a clear stand. Party unity scores measure the loyalties of members on roll calls in which a majority of one party opposed the majority of the other party.

Presidential support scores mix the important with less important decisions; they do not specify the substance of the legislation submitted to the Congress nor the ambition of a president's reach. Some administrations attempt to institute fundamental change; others are content with the status quo (see Tichenor, this volume). Presidential success also varies by time; presidents tend to do better in their first year in office and during their first terms. Still, these scores do present useful measures of party cohesion and unity.

Some presidents are ambitious. Lyndon Johnson, for example, backed the most far-reaching and the most liberal domestic and civil rights programs in the post–World War II period. At the same time, his administration was embroiled in the divisive war in Vietnam and was constantly before the Congress seeking greater funding and support. Yet the majority of Senate Republicans consistently voted in favor of the president's agenda. Johnson had a well-earned reputation as a master legislative strategist and coalition builder (Greenstein 2000).

Ronald Reagan's presidency—also one of substance and ambition, although from the other end of the ideological spectrum—favored significant redirections in the government's social and fiscal policies. Opposition or support for his policies among Democrats fluctuated substantially. A majority of Democrats supported his policies in both his first and last years in office, compared to approximately one-third during his second term (Dallek 1999).

The reasons for support are complicated, and the levels vary. Still, looking at the broad picture, the direction of support is as it should be in a policy-differentiated party system: the overwhelming majority of party members support their president's position and, more often than not, oppose those of the opposition party's president.

Party loyalty in Congress is high, averaging about 70 percent in party unity scores among each political party in each administration. It has become substantially higher in recent years due to the greater polarization of the congressional parties along ideological lines in the Reagan years and in the post–1994 Congress. In more recent administrations, party unity figures have risen to the high 80s.

Political party does matter in Congress. There is a policy-based difference between the parties. The parties oppose each other consistently. They also support the programs of presidents of the same party and, although the figures are not as strong, the majority within a party does oppose the programs of presidents of the other party.

On another level, Gerald Pomper has convincingly shown that the parties' legislative agendas and policy outputs are directly related to their electoral platforms (Pomper and Lederman 1980). Contrary to conventional wisdom, party platforms constitute meaningful statements of party positions, the differences between the party positions, the constituencies courted, and the objectives and approaches the parties will pursue once in office. There is broad consistency in party ideologies, most obviously in the treatment of traditional economic priorities that have long served to mark the parties' commitments and reflect their constituencies (Gerring 2001). The major parties are also consistently different in their responses to more contemporary social and lifestyle issues, such as rights of women and gays and lesbians.

The parties in their way, as crude and imperfect as they may be, do present conflicting approaches to government and do represent the interests of competing social and economic groups. After election, the parties' elected members pull together to enact their programs and to support presidents of their party and oppose those of the other. They offer programmatic alternatives to the voters and then attempt to legislate those commitments when elected. The parties act as reasonably cohesive policy machines linking electors, candidates, and issue votes. They provide a bond between the citizen base and policy positioning by the parties in office, a critical link in the chain of democratic representation.

POLITICAL PARTIES AND POLITICAL FUNDING

Accountability may have a different meaning—a financial obligation to campaign contributors. The funding of campaigns has been a perennial concern—the subject of sporadic reform efforts since the founding of the party system (Corrado 1993; Farrar-Myers and Dwyre 2001; Lubenow 2001; Bartels 2000a). The financing of political campaigns—both the extraordinary cost and the principal sources of funding—helps explain failures of both representation and accountability. The money does not come from a mass base of small contributors, but rather from the concentrations of economic power already dominant in the society. The consequence, in part, is party accountability to the major economic forces in society, resulting in an overrepresentation of some interests, and underrepresentation of many others. This imbalance frequently skews policy outcomes on behalf of those already better positioned in society.

Problems of democratic accountability are evident in the current state of campaign funding and the parties' financing. Campaigns are expensive and the costs have continued to escalate, reaching record levels in the 2000 campaign (Pomper 2001a; Crotty 2001). Furthermore, intended reforms have substantially failed in limiting costs and controlling individual contributions and overall campaign expenditures. These failures overshadow the political parties' significant and increasingly controversial role in political funding, in particular, in acting as fund-raising agencies for candidates and in promoting the reelection of incumbents (White and Shea 2000; Wattenberg 1991; Crotty 1977).

The 2000 election exemplifies the broad dimensions of the financing problem. It was the most expensive in history. Estimates have put the total spent on national races as high as $3 billion with another $1 billion spent on state races (Salant 2000). Some of the records broken (based on information from the Federal Election Commission) included the following: most money raised and spent by a single presidential candidate (George W. Bush); most money spent by a presidential candidate in the primaries (Bush); most federal matching funds ever awarded a presidential contender (Al Gore); most "soft money"— the focal point for recent reform efforts—by a political party (Republicans); most money raised by congressional candidates; most money raised and spent in an individual Senate race; most money raised and spent in an individual House race; most money raised in party fund-raisers. The results are impressive, but chances are that most, if not all, of these historic sums will be surpassed in the next election, and the elections after that, and so on.

CAMPAIGN FINANCE, REFORM, AND REPRESENTATION

The common assumption is that those who pay for the campaign expect their rewards through desired legislation, favorable administrative rulings, government contracts, personnel appointed to government and regulatory positions, and general assistance in achieving economic and policy ends. Against the backdrop of this assumption, the Center for Responsive Politics, a Washington-based citizens' watchdog group that monitors campaign expenditures, identifies the objectives of reform as the following:

> *political equality:* "Every person's vote should count the same as every
> other person's vote . . . wealth or lack of it, should not determine a
> person's opportunity of influence within the political system"; and
> *public accountability:* "If democracy has any meaning at all, it is clear
> that government must not only be representative of the people in its
> composition, but those in government must also *represent* the
> people—voicing their constituents' concerns and acting in their
> interests. It is the *public* interest . . . that must always take precedence
> over more narrow private interests." (Center for Responsive Politics
> 1996)

What can be said about the realization of those objectives? At this point everyone—Republicans, Democrats, candidates, and the public—would agree that the regulations on campaign financing have failed. Renewed efforts at reform are being made but are not likely to make a significant impact in the long run. Few have to date. The pull of money, the need for ever-increasing amounts of campaign funding, and the close association between funding, party, and candidate ensure that statutes are likely to be weakened by the courts, additional legislation, or rulings of the Federal Election Commission.

The history of these reforms is that they are eroded over time, their provisions often go ignored by candidates, and enforcement is lax or nonexistent.

A few facts: few Americans contribute to campaigns. Ninety-four to 96 percent made no contributions of any kind at any level for the three most recent presidential election cycles. Roughly one-third of 1 percent give contributions of $200 or more to congressional candidates, and individual contributions of less than $200 accounted for no more than one-fifth of the total funds spent. One zip code area in New York City gave more to congressional candidates than the total contributions of those living in twenty-four states. People earning more than $75,000 a year are 100 times more likely to contribute to political campaigns than those earning $15,000 a year. Mass giving is not the basis of campaign funding.

The presumption is that political contributions bring political favors. There may not be a direct payoff—a sum of money contributed in return for a given vote or a piece of legislation (in itself illegal)—but the expectation is that a recipient will be favorably disposed to a contributor and help promote his or her interests. At a minimum, this means providing the contributors with hearings on their concerns or, where useful, running interference with regulators or administrative agencies. Scandals from Watergate, to the Keating Five, to the Clinton administration's alleged interference with trade policy in exchange for foreign contributions, to Enron, all seem to indicate that funders anticipate favors.

Thomas Ferguson has taken this argument the furthest in his "investment theory" of politics. By tracing the source of campaign funding to the parties and their candidates, he argues, one can predict the issues both parties will push and their policy positions once in office. "The American political system is not . . . driven by votes. Public opinion has only a weak and inconstant influence on policy. The political system is largely investor-driven, and runs on enormous quantities of money." The policy agenda is attuned to the concerns of the investors and it is distinctly one-sided, resulting in "increasingly radical versions of 'laissez faire' economics . . . demands for tax 'relief,' freedom from regulation, cuts in social welfare expenditures, labor cost reductions and tighter control of increasingly decentralized production systems" (Ferguson 2001, 235–36; see also Ferguson 1995).

How campaigns are financed, where the money comes from, what restrictions are implemented, where the public funding is spent, all directly impact the political parties and may well be the single greatest influence on who is elected to serve in political office and the policy outcomes of the overall process. The present system yields limited party accountability and access biased in favor of those with the economic resources needed to fund campaigns.

Participation

In a democratic polity, citizen participation is a crucial measure of party performance. The parties' expected role is to mobilize a broad range of interests, involve those interests in campaigns and elections, and, through this process, develop stronger bonds between citizens and government.

Contestation and participation are keys to assessing the quality and vitality of a nation's commitment to democracy. Necessary conditions for a democracy include the equality of all citizens, the right to formulate their preferences and to voice them individually or collectively, and the recognition of each individual's preference without discrimination. "Regimes . . . vary in the proportion of the population entitled to participate on a more or less equal plane in controlling and contesting the conduct of the government . . . When a regime grants this right to some of its citizens, it moves toward greater public contestation . . . the larger the proportion of citizens who enjoy the right, the more inclusive the regime" (Dahl 1971, 4).

In reality, however, American policy making shows only a restricted public involvement. For many it is not enough. Benjamin Barber argues on behalf of "strong democracy" and advocates "a systematic program of participatory reform . . . Strong democracy looks to wage a second war for suffrage, a second campaign to win the substance of citizenship promised but never achieved by the winning of the vote" (1984, 264–66). Such views indicate the fundamental importance attached to the need for broad participation in political choices in a democracy and the adverse potential consequences of a restricted base of political involvement. (For a different argument, see Schumpeter 1950.)

The most inclusive and effective agency for ensuring such a degree of participation is the political party. The growth of parties is directly associated with the expansion of the electorate, contributing in turn to a more participatory-oriented and broadly democratic polity (Keyssar 2000; Crotty 1977). The logic of electoral success would presumably foster reaching and mobilizing the greatest number of voters in support of a party's or a candidate's cause. "The very nature of elections motivates political leaders to mobilize public involvement: More votes than the opposition means victory . . . the essential feature of electoral politics . . . is electoral mobilization" (Rosenstone and Hansen 1993, 161).

As obvious as this logic may appear, it is not empirically true (Conway 2001a, 200). A less apparent but forceful dynamic is at work here; parties attempt to reach those potential supporters *most likely to vote*, focusing campaigns on the "real electorate." Strategically, "political leaders do not try to mobilize everybody, and they do not try to mobilize all of the time. Mobilization . . . is not their real goal; they have little interest in citizen activism per se. Rather, they seek to use public involvement to achieve other ends: to win elections, to pass bills, to modify rulings, to influence policies" (Rosenstone and Hansen 1993, 30). Alternative party movements may be needed to expand the political universe.

POLITICAL PARTIES AND THE MOBILIZATION OF THE ELECTORATE

To put the matter up front, voter turnout is a chronic problem and one of the most extraordinary failures of political parties and the political system more generally. The United States consistently has had the lowest turnout of voters among industrialized democratic nations. This record belies the meaning of democracy—the participation of all, or as many as possible, in deciding the nation's direction.

E. E. Schattschneider called the low rate of participation in elections "the *sickness* of democracy." He raised the question, What is "the limit of tolerance of passive abstention" within the American system? No one has yet to answer it. But, as Schattschneider further asked: "Why should anyone worry?" His answer: "If we have lost the capacity to involve an ever-expanding public into the political system, it is obvious that American democracy has arrived at a turning point" (Schattschneider 1960, 97–98, 102; see also Barber 1998b).

The major way to stimulate significant change in public policy is through an expansion of the political community. Extensions of the electorate have historically been a by-product of the party conflict. Political parties are the principal agents for creating a more inclusive electorate and for expanding the frontiers of democratic decision making. Currently, they are not doing an acceptable job.

Over 60 percent (63 percent to 69 percent by some counts) of the eligible electorate voted in presidential contests of the 1960s. Since then, there has been a gradual but persistent decline in turnout. Roughly half the electorate now votes in presidential races (49.1 percent in 1996, 50.7 percent in 2000), and only one-third to 40 percent in midterm congressional races.

A distinct pattern divides participants and nonparticipants (Teixeira 1992). Those less likely to vote include those with the least formal education, those of lower socioeconomic status, minorities, younger people, and those not affiliated with a political party or having a low level of interest in campaigns or election outcomes. America shows a class-stratified electorate: those of higher socioeconomic status participate in politics; those of lower socioeconomic standing do not. In contrast, mass parties in other democracies organize lower socioeconomic groupings and mobilize them in elections, resulting in turnout rates similar to that of middle-class voters.

Other modes of political participation are similarly stratified. M. Margaret Conway writes: "Citizens of higher socioeconomic status are more likely to engage in several kinds of political activities, including organizational and campaign activities and contacting public officials as well as voting in elections. . . . They also perform each of these activities more frequently" (Conway 2001a, 21; see also Junn, this volume; Verba, Schlozman, and Brady 1995).

Registration barriers to the vote have lessened substantially in recent decades, although the American system of personal registration presents more of an obstacle than that experienced in other countries. The "Motor Voter" law enacted prior to the 1996 election added an estimated ten million new voters to the rolls. Yet as registration barriers have weakened since the 1960s, participation levels have not increased, holding at around one-half of those eligible in presidential contests (Flanigan and Zingale 1998, 46).

No one has a clear answer as to why this is or what can be done. Conway has shown that the strongest correlate of increased turnout, and the most effective way to get people to the polls, is through party- or candidate-sponsored door-to-door canvassing (Conway 2001a, 2001b). Personal contacting works, yet it is arguably the least used and most neglected aspect of the participation puzzle. In the words of Michael Dukakis, there has been a "virtual disappearance of genuine partisan grassroots politics in America" (Dukakis 2001, 3).

We see a party system more unified and cohesive at elite levels, and well designed to service such elites in election campaigns and in office, but one less effective at the mass level. The parties and candidates confine their campaign appeals to the known or most likely voters in the established voting universe, reluctant to venture into uncertain waters through expensive and unpredictable efforts to mobilize those with weaker political attachments. The result, in effect, is a middle-class electorate. Its interests are what both parties choose to address in campaigns, taking the safest road to electoral success, but one that excludes many of those otherwise eligible to vote.

Nonvoters are indirectly represented, if at all, in policy decisions, depending on the goodwill of officeholders to protect their interests and provide for their needs. Given the ferocity of political battles over the distribution of resources, it is not by accident that they lose out in most policy decisions and that they are the first targets for reductions in the benefits that they do receive (see Hirschmann, this volume, and Gans 1995). It is a vulnerable position and one fully exploited by those representing the privileged. Politicians need scapegoats in policy making. Those who do not vote are not part of the active electorate, wield no power of any consequence, nor exercise any potential sanctions over officeholders. Consequently, they constitute easy and inviting targets.

THIRD PARTYISM AS AN ALTERNATIVE TO THE MAJOR PARTIES

If the major parties fall short in broadening the bounds of participation, third parties or alternative party alignments might appear as a reasonable alternative. Historically, such movements have had an allure. Historian Lawrence Goodwin, writing on the Populists of the late nineteenth century, captures the sense of promise and democratic fulfillment such parties can offer. "Populism" he writes, was "the spirit of egalitarian hope . . . expansive, passionate, flawed, creative—above all, enhancing in its assertion of human striving" (Goodwin 1978, 295).

These sentiments expressed the type of ideals to which many third-party movements aspire: individual citizens banded together to electorally overthrow the old order as represented in the politics, economics, and political parties of the day. The goal was to realize the highest aspirations of the American democratic culture.

The reality is that such parties seldom if ever live up to their promises (Rosenstone, Behr, and Lazarus 1984). There have been many third and minor party movements, and few have enjoyed any electoral success or had any direct impact on policy making. To find up to twenty minor parties on the ballot of a presidential election is not unusual. To find any that qualify as "political parties" involving extended participatory or representative interests is equally rare.

The two most recent efforts of consequence have been Ross Perot's Reform Party (1992, 1996) and Ralph Nader's Green Party (2000). Perot's group was basically an extension of himself, his views, and his personal wealth. The movement managed to capture 20 percent of the popular vote in the 1992 presidential election, the most since Theodore Roosevelt's Bull Moose Party in 1912. In the 1996 election, the percentage of Perot's support dropped to 8 percent, still a remarkable showing. By the 2000 election the party, under new leadership (the party had split and, in a strange and controversial move, chose ultraconservative Pat Buchanan as its presidential candidate) had splintered and was vanishing into history, receiving less then 1 percent of the vote.

The Reform Party's success was unlikely and unexpected, yet it won no electoral votes. As with the vast majority of other third parties, it became one more well-intentioned but abortive attempt to provide an alternative to the major parties and to force an agenda. Perot's strength can be seen as a barometer of the major parties' weaknesses. Historically, third parties do well when there is a clear and widespread dissatisfaction with the two principal parties and their leadership.

One aspect of the Perot candidacy should give pause. Perot ignored traditional methods of campaigning—the rallies, speeches, pressing the flesh, and personal contact familiar to all campaigns and a critical link in person-to-person retail politics. Perot did little of this in 1992 and even less in 1996. His focus instead was on the union of technology and wealth. His personal fortune fueled the campaign. He then depended on television—free TV if offered, paid television if necessary—to get his message across. Traditional party operations—rooted in communities, its representation favoring local needs and broad recruitment efforts—were foreign to his campaign.

Perot essentially rendered parties irrelevant, except as targets for his campaign rhetoric. He circumvented the normal party structures with his message attacking their lack of credibility and relevance as, according to him, the cause of the nation's inability to meet its most critical problems. It is an appeal and an electoral strategy that other contenders to public office might use in the future and one that, if it enjoys increasing success, may well signal a further weakening of party politics.

Ralph Nader was another story. A consumer advocate with a national reputation for more than four decades, he ran as the Green Party's nominee. At first his campaign attracted little attention. He appealed to a liberal constituency, railed against both major parties as being in the pocket of corporate interests, and claimed they provided little real choice for Americans (Nader 2001).

Nader's message was a populistic blend of anticorporatism and pro-consumerism, pro-environment, and pro–women's rights. It was familiar to those who had followed his career and incorporated themes long endorsed by Democrats. Al Gore touched on similar issues at different points in the 2000 primary and general election campaigns but never consistently developed or identified with them. Had he done so—or, less likely, had the Republican candidate—Nader's support would have eroded.

Rather than identifying commonalties among third-party voters, a look at the Nader and Perot supporters indicates, in part, the range of types and functions of such parties in a determinedly two-party system. The Perot appeal was essentially based on a nonspecific "good government" reaction against what he (and his supporters) saw as corruption and incompetence in the contemporary political scene. Those who supported him tended to be moderates both in their political sympathies and in cultural matters (Menendez 1996). They had two other characteristics in common: weak ties to the body politic and a weak or nonexistent identification with the major parties. They displayed a vague discontent with the way things were.

Nader's constituency was quite different. He was a factional candidate, appealing most strongly to liberal Democrats. In their second choices, likely Nader voters favored Gore two to one. It was a liberal uprising against decades of centrist (the Clinton and Carter presidencies) to conservative/right wing tendencies (the Reagan years) in the parties and in government. Nader's candidacy was an effort to push the party system, and in particular Democrats, back to a more pro-government, pro-consumer, distribute-the-wealth direction. Nader has vowed to continue what he refers to as his "crusade" in future elections. More likely, his efforts will end up much as Perot's movement, a footnote to history in a two-party system.

Most minor parties are obscure ideological and single-issue groups, frivolous movements marginal to the political scene, and little known to the public. They are largely ignored by the mass media and are of little or no consequence to elections (the critical exception being Nader's impact on the Florida vote in the 2000 presidential election). These efforts indicate the irrelevance of such party efforts and the difficulty of contesting the major parties. At present it is virtually impossible to mount a successful campaign in opposition to the two major parties' dominance. In this regard, Perot's and Nader's efforts, whatever their failings, have still been remarkable. They may also serve as a barometer of public disaffection from the parties.

The dream dies hard, however. The commitment to a purer democratic form and a popular-based political movement, arising to challenge a corrupt and ineffective political system, has had a continuing appeal. George Wallace, John Anderson, Barry Commoner's Citizen Party in the early 1980s, former Sen. Eugene McCarthy's third and independent party movements of the 1960s and 1970s, and Perot's and Nader's efforts are but recent examples.

There appears to be a role for third and minor parties as vehicles for discontent and potential mobilizers of broader participation. They all dream the dream of the Republican Party of Lincoln, moving from minor to dominant party status in the American system. The fact that only one party has done it, however, indicates the odds.

The Future and Political Parties

The state of the parties serves as a guide to the effectiveness of the political system in meeting citizens' political expectations (Aldrich 1995; Coleman 1996; Maisel 2001; Cohen et al. 2001; Burnham 1982; Ginsburg and Stone 1996; Pomper 2001b). How relevant are contemporary political parties to the current issues of concern to broad constituencies? How accountable are they to the democratic public? Is the candidate-centered, permanent-campaign party system neglectful, if not destructive, of other valuable party contributions, such as voter mobilization and the organization of mass electorates? If so, what if anything can or should be done about it?

From a broad democratic perspective, parties are charged with bridging the gap between public officeholders and the mass citizenry in order to make a democracy representative. If this connection is absent, then the political system replicates the very problem the parties evolved to address, unrepresentative and unresponsive government. If the party elite is unbound by mass party views and unrepresentative of mass concerns, then the breakdown between the mass public and the political elite occurs not in the governing arena, but within the parties' own decision-making and accountability processes. The results could be serious and the consequences as fundamental as if the breakdown occurred within public institutions.

While not yet critical, this problem does bear watching. The party elites are still broadly representative of the rank and file and, even if primarily for elective purposes, still sensitive to their policy needs and their priorities. Would a different type of party system, however envisioned, better serve the nation's needs? If so, how could it be implemented? Although discussed in academic circles, there is no broad call for some form of multiparty system or preference voting. At present these possibilities are no more than speculative.

Questions do remain about the ability of the parties to deal with current policy issues. Of particular concern are the capacity of the parties to meet both economic problems—a globally interdependent economic world order and the increasing polarization of wealth in the United States—and political problems—a nation engaging in a war on terrorism and the pervasive mood of alienation and disillusionment in American politics.

MACROECONOMIC POLICY

Can the traditional party system cope with the demands of a globally interdependent economy? Political parties are instruments of national representation built on a domestic issue base. International party systems are visionary and impractical; they will not come to pass. If this is the case, how then do the parties represent public concerns and influence international policies that directly affect the livelihood of their constituents?

Macroeconomic policy and the direction of international trade and financing are not issues discussed, much less settled, in a broad public arena. Yet worldwide interdependence will set the economic character of the nation during the twenty-first century. Can political parties change appropriately so as to intelligently meet the demands of the new world order? Or are many of these issues beyond what parties, and by extension the mass public, can or should concern themselves with? If so, what then is the role of political parties in relation to the most fundamental economic and foreign policy issues in the coming decades? How will these issues affect the parties' contribution to the democratic tenets of representation, accountability, and participation?

In another economic context, can the political parties address the problem of an increasingly class-divided society experiencing an upward redistribution of wealth, a trend beginning in the 1970s, accelerating during the eighties, and continuing to this day (see McWilliams, this volume; Phillips 1990). The transformation is moving the United States from a country with one of the more equitable distributions of wealth in the period after World War II to the one with the largest gap between the rich and those of lesser means among industrial democratic nations. Parties contributed to these trends through conscious redesign of tax laws and social policies during the 1980s and 1990s. These laws could be revised, and government could again serve as the principal agent for the redistribution of wealth in a more equitable and, at least since the New Deal, more familiar manner.

PARTIES IN CONTEMPORARY POLITICS

American politics was permanently changed on September 11, 2001. Terrorism on the scale experienced on 9/11 constitutes a new challenge for the American people and for the parties. American political parties are not given to violence as a technique. They are conflict-avoidance and conflict-resolution mechanisms that operate best within a peaceful democratic setting. To function, they depend on the foundations of an open society: freedom of assembly, free speech, freedom of movement, a free press, the right to dissent and oppose, and the recognition of the primacy of human rights. How well will they operate in a "security state"? Their contribution will be to continue their representative, accountability, and participatory activities, although in a changed environment.

Even without the fears engendered by terrorism, alienation, frustration, disillusionment, apathy, and withdrawal in American politics appear pervasive. Findings that antiparty sentiments have increased in recent decades (Owen et al. 2001) seem more troubling when viewed against the lack of direction and inability to control larger economic, governmental, and broader social forces that seem to underlie modern life. What can be done about it?

Dahl believes that political parties directly contribute to the current malaise: "the capacity of our political parties to integrate diverse interests has dramatically declined . . . During the last several decades, at the electoral level they have become more fragmented than ever before . . . local, state and national party organizations have dissolved into loosely attached collections of individual political entrepreneurs who have their own organizations, agendas, and finances" (Dahl 1994, 1–2). Dahl rates the chances for meaningful reform of the parties "decidedly dim," although he would introduce the public funding of elections as one corrective.

The Future of the Parties

It may be that the political parties are the product of an older, slower, and more traditional age in American society. It may be that their ability to deal with contemporary social problems is severely limited. It may be, in short, that their day has passed. If so, what institutions would take their place? None appear on the horizon that can perform the functions necessary for a democratic order as well as parties have. It may also be that parties' problems are minor and transitory and that, as proved time and again throughout their history, they will adjust and adapt (see Aldrich 1995).

That future will depend greatly on the ability of the parties to promote increased public participation. All of the authors in this volume argue the significance of participation, but the forms it takes and the impact it makes (an empirical analysis) or should make (a normative judgment) vary considerably. Participation is affected by constitutional design (Hochschild, Hansen), basic structural factors (Junn), social inequalities (McWilliams, Hirschmann), civil liberty (Schochet), and the institutional processes of legislatures (Polsby, Rosenthal), the presidency (Tichenor), and the courts (Garrett, and Heumann and Cassak).

Participation in politics and policymaking is a multifaceted, kaleidoscopic and dynamic process contributing to a variety of outcomes. The basic premise of these authors is that it *should* be a factor—and for many in this volume, a determining force—in setting the nation's agenda and in representing the public's interests. The extent to which it achieves these ends is still debatable.

Given that uncertainty, what then can we say about the significance of the most important of the intermediary agencies—political parties—in performing their roles within the democratic system and in relation to the broader issue of the quality of democracy in twenty-first-century America? Quite obviously, the parties could do much better, particularly in regard to mobilization. Popular participation in political decision making may well be the weak link in contemporary American democratic governance. The institutions that have evolved to provide such involvement and the extent to which they perform this function rank among the most fundamental of contemporary concerns addressed by the presentations in this volume.

There is a new political order in the making, one whose outlines are not yet clear, but one likely to make unfamiliar demands on the party system. We may hope, as in the past, the parties will credibly provide representation, accountability, and mobilization. We may also hope that the past will prove a guide to the future: the parties will, over time, adapt and with luck prosper in the new society.

Chapter 12

Contentious Democracy

Presidential-Interest Group Relations in a Madisonian System

DANIEL J. TICHENOR

AMERICAN PRESIDENTIAL POWER has grown dramatically, if unevenly, over the past century. Economic crises, international relations, national security imperatives, and the advent of television as the ultimate bully pulpit have contributed to the drift of power from legislative to executive hands, a trend only reinforced by the terrorist assaults of September 11. Despite the philosophical tensions between executive leadership and democratic politics, ordinary citizens have increasingly viewed the U.S. presidency as a popular office capable of making the government responsive to democratic needs (Lowi 1985; Tulis 1987; Stuckey 1991; Genovese 2000). During these same years, an unprecedented array of organized interests became active in Washington (Tichenor and Harris 2003). This is especially true of the past three decades, which have accommodated staggering increases in the number, variety, and activities of interest groups engaged in national political life (Schlozman and Tierney 1986; Berry 1999).

The modern presidency and national interest group system loom today as dominant elements of the American political system. Remarkably, however, scholars have made little or no effort to investigate their pivotal interactions. To adequately assess the future of democratic politics in the United States, it is crucial to analyze the interplay of modern presidents and interest groups. This chapter examines how the relationship between presidents and interest groups generally influences the character and outcomes of American domestic policy making and, in particular, how that relationship affects nonincremental reform.

Committed democrats have ample reason to view presidential leadership and interest group lobbying alike with deep skepticism, if not hostility. Executive power fosters a passive and deferential citizenry that is ill-equipped to sustain the participatory lifeblood of democracy. Critics such as Thomas Paine warned early on that leadership is a "slavish custom" poorly suited for representative systems in which citizens are proprietors in government (Miroff 1993, 2). And to the extent that executive power is a necessary supplement to "rule by the people," it constitutes one of democracy's most glaring embarrassments. Likewise, interest groups are thought to subvert democracy by pursuing agendas that undermine the broader interests shared but poorly articulated by most ordinary citizens. Moreover, the uneven level and effectiveness of interest group representation in the Washington policy-making process at once reflects and reinforces deep-seated democratic inequalities.

Yet both presidential and interest group politics are at least theoretically capable of advancing democratic purposes. According to Woodrow Wilson, one of the principal founders of the modern presidency, the national electorate chooses a president to advance popular programmatic reforms often frustrated by conservative interests and political structures. Convinced that positive government was necessary to check the power of entrenched interests, he believed the president was uniquely positioned to serve as a democratic "spokesman for the real sentiment and purpose of the country, by giving direction to opinion" (Milkis 1993, 28). In sum, the unity and energy of the presidency make it a potentially powerful agent of the people when its incumbents attempt to overcome the American polity's many formalistic constraints for the sake of democratic ends.

A vibrant interest group system also holds democratic promise. Interest groups are expected to flourish in democracies precisely because they give people the freedom to organize for the purpose of influencing public policy. More significantly, interest groups provide a vehicle for connecting citizens to government. As Jeffrey Berry puts it, "They empower people by organizing those citizens with similar interests and expressing those interests to policymakers" (Berry 1999, 15).

As we shall see, the democratic possibilities of presidential and interest group politics are inescapably bound up together. This chapter first introduces a theoretical model of presidential interest group interactions in national policy making. Two important variables affect the likelihood that presidents and interest groups will support or frustrate one another in the pursuit of major policy innovation: whether powerful organized interests are affiliated or unaffiliated with the president's political party and whether historical circumstances afford the president a broad or narrow capacity to exercise policy leadership. This model generates four distinctive forms of presidential interest group interactions: collaborative breakthrough politics, adversarial breakthrough politics, collaborative politics-as-usual, and adversarial politics-as-usual. Subsequent sections of the chapter offer historical case studies that illuminate each type of interactive politics. Along the way, we shall find that presidents and interest groups regularly derail each other's most significant reform ambitions. It is little wonder that conflict and estrangement are recurrent if not inevitable features of presidential interest group relations in domestic policy making, as each actor blames the other for frustrating meaningful democratic change.

Contentious Elites: A Framework of Presidential Interest Group Relations

Ambivalence and contention are sewn into the nature of presidential interest group relations. Modern executives have numerous reasons either to openly battle with, or to keep their distance from, organized interests. Although millions of Americans financially support specific interest groups, the public regularly views organized interests in national politics with a level of contempt and suspicion comparable to that of our wary constitutional architects (Petracca 1992). As the only U.S. officials elected by the entire nation, modern presidents often have cast themselves as guardians of the common good at war with entrenched special interests. "Fifteen million people in the United States are represented by lobbyists," Harry S. Truman liked to say. "The other 150 million have only one man who is elected at large to represent them— that is, the President of the United States" (Deakin 1966). It is a seductive refrain intoned by most modern presidents. Conversely, administrations that seem too closely aligned with particular interest groups risk charges of serving special interests. George W. Bush learned this early in his presidency when his stands on issues such as arctic drilling, arsenic levels in drinking water, and global warming provoked criticism that he was cozying up to well-heeled corporate powers. Presidential aversion to organized interests is accentuated by the fact that entrenched Washington lobbies routinely frustrate the president's programmatic goals.

At the same time, interest groups have compelling reasons to concentrate their energies on government institutions other than the presidency. Relative to the Washington establishment's time horizons, presidents appear as something of political transients. While congressional members and federal bureaucrats typically enjoy long tenures in office, an individual president's hold on power is comparatively brief. Leaving aside the tempos of executive efficacy over the course of a single administration, the average tenure of postwar presidents is less than six years. Furthermore, gaining access to the White House can be a tall order for a lobbyist because of the enormous constraints on the time and attention of presidents and their key advisers. By contrast, the size and specialized work of Congress and federal agencies make them far more accessible to interest groups. As one political insider put it, "There are 535 opportunities in Congress and only one in the White House. Where would you put your effort?" (Light 1999). In short, interest group relationships with congressional members and federal bureaucrats are likely to be longer lasting and more reliable than those with White House officials.

Although the disincentives for close presidential interest group relations are considerable, rarely can either comfortably disregard the other. Indeed, they do so at their own political peril. Organized interests are significant elements of executive electoral coalitions. In an era of candidate-centered campaigns, interest groups provide money, organizational support, and votes for presidential hopefuls during their primary and general election bids (Wayne 1998). Once in office, modern presidents stake their claim as successful leaders largely on whether they regularly can build supportive coalitions for their policies. Along with political parties, organized interests can offer the White House a potent and efficient means of expanding support for the president's agenda in Congress and other venues. However, presidents must also consider that interest groups can just as surely serve as continuous sources of mobilized opposition.

For their part, interest groups cannot ignore the enormous power modern executives wield over public agenda-setting, policy formation, federal budgeting, and implementation. Presidents also have the capacity to alter the prevailing interest group system they encounter. They can encourage the creation of new organized interests, actively work to demobilize others, and even influence how interest groups frame their preferences in the first place (Ginsburg and Shefter 1988). The modern presidency presents interest groups with significant structural opportunities and constraints to which they must attend. Whether as allies or rivals, policy-minded presidents and interest groups cannot discount each other in a political system designed to "counteract ambition with ambition" (Hamilton and Madison 1961, 322).

Efforts to analyze presidential interest group relations are hampered by the fact that the presidency and the national interest group system are anything but static. Each evolves in terms of its size and influence. Moreover, these processes of change are not necessarily independent of one another; the presidential establishment plays some role in transformations of the interest group system and vice versa. There are several specific areas of study of presidential interest group relations, such as election campaigns, party politics, executive appointments, judicial nominations and confirmations, executive orders, and major legislation. But one way to generalize about the interactions between modern presidents and interest groups—that is, to identify patterns and draw analytical insights about their reciprocal relations—is to focus on two factors that help structure presidential interest group politics: (1) the relationship of interest groups to the president's party; and (2) the relative opportunities for presidential policy leadership.

It is an old saw of political science that vigorous political parties and interest groups are fundamentally at odds with one another (Dahl 1982, 190). In truth, both major American parties are linked to interest groups, and both nurture interest group coalitions that will help their candidates to win office and their officeholders to govern. "Whether observed in the electoral or lobbying arenas," Mark Peterson notes, "a significant portion of the interest group community reflects ideological positions, takes stands on the issues of the day, or represents constituencies whose orientations are at least compatible with one of the two major parties" (Peterson 1992a, 239–40).

While reassuring the general public of their eagerness to stand up to "special interests," modern presidents and their political advisers readily understand the importance of party-affiliated interest groups in constructing successful electoral coalitions and governing majorities. Franklin D. Roosevelt, for example, established mechanisms by which White House staff members could attend to the groups comprising his loose New Deal coalition, including organized labor, nationality groups, and small farmers (Pika 1987). Subsequent presidents have followed suit by placing at least some priority on interest group affairs for electoral and programmatic purposes and by institutionalizing presidential liaison with groups through both formal (for example, the Office of Public Liaison) and informal means (Patterson 1988).

Not all interest groups, of course, pursue access to or alliances with the White House. For ideological and strategic reasons, groups unaffiliated with the president's party may advance outsider strategies, such as campaigns to garner media attention and public support. For the purposes of our analytical model, the relationship of interest groups to the president's party (ranging from closely affiliated to staunchly unaffiliated) is crucial because it takes stock of both *collaborative* and *adversarial* forms of interaction.

What are the implications of collaborative and adversarial relations when the opportunities for modern executives to advance their domestic policy agendas are broad or narrow? Which interest groups fare better—those aligned with executives who dominate the policy-making process for a time or those actively opposed to weaker presidents who possess few chances for policy leadership? Which interest groups fare worse—those opposed to dominant executives or those aligned with politically vulnerable incumbents? Taking stock of variation in presidential leadership capacities allows us to address these compelling questions.

Among the most prominent factors shaping presidential opportunities to exercise policy leadership are levels of partisan and ideological support in Congress, electoral margins, public moods, popular approval levels, issue cycles, and economic and foreign policy crises (Hargrove and Nelson 1984; Mayhew 1991; Light 1999; Lammers and Genovese 2000). By most accounts, few presidents have enjoyed broad opportunities to dominate the policy-making process and to advance their reform agendas *(breakthrough politics)*. Presidential scholars tend to agree that the political context was exceptionally favorable for Woodrow Wilson, Franklin Roosevelt, Lyndon Johnson, and Ronald Reagan (at least for his first two years in office) to exercise policy leadership (Hargrove and Nelson 1984; Lammers and Genovese 2000). Most modern presidents have had to struggle with more challenging leadership circumstances in which their capacities to reshape public policy have been relatively narrow *(politics-as-usual)*.

As table 12.1 illustrates, four types of interactive politics emerge when we consider together the relationship of interest groups to the president's party (affiliated or unaffiliated) and the relative capacity of a president to exercise policy leadership (broad or narrow).[1]

One might expect *collaborative breakthrough politics* to be the most advantageous for interest groups based on the assumption that presidents with broad leadership capacities will handsomely reward their group allies. But more often than not, that is not the case. The logic of presidential dominance dictates that the fortunes of allied interest groups are contingent upon and subsumed by White House priorities. When the reform agendas of strong presidents and supportive interest groups closely overlap, groups are indeed likely to win important policy achievements. But they are just as likely to be marginalized when their goals are either contradictory or peripheral to presidential priorities. Where there are creative tensions, presidents trump group allies. The relationship of dominant executives to closely aligned interest groups also can entail significant White House sponsorship and control, resulting in a profound transformation of group identities and preferences. As the case of Franklin D. Roosevelt and the labor movement will illustrate, cooptation is often the price interest groups pay for their engagement in collaborative breakthrough politics.

As much as collaboration with strong presidents is less rewarding for in-

Table 12.1
Presidents and Interest Groups: A Model of Interactive Politics

		Relationship of Interest Groups to the President's Party	
		Affiliated *(Collaborative strategies)*	Unaffiliated *(Adversarial strategies)*
President's Capacity to Exercise Policy Leadership	Broad *(Breakthrough politics)*	Collaborative breatkthrough politics *Roosevelt: New Deal for labor*	Adversial breatkthrough politics *Reagan: Assault on liberal citizens groups*
	Narrow *(Politics-as-usual)*	Collaborative politics-as-usual *G.H.W. Bush: Clean air, rights of the disabled, and the competitiveness council*	Adversarial politics-as-usual *Clinton: Health care reform*

terest groups than often presumed, opposition to executives with enormous political capital is often less punishing than one might expect. To be sure, interest group opponents—those who challenge dominant presidents—may struggle to guard favorable policy outcomes of the past and are almost certain to find their long-term goals banished to the political wilderness. At the same time, they may also face formidable White House assaults. Yet the costs of *adversarial breakthrough politics* for interest group opponents are typically limited because of the fragmented structure of the U.S. political system. Even when confronted by powerful White House antagonism, adversarial groups often find alternative sources of support in Congress, the courts, or the bureaucracy. Indeed, White House antagonism may inspire sympathy for a threatened cause that groups can use to attract new supporters and to draw fresh resources. As we shall see, Ronald Reagan's largely unsuccessful campaign to demobilize liberal citizens groups concerned with the environment, consumer protection, civil rights, and other policy issues aptly captures these dynamics.

Breakthrough presidencies are the exception to the norm. Most modern presidents do not possess broad capacities to exercise policy leadership and must carefully ration their modest political resources (Neustadt 1990). *Collaborative politics-as-usual* poses a number of dilemmas for presidents and their interest group allies. Constrained presidents have particularly strong incentives to move to the political center to secure policy achievements and an independent public image. This frequently means offending affiliated groups. Presidents who pursue this tack may presume that, as captives of the president's party, affiliated groups have few alternatives but to maintain at least tacit support for the administration. While this political calculation is often sound, it does involve key risks. Affiliated groups may in fact take the dramatic step of openly breaking with an administration perceived as inattentive to its interests, as several prominent interest groups did when they supported insurgency campaigns late in the Jimmy Carter and George H. W. Bush presidencies.

But the costs of estrangement for presidents are usually more subtle. For example, when the Clinton White House alienated organized labor by successfully championing the North American Free Trade Agreement (NAFTA), one of the repercussions was that union chiefs refused to commit significant resources to help Bill Clinton secure his health care reform package. By contrast, if constrained presidents attempt to shore up support from their ideological base by advancing policy initiatives endorsed by affiliated interest groups, they face heavy criticism for betraying the public good on behalf of entrenched special interests.

One may safely predict that collaborative politics-as-usual will generally be inhospitable to affiliated groups seeking major policy innovations and more opportune for those content with incremental policy favors from a friendly administration. In a revealing case we shall examine below, the first Bush presidency ran afoul of many conservative allies when it endorsed popular centrist initiatives for improving air quality and ensuring stronger civil rights protections for the disabled. Tellingly, attempts by Bush officials to appease disgruntled business groups by softening the regulatory burdens of these reforms were thwarted after intense resistance from the media, interest group opponents, and congressional Democrats. Collaborative politics-as-usual is typically less rewarding for allied groups and more challenging for ordinary presidents than is often assumed.

Finally, *adversarial politics-as-usual* predictably affords oppositional interest groups extensive opportunities to frustrate the policy designs of politically constrained presidents by mobilizing grassroots resistance, exploiting alliances with supporters in other branches and levels of government, and pursuing other forms of veto politics. When the White House does not dominate the policymaking process, we also may anticipate that oppositional groups will play a significant role in helping to set the public agenda and to shape new policy initiatives.

Under these circumstances, constrained presidents may decide to follow the lead of unaffiliated interest groups championing popular causes. Significantly, the most prominent and ambitious policy reforms of presidents possessing ordinary leadership resources are usually defeated with ease within this environment of adversarial politics and fragmented power. As discussed in the pages that follow, the monumental demise of Clinton's health care reform plan affords a powerful illustration of adversarial politics-as-usual and the propensity of modern presidents and interest groups to frustrate each other's strongest democratic possibilities. Four case studies help capture these distinctive patterns of presidential interest group interactions.

Roosevelt and Industrial Unionism: Collaborative Breakthrough Politics

Interest groups are often attentive to new political openings for their policy goals. During the 1930s, organized labor could not resist linking its fortunes to the activist presidency of Franklin Roosevelt and his ambitious New Deal agenda. Labor leaders such as John L. Lewis of the United Mine Workers (UMW) particularly welcomed opportunities to translate New Deal legislative and administrative initiatives into growth for their unions, hoping to organize unskilled industrial workers who had been largely neglected by the American Federation of Labor (AFL).

In 1933, the Roosevelt administration invited a large number of organized interests—including business and labor groups—to participate in drafting the National Industrial Recovery Act (NIRA). Labor activists like W. Jett Lauck, a Lewis lieutenant, persuaded the White House to include a vague provision in NIRA, section 7(a), that recognized the right of workers to bargain collectively. Although corporate leaders were reassured by their lawyers that the provision included no administrative mechanism for enforcement, Lauck reported to Lewis that section 7(a) "will suit our purposes." After NIRA sailed through Congress, Lewis and other union organizers aggressively exploited the popularity of Roosevelt and NIRA to attract more miners to the UMW. "The president wants you to join the union," UMW literature and speakers told workers (Zeiger 1988). Tens of thousands of miners signed union cards and formed lodges with names such as "New Deal" and "Blue Eagle." After only one year of invoking the celebrated names of Roosevelt and the New Deal, the UMW's membership rolls had swollen from 150,000 to more than 500,000 (Leuchtenburg 1963, 106–7).

Lewis and other labor organizers orchestrated a dramatic break with the AFL in 1934, forming the Congress of Industrial Organizations (CIO) to represent millions of unskilled industrial workers (Leuchtenburg 1963). Publicly, CIO leaders professed unwavering support for Roosevelt and the New Deal. In private, they noted the aloof posture assumed by the White House when Sen. Robert Wagner (D-NY) championed legislation that would fundamentally protect unionizing efforts. Roosevelt tepidly endorsed the Wagner Act of 1935, organized labor's "Magna Carta," only at the eleventh hour (Miroff 1993). Although he understood that organized labor was a crucial element of his electoral and governing coalitions, the president took pains to publicly assert his independence of both labor and business interests. During major strikes, for example, Roosevelt was known to tell reporters that labor activists "did silly things," and he often sounded centrist tones in urging both employers and disgruntled laborers to embrace "common sense and good order" (Miroff 1993, 260–62).

Lewis and the CIO recognized Roosevelt's lack of enthusiasm for union radicalism. But they also appreciated that labor reforms such as the Wagner Act and the National Labor Relations Board (NLRB) were powerful catalysts for union organizing and collective bargaining. In 1936, Lewis, David Dubinsky, George Berry, Sidney Hillman, and other labor activists entered an electoral marriage of convenience between the CIO and the Democratic Party to reelect Roosevelt. CIO unions contributed significant financial and logistical support to the president's reelection campaign (Lewis's UMW was the Democratic Party's largest financial benefactor in 1936). In forming the Labor Nonpartisan League, however, Lewis hoped that union votes could be marshaled in future elections to support whichever party or candidate best served the CIO's interests (Leuchtenburg 1963).

After his landslide victory, it became clear that Roosevelt expected organized labor to follow his lead and not the reverse. Like other presidents who have dominated the policy process, Roosevelt intended to dictate the terms of any White House interest group alliances. Amid labor confrontations with steel manufacturers in 1937 and 1938, Roosevelt stunned many labor supporters when he commented on the killing of ten steelworkers who were demonstrating in Chicago against Republic Steel Corporation. Denouncing management and unions alike as sponsors of senseless violence, Roosevelt declared "a curse on both your houses." In a Labor Day radio address to millions of listeners, Lewis responded with a seething rebuke of the president: "It ill behooves one who has supped at labor's table and who has been sheltered in labor's house to curse with equal fervor and fine impartiality both labor and its adversaries when they become locked in deadly embrace" (Zeiger 1988, 105–6).

By the end of the 1930s, Lewis and a few other CIO leaders were convinced that the NLRB, the courts, and the White House were limiting the labor movement's larger aims. During the 1940 election, Lewis failed to derail FDR's reelection, fearing that it would bring about American entry into war and the concomitant demise of labor's agenda for progressive change. After failed efforts to launch a third party challenge and to back the Republican candidate Wendell Willkie in the 1940 election, Lewis stepped down as CIO president (Landy 1985; Zeiger 1988).

Eager to marginalize and defuse Lewis-style CIO militancy, the Roosevelt White House embraced moderate "labor statesmen" like Sidney Hillman, the president of the Amalgamated Clothing Workers of America, who helped form the CIO. Hillman, in contrast to Lewis, was an unflinching Roosevelt loyalist. He would oversee the creation of the CIO's Political Action Committee, which further cemented ties between organized labor and the Democratic Party.

After Pearl Harbor, war imperatives called for extraordinary industrial production and coordination. Labor leaders such as the new CIO president, Philip Murray, and Walter Reuther of the United Auto Workers proposed "industrial councils" that would facilitate efficient wartime production while giving organized labor real influence—along with business and government—in supervising industries and the workforce. The Roosevelt administration eschewed such ideas. In the end, the AFL, the CIO, and other unions agreed to a "no-strike pledge" during the war and merely hoped that war agencies would exercise their robust power over industrial workers benevolently (Brinkley 1995). "Instead of an active participant in the councils of industry," historian Alan Brinkley notes, "the labor movement had become, in effect, a ward of the state" (Brinkley 1995, 212). As the war drew to a close, Lewis's vision of an independent labor movement engaged in militant activities was overshadowed by broad CIO and AFL support for a more conciliatory posture. Heartened by the gains and protections secured during Roosevelt's administration, leaders of organized labor increasingly pinned labor's hopes on a permanent alliance with the Democratic Party.

Presidents with broad opportunities to shape domestic policy are unlikely to leave the interest group system the way they found it. Given their ample capacities to remake American politics and governance, it is hardly surprising that these executives are equally capable of reconstructing the interests that are close to them. Although Roosevelt did not explicitly favor union expansion or the meteoric rise of the CIO, his influence in these developments was unmistakable. Organized labor benefited greatly from its ties to a president blessed with an exceptional opportunity to advance major policy changes.

Roosevelt, however, exercised enormous control over the terms of their alliance and the nature of reform. Co-optation was the price of labor's programmatic collaboration, as union militancy and independence gave way to an increasingly moderate and bureaucratic style of labor organization.

Reagan's Assault on Liberal Citizen Groups: Adversarial Breakthrough Politics

Ronald Reagan, the first conservative modern president with abundant political capital, declared war on liberal advocacy groups early in his administration. Reaganites made no effort to conceal their disdain for liberal interest groups that they viewed as "a bunch of ideological ambulance chasers" who profited from bloated government and stood in the way of "regulatory relief" (Greve 1987). Government retrenchment, the Reagan White House resolved, would require a concerted effort to decrease the resources, size, and influence of liberal advocacy groups concerned with the environment, consumer protection, civil rights, poverty, and other policy issues. The Reagan administration set out to demobilize its interest group opponents in 1981 by cutting government programs favored by liberal groups, limiting their access to important federal agencies, and eliminating federal grants and contracts supporting their activities (Peterson 1992a).

The Reagan offensive was devastating for some advocacy groups, especially antipoverty organizations. The administration's social welfare budget cuts of 1981 spared programs aimed at the elderly, thereby neutralizing senior citizens lobbies that might have served as powerful allies to advocacy organizations for the poor. Instead, Reagan's effort to "defund the left" by eliminating government grant programs that supported liberal groups took its heaviest toll on a small cluster of poor people's lobbies (Imig 1996). Nevertheless, even as many antipoverty organizations shifted their energies from political advocacy to providing services, a number of groups concerned with the homeless made the Reagan administration's assault on the welfare state the focal point of contentious politics. Organizations associated with the emerging homeless movement of the 1980s engaged in confrontational anti-Reagan protests, building shanty-town "Reaganvilles" and staging demonstrations that drew extensive media attention, casting the White House as insensitive to the poor (Imig 1998). Ironically, the Reagan administration's constriction of older antipoverty organizations that dated back to the Great Society of Lyndon B. Johnson opened the door for new poor people's groups to challenge the president's agenda. Presidential antagonism inadvertently served as an impetus for liberal interest group formation.

Beyond its effective assault on a handful of antipoverty organizations, the White House plan to enervate liberal groups failed. Reagan strategists largely ignored the possibility that resourceful oppositional groups might transform the open hostility of a powerful conservative president into a catalyst for liberal organizational growth. National environmental groups, for example, prospered during the 1980s. Although denied access to once friendly federal agencies, environmental organizations launched an effective counter-mobilization that included aggressive fundraising, publicity, and coordinated action with congressional allies (Peterson and Walker 1986). As private donations to these groups increased markedly, environmental leaders quipped that Reagan's unpopular anticonservation secretary of the interior, James Watt, was the "Fort Knox of the environmental movement" (Greve 1987). Organizations like the Wilderness Society and the Sierra Club watched their membership rolls double in size between 1980 and 1985 (Waterman 1989; Bosso 1995). Finally, environmental groups drove from office two prominent Reagan appointees (Watt and Environmental Protection Agency Director Anne Gorsuch) and mounted a successful challenge to the administration's plans for environmental deregulation. Reagan's struggle with liberal citizens organizations highlights the resiliency of many oppositional groups even when they are under assault from breakthrough presidents. More precisely, adversarial breakthrough politics can present oppositional groups with opportunities for organizational expansion and influence when they enjoy strong mass-based constituencies and alternative sources of support within government.

Bush and Centrist Reform: Collaborative Politics-as-Usual

Presidents with narrow opportunities to exercise domestic policy leadership often have strong political incentives to embrace centrist reforms. By moving toward the political center, these presidents can gain credit among voters for advancing popular bipartisan initiatives. In the process, however, they may alienate their party's core interest group allies. George H. W. Bush's endorsements of popular bipartisan measures on the environment and civil rights illustrate this tradeoff.

Bush's policy leadership capacities were severely limited when he became president in 1989. His party held only 175 seats in the House of Representatives, the least of any modern president at the start of a term. Operating within this constrained political environment, the Bush administration hoped to prove its capacity to govern by introducing major environmental reform legislation that would draw considerable congressional, media, and popular support. During his 1988 election campaign, Bush pledged a "kinder and gentler" America and promised to be an "environmental president." As he proclaimed on the campaign trail, "Those who think we are powerless to do anything about the 'greenhouse effect' are forgetting about the 'White House effect'" (Holusha 1988).

Once in office, Bush stayed on the environmental bandwagon; like Nixon before him, Bush hoped to outmaneuver—or at least keep pace with—congressional Democrats on an issue of enormous popular concern. In July 1989, he sent to Congress an ambitious clean air bill. After successful negotiations with Senate majority leader George Mitchell (D-Maine) in early 1990, the Clean Air Act amendments of 1990 were enacted. The bill proved to be Bush's most significant policy achievement (Cohen 1992; Vig 2000). But along the way, the Bush administration was required to marginalize traditional Republican interest group allies in business and industry.

At about the same time, the Bush White House endorsed another major centrist reform, the Americans with Disabilities Act (ADA), solidly supported by the public and by liberal political actors but dreaded by many in the business community. The ADA sought to add the disabled to the groups protected against discrimination by the 1964 Civil Rights Act. At the urging of a broad coalition of interest groups associated with the disability, civil rights, and labor movements, the ADA also required that new or remodeled facilities be made accessible to disabled persons seeking jobs or hoping to make use of public accommodations; existing facilities were to be made accessible whenever "readily achievable." The potential financial costs arising from ADA requirements were enormous, and Bush officials attempted to dampen the blow on business interests by pressuring legislators to eliminate language from the bill permitting aggrieved parties to sue for damages. Congressional Democrats refused to make any concessions to the administration and passed the ADA unaltered. With polls indicating overwhelming public support for civil rights reform on behalf of the disabled, Bush signed the ADA into law (Mervin 1996).

Conservative critics assailed the Bush administration for approving the Clean Air Act Amendments and the ADA (Harris and Milkis 1996). Business groups and other conservative organizations warned administration officials that, at the start of a recession, new regulatory burdens placed "significant drags on the country's economic recovery" (Mervin 1996). Troubled by those attacks, Bush hoped to appease business groups outside the gaze of media attention by limiting the regulatory reach of the Clean Air Act, the ADA, and other initiatives in the implementation process. To this end, Bush created a Council on Competitiveness within the Executive Office of the President, chaired by Vice President Dan Quayle and charged to review regulations issued by bureaucratic agencies and make them less burdensome for relevant industry. "The president would say that if we keep our hand on the tiller in the implementation phase," recounted a member of the Council, "we won't add to the burdens of the economy" (Harris and Milkis 1996, 289).

In closed-door meetings, the Competitiveness Council focused on agency regulations that industry representatives complained were excessive. When the Department of Housing and Urban Development issued ADA-related regulations on how to make apartments more accessible to the disabled, for instance, the Competitiveness Council pressured the agency to ease the regulations at the behest of construction and real estate interests. As Jeffrey Berry and Kent Portney found, "The new rules were more sympathetic to the industry, and lobbyists for the home builders claimed that hundreds of millions of dollars would be saved each year in aggregate building costs" (Berry and Portney 1995, 320).

The success of some business groups in winning regulatory relief from the Bush administration illustrates perhaps the most promising strategy for interest group allies of practically constrained presidents to achieve incremental policy gains. Avoiding the glare of television lights, interest groups are most likely to benefit from collaborative politics-as-usual by mobilizing White House pressure on federal agencies for friendly implementation of existing laws. The Competitiveness Council, however, was ultimately unable to operate in secrecy. Its activities became increasingly hamstrung by liberal public interest groups, media scrutiny, and congressional opponents (Berry and Portney 1995).

As the Bush years suggest, the relationship between politically constrained presidents and the interest group coalitions of their party is often strained and unproductive. Tellingly, liberal interest groups closely aligned to the Democratic Party also were frustrated during the Clinton administration when popular centrist reforms were on the table. Clinton's support for the North American Free Trade Agreement (alienating organized labor), the Personal Responsibility and Work Opportunity Reconciliation Act (alienating antipoverty and civil rights groups), and the Defense of Marriage Act (alienating gay and lesbian groups) underscores the significant incentives for constrained executives to associate themselves with centrist initiatives even when they estrange interest group allies.

Clinton and Health Care Reform: Adversarial Politics-as-Usual

Shortly after his unexpected 1948 election, Harry S. Truman launched an aggressive campaign to secure national health insurance. Hoping to make the most of his modest political opportunity for programmatic leadership, Truman vigorously nurtured popular support for his ambitious health proposal. The

American Medical Association (AMA) and other groups that viewed national health insurance as an anathema to their interests launched an intense public relations campaign designed to depict Truman's plan as socialistic and corrosive of quality medical care. Spending what was then an unprecedented $1.5 million for its publicity counteroffensive, AMA ads forebodingly portrayed how national health insurance would place government bureaucrats between patients and their physicians. Already constrained by the slim Democratic majorities in Congress and by strong resistance from the conservative southern wing of his party, Truman was helpless to save his health plan when public support dwindled (Starr 1982).

More than four decades later, Bill Clinton, another Democrat constrained by limited political capacities to remake domestic policy, made universal health care coverage the centerpiece of his administration's reform agenda. He ran effectively on the issue during the 1992 election, receiving a warm reception from large numbers of voters who agreed that the health care system was in crisis. After a lengthy policy-planning process, Clinton unveiled his much-anticipated Health Security Act in late 1993, employing language intended to associate his proposal with one of the federal government's most popular programs, social security. In substance, the proposed act called for a new public-private partnership involving "managed competition" and employer mandates (Hacker 1997). Politically, it made important concessions to large companies and health care insurance providers to win their support, while promising universal coverage and restraints on soaring medical costs to attract the elderly, consumer groups, unions, religious organizations, and groups representing women, children, and minorities. When the AMA, the U.S. Chamber of Commerce, and several large employers voiced support for key features of the Health Security Act, the Clinton administration seemed to have assembled a powerful Left-Right coalition of unions, big business, health-care providers, and the elderly.

By mid–1994, Clinton's crusade for sweeping health care reform was dead. Explanation of the failure include the plan's eye-glazing complexity, resistance from Democrats on key congressional committees, Clinton's failure to streamline his policy agenda, his unwillingness to work with reform-minded Republicans, and high levels of public distrust in government (Schick 1995; Skocpol 1997; West and Loomis 1999). For our purposes, however, it is useful to concentrate on the significant role that Clinton's interest group adversaries played in derailing major health care reform.

Initially, the strongest group opposition to the administration's health care package came from two national organizations with large grassroots constituencies: the Health Insurance Association of America (HIAA) and the National Federation of Independent Businesses (NFIB). The HIAA represented midsized and small health insurance companies, many of which would go out of business if the Health Security Act were passed. Similarly, although large employers stood to benefit from the Clinton plan, small businesses represented by the NFIB found intolerable the proposal's mandate that employers pay 80 percent of employee health premiums (West and Loomis 1999, 78–82). The Pharmaceutical Research and Manufacturers of America (PRMA), representing drug companies that stood to lose profits under the Clinton scheme, also joined the cause. Then, late in 1993, Republican strategists led by William Kristol of the Project for the Republican Future began to persuade a broad set of conservative interest groups to mobilize in opposition to the Health Security Act. Anything but an all-out effort to defeat health care reform, Kristol argued, would seriously compromise the political future of the Republican Party and its interest group coalition. Passage of the Clinton plan, he insisted, would "relegitimize middle-class dependence for 'security' on government spending and regulation" and thereby revive the Democratic Party's appeal "as the generous protector of middle-class interests" (Skocpol 1997, 143–46). Before long, the Christian Coalition, anti-tax groups, and a variety of other conservative interest groups devoted new resources to kill health care reform, coordinating their activities with the HIAA, NFIB, and PRMA.

Clinton's interest group adversaries devoted considerable resources to advertising. The HIAA spent approximately $14 million on its public relations blitz, which included the famous "Harry and Louise" television ads promoting middle-class angst concerning the Clinton proposal. The PRMA devoted roughly $20 million to its political advertising campaign. The antireform advertising crusade was designed to minimize public concerns about a health crisis while arousing fears that the Health Security plan would compromise the quality of medical care, eliminate individual choice of health care providers, encourage bloated government, and dramatically increase taxes to cover the cost of universal coverage. For its part, the 600,000-member NFIB focused on grassroots mobilization, including direct mail and phone bank assaults on the Clinton plan. Against this backdrop, the White House received only modest support for its health care initiative from traditionally Democratic interest group allies. The AFL-CIO and other labor groups, for example, had already expended considerable resources fighting one of Clinton's treasured centrist achievements, NAFTA (West and Loomis 1999, 80–85).

Adversarial politics took its toll on public support for the health care reform, which drifted downward from 67 percent in a September 1993 *Washington Post/ABC News* poll to 44 percent in February 1994 (West and Loomis 1999, 92–93). Facing inevitable defeat, the Health Security Act was never put to a vote in either the House or the Senate. The failure of Clinton's major domestic policy initiative presaged the Republican takeover of Congress. Many analysts trace the demise of health care reform in 1993–94 to strategic missteps by the Clinton administration, of which there were many. Placed within the context of our theoretical model, however, Clinton's failure to achieve major health care reform reflects the formidable challenges faced by politically constrained presidents who pursue large-scale policy change. It also illustrates the enormous opportunities for interest group adversaries to block the programmatic ambitions of modern presidents in periods of politics-as-usual.

Reform and Contentious Democracy

Political interactions between presidents and national interest groups are a recurring and important feature of contemporary American political life. Studying presidential interest group relations in light of executive leadership opportunities and the partisan and ideological affiliations of interest groups permits us to draw comparisons and to recognize patterns across time.[2]

The existing scholarly literature tends to underscore the recent development of the institutional resources and political strategies with which the White House can deal with the interest group system.[3] These valuable empirical insights sometimes have led students of the presidency to perceive all modern presidents as being equally well situated to orchestrate successful relations with organized interests. According to Peterson, for instance, "modern presidents have the institutional means, and have demonstrated the willingness, to influence the interest group system to their own advantage"—including considerable resources to punish opponents and reward allies in the interest group community (1992a, 237).[4]

Our model of interactive politics offers a decidedly different portrait of presidential interest group relations, one in which modern executives are frequently confounded in their efforts both to coax allies into supportive coalitions and to thwart opposition groups. Except for rare moments of presidential dominance, interest groups engage in their own orchestration of effective strategic politics.

Presidents with transformational policy aspirations but ordinary leadership opportunities have routinely found interest group relations to be trying. Oppositional groups are usually well situated to frustrate the president's most ambitious programmatic goals, as Clinton's ill-fated crusade for health care reform illustrates. Nurturing and aiding interest group allies can also prove difficult for politically constrained presidents. These executives have strong incentives to endorse popular centrist measures where enactment allows them to point to tangible policy achievements. In the process, however, they routinely alienate affiliated interest groups, as Bush learned from his support of the Clean Air Act Amendments and ADA. Indeed, the political allure of such popular centrist initiatives frequently saps the ability of politically constrained presidents to build strong coalitions behind their more partisan measures.

During politics-as-usual periods, executives instead may quietly provide succor to their interest group allies through administrative means. The intense scrutiny devoted to White House activities by the media and organized opposition, however, means that such efforts can rarely remain secret. When publicized, they may subject the president to charges of catering to special interests and may be contested by interest group adversaries in federal courts and Congress. Although most interest groups allied to presidents with constrained leadership opportunities receive fewer tangible benefits than many assume, oppositional groups often find the adversarial politics that prevail during such presidencies to be hospitable to vibrant and effective activism. As interest groups opposed to Clinton's health program discovered in the 1994 midterm election, countermobilization can have surprising transformational possibilities.

Obviously, interest groups are most rewarded for collaborative relations with the White House during those fleeting periods when breakthrough presidents dominate American governance. Yet breakthrough presidents set the terms of collaboration, and allied interest groups whose goals may jeopardize more important White House objectives find themselves marginalized in the policy process. Even when the transformational goals of breakthrough presidents and allied interest groups are nearly the same, as was the case with Roosevelt New Dealers and labor activists in the 1930s, co-optation is typically the price these groups pay to secure dramatic gains for their constituencies.

It is also telling that the most recent breakthrough president, Ronald Reagan, dominated domestic policy making for only a year and that his interest group adversaries prospered during most of his tenure. The scale and variety of the interest group system during the past quarter century has been greater than ever before. This important development, as Graham K. Wilson argues, forces presidents today to contend with "a thicker structure of constraining institutions (in this case, interest groups)" (1996, 231). Thus, the promise of strained relations between modern presidents and interest groups is more certain than ever. As our investigation of presidential interest group relations suggests, the most significant and enduring bias of the American political system is its hostility toward nonincremental reform.

The framers of the U.S. Constitution could not have anticipated the unprecedented scope and content of presidential and interest group politics today, but it is a good bet that few would be troubled by the extra-constitutional checks that have accompanied their expansion. James Madison was the most celebrated constitutional architect to express profound ambivalence about executives and outright disdain for organized interests. Although he ultimately endorsed an energetic presidency because he thought it necessary to check potential legislative tyrannies and to promote national security, Madison still worried that executive power and leadership posed substantial perils for the future of representative government (suspicions that later hardened during the Federalist administrations of George Washington and John Adams). He also expressed great disdain for factions, selfish organized interests whose policy goals often proved costly or harmful to other groups. While recognizing that official restraints on the narcissistic pursuits of interest groups were "worse than the disease," Madison hoped to control the "effects" of factions via an extended sphere, separation of powers, checks and balances, and other innovations of modern political science.

The fact that the modern presidency and national interest group system now regularly bedevil one another is in many respects a most appropriate development for a national polity designed at the outset to fragment government power and to frustrate dramatic change. In short, contemporary presidential interest group relations represent a substantial Madisonian victory. The *democratic* meaning of these extra-constitutional checks, however, is more troublesome (see Hochschild and Hansen, this volume). The U.S. political system's bias against nonincremental reform can be viewed as a triumph of American democracy when it derails the perilous designs of tyrannical majorities, delays the most ill-advised whims of impetuous masses, or tempers the most dangerous ambitions of organized political elites and minorities. Yet inasmuch as these barriers to reform also reinforce oppressive inequalities for the nation's most disadvantaged members and often make government seem remote and unresponsive to middle-class Americans, they remain one of our most tenacious sources of democratic failure.

Conclusion

Perspectives on the Future of American Democratic Politics

MARC D. WEINER
GERALD M. POMPER

> *We live in an age of crisis. War is the bitterest expression of*
> *forces that were present before the war, that caused the*
> *outbreak of hostilities, and that will continue afterward.*
> *War settles . . . the power of leaders, but it does not provide*
> *constructive answers for the deeper questions. —*
> Pendelton Herring, 1944

PENDELTON HERRING'S observations of an age of crisis are no less true now than almost sixty years ago. The immediate and intense salience of terrorism in the post–9/11 era highlights rifts in our day-to-day partisan policy contests, bringing to the fore concerns for civil liberties, issues of racial classifications, and other manifestations of liberty and equality in American democratic politics. These, however, are but evidence of underlying disagreements in place well before September 11.

Since the close of the Second World War, America has seen interim crises—some long-lived, some brief but intense. The last fifty years have witnessed international conflagrations such as the cold war, the Korean police action, Vietnam, and the Gulf War, as well as the domestic conflicts of the McCarthy era, the widespread civil unrest of the 1960s, Watergate, the Iran-Contra affair, and the Clinton impeachment. Now, just after the turn of the millennium, we are beset by previously unimaginable terrorist attacks on our home soil.

In varying degrees, however, all ages are ages of crisis, and it is crisis that tests the mettle of our national ethos and our political culture. The current test shows the tremendous endurance and great flexibility of that mettle. National stability in the face of these crises has taught us the perpetual endurance of the principles that guide and bind our governing institutions together and the inherent flexibility of those institutions.

Despite all of the political wrangling and public hand-wringing of the current age of crisis, the scholars in this volume find stable, working institutions animating vital fundamental principles. And so perhaps the most important consideration for the future of American democratic politics in the post–9/11 world of terrorism is the continuity of our Madisonian constitutional framework, a workable mechanism enabling us to exercise diligence against outside threat and still live, work, love, and play in a free, liberal society.

Much cause for concern, however, remains. A stable government with power to overcome foreign threat and domestic disturbance is a necessary, but not sufficient, condition for realization of the fundamental principles of liberty and equality. As Herring implies, crises only exacerbate divisions already in place, and these strains are clearly evident in the post–9/11 world. Liberty is an American, even universal, ideal, but insecurity tempts a "flight from freedom." Inequalities that plagued the country at the founding still trouble us in modern forms. While slavery has been abolished, the franchise expanded, and civil rights and antidiscrimination legislation enacted, discrimination and racism persist. To the scholars in this volume, the United States must still work to realize the nation's founding truth of equal creation and to "secure the blessings of liberty."

At the end of the year-long symposium that forms the core of this volume, these authors discussed four common concerns for the future of American democratic politics: the balance of the constitutional separation of powers; the effect of terrorism-generated anxiety; concern for civil liberties; and issues of participation—partisanship, loyalty, and dissent. Their dialogues are excerpted below.

September 11 and the Balance of Institutional Power

The immediate governmental consequence of September 11, as in all crises, was a strengthening of the power of the presidency. Congress gave the executive extensive new powers under the Patriot Act, hundreds of aliens and American citizens of Arab descent were imprisoned, many without benefit of counsel or even release of their names. The courts were reluctant to intervene in this situation of emergency. These events posed major issues for the participants in the symposium.

MCWILLIAMS: War is always bad news for checks and balances. War always means executive authority, and it's even an authority that the Supreme Court tends to look at only retrospectively. So in the post–9/11 climate, there is likely to be a continuation of the expansion of the power of the executive.

ROSENTHAL: It is not only that war enhances executive power, but it is the nature of this war, too. It is an open-ended war, a war that isn't going to end. So indefinitely into the future, you can project there is going to be a need for security, the kind of security that the executive is charged with providing.

TICHENOR: And there is always profound tension between executive power and democracy. Expansive presidential leadership always threatens to make citizens spectators and followers rather than engaged participants. Yet the power seized by presidents during major wars is especially troubling not only because it undermines the authority of other democratic representatives to challenge executive dictates, but it enervates democratic liberty. Still worse, wartimes may nurture among insecure citizens a disquieting reliance upon and awe for unrestrained presidential force. Executive power in these circumstances poses one of democracy's greatest perils.

GARRETT: Shifting from the executive to the legislature, I'd like to focus on how 9/11 has affected both the inter- and intra-institutional developments that we've been discussing and what those effects mean for the future. There are at least three such effects. First, consider congressional oversight of the executive branch. It seems to me there are some really interesting questions relating to oversight posed by 9/11 and other recent circumstances. For example, what kind of documents can Congress demand from the executive branch? How much can Congress find out about what the vice president is doing, or about what Tom Ridge and the Office of Homeland Security are doing? How does the war on terrorism and increasing activity in the executive office of the president affect congressional oversight of the executive branch?

A second trend that we are seeing is the increasing use of omnibus acts in Congress, which involve legislative processes different from those of the "textbook Congress." With respect to the Patriot Act, for example, there wasn't much committee involvement.

CROTTY: . . . six weeks and it was out . . .

GARRETT: Right. And the decreasing importance of committees corresponds to the increasing use of task forces in Congress, and with more power being exerted by party leadership rather than through the relative public activities of traditional committees. What does that mean for the federal legislature? And for courts and agencies that rely in statutory interpretation and implementation on traditional kinds of legislative materials produced by committees but not by task forces or party leaders?

A third development that is relevant to the context of 9/11 is what this event means for the congressional budget process, which has been one of the most important aspects of the federal government since the mid–1980s. Before 9/11 we were going into an era of cash flow surpluses, but now we are returning to the world of large deficit spending. That will have a tremendous impact not just on the war on terrorism but also on domestic programs and what we do in the future in the budget process.

CROTTY: There is an irony in this situation. This Patriot Act in my opinion is so bad, it is such a combination of various things, that it will be going not as a single act, but as a series of cases, to the Supreme Court. That will have the unintended consequence of empowering the Court even more, allowing it to decide what will be done and what is acceptable and where the lines are going to be drawn. If anything, I expect the Supreme Court under this present situation to be even more influential, despite the disturbing trends we've discussed.

The Psychology of Vulnerability: Terrorism, Anxiety, and Democracy

In December of 2000, the country faithfully stood by as the presidential electoral contest demonstrated the institutional balance of power. Nine months later, as it sat watching in horror as the Twin Towers of the World Trade Center collapsed and the Pentagon burned, the country's attention—and attitude— shifted dramatically. The new focus gives rise to new concerns.

MANDEL: The question about the future of democratic politics is not the event of September 11 per se, but rather whether there's a real psychology of vulnerability, and, if so, what does that do to democratic politics? I would say there isn't such a psychology now, but if there were another attack, then the question of the future of democratic politics under a psychology of vulnerability would be very different.

POLSBY: How about a less alarmist view? We are hearing a lot of the rhetoric of total war, but it isn't a total war. There are good, sound, political reasons why the Republican Party wants to keep the president wrapped in the flag. The minute it becomes unraveled, the emperor will be very ill-clad indeed. So there are partisan reasons why the language of emergency is going to persist somewhat in the public sphere. But I don't see much to back it up really. I am ready to be convinced otherwise, but I don't see it.

SCHOCHET: The issue of the mentality of terror is very important. In a very real sense, reliance upon the government, upon the state, will increase when there is increasing anxiety among the citizenry. It is almost as if the people in Washington have been reading ancient and contemporary political philosophers who have argued this from antiquity to modernity. It seems that the Bush administration has set out to make the country anxious so that they can then enhance their political status. There is a kind of manufactured anxiety as a way of making sure the president remains clothed in the flag.

MCWILLIAMS: My memory is that repression in World War II was fairly strong, and in the 50s as well, and by comparison, this ain't it. In terms of government propaganda, you ain't seen nothing yet.

I do think that Ruth Mandel is right about the sense of vulnerability, but the other thing you have to plug in—because it makes a second potential threat more serious—is that there is a long-term cultural strain that results from a continuing sense of vulnerability.

And you can see it in all kinds of ways that we're penetrated and things we're subjected to. This concept is taken up in Paul Cantor's book *Gilligan Unbound,* which, among other things, is about how "Gilligan's Island" and "Star Trek" and "The Simpsons" and the "X-Files" all document the way in which popular culture shows, more and more, an America subject to incursion . . . America the vulnerable. If you think about . . .

POLSBY: . . . bomb shelters . . .

HOCHSCHILD: . . . or McCarthy . . .

POLSBY: McCarthy was a much more restricted phenomenon. But bomb shelters went into every school room. You would get under the desk, under the table.

SCHOCHET: Well, McCarthy was after World War II, and bomb shelters were in the 1950s . . .

POLSBY: In other words, the sense of vulnerability comes and goes.

HANSEN: One question about what vulnerability and insecurity are likely to do to our country deals with threats to liberty. I think we have something of a model in that Europe has decades of experience with political violence and terrorism. There are European states that have a much more statist history—with genuine conservative right wings, unlike the liberal right in the United States. We should ask whether those states, after decades of experience with terrorism, both from within and from outside, have less liberty than before? I am not so sure.

It seems to me that the primary European response to terrorism has been to pursue a foreign policy that from the United States looks craven and ready to give in to possible sponsors of terrorism. At least that is the view from the White House. So I am not so sure that I would expect that civil liberties and adherence to democratic norms in the United States would be more vulnerable than it would in Europe. In fact, following the European example, I think that 9/11 is probably going to have a greater effect on U.S. foreign policy than on domestic freedoms.

The War on Terrorism and Civil Liberties

This discussion of the psychology of vulnerability leads logically to a consideration of civil liberties. In order to enhance our sense of national security, what freedoms would the government infringe? And what would the public willingly surrender? This discussion directly involves concerns about racial and ethnic profiling. Less obviously, but still relevantly, it raises issues of national identity, patriotism, and even the symbolism of the American flag. These issues speak to distinctions, perhaps odd for a pluralistic society, between "us" and "them."

HIRSCHMANN: I question what the flag symbolizes and means in terms of people's activity. In so far as it is a substitution for participation, then I think flag-flying becomes problematic, because it is a way to make us think we are doing something instead of facing up to the fact that we are not participating, not doing anything. The question is what counts as participation, what should we be doing to have a good, strong democracy, what do we require of citizens by way of participation, what sorts of activities and actions should count. This ties into the argument about civil liberties. A lot of the time we don't worry about civil liberties because we just consider it inconvenient: it just gets relabeled as national security.

We've relabeled airport security as just an inconvenience; and the result is that civil liberties are, in a sense, taken off the table because we call it an inconvenience. We are taught, when you object to taking your shoes off in the airport, that you are getting hysterical about something that is not important. Is this the thin edge of the wedge, or can we say there is a line and we haven't crossed it yet, so we're safe?

POMPER: If you are going to call any restriction on your actions a significant invasion of liberty, then we are in a libertarian discourse. Taking your shoes off is not unrelated to a threat. There was somebody on a plane who was lighting their sneakers and would have caused a fire and explosion. You have to distinguish what are real invasions of liberty and what aren't.

Let me take your other point, too. Participation, you are right, should be effective, but then, what is that? I was a kid in the Second World War. We spent a lot of time gathering all sorts of stuff that, in retrospect, I wonder about. My mother used to keep fat from cooking, and we were left with all this fat. Only years later did I wonder, what they did with it. They couldn't have sent it overseas, it would have gotten rancid on the trip. But one reason was that it made people feel they were participating in the war effort.

HIRSCHMANN: I am not saying that taking off your shoes in itself is an invasion of liberty, but rather asking what that action means, and whether we shouldn't be having a conversation about what counts as participation, and be more self-conscious about what it is that we are doing. Do we just want to say this isn't that big a deal, and then the next thing, well, that isn't that big a deal, and then the next, that isn't that big. And we then slide into a substantial loss of liberty. Isn't that the conversation we want to have on the future of democratic politics? What is the line we don't want to cross?

HEUMANN: Well, by and large, Patriot Act aside—and that is a bad piece of legislation—it is quite remarkable how little trampling there has been on civil liberties. Take racial profiling at airports for example. There is a lot of resistance to it and to the secretary of transportation's support for it, who ironically was incarcerated during World War II in a Japanese relocation camp. But whether it is speech freedom or press freedom, in a lot of aspects we see a vindication of the concept of the elites as carriers of the creed of civil liberties; for the most part there has not been in practice a trampling of civil liberties. Now we don't know what the future will bring, but we have not seen a dramatic threat—obviously, nothing like World War II.

CASSAK: We have to wait and see exactly how the civil liberties issues play out. Take the case of military tribunals. They were first proposed in very general terms, exciting a lot of criticism and commentary, some of it positive, more of it negative. The Bush administration then clarified the procedures in response to some, though not all, of the criticism. But it is interesting that the first chance they had to apply it, which was the Moussaoui case, they elected not to use it. So, we don't yet have a full sense of exactly how 9/11 affected civil liberties. Some of the impact hasn't hit mainstream America, like the detention of a huge group of people, but most of them outside mainstream America.

Issues of Partisanship, Loyalty, and Dissent

The symposium's concern for civil liberties, then, was not about a single dramatic change, but rather—to paraphrase Justice William O. Douglas—of losing our liberties by littles. The small and incremental nature of these losses of liberty, and the need for a free citizenry to consciously monitor government actions in this regard, gave way to a wide-ranging discussion of the particular importance, post–9/11, of dissent in the national conversation.

MCWILLIAMS: The most notable thing about 9/11 is that, at least temporarily, it brought to an end the notion that government is the problem. We've got lots of people out there talking about in different ways how we've got to have more government. Republicans are even backing away from talking about privatization. But the general tendencies are to see government as at least more positive and more necessary, and to see ourselves as correspondingly more vulnerable. What is going to happen is going to depend a lot on how our encounter with terrorism plays out over the next months and years.

HIRSCHMANN: With regard to the expression of dissent, there are two possibilities: on one hand, it could be that what 9/11 has done is create an illusion that democracy is strengthening, but a reality that it is really weakening. On the other hand, there may be an inevitable backlash against the government through democracy. I can see protests and backlash against Bush as being a fundamentally democratic moment, an expression of the democratic potential, because people are coming forward and asserting rights and membership in the society. They can say, we are going to critique our government; it doesn't matter what the external circumstances are—and it would be a "real" democratic moment. It is when we say no, we have to be behind our president 100 percent, that we create an illusion that democracy is really strong, but in reality it is really weak, because we are not contesting, we are not questioning, we are not thinking critically about our institutions.

HANSEN: If one looks at historical patterns, even if the war on terrorism stays on the front burner and even if there are incidents after this, it may be not that the contestation and challenge will go away, but that their nature will change. Six months after Pearl Harbor there was plenty of contestation and challenge to the Roosevelt administration, both in terms of what it was doing domestically—the Republicans took this as an opportunity basically to dismantle the New Deal—and in terms of the way the Roosevelt administration was prosecuting the war. So I think we are likely to see very similar politics in this one.

Part of the reason why the administration's reaction to the revelations about the pre–September 11 reports from the FBI were so vociferous was that they see the situation now moving from the immediate aftermath, where the president wraps himself in the flag and enjoys a true rally effect, to one where we are in the normal politics of assessing responsibility and accountability. I think that is possible, even during wartime; there has been quite healthy conversation in the United States, even during times of total mobilization, as in World War II.

JUNN: Turning back to the flag, for a moment, I wonder about the extent to which this flag-waving phenomenon is a period effect that will be measurable in the future. After 9/11 there has been something of a flag obsession, and flying one is not only for older generations, but something ten- and seventeen-year-old kids are doing as well. Will flag-waving—this minimalist act of participation—have some positive effect on political awareness, engagement, and face-to-face contact with other people?

HOCHSCHILD: This flag discussion is really central to the larger question, what has the political leadership done as a consequence of the instinct of so many people to fly the flag. The answer is, not very much. There is a fair number of surveys that suggested that teenagers and young adults now suddenly feel patriotic and that they want to do something for their country, and that those sentiments were dissipated within the last month or two. I think that has a lot to do with party mobilization, which I think is absolutely a critical missing piece of this story. It probably has to do with elite signaling where, in the wake of 9/11, the president told us to go shopping rather than join the army or fix our local polluted swamp. It doesn't matter what it could have been, but it was economic, not civic, action he suggested.

But with regard to contempt for flag-waving, I think there's also a political argument to be made—that the left is never going to win anything if it is antifamily, antimorality, antireligion, and anticountry. The left can just forget it and talk to itself until the cows come home, end of story.

SCHOCHET: I want to pick up the point about loyalty in terms of the future of democracy. It seems to me that one of the aspects of democracy is its ability to engage in self-criticism and revision. And that requires a significant tolerance of dissent. That sharply conflicts with what we increasingly conventionally have come to mean by loyalty. Certainly, it's desirable to be loyal, but at the same time it's necessary to raise objections, to be critical, to maintain a state of critical inquiry, because the only time that that's an issue is in a time of crisis. It's only in a time of crisis that what the government is doing is called into question. That's why it's important to be a contrarian. The contrarian plays a very important inscrutable role in a democratic society. The contrarian calls us back to what we're about and what we're made of, no matter how objectionable his cause might be.

HOCHSCHILD: It seems to me equally possible as an empirical proposition that, rather than violating symbols that much of America passionately cares about—such as the flag—you will be a more effective critic and more people will listen because you understand what really matters to them, what your fellow citizens care about. Criticism, then, comes from within rather than from without. If you think about families, I will tolerate criticism from my daughter, whom I adore, that I would not tolerate from Carey McWilliams, who I esteem but don't adore. We all know that. But it seems to me the psychology of criticism from within could be more effective and more tolerable, and more intense.

The reason I care about this debate is because I discovered that I care a lot more about my country than I thought I did in the last twenty years, and that is important to discover. I think as a normative proposition, part of what this is about is where we think these things—loyalty to the nation, patriotism, identification with something called a state or nation fit in some pantheon of values as a democrat.

SCHOCHET: The American problem is unique, because we have no idea what, other than attachment to this geographic thing called America, we have in common. Historically, at least, we are the first nation or state to have been so constituted. We don't have religion, ethnicity, or even increasingly language in common. Yet, it is incumbent upon us to devise ways of making what we do have in common more important than what divides us without surrendering those things that do divide us. That, it seems to me, is distinctly American. I have no idea how to go about solving that or dealing with that, especially in a time of crisis, but I think it is something we must constantly be paying attention to. I think one of the ways we can at least confront it is by constantly telling ourselves various stories about who we are and where we came from and why it is important to have arrived where we are. And one of the stories I think we must tell ourselves is the story about the history of our liberties.

POMPER: One element common to all Americans is our political institutions. Those are symbolized, and the Pledge of Allegiance even says this, by the flag. The flag represents those institutions and the goals of liberty and justice, and so on. And if that is true, it's the political institutions which are the truly unifying bond. How, then, do we bring institutions back into this discussion?

Madisonianism Revisited

At the close of the symposium, the participants reflected a wary commendation of the nation's principles and its current institutions. America, post–9/11, was by no means nearly as oppressive as it might have been after the attacks. Our love of liberty, however, is only one possible explanation for the limited invasion of civil liberties. It may be that severe treatment of Arab Americans never materialized, for instance, only for prudential reasons, because we desperately need the international cooperation of the Arab world, both economically and strategically.

In their conclusions, the symposium members, as a group, also seemed sanguine on the continuing viability of Madisonianism. They forecast that Congress would intervene where necessary, that ambition would counteract ambition, that the courts or maybe local government would protect civil liberties, and that similar structural protections would remain effective. There was a distinct faith in the system of checks and balances, even more than on mass democratic attitudes. Some of these scholars expressed a fear of popular participation, asserting that it is to democracy's advantage that political elites manage the civil liberties questions, rather than letting those questions be

decided by potentially tyrannical majorities through opinion polls or such techniques as national referenda.

The conclusion, then, was that the Madisonian system, while somewhat
reworked from the founding, still operates to provide an adequate degree of
solution to the problems of popular government. This group of scholars, somewhat surprisingly, found a degree of comfort in that conclusion. We end with
Carey McWilliams's apt historical perspective:

> The Madisonian system always looks good when what it is doing is
> moderating your opponents, and it always looks bad when it is
> frustrating you. There is nothing wrong with the judgment that the
> Madisonian system is great when it is dealing with George W. Bush,
> and bad when it is dealing with his critics. That's the way it works.
> But you can't look at this administration and not recognize the
> profound ambivalences they have about this whole crisis.
>
> Let's suppose there was a more or less liberal Democratic
> administration that was resolved to pursue a war on terrorism. That
> would be a wonderful license for liberals to regulate all kinds of things
> that they could never get regulated in peacetime. Under the post–
> 9/11 circumstances, liberal Democrats would run with the ball even
> faster than Franklin Roosevelt. Financially, for example, they would
> have data on every overseas transfer and would shut down the banks
> of convenience, and so forth.
>
> One of the things that is interesting about this administration is
> that it doesn't want to do that. It resists pressure to totalize the war,
> because this is an administration that is devoted to scaling back the
> government. It really doesn't like this. This is a powerful part of what
> is happening.
>
> We should be reminded about the story of our liberties, the story
> that goes back to the origins of the American state. We should
> remember that we don't have a nation, we've got a state. That is what
> the Declaration of Independence is about.
>
> In 1776, Americans already enjoyed personal liberty. As British
> subjects, they enjoyed certainly more liberty than anybody else in the
> European world, and more liberty than the British enjoyed. True, we
> didn't count some of the people, and they didn't enjoy much liberty.
> But what was the issue in 1776, was it about our liberties? It was about
> something else; it was about something called self-government. The
> Declaration says we inalienably have liberties, but the real issue is our
> declared capacity to rule ourselves. Self-government is in some ways
> the American story. And maybe the question of our capacity to
> govern ourselves effectively is more interesting than the story of
> liberty.

Notes

Chapter 1 *Pluralism, Identity Politics, and Coalitions*

1. The melting pot has not been as benign in practice as this image suggests. It can be psychologically and legally coercive, as in "Americanization" programs of the early twentieth century (Gerstle 1997). Resistance to the overweening and offensive variants of melting-pot belief and practice provides much of the energy behind identity politics.

2. Topline results for the GSS and NES are available, respectively, in Davis, Smith, and Marsden (2001) and National Election Studies (1998); results for particular groups are from analyses by the author. Except where noted, I combined the GSS and NES (bi)annual surveys into three periods, 1972–80, 1982–90, 1992–2000. These periods coincide with the beginning of the GSS and with presidential elections that signaled the end of one political era and the beginning of another. The periods also yield large enough sample sizes for blacks and, sometimes, Hispanics. My thanks to Steven Minicucci, now of the Consortium on Financing Higher Education, for his invaluable research assistance.

3. Results are from GSS for 1994, 1996, and 2000; from *Washington Post* et al. (1999) for 1999; and from Gallup Organization (2001, 1:23) for 2001; analyses by author. There were too few Asian Americans in all of these surveys to report results.

4. GSS and NES. In the GSS, but not in the NES, the proportion of Latino conservatives, and the proportion of Latino Republicans, increased in the 1990s from the two previous decades. See also de la Garza et al. (1990); *Washington Post* et al. (1999; analyses by author). "Thinking by Ethnicity" (1998, 55–56) provides similar results for Americans with Mexican ancestry.

5. In addition to the usual "house effects," the number of reported Independents depends on how hard "leaners" are pushed to declare themselves as more Democratic than Republican or vice versa (NES and GSS).

6. David Hollinger, quoted here, opposes this view (Hollinger 2000, 58–59). Iris Young, among others, endorses it: "the traditional public realm of universal citizenship has operated to exclude persons associated with the body and feeling—especially women, Blacks, American Indians, and Jews. . . . The meaning of 'public' should be transformed to exhibit the positivity of group differences, passion, and play" (Young 1990, 97).

7. GSS 1994 (the sample contained fewer than sixty Hispanics). In 2001, only 12 percent of Asian Americans described themselves as "an American" tout court; an additional 50 percent thought of themselves as Asian American or, especially, [their ethnic group]-American (Lien 2001).

8. "A possible great and truly democratic commonwealth . . . would be . . . a democracy of nationalities, cooperating voluntarily and autonomously through common institutions in the enterprise of self-realization through the perfection of men according to their kind. . . . The political and economic life of the commonwealth is a single unit and serves as the foundation and background for the realization of the distinctive individuality of each *natio* that composes it and of the pooling of these in a harmony above them all" (Kallen 1998 [1924], 114–16). This phenomenon may also be described as nested identities, in which local or particularistic identities fit neatly within national or even international identities (Díez Medrano and Gutiérrez 2001).

9. In this 1994 survey, Anglos, blacks, and Latinos all were less likely to identify with Asian Americans than any other group, as the group with whom they feel the most in common—lending support to Kim's analysis of identity politics among Asian Americans. The 2000 GSS asked the same question and got similar results on this point. Only 22 percent of Anglos and 4 percent of blacks (among those giving substantive answers) claimed to have most in common with Asians; fully 50 percent of Anglos and 54 percent of blacks among those answering claimed to have least in common with Asians.

10. American Indians did not enter his discussion. Nor did Asians or Hispanics, since, with a few local exceptions, there were few immigrants from those parts of the world in the fifty years before Dahl wrote.

11. Blacks and Hispanics were still slightly more likely to report an increase than a decrease in racial tensions; the other two groups were about evenly split. All groups were most likely to report "stayed about the same."

     The National Conference for Community and Justice asked a similar question in 1993 and 2000 about current levels of "racial, religious, or ethnic tension." More blacks reported tension in 2000 than in 1993 at all four arenas (at work, with police, in their children's school, and in their neighborhood). Latinos expressed few differences except for a rise in tension with the police; Asians reported small but consistent rises in tension in all four arenas. We lack comparable data for whites, but in 2000 they generally reported less tension than all of the other groups for all four arenas. Nevertheless, except with regard to the police, no more than a quarter of respondents in all groups in both years reported racial, religious, or ethnic tension in their daily lives (National Conference for Community and Justice 1994; National Conference for Community and Justice 2000; analyses by author).

12. Contemporary analysts often reject the straight-line assimilation model in favor of a model of segmented assimilation, in which only some members of a new immigrant group move through the stages from poverty and (perhaps unwitting) identity politics to greater wealth and pluralism. The rest of the group, in this view, are likely to remain poor, isolated in ethnic enclaves, and politically inactive, at least in conventional electoral arenas. Even in this view, however, better-off immigrants are presumed to move from identity politics through coalition politics and, in some cases, into conventional interest-oriented politics (Portes and Rumbaut 2001; Jones-Correa 1998).

13. This point suggests a fourth type of coalition, which, if it thrives, will generate a new relationship between pluralism and identity politics. It is *conservative racial nationalism*, a combination of conservative policy positions and strong cultural nationalism or even racial separatism. It is the converse of the progressive rainbow coalition; I do not address it here because it is even less common and has demonstrated, so far, less political or substantive clout.

14. It was, however, fact recognized by Madison himself as well as other framers and

Alexis de Tocqueville. They were uncomfortable about the "white," uncertain about the "propertied," and oblivious about the "men" (Ellis 2001, chap. 3).

15. In many states, felons are excluded from the vote, and they are becoming a surprisingly important exception to any claim about "all adult citizens." A complete analysis would also need to address complications having to do with Native Americans, Mexican guest workers, and illegal immigrants.

Chapter 2   *Equality's Troubles*

1. Even a partisan of the state like Hegel, for example, taught principles that point toward the universal: "*we* know that all men absolutely (man *as man*) are free" (Hegel 1956, 19).
2. "As for you, modern peoples," Rousseau wrote, "you have no slaves, but you are slaves. You pay for their freedom with your own" (Rousseau 1978, 103).
3. On the general point, see *Federalist No. 70* (Hamilton et al. 1961, 471) following the argument in Locke's *Second Treatise on Civil Government*, §159–61 (Locke 1947, 203–4).
4. From 1997 to 2001, according to the Associated Press, support for labor rose from 45 percent to 50 percent; support for management fell from 37 percent to 27 percent (*New York Times*, September 2, 2001, 18Y).
5. For example, Engels spoke of "objective, external forces" coming "under the control of men themselves," with government eventually becoming "superfluous" (Engels 1939, 310, 307).
6. For an early example of this critique, see Lippmann (1925); the most devastating, relatively contemporary comment may be Vonnegut's (1980, 104).
7. There are a good many economists, of course, who are exceptions to this rule, in whole or in part (for example, see Sen 1999).

Chapter 3   *The Majoritarian Impulse and the Declining Significance of Place*

1. See conflicting evidence from different sources presented by Rosenstone and Hansen (1993, 61) and Schlozman, Verba, and Brady (1999).
2. Schattschneider himself drew the connection between local and national decision making and privatized and socialized conflict (1960, 10–11). Part of the critical reaction toward Robert A. Dahl's *Who Governs?* (1961) was also rooted in doubts that politics in a locale could ever be other than dominated by parochial interests whose intentions were the suppression of public debate. See, for example, Parenti (1970) and Baratz and Bachrach (1962).
3. According to Doug McAdam (1982, 120–25 and chap. 6), the ability to organize the movement at the local level was itself affected by national forces for racial liberalism. The New Deal, the cold war, and the ascent of racial liberals like Hubert H. Humphrey and Paul H. Douglas created a "political opportunity structure" conducive to optimism about the movement's ability to appeal successfully to a national constituency.
4. Fowler and Shaiko (1987) found that a majority of the membership of the Environmental Defense Fund thought of themselves as "contributors" rather than "members."
5. The most prominent exceptions are college students, whose peripatetic ways make them the roving workforce, the "roadies," of many a presidential campaign, and not a few other campaigns.
6. The same might be said of decisions that are made at the state level. Residents of

New Jersey and Connecticut, for instance, are disfranchised from participation in New York governments that tax the commuters among them. State governments make decisions that affect Americans well beyond the confines of state borders. For an interesting analysis of the implications of transcendent policies for the normative understanding of electoral institutions, see Thompson (2002).

7. For an interesting twist on the causes and effects of the surge in party discipline, see Pomper (1999). The ban on soft money in the pending 2002 campaign finance reform might be interpreted either as a lesson learned or as a warning confirmed. After unhappy experience, the optimists finally had to conclude that a provision meant to serve a commendable purpose, to strengthen the parties, had been turned to an ignoble purpose. The pessimists, on the other hand, found themselves right all along: money corrupts politics, they warned, no matter how it is channeled.

8. In the election cycles of the 1990s, for instance, Republican Party fundraising committees typically received more from individual donors both in absolute and relative terms. In the 1995–96 cycle, GOP committees received $362.1 million from individual contributors, for 86.9 percent of the total; Democratic Party committees received $171.3 million, for 77.3 percent of the total. An extensive study of contributors to presidential campaigns finds that the ideological match between candidate and contributor is crucial to the success of both "personal" and "impersonal" modes of campaign fundraising. See Brown, Powell, and Wilcox (1995).

9. It appears, in fact, that liberals have just done better at maintaining citizens groups than conservatives (Berry 1999b).

10. Innovations such as unrestricted absentee balloting and voting by mail have made it easier for people to vote—albeit illegally—in the nonresidential jurisdictions in which they have interests. One state voting official told me that she believed a significant number of "duplicate" voter registrations were in fact intentional, made by students who wished to vote at school and at home or by owners of second homes who wished to participate in both of the jurisdictions that taxed their property.

11. In the end, E. E. Schattschneider, the great skeptic of pluralism, was also a majoritarian more than a populist, or as he put it, a "realist." "Democracy," he wrote in a passage reminiscent of the "elitist" theorists, "is a competitive political system in which competing leaders and organizations define the alternatives of public policy in such a way that the public can participate in the decision-making process" (1960, 138). See also Schumpeter (1942, 269, and chap. 22) and Walker (1966).

Chapter 4   *The Future of Democratic Participation*

1. There are many good studies of immigration to the U.S. during the early twentieth century, among them King (2000) and Gerstle and Mollenkopf (2001).

2. Three classic studies in this scholarly tradition include Glazer and Moynihan (1963), Gordon (1964), and Epstein (1978).

3. Andersen's analysis (1979) of presidential voting between 1928 and 1936 identifies the political activation of immigrants as one of the chief reasons behind the New Deal realignment.

4. Jacobson (1999) provides an interesting account of these three groups. See also Ignatiev's analysis (1995) of the strategic significance for the Irish of racial conflict with African Americans in their struggle against nativism and quest for inclusion among whites. One fascinating reflection of the state's struggle with (and manipulation of) categorizing by race is the evolution of the race question in the

census, where Jews were once counted as "Hebrews" and South Asians as "Hindus." See Anderson (1988). In the 2000 Census, Americans were for the first time allowed to choose more than one racial category to represent themselves.

5. Verba and Nie (1972) were the first to demonstrate this finding with survey data from the U.S. population. See also Verba, Schlozman, Brady, and Nie (1993); Danigelis (1978, 1982); Dawson (1995); Dawson, Brown, and Allen (1990); Ellison and Gay (1989); Guterbock and London (1983); Leighley and Vedlitz (1999); Nelson (1979); Shingles (1981).

6. The Latino National Political Survey conducted interviews with a national sample of Latinos, focusing on Mexicans, Cubans, and Puerto Ricans. The research was conducted by Rodolfo de la Garza, Louis DeSipio, F. Chris Garcia, John Garcia, and Angelo Falcon, and the study is detailed in their 1992 book.

7. Jones-Correa's study of New York (1998) and Hardy-Fanta's work (1993) in Boston are two examples of work on Latinos. On Asian Americans, see Espiritu (1992) and Wei (1993). Some of the most interesting current research on racial and ethnic minorities in the United States is being done in sociology, where scholars are researching patterns of social and economic assimilation. See Portes (1996); Portes and Rumbaut (1996); Waters (1999); Foner (1987); Gans (1992); and the June/July 1999 issue of the *American Behavioral Scientist*.

8. The "second generation" project headed by John Mollenkopf of the CUNY Graduate Center is currently collecting data on the political activity of the children of immigrants in New York City. See also Lin and Jamal (1998) for a study of Arab immigrants; Minnite, Holdaway, and Hayduk (2000) on New York City residents; Ramakrishnan and Espenshade (2000) on generational voting patterns among minorities in the United States; and Wong (2000) on Mexican and Chinese immigrants in Los Angeles and New York.

9. In their "civic voluntarism" model, Verba, Schlozman, and Brady (1995) go beyond SES by unpacking the elements of resources, as time, money, and civic skills. In addition, Wolfinger and Rosenstone (1980, chap. 2) provide a good explanation of how and why formal education is so important to voting.

10. See chapter 6 in Nie, Junn, and Stehlik-Barry (1996) for a critique of the logic of the absolute education model and an explanation of rising aggregate levels of education amidst stagnant and declining political engagement.

11. Andrew Hacker uses this memorable phrase to describe the location of Asian Americans in the American educational system in his 1992 book.

12. "Special Report: Redefining Race in America," *Newsweek*, September 18, 2000.

13. Epstein defines *mischling* as "the offspring of marriages between Jew and Gentile who have usually been brought up on neither a Jewish nor a Christian tradition, and where the home environment has laid little emphasis on ethnic origins" (1978, 102).

14. The phrase, and the perspective, are from Charles Tilly (1998).

15. I will focus my attention here on the importance of education—as an indicator of class—to political participation in the United States. Formal education is not only the most widely used empirical measure of socioeconomic status and social class, but it is also the case that education occupies a particularly important place within the tradition of American democratic theory as a desirable prerequisite for political participation.

16. In support of IQ meritocracy theories, see Duncan, Featherman, and Duncan (1972); Duncan (1968); Herrnstein (1971); and Herrnstein and Murray (1994). Critiques of this perspective include Bell (1972); Olneck and Crouse (1979); and Krausz and Slomczynski (1985).

17. This "revisionist" perspective, consistent with Bowles and Gintis (1976), identifies

education as critical to the maintenance of capitalism. See also Willis (1977) for his analysis of how the "Hammertown lads" subjectively reproduce labor power through resistance to and rebellion from middle-class educational imperatives.

Chapter 5   *The Future of Liberty in American Democratic Politics?*

1. For example, freedom of religion was tied to resistance to Catholicism, which was feared in part because of the dangers of having private property confiscated by, or at least having to pay taxes to, a foreign power. The Exclusion Crisis in seventeenth-century England, for instance, was arguably less about religious freedom than it was about property rights, though religious toleration was a discourse that was used to complement, reinforce, and, according to some, mask this. See particularly Ashcraft (1986), Macpherson (1962), Schochet (1988, esp. 251–54), Schochet (2000), and Tully (1980).
2. It should be noted that Astell made this jibe not in the interest of equalizing liberty, but rather of pointing out hypocrisy. As a monarchist, it could be argued that Astell believed there was altogether too much concern with individual liberty and not enough with loyalty and obedience.
3. Contemporary Islamic fundamentalists similarly claim to reject freedom as a Western obsession; but many of them also seem to reject democracy, whereas the political ideal, if not the practice, of former communist countries was arguably a form of democracy, or rule "by the people."
4. For two very different approaches to this position within feminism, see, for instance, Brown (1995) and MacKinnon (1986). In terms of race, see Mills (1997). Cohen (1995) is an example of such expansion to class by a Marxist.
5. The one exception is expertise, because some people with specialized knowledge are more qualified to make certain decisions than are others. But even here, race, class, and gender inequities influence inequalities of power; if women or blacks are systematically denied access to certain kinds of knowledge, then they will not be "experts." Furthermore, the requirements of freedom demand that expertise should not translate into power to make choices for others, but only to influence debate and try to persuade others.
6. For a fuller discussion of this theme of freedom in U.S. welfare reform, see Hirschmann (2001).

Chapter 6   *The Rhetoric of Democratic Liberty*

It is a pleasure to acknowledge my indebtedness to Jonathan McFall for his—as usual—extraordinarily close reading and insightful suggestions, to Kiki Jamieson with whom I have often discussed many of these ideas over the past ten years and from whom I learned much, and, of course, to Rumm.

1. I acknowledge that there are circumstances that require one or the other of the terms, but these are due largely to usage, conventions, and the structure of the English language: lunch is "free" (or not), but, unless stolen, not "liberated"; sailors on shore leave are "at liberty" but not free; I may "take liberties" with a person's name by calling John "Jack" without permission or may be told to "feel free" to do so; there is no independent adjectival form of "liberty" that corresponds to "free" ("liberated" as a modifier is formed from the past tense of the verb "liberate"); and liberty tends to be the more elegant of the two. In all these cases, nuanced usages point to the absence, relaxation, or overcoming of restraints, not to conceptual distinctions. In most instances, *freedom* and *liberty* may properly be

used interchangeably with no loss or distortion of meaning. I am certain that there are more substantial reasons, but I suspect that part of the attempt to distinguish between them is due to something of a linguistic snobbery—perhaps unwitting—that holds the elegant, Latinate *liberty* in higher esteem than the more pedestrian, Germanic *freedom*, a snobbishness I sometimes share.

2. It referred, therefore, both to the independence of the *civitas* from foreign rule and to the personal status of not being enslaved.

3. No one, of course, claims that nonhuman animals should be participants in the public life of the political community. The point, rather, is that the needs and entitlements of animals should be addressed, just as the otherwise unarticulated needs of children and disabled persons should be brought to the attention of the community. Thus, while not directly related to political liberty, which is the unique preserve of humans, advocacy of "animal liberation" or "animal rights" does illustrate the larger process by which the category of bearer of natural human liberty has been extended beyond white males.

4. E.g., Hobbes in the *Leviathan*: "The Right of Nature . . . is the Liberty each man hath, to use his own power as he will himselfe. . . . Right consisteth in liberty to do, or to forbeare" (Hobbes 1651 [1991], 91 [chap. 14]); and H. L. A. Hart, who, after a careful analysis of the workings and presumptions of moral institutions and concepts, concluded "that if there are any moral natural rights at all, it follows that there is at least one natural right, the equal right of all men to be free" (Hart 1955, 175).

5. Another version, of course, is Abraham Lincoln's "conceived in liberty and dedicated to the proposition that all men are created equal."

6. Among the alleged costs of this liberalization are the decline of authority, the destruction of "civic virtue" and "community," the growth of sham participation, and the decline of equality as a social and political value. The first of these criticisms is often applied by conservatives to what is seen as excessive populism. The others are anticapitalist responses to the excesses of market-based practices and, recently, "globalization." Among the advantages claimed for economic globalization are that it will increase political participation and lead to democratic liberties throughout the world. The reply is that in these terms, a world economy advances the interests of the West, in particular the United States: under the guise of bringing democratic liberties and economic growth to the nonindustrial world, globalization exploits poor nations and strengthens oppressive states. Some of these issues are excellently discussed in Sassen (1996).

   The expansion of liberties and entitlements in democratic societies is not comparable to the lessening of restrictions in oppressive and nondemocratic regimes, where the new liberties apply to the entire society, or at least to its nonruling members. In states that are already democratic, the issue is not the end of repression but the expansion of liberties that are already in place by the elimination of specific exclusions or abuses.

7. Obviously, not all conflicts that satisfy these criteria require political resolution. Constitutional safeguards and provisions keep the state from attempting to regulate all the conflicts that might arise in the lives of its members; various practices and conventions help to limit the reach of political authority; and nonpolitical agencies settle many important—but "private"—disputes that occur in the normal course of events. Some conflicts, of course, are never resolved but are not sufficiently "important" to warrant the intervention of the state. But when the interests or concerns of others are at stake, when the conflict may be precedent-setting, when an unacceptable or unwarranted degree of coercion or

interference with fundamental rights or freedoms may be involved, and/or where there may be violations of what are taken to be the standards of justice, political resolution may be deemed necessary.

8. I am ignoring here the recent criticisms of neutrality as both a goal and a practice of (liberal) political decision making. The arguments are that neutrality is impossible to achieve and that the values of liberalism are themselves values about which liberal decision procedures cannot be neutral. Whatever their respective merits, neither criticism reaches my relatively weak claim that democratic legitimacy turns in part on the government's having no interest in the substantive outcome of the controversies it resolves.

9. It is undoubtedly for this reason that freedom did not appear in a recognizably modern or individualist form in the context of republicanism. Political freedom is one of the principal means of protecting and sustaining pluralism and diversity, and it was called into being, as it were, by that very diversity. There is little place for political freedom as the absence of restraints in a world that conceives of itself as homogeneous and tends to treat dissent as a kind of political heresy. Freedom is meant to legitimate departures from prevailing practices.

10. My use of this distinction is related to and partially derived from but not identical to the use of the same terminology in Williams (1956) and Attwooll (1977).

11. E.g., the unending chant of "Freedom, freedom, freedom" by Richie Havens at Woodstock, the ironic "Freedom's just another word for nothing left to lose" of Kris Kristofferson and Janis Joplin, and the insistence of The Young Rascals that "Deep in the valley, people got to be free." It is worth noting that recourse to freedom has virtually disappeared from recent popular music. One obvious reason for this difference is the fact that the period that gave rise to these and other such instances was intensely political in ways that the 1990s and early twenty-first century were not.

12. See, for instance, Macpherson (1966) for an attack on "bourgeois" or "liberal" democracy on the ground that its commitment to freedom is specious because it is class-based and inegalitarian and therefore undemocratic.

13. We can, of course, "operationalize" and even measure those practices that we have stipulated to be freedoms, which includes most of our legally protected rights and what we call "civil liberties." Beyond this, however, it is very difficult.

14. It was foreshadowed by Sabine (1952), whose usage was eclipsed by Berlin and is now all but forgotten.

15. To her credit, Hirschmann adds a new vitality to Berlin's distinction and forces a reconsideration of his conceptual claims. Nonetheless, I remain unpersuaded that "positive liberty" is a necessary, conceptually proper, or even a useful verbal construction.

16. There were important contextual reasons for the moves Hobbes made here, among them the need to subvert the newly emergent juridical vocabulary of rights and liberty by stealing it from the enemies of the monarchy and transforming it from an emancipatory, oppositional language to one that could be used in support of absolutism. Despite his unprecedented theoretical brilliance, Hobbes utterly failed in his attempt. No one—not even the proponents of narrowly construed negative liberty such as Isaiah Berlin, Jeremy Bentham (see Long 1977, 54–55, 74–75), and Benjamin Constant (1819)—has used that notion for any purpose other than to *limit* political authority. It is among the great ironies in the history of political thought that irrespective of these facts, the Hobbesian version of the theory survives as the model.

17. Of these three, Unger is the most egregious in his caricature of "liberalism" in order to attack it. George and Garvey are more subtle, but they too end up with

oversimplified presentations of liberalism as narrowly self-regarding autonomy that they then criticize from a shared perspective rooted in notions of human goodness and natural law. None of these critics is ultimately willing to accept the ineliminable pluralism that is at the heart of liberalism; they appear to prefer the homogeneous political perfectionism that liberalism has consistently opposed.

18. I follow here some of the arguments against Berlin in McCallum (1967) but not those of Taylor ([1979] 1985), which I think are wide of the mark, in part because of the presumption that humans are "purposive beings" (219).

19. This seems to be at the heart of what is often meant by "culture" and by the notion of "social construction," that it is in the nature of human life to be restrained by unavoidable and ineliminable *external* factors. "Consciousness," one of the important and celebrated hallmarks of "modernity," would include an awareness of this inherent limitation, as philosophers and social critics have not failed to remind us since the Enlightenment, when they ask us to consider how free we *really* are.

20. They are also concerned to argue that the "liberal" emphasis upon freedom promotes self-interest and undermines other-regardingness, but that is part of an attack on "negative freedom" that I do not consider here.

21. So-called classical liberals of the laissez-faire variety share this position with modern antiliberals, with the important difference that these self-styled "classical liberals" do not care for equality and see the apparent incompatibility as a strength.

22. *http://www.npr.org/news/specials/civillibertiespoll/011130.poll.html.*

Chapter 7 *The Future of Legislatures in Democratic Politics*

1. On page 405 Jones writes,

   Recent reforms (growth in staff, expanded use of the legislative veto, a more comprehensive and coordinated budgetary procedure) encourage even more direct and systematic congressional participation in program execution. Interestingly, these changes appear to have been made to a substantial degree as a consequence of perceived excesses by the president—particularly during the Johnson and Nixon administrations. That is, Congress was moved to expand its capabilities to deal with all aspects of foreign and domestic issues because many members came to believe that Presidents Johnson and Nixon had exceeded their authority.

   Also see Jones (1981).

2. Abolished by Newt Gingrich's Revolution in 1995, the OTA was given seventeen full-time equivalents for Fiscal Year 1996 in order to close down the organization.

3. In the 1960s, Alexander Heard wrote: "Mr. Unruh is perhaps the most prominent state legislator in the United States. His California Legislature has perhaps done more to improve its capacity to meet the extraordinary problems it faces than has any other. Mr. Unruh was reported as saying there was a national awareness of the ineptitude of state legislatures. In a competitive mood that those familiar with California state politics will understand, he ruefully observed that state legislatures are being outshone by the executive branches in their states" (1966, 158). See also the Citizens Conference on State Legislatures (1971). These changes were also stimulated by work led by Don Herzberg at the Eagleton Institute at Rutgers.

4. The Supreme Court ruled that absent a constitutional amendment, "neither states nor Congress may limit the number of terms that members of Congress can serve."

5. The main decisions were *Baker v. Carr* (1962), which took jurisdiction in state

apportionment cases; *Wesberry v. Sanders* (1964), which required substantial equality of populations within U.S. House districts; and *Reynolds v. Sims* (1964), which forced the apportionment of both houses of bicameral state legislatures on the same proportional basis. For a thorough discussion of these and other cases, see Robert G. Dixon's *Democratic Representation* (1968). In *Wells v. Rockefeller* (1969), the Court defined more exactly—and more narrowly—what "substantial equality" meant (see Polsby 1971). The line of cases continues to grow. For more recent commentary see Grofman, Lijphardt, McKay, and Scarrow (1982). In *Mahan v. Howell* (1973), the court forced the state of Virginia closer to "one person, one vote" in state districts. In *Karcher v. Daggett* (1983) the Court demanded that congressional districts be more exactly equal in population than the U.S. Census is capable of warranting. In *Shaw v. Reno* (1993), the Court held that while race could be considered in drawing congressional district lines it could not be a decisive factor.

6. *Table 7.1.*
   Decline of U.S. Agricultural Population, 1900–1990, Percentage of Population Living on a Farm

	1900	1920	1940	1950	1960	1980	1990
Non-South	32.1	22.2	17.1	11.4	6.3	2.7	1.7
South	60.8	55.3	42.0	27.2	11.2	2.8	1.3

Sources: Total state populations (the denominator): 1900–1960 from *Historical Statistics of the United States, Colonial Times to 1970* (Washington, D.C.: Bureau of the Census, 1975), 10, 24–37; 1980 and 1990, *1996 Statistical Abstract of the United States* (Washington, D.C.: Bureau of the Census, 1996), 28. Farm population (numerator): 1900–1950, *Historical Statistics of the United States: Colonial Times to 1970* (Washington, D.C.: Bureau of the Census, 1975), 458. 1960: *Census of Population 1960: Vol. I, Characteristics of the Population*, U.S. Summary, table 155; state totals, table 95. 1980: Bureau of the Census Report, *Estimates of the Number of Farm Residents*. Provided by Economic Research Service, U.S. Department of Agriculture. 1990: *Census of Population 1990: Social and Economic Characteristics Report* CP–2–1 (Washington, D.C.: Bureau of Census, U.S. Summary. Table 15, state totals, table 4. South = eleven states of the Confederacy.

Table 7.2.
Urban and Rural Distribution of the U.S. Population in each Census since 1940

Year	Total	Urban Number	Percent	Rural Number	Percent
1940	132,164,569	74,705,338	56.5	57,459,231	43.5
1950	151,325,798	96,846,817	64.0	54,478,981	36.0
1960	179,323,175	125,268,750	69.9	54,054,425	30.1
1970	203,302,031	149,646,629	73.6	53,565,297	26.4
1980	226,542,199	167,050,992	73.7	59,494,813	26.3
1990	248,709,873	187,053,487	75.2	61,656,386	24.8

Source: U.S. Census Bureau, table 16, 1990 CPH–2–1; table 25, 1990 CPH–2–1; and table 13, 1980 PC80–1–1.

7. There are currently thirty-seven African Americans in Congress, thirty-six of whom are Democrats.

Table 7.3.
Number of African Americans elected to each Congress since 1980

1980	1982	1984	1986	1988	1990	1992	1994	1996	1998	2000
17	20	19	22	23	25	38	38	37	37	37

Chapter 9   *The Impact of* Bush v. Gore *on Future Democratic Politics*

1. See also Burgess (1888) explaining the act and discussing its legislative history.
2. The focus of this chapter is on the involvement of the federal judiciary and thus the question of the propriety of state court involvement is not directly discussed. The roles played by the two courts are different in ways important to the analysis. The U.S. Supreme Court intervened in the election so that it acted instead of Congress; its involvement rendered congressional involvement superfluous. The Florida Supreme Court did not act as a substitute for the political branches; rather, the courts served in an oversight capacity, assessing and guiding the administration of the state election code. Some, including Justice Rehnquist in his concurrence in *Bush v. Gore,* have argued that the state supreme court erred in its oversight role (Epstein 2001, 22–35). Others have defended the Florida Supreme Court's interpretation of the election code as employing acceptable methods of statutory construction (Kramer 2001b, 130–35). Whether one agrees with the defenders of the state justices or their detractors, the state judiciary would have allowed the continued involvement of some state political actors and, regardless of the outcome of any recounts, would not have preempted the U.S. Congress from serving as the final arbiter of the election contest.
3. See also *United States v. Morrison,* 529 U.S. 598 (2000) (also using legislative record review in the context of the Violence Against Women Act). For further critiques of these cases, see Frickey and Smith (2002) and Kramer (2001a, 137–53).
4. *Emergency Supplemental Appropriations Act—Response to Terrorist Attacks on September 11, 2001,* PL 107–38; *Authorization for Use of Military Force,* 2001, PL 107–40; *Air Transportation Safety and Stabilization Act,* 2001, PL 107–42.
5. It appears that at least with respect to the airline bailout bill, a few other members worked as key negotiators. Some reports identify, in addition to Daschle, Representative Blunt, the House Majority Deputy Whip, Senator Hollings, the Chair of the Senate Commerce Committee, and OMB Director Mitch Daniels as the policymakers who negotiated and drafted the bills (Benton and Cohn 2001).
6. Some of the arguments here are developments and extensions from Garrett (2001a, 2001b).
7. There is disagreement about the seriousness of the election dispute in 1876. Senator Ingalls, in debate over the Electoral Count Act, argued that the disputes of 1800 and 1876 brought the country "to the very verge and brink of revolution" (*Cong. Rec.,* 49th Cong., 1st sess., 1886, 17 Ingalls, 1886, 2:1025). Certainly, these nineteenth-century episodes were much more serious threats to the country, in part because of surrounding events, than the 2000 election, and yet both were resolved by the political branches without catastrophic results.
8. *U.S. Code,* Title 3, sec. 5, provides a rule of decision for Congress so that "[i]f any State shall have provided, by laws enacted prior to the day fixed for the appointment of the electors, for its final determination of any controversy or contest concerning the appointment of all or any of the electors of such State, by judicial or other methods or procedures, and such determination shall have been

made at least six days before the time fixed for the meeting of the electors, such determination made pursuant to such law so existing on said day, and made at least six days prior to said time of meeting of the electors, shall be conclusive, and shall govern in the counting of the electoral votes as provided in the Constitution, and as hereinafter regulated, so far as the ascertainment of the electors by such State is concerned."

9. On this latter point, see Sherman (1886), listing other "supposable cases" and acknowledging that the act does not provide rules for all of them.

Chapter 10   *The Supreme Court and* Bush v. Gore

1. The initial literature has included works by judges, legal scholars, political scientists, historians, and journalists. See, for example, Posner (2001); Ceaser and Busch (2001); Gillman (2001); Sunstein and Epstein (2001); Rakove (2001); Dionne and Kristol (2001); the *New York Times* (2001); Dershowitz (2001); *Washington Post* (2001); and Ackerman (2002). It has also been subjected to wide treatment in law reviews, including symposia in the *University of Chicago* and *Florida State University Law Reviews* (2001). To cite only a few of the many excellent law review articles, see Klarman (2001); Balkin (2001); Tushnet (2001); and Scheppele (2001).

2. For example, Calabresi (Ackerman 2002, 129–44) argues that Congress, or any one of a number of other elected officials, rather than the Court, should have resolved the 2000 election dispute because the case presented a "political question," rather than a properly justifiable controversy. Some have touched briefly upon whether Congress should have resolved the election dispute, addressing the issue as a companion or side issue to other considerations. See, for example, Levinson and Young (2001); Tushnet (Ackerman, 2002, 173); Gillman (2001, 191–95). Not everyone, however, views Congress as the appropriate entity to resolve the impasse (Posner 2001, 132–47; Sunstein and Epstein 2001, 216–18).

3. We think Garrett is correct to dismiss an argument that has gotten surprisingly wide currency—the notion that intervention by the Supreme Court was necessary to avoid a constitutional or political crisis. At the heart of this argument is an irony that few of its proponents acknowledge or address: a resort to Congress to resolve close or contested elections is exactly the solution embodied in the Constitution. Considering that the closest we came to civil unrest was the less-than-spontaneous demonstration by imported Republican campaign workers outside the location where they were recounting votes in Miami, the worst that would have befallen our society if the Supreme Court had not stopped the recounts was a few weeks of intermittent guerilla warfare between ambassadors-in-waiting for the two parties.

4. As the majority explained its dilemma, "None are more conscious of the vital limits on judicial authority than are the members of this Court, and none stand more in admiration of the Constitution's design to leave the selection of the President to the people, through their legislatures, and to the political sphere. When contending powers, however, invoke the process of the courts, however, it becomes our unsought responsibility to resolve the federal and constitutional issues the judicial system has been forced to confront" (*Bush v. Gore*, 531 U.S. 98, 111). For a response to the idea that the Court was *forced* to take the case, see Kramer (2001, 156–58).

5. On the election of 1800 and the sense of crisis and intrigue following the tie for electoral college votes by Jefferson and Burr, see Elkins and McKitrick (1993, 746–50); Freeman (2001, 199–261); and Sharp (1993, 250–75).

6. Passage of the Twelfth Amendment was also driven by the fact that, with the emergence of political parties, the original system for deciding elections (with the winner of the majority of the electoral votes ascending to the presidency and the winner of the second most assuming the vice-presidency) could have unintended consequences, such as an administration in which members of competing parties occupied the two offices (Currie 1997, chap. 2; Kyvig 1996, 114–19).

7. See Dangerfield (1965, 212–30); Peterson (1987, 116–29). For a different assessment of the corruption to be found in the 1824 election, see Remini (1991, 251–72).

8. For somewhat differing views on the electoral deadlock and the negotiations and forces that led to a solution, see Polakoff (1973) and Woodward (1951).

9. The phrase is taken from Balkin (2001).

10. See remarks of Senator Sherman quoted in Karlan (Rakove 2001).

11. Article II of the Constitution clearly commits the resolution to Congress when the election is deadlocked because no candidate received a majority of the electoral votes—the situation in 1800 and 1824—but it is not at all clear that the text of the Constitution provides a similar commitment regarding resolution of contested electoral votes in the first place—the situation in 1876 and 2000 (Calabresi essay in Ackerman 2002; Levinson and Young 2001, 959–60). Indeed, the debates over the Electoral Count Act indicate that leaving such disputes to the Supreme Court was one option that was considered but rejected in favor of having Congress decide.

12. For example, if there are two competing slates of electors, Congress is directed to count "those electors . . . whose title as electors the two Houses, acting separately shall concurrently decide is supported by the decision of such State so authorized by its law." And if there was no clear determination by the State, then Congress is to count "those votes, and only those votes . . . which the two Houses shall concurrently decide were cast by lawful electors appointed in accordance with the laws of the State, unless the two Houses, acting separately, shall concurrently decide such votes not to be the lawful votes of the legally appointed electors of such State" (3 USC 15). For an argument that this *is* all the Congress would consider had resolution of the deadlocked 2000 election fallen to it, see Friedman (2001). Friedman, however, did not expressly reject, or even address, the argument we make here—that political considerations might play a role in the decisions that members of Congress would reach.

13. For example, if the Florida legislature had done an end run around the courts and decided to resolve the matter by simply sending its own slate, as some of the state legislators threatened to do, that slate might well have had an argument that it was entitled to recognition as electors under section 15. See also Posner (2001), arguing that the vote in Florida was so close that it would have been impossible to determine who actually received more votes.

14. Treating Congress's decision as nothing more than an effort to answer specific points about state election law raises other important questions, including whether that decision is then subject to judicial review and whether Congress must work from different considerations when electoral votes are in dispute than when no candidate received a majority of electoral votes.

15. On republicanism in the founding era, see Wood (1992, 92–225) and Sunstein (1988, 1539–90). For correctives or qualifiers on the usefulness of republicanism as a concept, see Kerber (1988, 1663–72) and Rogers (1992, 11–38).

16. This, in turn, raises its own interesting irony. If members of Congress, voting on whom to elect as president in the scenario presented, are limited only to considerations of "high politics," any member who deviated and entertained more

partisan or mundane considerations such as those usually at work as part of the normal vote-trading found in the legislative process would be subject to criticism for *not* deviating from his or her conventional role. That would be the exact opposite of the criticism leveled at the Supreme Court in *Bush v. Gore*, to the extent that the Court has been criticized for *not* adhering to the "traditional" judicial model of deciding cases based on established principles and without political influence.

17. For some particularly scathing critiques of the decision, see Rubenfeld (Ackerman 2002), Kramer (Rakove 2001), and Balkin (2001).

18. For years before it rendered its decision in *Erie RR v. Tompkins* (1938), the Court adumbrated its conclusion (Purcell 2000). This is in sharp contrast to how the Court handled equal protection in *Bush v. Gore*.

19. One might be justified in thinking that the situation in *Bush v. Gore* did not present an opportunity for a well-reasoned opinion acceptable to all. Nonetheless, for an interesting effort to craft such an opinion, see Guido Calabresi (Ackerman 2002, 67–83). However, some legal scholars have argued that the test for legitimacy of a Supreme Court decision rests not on the quality of its reasoning, but rather on how well it is accepted by the broader public (Friedman 2001, 1383; Klarman 2001).

20. Gillman (2001, 151–58) briefly summarizes the reaction. Those who applaud the result, without endorsing the Court's reasoning, include Posner (2001) and Sunstein and Yoo (Sunstein and Epstein 2001), while McConnell (Sunstein and Epstein 2001) supports at least some of the Court's reasoning.

21. On the initial reaction to the *Brown* decision, the literature is voluminous, but for excellent overviews see Kluger (1977), Patterson (2001), and Wilkerson (1979).

22. On *Roe v. Wade*, see Ely (1973, 920–49). Regarding the *Miranda* decision, see Malone (Leo and Thomas 1998), who claims that *Miranda* quickly became "the most reviled decision ever issued by the Supreme Court in a criminal case," and who notes that "[a]ll this controversy was over a decision that required police departments to do what many law enforcement agencies already practiced" (75).

23. See, e.g., *Planned Parenthood of Southeastern Pennsylvania v. Casey* (1992) and *Dickerson v. United States* (2000).

24. Karlan (Rakove 2001) calls the case unprecedented in the "colloquial" sense of the word, because no prior case decisions supported the Court's ruling, but finds the decision part of a line of cases involving "structural equal protection" in which "the Court uses the [equal protection] clause to regulate the institutional arrangements within which politics is conducted, rather than to protect the rights of specific individuals or groups" (195). On the alignment of the justices, see Kramer (2001), who notes that "[n]ot only were the Court's two most liberal members, Justices Stevens and Ginsburg, in dissent, but the five most conservative Justices suddenly embraced Warren Court principles they have spent their whole careers trying to undo" (154 n. 659).

25. It is true, of course, that the Court's decision frames the issues as matters of law—involving Article II of the Constitution and the Equal Protection Clause—rather than "political" considerations (Gillman 2001, 172–73). But if that were remotely persuasive to most of the political scientists and legal commentators who have weighed in on the decision, the reaction to the Court's decision would have been very different.

26. Probably the most certain long-term effects coming out of the election of 2000 will be efforts to reform the laws and technologies involved in voting, and, ad-

mittedly less likely, reconsideration and abolition of the Electoral College. But those consequences seem attributable more to the election mess that gave rise to *Bush v. Gore* rather than a response to the decision itself.

27. Consider, for example, *Brown v. Board of Education* (1954) and *United States v. Nixon* (1974), both examples of unanimous decisions aimed at encouraging public acceptance, even at the expense of a clear and unequivocal ruling, at least in the *Brown* case.

28. However, see Klarman (2001) hypothesizing that one reason that the opinion will not affect the Court's long-term reputation is that the issues involved are so obscure and unlikely to repeat themselves.

29. Ackerman (2002, 200–202) makes a comparable point, stressing more how Congress might handle future judicial appointments in light of *Bush v. Gore*. However, not everyone is persuaded that the handling of *Bush v. Gore* by itself was needed to provoke pitched battles over future judicial nominations by a Democratically controlled Senate (Gillman 2001, 199–200).

30. It is interesting to note that the editors of the *American Heritage Dictionary*, comparing the impact on our lexical currency of "9/11" to that of "Bush v. Gore," observed that "[n]o one asks about chads anymore" (Scott 2002).

Chapter 11   *Democratic Ends and Political Parties in America*

I owe a particular debt of gratitude to Gerald M. Pomper for his contributions to this essay.

1. This elegant imperative is at the core of Robert Dahl's lifelong concern with democracy (Dahl 1971, 1989, 1994, 1998).

2. This discussion reflects the long-standing debate on party responsibility (Pomper 2001b; American Political Science Association 1950; White and Mileur 1992). Electoral accountability was central to the arguments over party responsibility. The issue was not whether it was a valuable and necessary asset in a democratic society, but the extent to which it could be realized in the federated, multicentered, and weakly organized party system found in the United States. Parties have to be "responsible" in the sense that they link voters and their views through campaigns and candidates to policy outcomes. These can be measured, if crudely, through indicators of party coherence and like-mindedness in voting on policy issues.

Chapter 12   *Contentious Democracy*

1. For an excellent typology of interest group liaison (governing party, consensus building, outreach, and legitimation), see Peterson (1992b).

2. This approach is similar to Stephen Skowronek's (1993) emphasis on regime cycles in that it enables us to analytically link together presidents from different historical periods facing similar political circumstances.

3. The best review of this literature is offered by Pika (1999).

4. It is telling in this regard that Peterson focuses on the political activities of Lyndon Johnson and Ronald Reagan, presidents with exceptional opportunities to advance policy breakthroughs (Peterson 1992a, 237).

Works Cited

Abramowitz, Alan. 1994. "Issue Evolution Reconsidered." *American Journal of Political Science* 38(1):1–24.

Ackerman, Bruce. 2001. "The Court Packs Itself." *American Prospect* (February): 48.

———, ed. 2002. *Bush v. Gore: The Question of Legitimacy*. New Haven: Yale University Press.

Adams, George Everett. 1886. Representative Adams of Illinois speaking against the Electoral Count Act. 49th Cong., 2d sess., *Cong. Rec.*, 1886, vol. 18, pt. 1.

Air Transportation Safety and Stabilization Act. 2001. U.S. Public Law 107–42, 107th Cong., 1st sess., September 22; *U.S. Statutes at Large* 115: 230.

Alba, Richard D. 1990. *Ethnic Identity: The Transformation of White America*. New Haven: Yale University Press.

Alba, Richard, and Victor Nee. 1997. "Rethinking Assimilation Theory for a New Era of Immigration." *International Migration Review* 31(4):826–74.

Albiston, Catherine R., and Laura Beth Nielsen. 1995. "Welfare Queens and Other Fairly Tales: Welfare Reform and Unconstitutional Reproductive Controls." *Howard Law Journal* 38, no. 3:473–519.

Aldrich, John. 1995. *Why Parties?* Chicago: University of Chicago Press.

American Political Science Association. 1950. *Toward a More Responsible Two-Party System*. New York: Rinehart.

Andersen, Kristi. 1979. *The Creation of a Democratic Majority, 1928–1936*. Chicago: University of Chicago Press.

Anderson, Margo J. 1988. *The American Census: A Social History*. New Haven: Yale University Press.

Apple, R. W. 2001. "Big Government Is Back in Style." *New York Times*, November 23, B2.

Arendt, Hannah. 1965. *On Revolution*. New York: Viking Press.

Aristotle. 1977. *Politics*. Trans. H. Rackham. Cambridge, Mass.: Harvard University Press.

Arkansas Educational Television Commission v. Forbes. 523 U.S. 666 (1998).

Ashcraft, Richard. 1986. *Revolutionary Politics and Locke's Two Treatises of Government*. Princeton, N.J.: Princeton University Press.

Astell, Mary. 1996. "Reflections upon Marriage." In *Political Writings*, ed. Patricia Springborg. New York: Cambridge University Press.

Attwooll, Elspeth. 1977. "Liberties, Rights, and Powers." In *Perspectives in Jurisprudence*. Glasgow: University of Glasgow Press.

Authorization for Use of Military Force. 2001. U.S. Public Law 107–40. 107th Cong., 1st sess., September 18; *U.S. Statutes at Large* 115:224.

Baker v. Carr. 389 U.S. 186 (1962).

Balanced Budget and Emergency Deficit Control Act of 1985, U.S. Code. Title 2 secs. 900–907d, 922.

Balkin, Jack M. 2001. "*Bush v. Gore* and the Boundary between Law and Politics." *Yale Law Journal* 110:1407–58.

Baratz, Peter, and Morton Bachrach. 1962. "The Two Faces of Power." *American Political Science Review* 56 (December): 947–52.

Barber, Benjamin. 1984. *Strong Democracy: Participatory Politics for a New Age.* Berkeley: University of California Press.

———. 1998a. "Big = Bad, Unless It Doesn't." *New York Times,* April 16, A23.

———. 1998b. *A Passion for Democracy.* Princeton, N.J.: Princeton University Press.

Barkow, R. E. 2002. "More Supreme than Court? The Fall of the Political Question Doctrine and the Rise of Judicial Supremacy." *Columbia Law Review* 102 (2002): 237–336.

Barnett, Ola W., and Alyce D. LaViolette. 1993. *It Could Happen to Anyone: Why Battered Women Stay.* Newbury Park, Calif.: Sage Publications.

Barone, Michael. 2001. *The New Americans: How the Melting Pot Can Work Again.* Washington: Regnery.

Bartels, Larry M. 2000a. "Campaign Reform: Insights and Evidence." In Larry M. Bartels and Lynn Vavreck, eds. *Campaign Quality: Standards for Evaluation, Benchmarks for Reform.* Ann Arbor: University of Michigan Press.

———. 2000b. "Partisanship and Voting Behavior, 1952–1996." *American Journal of Political Science* 44: 35–50.

Baumgartner, Frank R., and Beth L. Leech. 1998. *Basic Interests: The Importance of Groups in Politics and in Political Science.* Princeton, N.J.: Princeton University Press.

Becker, Gary. 1993. *Human Capital: A Theoretical and Empirical Analysis with Special Reference to Education.* 3d ed. Chicago: University of Chicago Press.

Becker, Ted, and Christa Daryl Slaton. 2000. *The Future of Teledemocracy.* Westport, Conn.: Praeger.

Beiner, Ronald. 1992. *What's the Matter with Liberalism?* Berkeley: University of California Press.

Bell, Daniel. 1972. "On Meritocracy and Equality." *Public Interest* 29:29–68.

Bennett, W. Lance. 1998. "The Uncivil Culture: Communication, Identity and the Rise of Lifestyle Politics." *Political Science* 31:741–62.

Benton, J. C., and P. Cohn. 2001. "Hill Clears Aid for Airlines." *CQ Weekly,* September 22, 2206–7.

Berelson, Bernard R., Paul F. Lazarsfeld, and William N. McPhee. 1954. *Voting: A Study of Opinion Formation in a Presidential Campaign.* Chicago: University of Chicago Press.

Berlin, Isaiah. 1958. *Two Concepts of Liberty.* Oxford: Oxford University Press.

———. 1969. *Four Essays on Liberty.* Oxford: Oxford University Press.

Bernstein, Nina. 2001. "As Welfare Comes to an End, So Do the Jobs." *New York Times,* December 17.

Bernstein, Richard. 1994. *Dictatorship of Virtue: Multiculturalism and the Battle for America's Future.* New York: Knopf.

Berry, Jeffrey M. 1977. *Lobbying for the People: The Political Behavior of Public Interest Groups.* Princeton, N.J.: Princeton University Press.

———. 1999a. "The Rise of Citizens Groups." In *Civic Engagement in American Democracy,* ed. Theda Skocpol and Morris P. Fiorina, 367–93. Washington: Brookings Institution.

———. 1999b. *The New Liberalism: The Rising Power of Citizens Groups.* Washington: Brookings Institution.

Berry, Jeffrey M., and Kent Portney. 1995. "Centralizing Regulatory Control and Interest Group Access: The Quayle Council on Competitiveness." In *Interest Group Politics*, ed. Alan Cigler and Burdett Loomis. Washington: Congressional Quarterly Press.

Bessette, Joseph M. 1994. *The Mild Voice of Reason*. Chicago: University of Chicago Press.

Bibby, John F. 1999. "Party Networks: National-State Integration, Allied Groups, and Issue Activists." in *The State of the Parties: The Changing Role of Contemporary American Parties*, ed. John C. Green and Daniel M. Shea, 86–104. Lanham, Md.: Rowman & Littlefield.

"Blacks, Yes; Democrats, Maybe." 1998. *Economist*, July 18, 25–26.

Blau, Peter M., and Otis Dudley Duncan. 1967. *The American Occupational Structure*. New York: Wiley.

Board of Trustees of the University of Alabama v. Garrett. 531 U.S. 356 (2001).

Bobo, Lawrence, and Franklin D. Gilliam Jr. 1990. "Race, Socio-Political Participation, and Black Empowerment." *American Political Science Review* 84:377–93.

Bosso, Christopher. 1995. "The Color of Money: Environmental Groups and the Color of Money." In *Interest Group Politics*, ed. Allan Cigler and Burdett Loomis. Washington: Congressional Quarterly Press.

Bourdieu, Pierre. 1987. *Distinction: A Social Critique of the Judgment of Taste*. Trans. Richard Nice. Cambridge, Mass.: Harvard University Press.

———. 1989. *The State Nobility*. Trans. Lauretta C. Clough. Palo Alto, Calif.: Stanford University Press.

———. 1990. *Reproduction in Education, Society, and Culture*. 2d ed. Beverly Hills, Calif.: Sage Publications.

Bowles, Samuel, and Herbert Gintis. 1976. *Schooling in Capitalist America: Educational Reform and the Contradictions of Economic Life*. New York: Basic Books.

———. 1999. *Recasting Egalitarianism: New Rules for Markets, States and Communities*. London: Verso.

Brady, Henry. 2001. Trust the People: Political Party Coalitions and the 2000 Election. Berkeley: University of California at Berkeley, Survey Research Center.

Brady, Henry E., Kay Lehmann Schlozman, and Sidney Verba. 1999. "Prospecting for Participants: Rational Expectations and the Recruitment of Political Activists." *American Political Science Review* 93 (March): 153–68.

Brinkley, Alan. 1995. *The End of Reform: New Deal Liberalism in Recession and War*. New York: Knopf.

Broder, David S. 1972. *The Party's Over: The Failure of Politics in America*. New York: Harper & Row.

———. 2000. *Democracy Derailed: Initiative Campaigns and the Power of Money*. New York: Harcourt.

———. 2001. "The Trust Factor." *Washington Post*, October 3, A31.

Brody, Richard. 1978. "The Puzzle of Participation." In *The New American Political System*, ed. Anthony King. Washington: American Enterprise Institute.

Brown v. Board of Education. 347 U.S. 483 (1954).

Brown, Clifford W., Jr., Linda W. Powell, and Clyde Wilcox. 1995. *Serious Money: Fundraising and Contributing in Presidential Nomination Campaigns*. New York: Cambridge University Press.

Brown, Wendy. 1995. *States of Injury: Power and Freedom in Late Modernity*. Princeton, N.J.: Princeton University Press.

Browne, Thomas McLelland. 1884. Representative Browne of Indiana speaking against the Electoral Count Act. 48th Cong., 1st sess., *Cong. Rec.*, 1884, vol. 15, pt. 5.

Brunt, P. A. 1988. *The Fall of the Roman Republic and Related Essays*. Oxford: Oxford University Press.

Buckley v. Valeo. 424 U.S. 1 (1976).

Buffett, Warren. 2000. "The Billionaire's Buyout Plan." *New York Times*, September 10, WK 17.

Bullock, Charles S., and Mark J. Rozell, eds. 1998. *The New Politics of the Old South.* Lanham, Md.: Rowman & Littlefield.

Burgess, J. W. 1888. "The Law of the Electoral Count." *Political Science Quarterly* 3 (1888): 633–53.

Burnham, Walter Dean. 1970. *Critical Elections and the Mainsprings of American Politics.* New York: W. W. Norton.

———. 1982. *The Current Crisis in American Politics.* Oxford: Oxford University Press.

Burns, Nancy E., Kay Lehman Schlozman, and Sidney Verba. 2001. *The Private Roots of Public Action: Gender, Equality, and Political Participation.* Cambridge, Mass.: Harvard University Press.

Bush v. Gore. 531 U.S. 98 (2000).

Bush v. Gore. 531 U.S. 1046 (2000)

"Bush v. Gore Issue Symposium." 2001. *Florida State University Law Review* 29 (spring): 325–1029.

Bush v. Palm Beach County Canvassing Board. 531 U.S. 70 (2000) (per curiam).

Butler, Judith. 1990. *Gender Trouble: Feminism and the Subversion of Identity.* New York: Routledge.

Buzbee, W. W., and R. A. Schapiro. 2001. "Legislative Record Review." *Stanford Law Review* 54: 87–161.

California Democratic Party v. Jones. 530 U.S. 567 (2000).

Calvo, Maria A., and Steven J. Rosenstone. 1989. *Hispanic Political Participation.* San Antonio, Tex., Southwest Voter Research Institute.

"Campaign 2000 Roundup." 2000. *Harrisburg Patriot*, February 26.

Cantor, Paul A. 2001. *Gilligan Unbound: Pop Culture in the Age of Globalization.* Lanham, Md.: Rowman & Littlefield.

Carey, John M., Richard Niemi, and Lynda Powell. 1998. "The Effects of Term Limits on State Legislatures." *Legislative Studies Quarterly* 23 (May): 271–300.

Carmines, Edward, and James Stimson. 1989. *Issue Evolution: Race and the Transformation of American Politics.* Princeton, N.J.: Princeton University Press.

Casey, Kathleen J., and Susan J. Carroll. 2001. "Welfare Reform and the 104th Congress: Institutional Position and the Role of Women." In *Women and Welfare: Theory and Practice in the United States and Europe*, ed. Nancy J. Hirschmann and Ulrike Liebert. New Brunswick: Rutgers University Press.

Ceaser, James, and Andrew Busch. 2001. *The Perfect Tie: The True Story of the 2000 Presidential Election.* Lanham, Md.: Rowman & Littlefield.

Center for Responsive Politics. 1996. *Money in Politics.* Washington: Center for Responsive Politics.

Charge of the Commons. 1648. *The Charge of the Commons of England, against Charles Stuart, King of England.* London.

Chesterton, Gilbert Keith. 1922. *What I Saw in America.* New York: Dodd Mead.

Citizens Conference on State Legislatures. 1971. *State Legislatures: An Evaluation of Their Effectiveness.* New York: Praeger Publishers.

Cogan, J. F. 1994. "The Dispersion of Spending Authority and Federal Budget Deficits." In *The Budget Puzzle: Understanding Federal Spending*, ed. J. F. Cogan, T. J. Muris, and A. Schick, 16–40. Stanford, Calif.: Stanford University Press.

Cohen, G. A. 1995. *Self-Ownership, Freedom, and Equality.* Cambridge, UK: Cambridge University Press.

Cohen, Jeffrey A., Richard Fleisher, and Paul Kantor, eds. 2001. *American Political Parties: Decline or Resurgence?* Washington: Congressional Quarterly Press.

Cohen, Richard E. 1987. "The Hill People." *National Journal* 19 (May): 1170–71.

———. 1992. *Washington at Work: Back Rooms and Clean Air.* New York: Macmillan.

———. 2001. "The Past as Prologue." *National Journal* (September 29): 3000–3002.

Coleman, John J. 1996. *The Decline of the Party in America.* Princeton, N.J.: Princeton University Press.

Colker, R., and J. J. Brudney. 2001. "Dissing Congress." *Michigan Law Review* 100: 80–144.

Collins, Randall. 1979. *The Credential Society: A Historical Sociology of Education and Stratification.* New York: Academic Press.

Committee for the Study of the American Electorate. 2001. "Two Pro-Participation Reforms Actually Harm Voter Turnout." Washington: Committee for the Study of the American Electorate.

Connelly, Marjorie. 2000. "Who Voted: A Portrait of American Politics, 1976–2000." *New York Times,* November 12.

Constant, Benjamin. 1819. "The Liberty of the Ancients Compared with that of the Moderns." Reprinted in his *Political Writings,* ed. Biancamaria Fontana. Cambridge, UK: Cambridge University Press, 1988.

Constitution Project. 2001. "Recommendations for Congressional Action." Washington: Constitution Project.

Converse, Philip E. 1972. "Change in the American Electorate." In *The Human Meaning of Social Change,* ed. Angus Campbell and Philip E. Converse. New York: Russell Sage Foundation.

Conway, M. Margaret. 2001a. "Political Mobilization in America." In *The State of Democracy in America,* ed. William Crotty. Washington D.C.: Georgetown University Press.

———. 2001b. "Political Participation in American Elections: Who Decides What?" in *America's Choice 2000,* ed. William Crotty. Boulder, Colo.: Westview Press.

Cooper, Joseph. 1999. *Congress and the Decline of Public Trust.* Boulder, Colo.: Westview Press.

Cornell, Drucilla. 1999. *At the Heart of Freedom.* Princeton, N.J.: Princeton University Press.

Corrado, Anthony. 1993. *Paying for Presidents.* New York: Twentieth Century Fund.

Correspondents of the New York Times. 2001. *Thirty-six Days: The Complete Chronicle of the 2000 Presidential Election Crisis.* New York: Times Books.

Cowell, Alan. 2002. "Europe Is Rubbing Its Eyes at the Ascent of the Right." *New York Times,* May 18, A3.

Cox, Archibald. 1976. *The Role of the Supreme Court in American Government.* New York: Oxford University Press.

Cremin, Lawrence A. 1961. *The Transformation of the American School: Progressivism in American Education.* New York: Alfred Knopf.

Croce, Benedetto. 1941. *History as the Story of Liberty.* Trans. Sylvia Sprigge. New York: W. W. Norton.

Crotty, William J. 1977. *Political Reform and the American Experiment.* New York: Thomas Y. Crowell.

———. 1984. *American Political Parties in Decline.* 2d ed. Boston: Little, Brown and Co.

———. 2001. "The Election of 2000: Close, Chaotic and Unforgettable." In *America's Choice 2000,* ed. William Crotty, 1–35. Boulder, Colo.: Westview Press

Crotty, William J., John S. Jackson III, and Melissa Kary Miller. 1999. "Political Activists Over Time: 'Working Elites' in the Party System." In *Comparative Political Parties and Elites,* ed. Birol Yesilada, 259–86. Ann Arbor: University of Michigan Press.

Currie, David P. 1997. *The Constitution in Congress: The Jeffersonians, 1801–1829*. Chicago: University of Chicago Press.

Dahl, Robert. 1961. *Who Governs? Democracy and Power in an American City*. New Haven: Yale University Press.

———. 1967. *Pluralist Democracy in the United States*. Chicago: Rand McNally.

———. 1971. *Polyarchy*. New Haven: Yale University Press.

———. 1982. *Dilemmas of Pluralist Democracy*. New Haven: Yale University Press.

———. 1989. *Democracy and Its Critics*. New Haven: Yale University Press.

———. 1994. *The New American (Dis)Order*. Berkeley: University of California Press.

———. 1998. *On Democracy*. New Haven: Yale University Press.

Dallek, Robert. 1999. *Ronald Reagan: The Politics of Symbolism*. With a new preface. Cambridge, Mass.: Harvard University Press.

Dalton, Russell J. 2002. *Citizen Politics in Western Democracies*. Chatham, N.J.: Chatham House Publishers.

Dangerfield, George. 1965. *The Awakening of American Nationalism, 1815–1828*. New York: Harper & Row.

Danigelis, Nicholas L. 1978. "Black Political Participation in the United States: Some Recent Evidence." *American Sociological Review* 43:756–71.

———. 1982. "Race, Class, and Political Involvement in the U.S." *Social Forces* 61:532–50.

Davis, James, Tom Smith, and Peter Marsden. 2001. *General Social Surveys, 1972–2000: Cumulative Codebook*. Chicago: National Opinion Research Center.

Dawson, Michael. 1995. "Desperation and Hope: Competing Visions of Race and American Citizenship." University of Chicago unpublished manuscript.

Dawson, Michael C., Ronald E. Brown, and Richard L. Allen. 1990. "Racial Belief Systems, Religious Guidance and African-American Political Participation." *National Political Science Review* 2:22–44.

Dawson, Michael, Ronald E. Brown, and James Jackson. 1993. *National Black Politics Study*. Study No. 2018. Ann Arbor: University of Michigan, Inter-University Consortium for Political and Social Research.

de la Garza, Rodolfo O. 1994. "The Effects of Primordial Claims, Immigration and the Voting Rights Act on Mexican American Politics." In *Minority Urban Coalitions in the 1990's*, ed. Wilbur Rich, 163–76. Westport, Conn.: Praeger.

———. 1995. "The Effect of Ethnicity on Political Culture." In *Classifying By Race*, ed. Paul E. Peterson. Princeton, N.J.: Princeton University Press.

de la Garza, Rodolfo O., and Louis DeSipio, eds. 1999. *Awash in the Mainstream: Latino Politics in the 1996 Election*. Boulder, Colo.: Westview Press.

de la Garza, Rodolfo O., Louis DeSipio, F. Chris Garcia, John Garcia, and Angelo Falcon, eds. 1992. *Latino Voices: Mexican, Puerto Rican and Cuban Perspectives on American Politics*. Boulder, Colo.: Westview Press.

de la Garza, Rodolfo O., Angelo Falcon, F. Chris Garcia, and John Garcia, eds. 1990. *Latino National Political Survey, 1989–1990*. Study No. 6841. Ann Arbor: Inter-University Consortium for Political and Social Research.

Deakin, James. 1966. *The Lobbyists*. Washington: Public Affairs Press.

Dershowitz, Alan M. 2001. *Supreme Injustice: How the High Court Hijacked the Election of 2000*. New York: Oxford University Press.

DeSipio, Louis. 1996. *Counting on the Latino Vote: Latinos As a New Electorate*. Charlottesville: University of Virginia Press.

Dewey, John. 1916. *Democracy and Education: An Introduction to the Philosophy of Education*. New York: Macmillan.

———. 1927. *The Public and Its Problems*. New York: Holt.

Dibble, Samuel. 1886. Representative Dibble of South Carolina speaking against the Electoral Count Act. 49th Cong., 2d sess., *Cong. Rec.*, 1886, vol. 18, pt. 1.

Dickerson v. United States. 530 U.S. 428 (2000).

Dickinson, Matthew J. 1996. *Bitter Harvest: FDR, Presidential Power, and the Growth of the Presidential Branch.* Cambridge, UK: Cambridge University Press.

Díez Medrano, Juan, and Paula Gutiérrez. 2001. "Nested Identities: National and European Identity in Spain." *Ethnic and Racial Studies* 24(5):753–78.

DiMaggio, Paul, John Evans, and Bethany Bryson. 1996. "Have Americans' Social Attitudes Become More Polarized?" *American Journal of Sociology* 102(3):690–755.

Dionne, E. J., and William Kristol, eds. 2001. *Bush v. Gore: The Court Cases and the Commentary.* Washington: Brookings Institution Press.

Dixon, Robert G. 1968. *Democratic Representation.* New York: Oxford University Press.

Donohue, John. 2001. "Is Government the Good Guy?" *New York Times*, December 13, A39.

Drake, Paul W., and Matthew D. McCubbins, eds. 1998. *The Origins of Liberty: Political and Economic Liberalization in the Modern World.* Princeton, N.J.: Princeton University Press.

Drew, Elizabeth. 1983. *Politics and Money: The New Road to Corruption.* New York: Macmillan.

Dukakis, Michael. 2001. "Politics and Policy for a New Century." In *The State of Democracy in America*, ed. William Crotty, 1–6. Washington: Georgetown University Press.

Duncan, Otis Dudley. 1968. "Ability and Achievement." *Eugenics Quarterly* 15:1–11.

Duncan, Otis Dudley, David L. Featherman, and Beverly Duncan. 1972. *Socioeconomic Background and Achievement.* New York: Seminar Press.

Easton, David. 1965. *A Systems Analysis of Political Life.* New York: John Wiley and Son.

Edin, Kathryn. 1991. "Surviving the Welfare System: How AFDC Recipients Make Ends Meet in Chicago." *Social Problems* 38, 4:462–74.

———. 2001. "Statement of Kathryn Edin." In *Testimony Before the Subcommittee on Human Resources of the House Committee on Ways and Means: Hearing on Welfare and Marriage Issues*, May 22. At http://waysandmeans.house.gov/humres/107cong/5-22-01/5-22edin.htm.

Edin, Kathryn, and Laura Lein. 1997. *Making Ends Meet: How Single Mothers Survive Welfare and Low-Wage Work.* New York: Russell Sage Foundation.

Electoral Count Act. 1887. *U.S. Code.* Title 3, secs. 1–18.

Elhuage, Einer. 1998. "What Term Limits Do that Ordinary Voting Cannot." *Policy Analysis Series*, no. 328. Washington: Cato Institute.

Elkins, Stanley, and Eric McKitrick. 1993. *The Age of Federalism: The Early American Republic, 1788–1800.* New York: Oxford University Press.

Ellis, Joseph. 2001. *Founding Brothers: The Revolutionary Generation.* New York: Knopf.

Ellis, Richard J. 2002. *Democratic Delusions: The Initiative Process in America.* Lawrence: University Press of Kansas.

Ellison, Christopher G., and David A. Gay. 1989. "Black Political Participation Revisited: A Test of Compensatory, Ethnic Community, and Public Arena Models." *Social Science Quarterly* 70:101–19.

Ellul, Jacques. 1964. *The Technological Society.* Trans. John Wilkinson. New York: Vintage.

Elster, Jon. 1983. *Sour Grapes.* New York: Cambridge University Press.

Ely, John Hart. 1973. "The Wages of Crying Wolf: A Comment on Roe v. Wade." *Yale Law Journal* 82:920–49.

Emergency Supplemental Appropriations Act—Response to Terrorist Attacks on September 11, 2001. 2001 U.S. Public Law 107–38. 107th Cong., 1st sess., September 18; *U.S. Statutes at Large* 115:220.

Engels, Friedrich. 1939. *Anti-Dühring*. Trans. Emile Burns. New York: International Publishers.

Epstein, A. L. 1978. *Ethos and Identity: Three Studies in Ethnicity*. Chicago: Aldine.

Epstein, Leon. 1967. *Political Parties in Western Democracies*. New York: Praeger.

Epstein, R. A. 2001. "'In Such Manner as the Legislature Thereof May Direct': The Outcome in *Bush v. Gore* Defended." In *The Vote: Bush, Gore and the Supreme Court*, ed. C. R. Sunstein and R. A. Epstein, 13–37. Chicago: University of Chicago Press.

Erie RR v. Tompkins. 304 U.S. 64 (1938).

Espiritu, Yen Le. 1992. *Asian American Panethnicity: Bridging Institutions and Ideas*. Philadelphia: Temple University Press.

Etzioni, Amitai. 2001. *The Monochrome Society*. Princeton, N.J.: Princeton Uni-versity Press.

Fanon, Frantz. 1968. *The Wretched of the Earth*. New York: Grove Press.

Farrar-Myers, Victoria A., and Diana Dwyre. 2001. "Parties and Campaign Finance." In *American Political Parties: Decline or Resurgence?*, ed. Jeffrey A. Cohen, Richard Fleisher, and Paul Kantor, 138–61. Washington: Congressional Quarterly Press.

Ferguson, Thomas. 1995. *Golden Rule: The Investment Theory of Party Competition and the Logic of Money-Driven Political Systems*. Chicago: University of Chicago Press.

———. 2001. "Blowing Smoke: Impeachment, the Clinton Presidency, and the Political Economy." In *The State of Democracy in America*, ed. William Crotty. Washington: Georgetown University Press.

Finkel, Steven E. 1985. "Reciprocal Effects of Participation and Political Efficacy: A Panel Analysis." *American Journal of Political Science* 29 (November): 891–913.

Fitts, M. A. 1990. "Can Ignorance Be Bliss? Imperfect Information as a Positive Influence in Political Institutions." *Michigan Law Review* 88:917–82.

Flanigan, William H., and Nancy Zingale. 1998. *Political Behavior of the American Electorate*. 9th ed. Washington: Congressional Quarterly Press.

Foner, Nancy. 1987. "The Jamaicans: Race and Ethnicity among Migrants in New York City." In *New Immigrants in New York*, ed. Nancy Foner. New York: Columbia University Press.

Foucault, Michel. 1990. *The History of Sexuality: Vol. I, an Introduction*. New York: Vintage Books.

Fowler, Linda L., and Ronald G. Shaiko. 1987. "The Grass Roots Connection: Environmental Activists and Senate Roll Calls." *American Journal of Political Science* 31 (August): 484–510.

Fox, Harrison W., Jr., and Susan Webb Hammond. 1977. *Congressional Staffs: The Invisible Force in American Lawmaking*. New York: Free Press.

Franklin, Benjamin. 1759. "An Historical Review of the Constitution and Government of Pennsylvania, from Its Origin." Ed. Richard Jackson. London: Arno Press.

Freeman, Joanne B. 2001. *Affairs of Honor: National Politics in the New Republic*. New Haven: Yale University Press.

Frickey, P. P., and S. S. Smith. 2002. "Judicial Review, the Congressional Process, and the Federalism Cases: An Interdisciplinary Critique." *Yale Law Journal* 111:1707–56.

Friedman, Barry. 2001. "The History of the Countermajoritarian Difficulty, Part Three: The Broader Public." *New York University Law Review* 76:1383, 1387.

Gallup Organization. 2001. *Gallup Poll Social Series: Minority Rights and Relations*. Princeton: Gallup Organization.

Gallup/CNN/U.S.A. Today. 1995. Poll, June 5–6.

Gans, Herbert J. 1992. "Second Generation Decline: Scenarios for the Economic and Ethnic Futures of Post–1965 American Immigrants." *Ethnic and Racial Studies* 15:173–92.

———. 1995. *The War against the Poor*. New York: Basic Books.

Garcia, F. Chris. 1988. *Latinos and the Political System*. South Bend, Ind.: University of Notre Dame Press.

———, ed. 1997. *Pursuing Power: Latinos and the Political System*. South Bend, Ind.: University of Notre Dame Press.

Garrett, Elizabeth. 1998a. "Harnessing Politics: The Dynamics of Offset Requirements in the Tax Legislative Process." *University of Chicago Law Review* 65:501–69.

———. 1998b. "Rethinking the Structures of Decision Making in the Federal Budget Process." *Harvard Journal on Legislation* 35:387–445.

———. 2001a. "Institutional Lessons from the 2000 Presidential Election." *Florida State University Law Review* 29:975–93.

———. 2001b. "Leaving the Decision to Congress." In *The Vote: Bush, Gore, and the Supreme Court*, ed. C. R. Sunstein and R. A. Epstein, 38–54. Chicago: University of Chicago Press.

Garvey, John H. 1996. *What Are Freedoms For?* Cambridge, Mass.: Harvard University Press.

Genovese, Michael. 2000. *Power and the American Presidency, 1789–2000*. New York: Oxford University Press.

George, Robert P. 1993. *Making Men Moral: Civil Liberties and Public Morality*. Oxford: Oxford University Press.

Gerring, John. 1999. "Culture versus Economics: An American Dilemma." *Social Science History* 23 (summer): 129–72.

———. 2001. *Party Ideologies in America, 1928–1996*. Cambridge, UK: Cambridge University Press.

Gerstle, Gary. 1997. "Liberty, Coercion, and the Making of Americans." *Journal of American History* 84(2):524–58.

Gerstle, Gary, and John Mollenkopf. 2001. *E Pluribus Unum? Contemporary and Historical Perspectives on Immigrant Political Incorporation*. New York: Russell Sage Foundation.

Gibson, James L., Gregory Caldeira A., and Lester Spense. 2001. "The Supreme Court and the U.S. Presidential Election of 2000: Wounds, Self-Inflicted or Otherwise." Working paper, Weidenbaum Center on the Economy, Government, and Public Policy, Washington University, St. Louis, Mo.

Gillman, Howard. 2001. *The Votes that Counted: How the Court Decided the 2000 Presidential Election*. Chicago: University of Chicago Press.

Gimpel, James G. 1999. *Separate Destinations: Migration, Immigration, and the Politics of Places*. Ann Arbor: University of Michigan Press.

Ginsberg, Benjamin, and Alan Stone, eds. 1996. *Do Elections Matter?* 3d ed. Armontz, N.Y.: M. E. Sharpe.

Ginsburg, Benjamin, and Martin Shefter. 1988. "The Presidency and the Organization of Interests." In *The Presidency and the Political System*, ed. Michael Nelson. Washington: Congressional Quarterly Press.

Gitlin, Todd. 1995. *The Twilight of Common Dreams*. New York: Metropolitan Books.

Glazer, Nathan, and Daniel Patrick Moynihan. 1963. *Beyond the Melting Pot*. Cambridge, Mass.: Harvard University Press.

Goodwin, Lawrence. 1978. *The Populist Movement*. Oxford: Oxford University Press.

Gordon, Milton. 1964. *Assimilation in American Life: The Role of Race, Religion, and National Origins*. New York: Oxford University Press.

Gough, J. W. 1955. *Fundamental Law in English Constitutional History*. Oxford: Clarendon Press.

Grann, David. 1998. "Close Races." New Republic (March 9): 11–12.

Greene, Abner. 2001. Understanding the 2000 Election: A Guide to the Legal Battles that Decided the Presidency. New York: New York University Press.

Greenstein, Fred I. 2000. The Presidential Difference. Princeton, N.J.: Princeton University Press.

Greve, Michael S. 1987. "Why 'Defunding the Left' Failed." Public Interest 89:88–96.

Grimsley, Kirstin Downey. 1998a. "Beep Her to Get the Fax about the Voice Mail on Her E-Mail." Washington Post National Weekly, June 1, 30.

———. 1998b. "Leaner—and Definitely Meaner." Washington Post National Weekly, July 20–27, 21.

Grofman, Bernard, Arend Lijphardt, Robert McKay, and Howard Scarrow. 1982. Representation and Redistricting Issues. Lexington, Mass.: Lexington Books.

Grossman, Lawrence K. 1995. The Electronic Republic. New York: Viking.

Guinier, Lani, and Gerald Torres. 2002. The Miner's Canary: Enlisting Race, Resisting Power, Transforming Democracy. Cambridge, Mass.: Harvard University Press.

Gunther, Gerald. 2000. "A Risky Moment for the Court." New York Times, December 1, A37.

Guterbock, Thomas M., and Bruce London. 1983. "Race, Political Orientation, and Participation: An Empirical Test of Four Competing Theories." American Sociological Review 48:439–53.

Hacker, Andrew. 1992. Two Nations: Black and White, Separate, Hostile, Unequal. New York: Scribner's.

Hacker, Jacob. 1997. Road to Nowhere: The Genesis of President Clinton's Plan for Health Security. Princeton, N.J.: Princeton University Press.

Hager, George. 1999. "While the Rich Get Richer." Washington Post National Weekly, September 13, 19.

Hallow, Ralph. 1997. "GOP Starts Minority Outreach." Washington Times, September 17, A4.

Hamilton, Alexander, James Madison, and John Jay. 1961. The Federalist Papers. Ed. Clinton Rossiter. New York: New American Library.

Hansen, John Mark. 2002. "Early Voting, Unrestricted Absentee Voting, and Voting by Mail." In National Commission on Federal Election Reform, To Assure Pride and Confidence in the Electoral Process, 163–79. Washington: Brookings Institution.

Hardy-Fanta, Carol. 1993. Latina Politics, Latino Politics. Philadelphia: Temple University Press.

Hargrove, Erwin, and Michael Nelson. 1984. Presidents, Politics and Policy. New York: Knopf.

Harmon, Amy. 2001. "Exploration of World Wide Web Tilts from Eclectic to Mundane." New York Times, August 26, A1.

Harris, Fredrick C. 1994. "Something Within: Religion as a Mobilizer of African-American Political Activism." Journal of Politics 56:42–68.

Harris, Richard, and Sidney Milkis. 1996. The Politics of Regulatory Change: A Tale of Two Agencies. New York: Oxford University Press.

Harrison, J. 2000. "Nobody for President." Journal of Law and Politics 16:699–715.

Hart, H. L. A. 1955. "Are There Any Natural Rights?" Philosophical Review 64:175–91.

Hart, John. 1987. The Presidential Branch. New York: Pergamon Press.

Hartmann, Heidi, and Hsaio-Ye Yi. 2001. "The Rhetoric and Reality of Welfare Reform." In Women and Welfare: Theory and Practice in the United States and Europe, ed. Nancy J. Hirschmann and Ulrike Liebert. New Brunswick: Rutgers University Press.

Hasen, Richard. 2001. "Bush v. Gore and the Future of Equal Protection Law in Elections." Florida State University Law Review 29:377, 380–86.

Heard, Alexander. 1966. "Reform: Limits and Opportunities." In *State Legislatures in American Politics*, ed. Alexander Heard. Englewood Cliffs, N.J.: Prentice-Hall.

Heckman, James, and James Snyder. 1997. "Linear Probability Models of the Demand for Attributes with and Empirical Application to Estimating the Preferences of Legislators." *Rand Journal of Economics* 28:S142–S189.

Hegel, G. W. F. 1956. *The Philosophy of History*. Trans. J. Sibree. New York: Dover.

Herbert, Bob. 1999. "A Nation Loosening Its Bonds." *New York Times*, August 26, A17.

Herring, Pendelton. 1944. "Executive-Legislative Responsibilities." In *American Political Science Review* 38 (December):1153–65.

Herrnson, Paul S. 1988. *Party Campaigning in the 1980s*. Cambridge, Mass.: Harvard University Press.

Herrnson, Paul S., and Diana Dwyre. 1999. "Party Issue Advocacy in Congressional Election Campaigns." In *The State of the Parties: The Changing Role of Contemporary American Parties*, ed. John C. Green and Daniel M. Shea, 86–104. 3d ed. Lanham, Md.: Rowman & Littlefield.

Herrnstein, Richard J. 1971. *IQ in the Meritocracy*. Boston, Mass.: Little Brown.

Herrnstein, Richard J., and Charles Murray. 1994. *The Bell Curve: Intelligence and Class Structure in American Life*. New York: Free Press.

Hibbing, John R., and Elizabeth Theiss-Morse. 1995. *Congress as Public Enemy*. Cambridge, UK: Cambridge University Press.

———. 2002. *Stealth Democracy: Americans' Beliefs about How Government Should Work*. Cambridge, UK: Cambridge University Press.

Hing, Bill Ong. 1997. *To Be an American: Cultural Pluralism and the Rhetoric of Assimilation*. New York: New York University Press.

Hirschmann, Nancy J. 2001. "A Question of Freedom, A Question of Rights? Women and Welfare." In *Women and Welfare: Theory and Practice in the United States and Europe*, ed. Nancy J. Hirschmann and Ulrike Liebert. New Brunswick: Rutgers University Press.

———. 2003. *The Subject of Liberty: Toward a Feminist Theory of Freedom*. Princeton, N.J.: Princeton University Press.

Hobbes, Thomas. [1651] 1991. *Leviathan*. Richard Tuck, ed. Cambridge, UK: Cambridge University Press.

Hollinger, David. 2000. *Postethnic America: Beyond Multiculturalism*. 2d ed. New York: Basic Books.

Holusha, John. 1988. "Bush Pledges Aid for Environment," *New York Times*, September 22, 1.

Huckfeldt, Robert. 1979. "Political Participation and the Neighborhood Context." *American Journal of Political Science* 23 (August): 579–92.

Huckfeldt, Robert, and John Sprague. 1992. "Political Parties and Electoral Mobilization: Political Structure, Social Structure, and the Party Canvass." *American Political Science Review* 86 (March): 70–86.

Hunter, James Davison. 1983. *American Evangelicalism: Conservative Religion and the Quandary of Modernity*. New Brunswick: Rutgers University Press.

———. 1991. *Culture Wars: The Struggle to Divide America*. New York: Basic Books.

———. 2000. "Bowling with the Social Scientists." *Weekly Standard*, August 28–September 4, 31.

Ignatiev, Noel. 1995. *How the Irish Became White*. New York: Routledge.

Imig, Douglas R. 1996. *Poverty and Power: The Political Representation of Poor Americans*. Lincoln: University of Nebraska Press.

———. 1998. "American Social Movements and Presidential Administrations." In *Social Movements and American Political Institutions*, ed. Ann Costain and Andrew McFarland. Lanham, Md.: Rowman & Littlefield.

Ingalls, John J. 1886. Senator Ingalls of Kansas speaking on the Electoral Count Act. 49th Cong., 1st sess., *Cong. Rec.*, vol. 17, pt. 1.

Inglehart, Ronald. 1997. *Modernization and Postmodernization.* Princeton, N.J.: Princeton University Press.

"Interest Groups." 2000. In *Encyclopedia of Associations.* 34th ed. Detroit: Gale Research Co.

Jackson, James. 1984. *National Black Election Panel Study, 1984 and 1988,* Study No. 9954. Ann Arbor: University of Michigan, Inter-University Consortium for Political and Social Research.

Jackson, John S., III, and William Crotty. 2001. *The Politics of Presidential Selection.* 2d ed. New York: Longman.

Jacobson, Gary C. 1985. "The Republican Advantage in Campaign Finance." In *The New Directions in American Politics,* ed. John E. Chubb and Paul E. Peterson, 143–73. Washington: Brookings Institution.

Jacobson, Matthew Frye. 1999. *Whiteness of a Different Color: European Immigrants and the Alchemy of Race.* Cambridge, Mass.: Harvard University Press.

Jacoby, Russell. 1994. *Dogmatic Wisdom: How the Culture Wars Divert Education and Distract America.* New York: Doubleday.

Jefferson, Thomas. 1944. *Life and Selected Writings of Thomas Jefferson.* Ed. Adrienne Koch and William Peden. New York: Modern Library.

Jencks, Christopher. 1992. *Rethinking Social Policy: Race, Poverty and the Underclass.* Cambridge, Mass.: Harvard University Press.

Johnson, Paul E. 1998. "Interest Group Recruiting: Finding Members and Keeping Them." In *Interest Group Politics,* ed. Allan J. Cigler and Burdett A. Loomis, 35–62. 5th ed. Washington: Congressional Quarterly Press.

Jones, Charles O. 1981. "Congress and the Presidency." In *The New Congress,* ed. Thomas E. Mann and Norman J. Ornstein, 223–49. Washington: American Enterprise Institute for Public Policy Research.

———. 1982. *The United States Congress: People, Places and Policy.* Homewood, Ill.: Dorsey.

Jones-Correa, Michael. 1998. *Between Two Nations: The Political Predicament of Latinos in New York City.* Ithaca, N.Y.: Cornell University Press.

Jouvenel, Bertrand de. 1993. *On Power: Its Natural History and Growth.* Trans. J. W. Huntington. Indianapolis: Liberty Fund.

Junn, Jane. 1999. "Participation in Liberal Democracy: The Political Assimilation of Immigrants and Ethnic Minorities in the United States." *American Behavioral Scientist* 42:1417–38.

Kahn, Herman. 1975. "On Studying the Future." In *Handbook of Political Science,* ed. Fred I. Greenstein and Nelson W. Polsby, 7:405–43. Reading, Mass.: Addison-Wesley.

Kallen, Horace. 1998 [1924]. *Culture and Democracy in the United States.* New Brunswick, N.J.: Transaction Books.

Karcher v. Daggett. 462 U.S. 725 (1983).

Keller, Morton. 1977. *Affairs of State.* Cambridge, Mass.: Harvard University Press.

Kerber, Linda. 1988. "Making Republicanism Useful." *Yale Law Journal* 97:1663–72.

Kernell, Sam. 1973. "Comment: A Re-Evaluation of Black Voting in Mississippi." *American Political Science Review* 67 (December): 1307–18.

Keyssar, Alexander. 2000. *The Right to Vote: The Contested History of Democracy in the United States.* New York: Basic Books.

Kilborn, Peter T. 2001. "Recession Is Stretching the Limit on Welfare Benefits." *New York Times,* December 9.

Kilborn, Peter T., and Lynette Clemetson. 2002. "Gains of 90's Did Not Lift All, Census Shows." *New York Times*, June 5.

Kim, Claire. 1999. "The Racial Triangulation of Asian Americans." In *Politics and Society* 27(1):103–36.

King Charles His Tryal. 1649. *King Charles His Tryal: or, A Perfect Narrative of the Whole Proceeding the High Court of Justice*. London.

King, Desmond. 2000. *Making Americans: Immigration, Race, and the Origins of the Diverse Democracy*. Cambridge, Mass.: Harvard University Press.

Kirkpatrick, Jeane. 1976. *The New Presidential Elite*. New York: Russell Sage and Twentieth Century Fund.

Klarman, Michael. 2001. "*Bush v. Gore* through the Lens of Constitutional History." *California Law Review* 89:1721–65.

Kluger, Richard. 1977. *Simple Justice*. New York: Vintage Books.

Kollman, Ken. 1998. *Outside Lobbying: Public Opinion and Interest Group Strategies*. Princeton, N.J.: Princeton University Press.

Kotkin, Joel, and David Friedman. 1998. "Don't Pop the Champagne Yet." *Washington Post National Weekly*, June 1, 17.

Kousser, Thad. 2002. "Redesigning Democracies: How Term Limits and Professionalization Reshape America's State Legislatures." Ph.D. diss., University of California, Berkeley.

Kozol, Jonathan. 1991. *Savage Inequalities: Children in America's Schools*. New York: Crown Publishers.

Kramer, Larry. 2001a. "The Supreme Court 2000 Term Forward: We the Court." *Harvard Law Review* 115:4–169.

———. 2001b. "The Supreme Court in Politics." In *The Unfinished Election of 2000*, ed. J. N. Rakove, 105–57. New York: Basic Books.

Krausz, Tadeusz, and Kazimierz M. Slomczynski. 1985. "How Far to Meritocracy? Empirical Tests of a Controversial Thesis." *Social Forces* 63:623–42.

Krueger, Alan. 2001. "Economic Scene." *New York Times*, August 16, C2.

Krugman, Paul. 2000. "Once and Again." *New York Times*, January 2, WK 9.

———. 2002a. "America the Polarized." *New York Times*, January 4, A21.

———. 2002b. "Spreading It Around," *New York Times*, January 25, A23.

Kyvig, David E. 1996. *Explicit and Authentic Acts: Amending the U.S. Constitution*. Lawrence: University of Kansas Press.

Lammers, William, and Michael Genovese. 2000. *The Presidency and Domestic Policy*. Washington: Congressional Quarterly Press.

Landy, Marc. 1985. "FDR and John L. Lewis and the Lessons of Rivalry." In *Modern Presidents and the Presidency*, ed. Marc Landy, 106–12. Lexington, Mass.: D.C. Heath.

Lawrence, David G. 2001. "On the Resurgence of Party Identification in the 1990s." In *American Political Parties: Decline or Resurgence?* ed. Jeffrey A. Cohen, Richard Fleisher, and Paul Kantor, 30–54. Washington: Congressional Quarterly Press

Lazarsfeld, Paul F., Bernard R. Berelson, and Hazel Gaudet. 1948. *The People's Choice: How the Voter Makes Up His Mind in a Presidential Campaign*. New York: Columbia University Press.

Lee, Taeku. 1998. "The Backdoor and the Backlash: Campaign Finance and the Political Opinions of Chinese Americans." Paper presented at the annual meeting of the American Political Science Association, Boston, Mass.

Leighley, Jan E., and Arnold Vedlitz. 1999. "Race, Ethnicity and Political Participation: Competing Models and Contrasting Explanations." *Journal of Politics* 61:1092–1114.

Lein, Laura, Susan E. Jacquet, Carol M. Lewis, Patricia R. Cole, and Bernice B. Williams. 2001. "With the Best of Intentions: Family Violence Option and Abused Women's Needs." *Violence Against Women* 7, 2:193–210.

Leo, Richard A., and George C. Thomas III. 1998. *The Miranda Debate: Law, Justice, and Policing*. Boston: Northeastern University Press.

Lerner, Robert, Althea K. Nagai, and Stanley Rothman. 1996. *American Elites*. New Haven: Yale University Press.

Leuchtenburg, William. 1963. *Franklin Roosevelt and the New Deal*. New York: Harper & Row.

Levinson, Sanford, and Ernest Young. 2001. "Who's Afraid of the Twelfth Amendment?" *Florida State University Law Review* 29:925, 959–61.

Levison, Andrew. 2001. "Who Lost the Working Class?" *The Nation* (May 14): 25–32.

Lieberman, Robert. 1998. *Shifting the Color Line: Race and the American Welfare State*. Cambridge, Mass.: Harvard University Press.

Lien, Pei-te. 1994. "Ethnicity and Political Participation: A Comparison between Asian and Mexican Americans." *Political Behavior* 16:237–64.

———. 1997. *The Political Participation of Asian Americans*. New York: Garland.

———. 2001. The "Quiet Minority" Speaks Up! Salt Lake City: University of Utah, Department of Political Science.

Light, Paul C. 1999. *The President's Agenda*. Baltimore: Johns Hopkins University Press.

Lin, Ann, and Amany Jamal. 1998. Arab-Americans and Political Participation. Paper presented at the Annual Meeting of the American Political Science Association, Boston.

Linz, Juan, and Arturo Valenzuela, eds. 1994. *The Failure of Presidential Democracy*. Baltimore: Johns Hopkins University Press.

Lippmann, Walter. 1925. *The Phantom Public*. New York: Macmillan.

Lipsky, Michael. 1968. "Protest as a Political Resource." *American Political Science Review* 62 (December): 1144–58.

Little, Thomas, and George Peery. 2000. Views from the Bridge: Legislative Leaders' Perceptions of Institutional Power in the Stormy Wake of Term Limits. Paper presented at "Coping with Term Limits: Ohio and the Nation," April, Columbus, Ohio.

Locke, John. 1947. *Two Treatises on Government*. Ed. Thomas Cook. New York: Hafner.

———. 1960. *Two Treatises of Government*. Ed. Peter Laslett. New York: New American Library.

Long, Douglas G. 1977. *Bentham on Liberty: Jeremy Bentham's Idea of Liberty in Relation to His Utilitarianism*. Toronto: University of Toronto Press.

Lowi, Theodore J. 1979. *The End of Liberalism: The Second Republic of the United States*. 2d ed. New York: W. W. Norton.

———. 1985. *The Personal President: Power Invested, Promise Unfulfilled*. Ithaca: Cornell University Press.

———. 1998. "Think Globally, Lose Locally." *Boston Review*, April/May, 4–10.

Lubenow, Gerald C., ed. 2001. *A User's Guide to Campaign Finance Reform*. Lanham, Md.: Rowman & Littlefield.

Mackenzie, G. Calvin. 1996. *The Irony of Reform: The Roots of American Political Disenchantment*. Boulder: Westview.

MacKinnon, Catherine. 1986. *Feminism Unmodified: Discourses on Life and Law*. Cambridge, Mass.: Harvard University Press.

Macmahon, Arthur. 1943a. "Congressional Oversight of Administration: The Power of the Purse—I." *Political Science Quarterly* 58 (June): 161–90.

———. 1943b. "Congressional Oversight of Administration: The Power of the Purse—II." *Political Science Quarterly* 58 (September): 380–414.

Macpherson, C. B. 1962. *Political Theory of Possessive Individualism: Hobbes to Locke.* New York: Oxford University Press.

———. 1966. *The Real World of Democracy.* Oxford: Oxford University Press.

Madison, James. 1792. "Who Are the Best Keepers of the People's Liberties?" *National Gazette*, December 22. Reprinted in James Madison, *Writings.* Ed. Jack N. Rakove. New York: Library of America, 1999.

———. 1966. *Notes of Debates in the Federal Convention of 1787.* Ed. Adrienne Koch. Athens: Ohio University Press.

Madrick, Jeff. 2001. "Economic Scene." *New York Times*, November 29, C2.

Magleby, David B. 1984. *Direct Legislation: Voting on Ballot Propositions in the United States.* Baltimore, Md.: Johns Hopkins University Press.

Mahan v. Howell. 410 U.S. 315 (1973).

Mahoney, Martha R. 1994. "Victimization or Oppression? Women's Lives, Violence, and Agency." In *The Public Nature of Private Violence*, ed. Martha Albertson Fineman and Roxanne Mykitiuk. New York: Routledge.

Maisel, Sandy L. 2001. "American Political Parties: Still Central to a Functioning Democracy?" In *American Political Parties: Decline or Resurgence?* ed. Jeffrey A. Cohen, Richard Fleisher, and Paul Kantor, 103–21. Washington: Congressional Quarterly Press.

Malbin, Michael J. 1980. *Unelected Representatives: Congressional Staff and the Future of Representative Government.* New York: Basic Books.

Markoff, John. 2000. "A Newer, Lonelier Crowd Emerges in Internet Study." *New York Times*, February 16, A1.

Marx, Karl. 1978. "The German Ideology." In *The Marx-Engels Reader*, ed. Robert C. Tucker. 2d ed. New York: W. W. Norton.

Matthews, Richard. 1995. *If Men Were Angels: James Madison and the Heartless Empire of Reason.* Lawrence: University Press of Kansas.

Mayhew, David. 1991. *Divided We Govern.* New Haven: Yale University Press.

McAdam, Doug. 1982. *Political Process and the Development of Black Insurgency, 1930–1970.* Chicago: University of Chicago.

McCallum, Gerald I., Jr. 1967. "Negative and Positive Freedom." *Philosophical Review* 76:312–24; reprinted in Laslett et al., 1972, 24.

McCarty, Nolan, Keith Poole, and Howard Rosenthal. 2003. Political Polarization and Income Inequality. Princeton, N.J.: Princeton University Press, Department of Politics.

McClosky, Herbert, et al. 1960. "Issue Conflict and Consensus among Party Leaders and Followers." *American Political Science Review* 54:406–27.

McConnell, Grant. 1966. *Private Power and American Democracy.* New York: Alfred A. Knopf.

McGerr, Michael E. 1986. *The Decline of Popular Politics: The American North, 1865–1928.* New York: Oxford University Press.

Menendez, Albert J. 1996. *The Perot Voters.* Amherst, N.Y.: Prometheus Books.

Mervin, David. 1996. *George Bush and the Guardianship Presidency.* New York: St. Martin's Press.

Meyers, Marvin, ed. 1981. *The Mind of the Founder.* Hanover: University Press of New England.

Milkis, Sidney. 1993. *The President and the Parties.* New York: Oxford University Press.

Mill, John Stuart. 1992. *On Liberty in Mill, On Liberty and Other Essays.* Ed. John Gray. New York: Oxford University Press.

Miller, Warren E. 1987. *Without Consent: Mass-Elite Linkage in Presidential Politics.* Lexington: University Press of Kentucky.

———. 1994. "Party Identification and the Electorate of the 1990s." In *The Parties Respond*, ed. L. Sandy Maisel. 2d ed. Boulder, Colo.: Westview Press.

Miller, Warren E., and J. Merrill Shanks. 1996. *The New American Voter*. Cambridge, Mass.: Harvard University Press.

Miller, Warren E., and M. Kent Jennings. 1986. *Parties in Transition: A Longitudinal Study of Party Elites and Party Supporters*. New York: Russell Sage Foundation.

Mills, Charles W. 1997. *The Racial Contract*. Ithaca: Cornell University Press.

Mincer, Jacob. 1974. *Schooling, Experience, and Earnings*. New York: Columbia University Press.

Minnite, Lorraine, Jennifer Holdaway, and Ronald Hayduk. 2000. The Political Participation of Immigrants in New York. Paper presented at the CUNY Graduate Center conference on Immigrant Political Participation, New York.

Miranda v. Arizona, 384 U.S. 436 (1966).

Miroff, Bruce. 1993. *Icons of Democracy: American Leaders as Heroes, Aristocrats, Dissenters, and Democrats*. New York: Basic Books.

Montoya, Lisa. 1996. "Latino Gender Differences in Public Opinion: Results from the Latino National Political Survey." *Hispanic Journal of Behavioral Science* 18 (May): 255–76.

Moore, Barrington, Jr. 1966. *The Social Origins of Democracy and Dictatorship: Lord and Peasant in the Making of the Modern World*. Boston: Beacon Press.

Murphy, Kevin. 1990. "The Education Gap Rap." *American Enterprise* 1:62–63.

Murray, Charles. 1994. *Losing Ground: American Social Policy, 1950–1980*. New York: Basic Books.

Nader, Ralph. 2001. *Crashing the Party: How to Tell the Truth and Still Run for President*. New York: St. Martin's Press.

Namier, Lewis. 1929. *The Structure of Politics at the Accession of George III*. London: Macmillan.

National Commission on Federal Election Reform. 2002. *To Assure Pride and Confidence in the Electoral Process*. Washington: Brookings Institution.

National Conference for Community and Justice. 1994. *Taking America's Pulse: The Full Report of the National Conference Survey on Inter-Group Relations*. New York: National Conference for Community and Justice.

———. 2000. *Taking America's Pulse II: A Survey of Intergroup Relations*. New York: National Conference for Community and Justice.

National Election Studies, Center for Political Studies. 1998. *NES Guide to Public Opinion and Electoral Behavior*. Ann Arbor: University of Michigan, Center for Political Studies.

National Task Force on Election Reform. 2001. "Election 2000: Review and Recommendations of the Nation's Elections Administrators." Houston: Election Center.

Neal, Terry, and Thomas Edsall. 1998. "Democrats Fear Loss of Black Loyalty." *Washington Post*, August 3, A1, A6.

Nelson, Dale C. 1979. "Ethnicity and Socioeconomic Status as Sources of Participation: The Case for Ethnic Political Culture." *American Political Science Review* 73:1024–38.

Neustadt, Richard E. 1990. *Presidential Power and the Modern Presidents*. New York: Free Press.

Nie, Norman H., Jane Junn, and Kenneth Stehlik-Barry. 1996. *Education and Democratic Citizenship in America*. Chicago: University of Chicago Press.

Norton, Eleanor Holmes. 1997. Statement at Hearings on Federal Measures of Race and Ethnicity and the Implications for the 2000 Census, House of Representatives, 105th Cong., 1st sess., 259–61.

Nussbaum, Martha. 2001. *Women and Human Development: The Capabilities Approach.* New York: Cambridge University Press.

Okin, Susan Moller. 1989. *Justice, Gender, and the Family.* New York: Basic Books.

Oliver, J. Eric. 1996. "The Effects of Eligibility Restrictions and Party Activity on Absentee Voting and Overall Turnout." *American Journal of Political Science* 40 (May): 498–513.

———. 2001. *Democracy in Suburbia.* Princeton, N.J.: Princeton University Press.

Oliver, Mike, and Colin Barnes. 1998. *Disabled People and Social Policy: From Exclusion to Inclusion.* New York: Addison Wesley Longman.

Olneck, Michael R., and James Crouse. 1979. "The IQ Meritocracy Reconsidered: Cognitive Skill and Adult Success in the United States." *American Journal of Education* 88:1–31.

Omi, Michael, and Howard Winant. 1994. *Racial Formation in the United States: From the 1960s to the 1990s.* New York: Routledge.

Orloff, Ann Shola. 2001. "Ending the Entitlements of Poor Single Mothers: Changing Social Policies, Women's Employment and Caregiving in the Contemporary United States." In *Women and Welfare: Theory and Practice in the United States and Europe,* ed. Nancy J. Hirschmann and Ulrike Liebert. New Brunswick: Rutgers University Press.

Ornstein, Norman J., Thomas E. Mann, and Michael J. Malbin. 1997. *Vital Statistics on Congress, 1997–98.* Washington: Congressional Quarterly Press.

Owen, Diana, Jack Dennis, and Casey Klofstad. 2001. "Public Support for the Party System in the United States." In *The State of Democracy in America,* ed. William Crotty. Washington: Georgetown University Press.

Parenti, Michael. 1970. "Power and Pluralism: A View from the Bottom." *Journal of Politics* 32 (August): 501–30.

Parks, D. J. 2001. "Emergency Spending Measure Puts Bush Budget Chief on the Spot." *Congressional Quarterly Weekly,* October 20, 2465–67.

Pateman, Carole. 1970. *Participation and Democratic Theory.* New York: Cambridge University Press.

———. 1985. *The Problem of Political Obligation: A Critique of Liberal Theory.* Berkeley: University of California Press.

Patterson, Bradley. 1988. *The Ring of Power.* New York: Basic Books.

Patterson, James. 2001. *Brown v. Board of Education: A Civil Rights Milestone and Its Troubled Legacy.* New York: Oxford University Press.

Pearlstein, Steven. 2000. "The New Politics of Globalization." *Washington Post National Weekly,* October 9, p. 18.

Pertschuck, Michael. 1982. *Revolt against Regulation: The Rise and Pause of the Consumer Movement.* Berkeley: University of California Press.

Peterson, Mark. 1992a. "Interest Mobilization and the Presidency." In *The Politics of Interests: Interest Groups Transformed,* ed. Mark Petracca. Boulder, Colo.: Westview.

———. 1992b. "The Presidency and Organized Interests: White House Patterns of Interest Group Liaison." *American Political Science Review* 86 (September): 3–22.

Peterson, Mark, and Jack Walker. 1986. "Interest Group Responses to Partisan Change." In *Interest Group Politics,* ed. Allan Cigler and Burdett Loomis, 161–82. Washington: Congressional Quarterly Press.

Peterson, Merrill. 1987. *The Great Triumvirate: Webster, Clay and Calhoun.* New York: Oxford University Press.

Petracca, Mark. 1992. "The Rediscovery of Interest Group Politics." In *The Politics of Interests: Interest Groups Transformed,* ed. Mark Petracca. Boulder, Colo.: Westview.

———. 1996. "A Legislature in Transition: The California Experience with Term

Limits." *Institute of Governmental Studies Working Paper* 96–19. Berkeley: University of California, Institute of Governmental Studies.

———. 1998. "California's Experience with Legislative Term Limits." *Term Limits Outlook Series* 6 (3). Washington: U.S. Term Limits.

Petracca, Mark P., and Pamela A. Smith. 1990. "How Frequent Is Frequent Enough? An Appraisal of the Four-Year Term for House Members." *Congress and the Presidency* 17 (spring): 45–66.

Pettit, Philip. 1997. *Republicanism: A Theory of Freedom and Government.* Oxford: Oxford University Press.

———. 2001. *A Theory of Freedom: From the Psychology to the Politics of Agency.* New York: Oxford University Press.

Phillips, Ann. 1999. *Which Equalities Matter?* Cambridge, Mass.: Polity Press.

Phillips, Kevin. 1990. *The Politics of Rich and Poor.* New York: Harper.

Pika, Joseph. 1987. "Interest Groups and the White House under Roosevelt and Truman." *Political Science Quarterly* 102:647–68.

———. 1999. "Interest Groups: A Doubly Dynamic Relationship." In *Presidential Policymaking: An End-of-Century Assessment*, ed. Steven Shull. New York: M. E. Sharp.

Pildes, R. H. 2001. "Democracy and Disorder." In *The Vote: Bush, Gore and the Supreme Court*, ed. C. R. Sunstein and R. A. Epstein, 140–64. Chicago: University of Chicago Press.

———. 2002. "Constitutionalizing Democratic Politics." In *A Badly Flawed Election: Debating Bush v. Gore, the Supreme Court, and American Democracy*, ed. R. Dworkin, 155–86. New York: New Press.

Pitkin, Hanna Fenichel. 1988. "Are Freedom and Liberty Twins?" 16, 523–52.

Planned Parenthood of Southeastern Pennsylvania v. Casey. 503 U.S. 833 (1992).

Plessy v. Ferguson. 163 U.S. 537 (1896).

Polakoff, Keith Ian. 1973. *The Politics of Inertia: The Election of 1876 and the End of Reconstruction.* Baton Rouge: Louisiana State University Press.

Political Staff of the Washington Post. 2001. *Deadlock: The Inside Story of America's Closest Election.* New York: Public Affairs Press.

Polsby, Nelson W. 1970. "Strengthening Congress in National Policy-Making." *Yale Review* 59 (June): 481–97.

———. 1975. "Legislatures." In *Handbook of Political Science*, ed. Fred I. Greenstein and Nelson W. Polsby, 5:257–319. Reading, Mass.: Addison-Wesley.

———. 1993. "Restoration Comedy." (Review of George F. Will's *Restoration: Congress, Term Limits, and the Recovery of Deliberative Democracy*. New York: Free Press, 1992). *Yale Law Journal* 102 (April): 1515–26.

———, ed. 1971. *Reapportionment in the 1970s.* Berkeley: University of California Press.

Pomper, Gerald M. 1999. "Parliamentary Government in the United States?" in *The State of the Parties: The Changing Role of Contemporary American Parties*, ed. John C. Green and Daniel M. Shea, 251–70. 3d ed. Lanham, Md.: Rowman & Littlefield.

Pomper, Gerald. 2001a. *The Election of 2000.* New York: Chatham House.

———. 2001b. "Party Responsibility and the Future of American Democracy." In *American Political Parties: Decline or Resurgence?* ed. Jeffrey A. Cohen, Richard Fleisher, and Paul Kantor, 162–86. Washington: Congressional Quarterly Press.

Pomper, Gerald, with Susan S. Lederman. 1980. *Elections in America*, 2d ed. New York: Longman.

Popenoe, David. 2001. Testimony before the Subcommittee on Human Resources of the House Committee on Ways and Means: Hearing on Welfare and Marriage Issues, May 22. At http://waysandmeans.house.gov/humres/107cong/5–22–01/5–22pope.htm.

Popkin, Samuel I. 1994. *The Reasoning Voter.* Chicago: University of Chicago Press.

Portes, Alejandro, ed. 1996. *The New Second Generation.* New York: Russell Sage Foundation.

Portes, Alejandro, and Rubén G. Rumbaut. 1996. *Immigrant America: A Portrait,* 2d ed. Berkeley: University of California Press.

———. 2001. *Legacies: The Story of the Immigrant Second Generation.* Berkeley and New York: University of California Press and Russell Sage Foundation Press.

Posner, Richard A. 2001a. "Florida 2000: A Legal and Statistical Analysis of the Election Deadlock and the Ensuing Litigation." *Supreme Court Review* 2000:1–60.

———. 2001b. *Breaking the Deadlock: The 2000 Election, the Constitution, and the Courts.* Princeton, N.J.: Princeton University Press.

Powers, Richard. 1998. "Losing Our Souls, Bit by Bit." *New York Times,* July 15, A19.

Price, David. 1972. *Who Makes the Laws? Creativity and Power in Senate Committees.* Cambridge, Mass.: Schenkman Publishing Co.

Purcell, Edward A. 2000. *Brandeis and the Progressive Constitution.* New Haven: Yale University Press.

Putnam, Robert D. 2000. *Bowling Alone: The Collapse and Revival of American Community.* New York: Simon and Schuster.

———. 2002. "Bowling Together." *American Prospect* (February 12): 20–22.

Rakove, Jack, ed. 2001. *The Unfinished Election of 2000.* New York: Basic Books.

Ramakrishnan, S. Karthick, and Thomas J. Espenshade. 2000. Political Participation and Immigrant Incorporation: Generational Status and Voting Behavior in U.S. Elections. Paper presented at the Annual Meeting of the Midwest Political Science Association, Chicago.

Ravitch, Dianne, and Chester F. Finn. 1988. *What Our Seventeen-Year-Olds Know.* New York: Basic Books.

Rawls, John. 1993. *Political Liberalism.* New York: Columbia University Press.

———. 1999. "Justice as Fairness: Political, Not Metaphysical." In *Collected Papers,* ed. Samuel Freeman. Cambridge, Mass.: Harvard University Press.

Rehfeld, Andrew. 2001. "Silence of the Land: On the Historical Irrelevance of Territory to Congressional Districting and Political Representation in the United States." *Studies in American Political Development* 15 (spring): 53–87.

Reich, Robert. 1999. "Making Room on the Up Elevator." *Washington Post National Weekly,* May 24, p. 23.

Reichley, A. James. 1985. "The Rise of National Parties." In *New Directions in American Politics,* ed. John E. Chubb and Paul E. Peterson, 175–200. Washington: Brookings Institution.

Remini, Robert. 1991. *Henry Clay: Statesman for the Union.* New York: W. W. Norton.

Reynolds v. Sims. 377 U.S. 533 (1964).

Rich, Frank. 2001. "War Is Heck." *New York Times,* November 10, A23.

Roe v. Wade. 410 U.S. 113 (1973).

Rogers, Daniel T. 1992. "Republicanism: The Career of a Concept." *Journal of American History* (June): 11–38.

Rogers, Lindsay. 1941. "The Staffing of Congress." *Political Science Quarterly* 56 (March): 1–22.

Rogers, Reuel. 2000. Between Race and Ethnicity: Afro-Caribbean Immigrants, Afro-Americans, and the Politics of Incorporation. Ph.D. diss., Princeton University.

Rogin, Michael Paul. 1992. "JFK: The Movie," *American Historical Review* 97: 502–5.

Rohde, David W. 1991. *Parties and Leaders in the Postreform House.* Chicago: University of Chicago Press.

Roper, Steven D. 2002. "Are All Semi-Presidential Regimes the Same?" *Comparative Politics* 34 (April): 253–72.

Rosen, Jeffrey. 2000. *The Unwanted Gaze: The Destruction of Privacy in America*. New York: Random House.

Rosenstone, Steven J., and John Mark Hansen. 1993. *Mobilization, Participation, and Democracy in America*. New York: Macmillan.

Rosenstone, Steven J., Roy L. Behr, and Edward H. Lazarus. 1984. *Third Parties in America*. Princeton, N.J.: Princeton University Press.

Rosenthal, Alan. 1998a. *The Decline of Representative Democracy*. Washington: Congressional Quarterly Press.

———. 1998b. "The Good Legislature: Getting Beyond 'I know It When I see It.'" *APSA Legislative Studies Section Newsletter, Extension of Remarks*, July 2–6.

———. 2001. *The Third House: Lobbyists and Lobbying in the States*. 2d ed. Washington: Congressional Quarterly Press.

Rosenthal, Alan, Burdett Loomis, John R. Hibbing, and Karl Kurtz. 2003. *Republic on Trial: The Case for Representative Democracy*. Washington: Congressional Quarterly Press.

Rothenberg, Lawrence S. 1988. "Organizational Maintenance and the Retention Decision in Groups." *American Political Science Review* 82 (December): 1129–52.

Rothman, David J. 1966. *Politics and Power: The United States Senate, 1869–1901*. Cambridge, Mass.: Harvard University Press.

Roudebush v. Hartke. 405 U.S. 15 (1972).

Rousseau, Jean Jacques. 1978. *On the Social Contract*. Trans. Judith R. Masters. New York: St. Martin's.

Runciman, W. G. 1966. *Relative Deprivation and Social Justice: A Study of Attitudes toward Social Inequality in Twentieth-Century England*. Berkeley: University of California Press.

Sabato, Larry J. 1983. "Political Consultants and the New Campaign Technology." In *Interest Group Politics*, ed. Allan J. Cigler and Burdett A. Loomis, 145–68. 1st ed. Washington: Congressional Quarterly Press.

Sabine, George H. 1952. "Two Democratic Traditions." *Philosophical Review* 61:451–74.

Salamon, Lester M., and Stephen Van Evera. 1973a. "Fear, Apathy, and Discrimination: A Test of Three Explanations of Political Participation." *American Political Science Review* 67 (December): 1288–1306.

———. 1973b. "Fear Revisited: Rejoinder to 'Comment' by Sam Kernell." *American Political Science Review* 67 (December): 1319–26.

Salant, Jonathan D. 2000. "Record $3 Billion in Campaign Funds to Be Spent in 2000." *Boston Globe*, November 9.

Sandel, Michael. 1994. "Book Review: *Political Liberalism*." *Harvard Law Review* 107:1765–96.

———. 1996. *Democracy's Discontent: America in Search of a Public Philosophy*. Cambridge, Mass.: Harvard University Press.

Sassen, Saskia. 1996. *Losing Control? Sovereignty in an Age of Globalization*. New York: Columbia University Press.

Scammon, Richard M., and Ben J. Wattenberg. 1970. *The Real Majority*. New York: Coward-McCann.

Schattschneider, E. E. 1960. *The Semi-Sovereign People: A Realist's Theory of Democracy*. Hinsdale, Ill.: Dutton Press.

Scheppele, Kim. 2001. "When the Law Doesn't Count: The 2000 Election and the Failure of the Rule of Law." *University of Pennsylvania Law Review* 149:1361–1437.

Schick, Allan. 1995. "How a Bill Didn't Become a Law." In *Intensive Care: How Congress Shapes Health Policy*, ed. Thomas Mann and Norman Ornstein. Washington: Brookings Institution.

Schlesinger, Arthur. 1992. *The Disuniting of America*. New York: W. W. Norton.

Schlozman, Kay Lehman, and John Tierney. 1986. *Organized Interests and American Democracy*. New York: Harper & Row.

Schlozman, Kay Lehman, Sidney Verba, and Henry E. Brady. 1999. "Civic Participation and the Equality Problem." In *Civic Engagement in American Democracy*, ed. Theda Skocpol and Morris P. Fiorina, 427–59. Washington: Brookings Institution.

Schmale, Wolfgang. 1996. "'Liberty Is an Inestimable Thing': Some Unexpected 'Laboratories' of Human Rights in France and Germany." In *The Individual in Theory and Practice*, ed. Janet Coleman. Oxford: Oxford University Press.

Schmitt, Eric. 2001. "Hispanic Voter Is Vivid in Parties' Crystal Ball." *New York Times*, April 9, A14.

Schochet, Gordon J. 1988. *The Authoritarian Family and Political Attitudes in Seventeenth-Century England: Patriarchalism in Political Thought*. New Brunswick: Transaction Books.

———. 1990. "Intending (Political) Obligation: Hobbes on the Voluntary Basis of Society." In *Thomas Hobbes and Political Theory*, ed. Mary Dietz. Lawrence: University Press of Kansas.

———. 1992a. "From Persecution to 'Toleration.'" In *Liberty Secured? British Freedom before and after 1688*, ed. James Jones. Stanford: Stanford University Press.

———. 1992b. "John Locke and Religious Toleration." In *The Revolution of 1688–89: Changing Perspectives*, ed. Lois G. Schwoerer. Cambridge, UK: Cambridge University Press.

———. 1994. "Why Should History Matter? Political Theory and the History of Political Discourse." In *The Varieties of British Political Thought*, ed. J. G. A. Pocock, Gordon Schochet, and Lois G. Schwoerer. Cambridge, UK: Cambridge University Press.

———. 2000. "'Guards and Fences': Property and Obligation in Locke's Political Thought." *History of Political Thought* 21, 3:365–89.

———. 2003. "The Politics of Tradition and Tradition as Politics." In *Questions of Tradition*, ed. Mark Phillips and Gordon Schochet. Toronto: University of Toronto Press.

Schultz, Theodore W. 1971. *Investment in Human Capital: The Role of Education and Research*. New York: Free Press.

Schuman, Howard. 1981. *Questions and Answers in Attitude Surveys: Experiments on Question Form, Wording, and Context*. New York: Academic Press.

Schumpeter, Joseph. 1942. *Capitalism, Socialism, and Democracy*. New York: Harper & Row.

Scott, Janny. 2002. "Words of 9/11 Go from the Coffee Shops to the Dictionary." *New York Times*, February 24, p. 1.

Sears, David, Jack Citrin, Sharmaine Cheleden, and Colette van Laar. 1999. "Cultural Diversity and Multicultural Politics: Is Ethnic Balkanization Psychologically Inevitable?" In *Cultural Divides: Understanding and Overcoming Group Conflict*, ed. Deborah Prentice and Dale Miller, 35–79. New York: Russell Sage Foundation Press.

Seccombe, Karen. 1999. *So You Think I Drive a Cadillac? Welfare Recipients' Perspectives on the System and Its Reform*. Boston: Allyn and Bacon.

Sen, Amartya. 1999. *Development as Freedom*. New York: Alfred A. Knopf.

Senate Judiciary Committee. 2001. *Anti-Terrorism Policy Review*. 107th Cong., 1st sess. December 6.

Sewell, William H., and Robert M. Hauser. 1975. *Education, Occupation, and Earnings*. New York: Academic Press.

Sewell, William H., Robert M. Hauser, and David L. Featherman, eds. 1976. *Schooling and Achievement in American Society*. New York: Academic Press.

Sharp, James R. 1993. *American Politics in the Early Republic: The New Nation in Crisis.* New Haven: Yale University Press.

Shaw v. Reno. 509 U.S. 630 (1993).

Sherman, John. 1886. Senator Sherman of Ohio speaking on the Electoral Count Act. 49th Cong., 1st sess., *Cong. Rec.*, 1886, vol. 17, pt. 1.

Shingles, Richard D. 1981. "Black Consciousness and Political Participation: The Missing Link." *American Political Science Review* 75:76–91.

Skinner, Quentin. 1984. "The Ideal of Negative Liberty: Philosophical and Historical Perspectives." In *Philosophy in History: Essays on the Historiography of Philosophy,* ed. Richard Rorty, J. B. Schneewind, and Quentin Skinner. Cambridge, UK: Cambridge University Press.

———. 1998. *Liberty before Liberalism.* Cambridge, UK: Cambridge University Press.

Skocpol, Theda. 1995. *Protecting Soldiers and Mothers: The Political Origins of Social Policy in the U.S.* Cambridge, Mass.: Harvard University Press.

———. 1997. *Boomerang: Health Care Reform and the Turn Against Government.* New York: W. W. Norton.

———. 1999a. "How Americans Became Civic." In *Civic Engagement in American Democracy,* ed. Theda Skocpol and Morris P. Fiorina, 27–80. Washington: Brookings Institution.

———. 1999b. "Advocates without Members: The Recent Transformation of American Civic Life." In *Civic Engagement in American Democracy,* ed. Theda Skocpol and Morris P. Fiorina, 461–509. Washington: Brookings Institution.

Skocpol, Theda, Marshall Ganz, and Ziad Munson. 2000. "A Nation of Organizers: The Institutional Origins of Voluntarism in America." *American Political Science Review* 94 (September): 527–46.

Skowronek, Stephen. 1993. *The Politics Presidents Make.* Cambridge, Mass.: Harvard University Press.

Smith, Rogers. 1997. *Civic Ideals: Conflicting Visions of Citizenship in U.S. History.* New Haven: Yale University Press.

Somers, Herman. 1950. *Presidential Agency: OWMR, the Office of War Mobilization and Reconversion.* Cambridge, Mass.: Harvard University Press.

Sorauf, Frank J. 1988. "Parties and Political Action Committees in American Politics." In *When Parties Fail: Emerging Alternative Organizations,* ed. Kay Lawson and Peter H. Merkl, 282–306. Princeton, N.J.: Princeton University Press.

———. 1992. *Inside Campaign Finance: Myths and Realities.* New Haven: Yale University Press.

Spalter-Roth, Roberta M., and Heidi I. Hartman. 1994. "AFDC Recipients as Care-Givers and Workers: A Feminist Approach to Income Security Policy for American Women." *Social Politics: International Studies in Gender, State, and Society* 1:190–210.

Starr, Paul. 1982. *The Social Transformation of American Medicine.* New York: Basic Books.

Stille, Alexander. 2001. "Grounded by an Income Gap." *New York Times,* December 15, A17.

Stuckey, Mary. 1991. *The President as Interpreter-in-Chief.* Chatham, N.J.: Chatham House Press.

Sundquist, James L. 1982. "Party Decay and the Capacity to Govern." In *The Future of American Political Parties,* ed. Joel L. Fleishman, 42–69. New York: Prentice-Hall.

Sunstein, Cass. 1988. "Beyond the Republican Revival." *Yale Law Journal* 97:1539–90.

———. 2001a. "Order without Law." In *The Vote: Bush, Gore and the Supreme Court,* ed. C. R. Sunstein and R. A. Epstein, 205–22. Chicago: University of Chicago Press.

―――. 2001b. *Republic.com*. Princeton, N.J.: Princeton University Press.

Sunstein, Cass, and Richard Epstein, eds. 2001. *The Vote: Bush, Gore and the Supreme Court*. Chicago: University of Chicago Press.

"Symposium, Bush v. Gore." 2001. *University of Chicago Law Review* 68 (summer): 613–792.

Tahmineioglu, Eva. 2001. "Vigilance in the Face of Layoff Rage." *New York Times*, August 1, C1.

Tam, Wendy. 1995. "Asians—A Monolithic Voting Bloc?" *Political Behavior* 17:223–49.

Tamás, G. M. 2000. "On Post-Fascism." *Boston Review* (summer): 46.

Tate, Katherine. 1993. *From Protest to Politics: The New Black Voters in American Elections*. Cambridge, Mass.: Harvard University Press.

―――. 1996. *National Black Election Study, 1996*. Ann Arbor: University of Michigan, Inter-University Consortium for Political and Social Research.

Taylor, Charles. 1979 [1985]. "What's Wrong with Negative Liberty." Reprinted in idem, *Philosophy and the Human Sciences*. Cambridge, UK: Cambridge University Press.

Teixeira, Ruy. 1992. *The Disappearing American Voter*. Washington: Brookings Institution.

The Old Whig: or, The Consistent Protestant (London), Thursday, March 16, 1737–38.

"Thinking by Ethnicity." 1998. *Public Perspective* 9:55–57.

Thomas, Clive S., and Ronald J. Hrebenar. 1999a. "Interest Groups in the States." In *Politics in the American States: A Comparative Analysis*, ed. Virginia Gray, Russell L. Hanson, and Herbert Jacob. 7th ed. Washington: Congressional Quarterly Press.

―――. 1999b. "Who's Got Clout? Interest Group Power in the States." *State Legislatures* (April): 30–34.

Thompson, Dennis F. 2002. *Just Elections: Creating a Fair Electoral Process in the United States*. Chicago: University of Chicago Press.

Thompson, Joel, and Gary Moncrief. 2000. Lobbying Under Limits: Interest Group Perspectives on the Effects of Term Limits. Paper Presented at "Coping with Term Limits: Ohio and the Nation," April, Columbus, Ohio.

Tichenor, Daniel, and Richard Harris. Forthcoming. "Organized Interests and American Political Development." *Political Science Quarterly*.

Tilly, Charles. 1998a. *Durable Inequality*. Berkeley: University of California Press.

―――. 1998b. "Where Do Rights Come From?" In *Democracy, Revolution, and History*, ed. Theda Skocpol. Ithaca: Cornell University Press.

Timmons v. Twin Cities Area New Party. 520 U.S. 351 (1997).

Tocqueville, Alexis de. 1980. *Democracy in America*. Trans. Henry Reeve. New York: Knopf.

Tolman, Richard M., and Daniel Rosen. 2001. "Domestic Violence in the Lives of Women Receiving Welfare." *Violence against Women* 7, no. 2.

Tulis, Jeffrey. 1987. *The Rhetorical Presidency*. Princeton, N.J.: Princeton University Press.

Tully, James. 1980. *Discourse on Property: John Locke and His Adversaries*. New York: Cambridge University Press.

Tushnet, Mark. 2001. "Renormalizing Bush v. Gore: An Anticipatory Intellectual History." *Georgetown Law Journal* 90:113–26.

Tversky, Amos, and Daniel Kahneman. 1974. "Judgments under Uncertainty: Heuristics and Biases." *Science* 185 (September): 1124–31.

Tyler, Tom. 1992. *Why People Obey Law*. New Haven: Yale University Press.

―――. 2000. "Social Justice: Outcome and Procedure." *International Journal of Psychology* 35:117–25.

Uchitelle, Louis. 1999. "The American Middle, Just Getting By." *New York Times*, August 1, BU1.

Uhlaner, Carole J., Bruce E. Cain, and D. Roderick Kiewiet. 1989. "Political Participation of Ethnic Minorities in the 1980s." *Political Behavior* 11:195–232.

Unger, Roberto M. 1975. *Knowledge and Politics.* New York: Free Press.

United States v. Morrison. 529 U.S. 598 (2000).

United States v. Nixon. 418 U.S. 683 (1974).

U.S. Term Limits, Inc. v. Thornton. 514 U.S. 779 (1995).

Verba, Sidney, and Norman H. Nie. 1972. *Participation in America.* New York: Little Brown.

Verba, Sidney, Kay Lehman Schlozman, and Henry E. Brady. 1995. *Voice and Equality: Civic Voluntarism in American Politics.* Cambridge, Mass.: Harvard University Press.

Verba, Sidney, Kay Lehman Schlozman, Henry E. Brady, and Norman H. Nie. 1993. "Race Ethnicity and Political Resources: Participation in the United States." *British Journal of Political Science* 23:453–97.

Vermeule, A. 2001. "Veil of Ignorance Rules in Constitutional Law." *Yale Law Journal* 111:399–433.

Vig, Norman. 2000. "Presidential Leadership and the Environment from Reagan to Clinton." In *Environmental Policy*, ed. Norman Vig and Michael Kraft. Washington: Congressional Quarterly Press.

Vonnegut, Kurt. 1980. *Player Piano.* New York: Dell.

Walker, Jack L. 1966. "A Critique of the Elitist Theory of Democracy." *American Political Science Review* 60 (June): 285–95.

Walker, Jack L., Jr. 1983. "The Origins and Maintenance of Interest Groups in America." *American Political Science Review* 77 (June): 390–406.

Warren, Mark. 2001. *Dry Bones Rattling: Community Building to Revitalize American Democracy.* Princeton, N.J.: Princeton University Press.

Washington Post, Kaiser Family Foundation, and Harvard University School of Public Health. 1995. *The Four Americas: Government and Social Policy through the Eyes of America's Multi-racial and Multi-ethnic Society.* Washington, D.C.: *Washington Post*.

———. 1999. *Survey of Latinos in America.* Washington, D.C.: PKH.

———. 2001. *Racial Attitudes Survey.* Washington, D.C.: PKH.

Waterman, Richard. 1989. *Presidential Influence and the Administrative State.* Knoxville: University of Tennessee Press.

Waters, Mary C. 1990. *Ethnic Options: Choosing Identities in America.* Berkeley: University of California Press.

———. 1999. *Black Identities: West Indian Immigrant Dreams and American Realities.* Cambridge, Mass.: Harvard University Press.

Wattenberg, Martin P. 1990. *The Decline of American Political Parties: 1952–1988.* Cambridge, Mass.: Harvard University Press.

———. 1991. *The Rise of Candidate-Centered Politics.* Cambridge, Mass.: Harvard University Press.

Wayne, Stephen. 1998. "Interest Groups on the Road to the White House: Traveling Hard and Soft Routes." In *The Interest Group Connection*, ed. Paul Herrnson, Ronald Shaiko, and Clyde Wilcox, 65–79. Chatham, N.J.: Chatham House Publishers.

Weatherford, M. Stephen. 1982. "Interpersonal Networks and Political Behavior." *American Journal of Political Science* 26 (February): 117–43.

Wechsler, Herbert. 1959. "Toward Neutral Principles of Constitutional Law." *Harvard University Law Review* 73:1–35.

Wei, William. 1993. *The Asian American Movement*. Philadelphia: Temple University Press.

Wells v. Rockefeller. 389 U.S. 421 (1969).

Wesberry v. Sanders. 376 U.S. 1 (1964).

West, Darrell, and Burdett Loomis. 1999. *The Sound of Money*. New York: W. W. Norton.

White, John Kenneth, and Daniel M. Shea. 2000. *New Party Politics*. New York: Bedford/St. Martin's Press.

White, John Kenneth, and Jerome M. Mileur, eds. 1992. *Challenges to Party Government*. Carbondale: Southern Illinois University Press.

Whitlock, Brand. 1925. *Forty Years of It*. New York: Appleton.

Wilkerson, Harvie, III. 1979. *From Brown to Bakke*. New York: Oxford University Press.

Williams, Bernard. 2001. "From Freedom to Liberty: The Construction of a Political Value." *Philosophy and Public Affairs* 30:3–26.

Williams, Glanville. 1956. "The Concept of Legal Liberty." *Columbia Law Review* 56:1129–50. Reprinted in Robert S. Summers, ed., *Essays in Legal Philosophy* (Oxford: Blackwell, 1970).

Williams, Rhonda. 1987. "Culture as Human Capital: Methodological and Policy Implications." *Praxis International* 7, 2:152–63.

Willis, Paul. 1977. *Learning to Labor: How Working Class Kids Get Working Class Jobs*. New York: Columbia University Press.

Wilson, Graham K. 1996. "The Clinton Administration and Interest Groups." In *The Clinton Presidency: First Appraisals*, ed. Colin Campbell and Bert Rockman. Chatham, N.J.: Chatham House.

Wilson, James Q. 2000. "Democracy for All?" *Commentary* (March): 25–28.

Wilson, William J. 1999. *The Bridge over the Racial Divide: Rising Inequality and Coalition Politics*. Berkeley: University of California Press.

Wilson, Woodrow. 1885. *Congressional Government*. Boston: Houghton Mifflin.

Wirszubski, Charles. 1968. *Libertas as a Political Idea at Rome during the Late Republic and Early Principate*. Cambridge, UK: Cambridge University Press.

Wolfe, Alan. 1998. *One Nation After All*. New York: Viking.

Wolff, Edward. 2002. *Top Heavy*. New York: New Press.

Wolfinger, Raymond E., and Steven J. Rosenstone. 1980. *Who Votes?* New Haven: Yale University Press.

Wolin, Sheldon S. 2002. *Tocqueville between Worlds*. Princeton, N.J.: Princeton University Press.

Wollstonecraft, Mary. 1982. *A Vindication of the Rights of Woman*, ed. Miriam Brody Kramnick. New York: Viking Penguin.

Wong, Janelle S. 2000. Institutional Context and Political Mobilization among Mexican and Chinese Immigrants in New York and Los Angeles. Paper presented at the CUNY Graduate Center conference on immigrant political participation, New York.

Wood, Gordon. 1992. *The Radicalism of the American Revolution*. New York: A. A. Knopf.

Woodward, C. Vann. 1951. *Reunion and Reaction: The Compromise of 1877 and the End of Reconstruction*. Boston: Little Brown.

Young, Iris Marion. 1990. *Justice and the Politics of Difference*. Princeton, N.J.: Princeton University Press.

Zeiger, Robert. 1988. *John L. Lewis: Labor Leader*. Boston: Twayne.

Index